Global Economic Meltdown

Volume – 1

Manoranjan Sharma
K.R. Gupta

ATLANTIC
PUBLISHERS & DISTRIBUTORS (P) LTD

Published by
ATLANTIC
PUBLISHERS & DISTRIBUTORS (P) LTD
7/22, Ansari Road, Darya Ganj, New Delhi-110002
Phones : +91-11-40775252, 23273880, 23275880, 23280451
Fax : +91-11-23285873
Web : www.atlanticbooks.com
E-mail : orders@atlanticbooks.com

Branch Office
5, Nallathambi Street, Wallajah Road, Chennai-600002
Phones : +91-44-64611085, 32413319
E-mail : chennai@atlanticbooks.com

ISBN 978-81-269-1779-2 (Vol. I)
ISBN 978-81-269-1781-5 (Set)

Printed in India at Glorious Printers, A-13, D.S.I.D.C.,
Jhilmil Industrial Area, Delhi-110095

Contents

VOLUME 2

Preface

Diverse economies have been devastated by severe financial crisis. Of the 45 countries rocked by systemic banking crises during 1980s and 63 countries during 1990s, mention may here be made of Mexican crisis of 1994, Bulgarian crisis of (1996/97), financial crisis in Thailand (1997/98), Russian/ Brazilian crisis of 1998/99 and the Argentinian banking infirmities. The reconstruction costs were high, e.g. 55 per cent of GDP in Argentina, over 50 per cent of GDP in Indonesia, 42 per cent of GDP for Thailand and about 35 per cent of GDP in Korea.

The recent global financial meltdown, which was initially triggered by the subprime crisis subsequently encompassed subprime and prime mortgages, home equity loans, commercial real estate, unsecured consumer credit, leveraged loans, municipal bonds, industrial and commercial loans, corporate bonds and derivative markets. With the collapse of Lehman Brothers on 23 September 2008, the financial crisis morphed into a truly global economic downturn. A comprehensive quantitative and statistical analysis by Carmen M. Reinhart and Kenneth S. Rogoff (Centuries of Financial Folly) demonstrated that the credit crunch of 2007 led to the financial crash of 2008 and the recession of 2009.

The stunning sequence of the "Second Great Contraction"—the subprime meltdown in the United States that originated in 2007—included collapse of Fannie Mae, Freddie Mac, AIG, Lehman Brothers and Merrill Lynch with revenues aggregating nearly $ 322 billion in 2007, followed by Washington Mutual (WaMu) and Wachovia. Lehman Brothers' $ 639 billion bankruptcy heralded more dramatic banking system failure. The balance sheet of Lehman Brothers was widely derided, including the following scathing criticism: "Whatever was on the left-hand side (liabilities) was not right and whatever was on the right-hand side (assets) was not left". Over $ 2 trillion of America's troubled loans and likely losses stemmed from illiquid, complex and hard-to-price detritus of the mortgage bust, growing delinquencies of non-housing loans and collapse of "securitization".

The ease with which the world's most powerful institutions were brought to the precipice and the economic crises that swept across the world were symptomatic of a larger malaise: the devastating crisis of confidence. Increasing complexity, loss of control and regulation were clearly reflected in debilitated rich world's financial system, plummeting stock markets, stoppage of inter-bank lending, closure of money and credit markets with skyrocketing interest rates, fear of a generalised run on the banking system and the shadow banking system being particularly vulnerable on short-term liabilities.

And, pray, how did the world come to such a pass? In view of the complex and multi-layered issues at work, assessments vary. The balance of opinion, however, attributes diverse reasons such as lax lending standards, poorly underwritten subprime mortgages, underestimation of risk pervading financial markets, inadequate quantity and quality of capital, insufficient liquidity buffers, the complex nature of the derivatives and high degree of leveraging on poor, light or even absent collateral. There were also issues of unrestrained speculation, shockingly sizeable exposures of large financial institutions to some of the debt instruments and derivatives and gross asset-liability mismatches. Inadequate coverage of certain risks in the elusive search for 'beta', absence of a regulatory framework for addressing systemic risks, proliferation of opaque and poorly understood financial products in search of yields, perverse incentive structure in securitisation process, lack of transparency in OTC markets particularly the CDS, grossly ineffective regulation and supervision also played a role in precipitating the crisis. While reasons such as a macroeconomic imbalance, a regulatory problem, an ethical problem and an incentive problem are indeed valid, the basic flaw was the completely mistaken belief in the hypothesis that strong institutions make a strong system and the conspicuous absence of a framework to deal with systemic risk.

Banking crises caused by macroeconomic vulnerability and the fragility of banking and finance has led to increased frequency and severity of systemic crisis. These crises were trigerred by financial liberalization. Financial stability, as reflected in financial soundness indicators (FSIs), assumes not just strong banks but also prudent fiscal and monetary policies.

There has been a heightened consciousness of the role of central banks because in an integrated global financial system, the vulnerabilities of any player are quickly transmitted to other economies. Accordingly, banks must develop a near foolproof system, with adequate supervisory and regulatory safeguards. But financial liberalisation tends to increase financial fragility. Increased 'moral hazard' is attributed to low bank franchise value in explaining why financial liberalisation tends to make bank crises more likely. Increased market exposure of the financial system and its vulnerability to macroeconomic shocks make it difficult to check speculative pressures of global financial markets.

Given the inherently risky nature of banking and the double whammy affecting banks (banks' assets under constant threat of depreciation, liabilities, i.e. deposits vulnerable because of the possibility of sudden withdrawal), banks must plough back profits through reserves for expansion and provide for losses and current and contingent expenses, while meeting the needs of their customers. The need for maintaining capital is often based on capital performance and financial flexibility in the decision-making process.

Systemic risk has been differently defined because of the semantic difficulty in conveying various meanings and different connotations implicit in the term. Consequently, attempts need to be made to formulate a working definition of systemic risk in the light of continuity and change in the definition of the term in the long haul without being dogmatic. The working definition provided by the IMF/FSB/BIS is "the risk of disruption to the flow of financial services that is (i) caused by an impairment of all or parts of the financial system; and has (ii) the potential to have serious negative consequences for the real economy". In other words, systemic risk is associated with negative externalities and/or market failure. Consequently, a financial institution's failure or malfunction may impair the operation of the financial system and/or the real economy. While the cross-sectional dimension examines the distribution of risk within the system at any given point in time because of the inter-connectedness of institutions, balance sheet entanglements, common exposures, and sometimes, even common business models of financial institutions; the time dimension deals with the temporal evolution of aggregate risks in the financial system, i.e. the pro-cyclicality issues. The cumulative impact of these and other developments has morphed the business of banking and finance, and the accompanying risk management into a complex structure.

Accordingly, risk management in an environment of dynamic global markets should not unduly rely on any particular model or a single methodology. And complex financial models should not substitute 'thinking'. What matters is not the model with macros upon macros built into it, but a clear understanding of the key drivers of the valuation of the asset. With a firm grip on the key drivers, even an extremely basic model can help to derive useful inferences. Such inferences and agile solutions enable senior management and board of directors to take the appropriate decisions at the right time.

The process of comprehensive risk management, unlike the silo approach, should address all risks and their inter-linkages to prevent crony capitalism, collapse of corporate governance, poor regulation, banking imprudence and lack of accountability across levels. This requires a paradigm shift from a mere compliance and audit mindset to a mature state of imbibing a culture that complements other efforts for reducing and mitigating risk. A moving-wheel based approach for risk management requires Enterprise-wide Risk Management (ERM) and Enterprise Collateral Management.

Irrational Exuberance

The effects of this slowdown were particularly far-reaching because this slowdown was truly global. While all markets were adversely impacted, the US mortgage market was particularly susceptible to growing macroeconomic weaknesses. The markedly different institutional settings in US and elsewhere influenced different responses and interaction between these institutions largely caused different outcomes. The US mortgage market was distinguished by excessive US housing construction, much greater easing in US's lending standards and loans and quick rise in mortgage arrears rates. The super-bubble, which was caused by increasing credit expansion, globalization of financial markets, progressive removal of financial regulations and accelerating financial innovations, clearly underscored the vulnerability of the US's financial system. But pre-crisis, the US Federal Reserve adopted what is widely known as "the mopping up approach". In terms of this static approach, the central bank should not react to asset prices and situations that it regarded as bubbles until the bubble bursts. Subsequent to the crisis, however, there has been a marked difference in the perception about the response of monetary policy to asset price bubbles, the need to employ macro-prudential supervision, and the use of regulatory measures to supplement the effects of interest rates on asset prices.

The approach, which was principally driven by 'elimination of risk' created by 'originate and distribute' model, crashed because the securitisation model, instead of reducing the risk, increased it by setting up structured products based on low-cost debt. Further, risk-rating institutions failed to properly rate complex securities and executive compensation structure encouraged absurdly high returns.

Professor Robert Shiller (*Irrational Exuberance*) linked the subprime crisis to the irrational exuberance that caused stock bubble in 1990s and housing bubble between 2000 and 2007. Since illiquid, opaque toxic assets congested credit and broader capital markets, Shiller suggested "truly aggressive measures".

The Quagmire of Credit Boom on Top of the Housing Bubble

The basic contributory factor of this credit implosion was the "easy money" policies of government. In absolute terms, the credit boom on top of the housing bubble was unparalleled. This was a recipe for disaster. For, cross-country empirical evidences clearly reveal that financial crashes do not occur randomly but generally follow booms. In bringing about financial crises, factors such as domestic credit/GDP, inflation, banking crisis, foreign exchange reserves, fiscal balance/GDP and bank reserves/bank assets play a precipitating role.

At the time of the onset of the crisis, finance and insurance accounted for 8 per cent of America's GDP, double their share in 1960s. Retrospectively, the rise in house prices in America in a benign environment of declining real incomes, deregulation, low interest rates, surplus funds and lax regulations were clearly unsustainable. Similarly, the regulators, policymakers and even those at the helm of affairs were oblivious to the imminent dangers of a looming financial crisis in the US, Britain, Spain and Ireland in particular. For example, between 1996 and 2006, the cumulative real-price increase in the US housing market was a whopping 92 per cent, more than three times the 27 per cent increase between 1890 and 1996. Cross-country empirical evidences strongly suggest that unusually high levels of domestic credit customarily work as an indicator of the fragility of the banking sector. Yet financial analysts and supposedly well-informed commentators scoffed at these and other grim portents such as the spiralling of US external and domestic debt.

While a causative factor for the global financial turbulence was widely attributed to the financial industry, investment in hedge funds accounted for less than 5 per cent of total institutional investment and strategies with high exposure to credit risk accounted for 20 per cent or less of assets invested in hedge funds (Amenc, N. "Three Early Lessons from the Subprime Lending Crisis: A French Answer to President Sarkozy". EDHEC Position Paper, August 2007). Accordingly, it is inconceivable that all transfers of credit risk could have been done with hedge funds alone as counterparties. Banks were debilitated by huge investment in asset-backed securities in illiquid structured credit products. The underlying forces at work led to a perception of insolvency of these banks to their counterparties in the money market necessitating the massive intervention of central banks. What a remarkable alchemy it was that central banks were asked to rescue "speculators" and thus risk increased moral hazard.

The US remained at the financial quake's "epicenter". The backwash effect of the American financial crisis, however, devastated financial institutions in other countries "reflecting the same overly benign global financial conditions, an inattention to appropriate risk management systems, and lapses in prudential supervision". Inextricably linked events and developments such as the role of speculation, grossly faulty risk management system of financial institutions, absence of genuine integration of the leverage effect of banks by the Value at Risk (VaR) and the failure of the strategy to diminish systemic risk eventually resulted in mounting delinquencies and trigerred a vicious downward spiral leading to the world banking system going into a tailspin.

To be sure, most economists failed to predict the intensity and scale of the worst US financial turbulence after the subprime mortage crises, since the Great Depression. It was not understood then—and could only be grasped much later—that this conspicuous failure together with the absence of effective firewall required to avoid the financial debacle led to banks both in the US and elsewhere going insolvent because of the interdependent and dynamic nature of the world markets.

Crisis of Capitalism—Continuity and Change

Considered in a proper historical and comparative perspective, the process and pattern of globalization and financial development has been susceptible to crises. The thesis of the inherent nature of crisis in the capitalist system, the malaise in the financial sector, systemic banking crises and financial volatility, inevitability of the boom-and-bust cycles can be substantiated both by incisive Marxian analysis and the fact that not just the capitalist system but also even relatively mature financial systems lurched from one crisis to another in "centuries of financial folly". Luc Laeven and Fabian Valencia have demonstrated in their paper "Systemic Banking Crises: A New Database" (International Monetary Fund Working Paper WP/08/224, October, 2008) that financial meltdowns occurred repeatedly in diverse countries ranging from Sweden to Argentina, from Russia to Korea, from the United Kingdom to Indonesia, and from Japan to the United States. Clearly, then, the recurring cycle of financial crises transcends particular instruments, institutions, individuals or information.

While there certainly are significant differences in various crises, the common thematic pattern that emerges stresses commonality of elements. Such elements of the overarching macroeconomic environment include overheating of markets, excessive leveraging of debt, credit booms, miscalculations of risk, rapid outflows of capital from a country, unsustainable macroeconomic policies, off-balance sheet operations by banks, inexperience with new financial instruments, and deregulation without sufficient market monitoring and oversight.

"Pump-priming" and "animal spirits"

Traditionally, the Keynesian thesis of "pump-priming" stressed the criticality of government spending in enhancing demand. But consumers and businesses are rational and farseeing, and not likely to be rushed into recession. Further, the government could not spend its way out of a recession because consumers realize that extra government spending now would necessitate higher taxes in the future.

Professors George Akerlof and Shiller showed that the Keynesian thesis continued to be contextually relevant and fiscal stimulus had an important part in the route back from the precipice. They demonstrated that conventional macroeconomics is based on people and businesses being rational actors. But this model crumbles during booms and busts necessitating thrust on non-economic motivations and irrational behaviour "animal spirits" (i.e. the optimism and confidence that allow business owners to invest for the future). Akerlof and Shiller's much broader definition of animal spirits included "confidence, fairness, corruption and antisocial behaviour" and "stories". They advanced the notion of a "confidence multiplier" (government action to boost confidence can impact greater than the original effort) broadly similar to the concept of a "fiscal multiplier" (government spending widely impacting growth).

Reinhart and Rogoff clearly brought out that deep and prolonged asset market collapses are accompanied by steep declines in output and employment. What makes matters worse is that simultaneously, the government debt explodes, not primarily because of the cost of bailouts, but because of the collapse of tax revenues. While some of these factors could well be individually contained within manageable proportions, it is extremely difficult to check the rot by managing all these developments at the same time because the effects on unemployment, house prices and output last for years.

Synchronised Global Cooperation—Together We Can!

The severity and suddenness of the crisis generated "economic nationalism" and "neo-protectionism" across countries. The preliminary report of the UN Experts Commission supported many G-20 initiatives and those of the international lending institutions but it urged stronger measures for developing countries because of their manifest resource crunch. Avoiding of another debt crisis requires liberal grants without stiff conditionalities and imposed financial deregulation. A World Bank study revealed that 17 of 20 countries undertook new protectionist measures, particularly the US with "buy American" provision as part of its stimulus package. Subsidies are even more destructive than tariffs because rich countries can better afford them.

A common thematic pattern that clearly emerges out of the G-20 agenda is the imperative necessity of global cooperation in fully meeting the challenges of today and the expectations of tomorrow. The crisis also reinforced the basic message that since no country can be an island in the third millennium because of the deepening integration of countries into the global economic and financial system, the notion of a "development" agenda (and the implied asymmetry of power and influence between developed and developing countries) must give way to the concept of a "shared global agenda" across nation-states. This "shared global agenda", which has to be founded on cooperation among nations in their own interests and in the interest of global stability and prosperity, may apparently seem to be a tall order because of the near-term conflict of interests and seeming irreconcilable objectives. An incisive, objective analysis, however, clearly brings out that disjointed and fragmented responses will lead to worse outcomes for everyone and therefore, the steadfast pursuit of a synchronised approach has to be the way forward.

Compelling Need for Course Correction

The genesis of the financial sector imbroglio lay in "global imbalance", which was characterized by high savings and large current account surpluses in China and some other countries co-existing with debt financed over-consumption leading to large U.S. deficits. Plainly, this situation of huge disequilibrium because of excessive consumerism, which rose from 2/3 of the GNP to almost 3/4 of the American GNP, and the benign macroeconomic environment of high global output growth, low inflation and absurdly low interest rates, was unsustainable. In the interregnum, the explosion of world macro-imbalances of wealth and income, current account, and financial sector led to under-pricing of risks and the elusive search for beta and progressively rising yield fostered financial innovation as Wall Street boomed and financial wheeler-dealers made huge windfall profits.

Enormously corrosive mistrust became all pervasive in a catastrophic environment of increasing interdependence of the countries and globalisation. While government regulation and oversight are prerequisites to a functioning market economy, excessive regulation and concomitant red-tapism stifles innovation. Excessive risk-taking, credit default swapping and leveraging were also attempts to bypass rules. The failure of regulation to keep pace with an increasingly out-of-control financial system, the inability of the supervisors to fully understand the systemic implications of the toxic instruments together with the deadly combination of loose money and light regulations set the United States, and the world as a whole, up for the greatest financial crisis since the 1930s.

In view of the all-round havoc wreaked by this crisis, there has been a justifiable streamlining and tightening of the broadened regulatory architecture under Basel III to restrict the banks from indulging in unhealthy and imprudent practices with great cascading effects on the economies around the world. But coordinated regulation of the financial services industry must not degenerate into submission. For, finance does allocate resources almost optimally. Hence, the multi-pronged regulation reform strategy must mark an end to America's fragmented system of oversight and capital requirements biased against booms and flex with busts. There is also a compelling need for greater transparency, better accounting valuation of risks, and clearing houses and exchanges must make derivatives safer and less opaque.

Basel III has disconcerting implications, not just for the higher capital adequacy regulations, but also for close supervision of institutions like AIG, considered too big to fail (TBTF) and the concomitant issue of moral hazard. While BRIC countries are characterized by marked differences in terms of various parameters, there is a compelling need for the development of a regulatory and legal resolution mechanism, whereby an institution can be liquidated in an orderly process. This is difficult, particularly for global banks, which operate in many jurisdictions and under different sets of laws and organisational frameworks. Professor Fischer's rough rule of thumb to address the issue of the moral hazard in a variety of financial crises suggests: "If you find yourself on the verge of imposing massive costs on an economy—that is on the people of a country or countries—by precipitating a crisis in order to prevent moral hazard.... You should not take the action that imposes those costs."

Strategic Options and Choices

A strategic plan to address financial and macroeconomic instability must include both a short-term programme of survival and long-term structural changes. While the "range of legislative and policy changes" required widely differ, basic elements include uniformity of international standards; universal applicability of the new regulatory system; strengthened prudential oversight of banks and other financial institutions and adoption of best practice models. Such measures may seem to be far too radical to be implemented immediately. But these measures are necessary in the context of the vicious circle of deleveraging, asset collapses, margin calls, and cascading falls in asset prices well below fundamentals, and panic.

Impact on Developing Economies

The crisis affected developing countries through financial contagion and stock market spillovers and transmission of economic downturn in developed countries through trade and trade prices, remittances, FDI and equity investment. With robust annual GDP growth of 7.5 per cent over the past decade, two and a half times faster than the rest of the world, Asian Emerging Market Economies (EMEs) have been the engine of world growth. EMEs were considered 'decoupled' from advanced economies because of their substantial foreign exchange reserves, self-sufficiency of resources, improved policy framework, robust corporate balance sheets and relatively healthy banking sector. But capital flow reversals, sharp widening of spreads on sovereign and corporate debt and abrupt currency depreciations highlighted inherent fallacies of the 'decoupling theory'.

Asian countries faced their own set of challenges. Vulnerabilities in Asia increased considerably in terms of several development indicators such as commodity price sensitivity, current account balance, gross reserves to short term external debt, net external position vis-à-vis BIS reporting banks, growth in credit to the private sector, equities, inflation and real policy rate. ADB reduced growth projections of many Asian economies, including India's because of larger convergence in business cycle in terms of growth of real GDP, inflation and interest rates. All-round devastation was clearly discernible in the decline of 20-40 per cent in imports and exports of Japan, Singapore, China and Vietnam. China, India and Korea eased their monetary stance. But the space for monetary maneuverability was extremely limited in countries like Pakistan, Philippines and Viet Nam, which were characterized by macroeconomic difficulties and double-digit inflationary price spiral.

The contagion in the global financial markets was transmitted to Asia and spillage of subprime domino affected stability of capital flows, housing and equity markets, banking industry, capital market development, stock markets, inflation, aid and poverty alleviation, construction-led growth and microfinance, necessitating immediate synchronised action at national, regional and global levels to stimulate domestic demand by shifting from increasingly capital-intensive manufacturing towards labour-intensive services and thus spurring economic recovery.

Implications for Indian Macroeconomic Growth

In an increasingly interdependent financial world, the global economic meltdown has had a cascading effect on the economies across the development spectrum. Despite the turmoil in global financial markets, India emerged relatively unscathed from the global financial crisis because of its democratic polity, sequential economic reforms, prudential regulations and RBI's calibrated policies. Domestic demand was the key growth driver with merchandise exports contributing less than 15 per cent of GDP in FY 08 and Indian financial market remains more circumspect than the western regulators. While trade to GDP ratio rose from 21.2 per cent in 1997-98 to 34.7 per cent in 2007-08, ratio of trade and capital flows to GDP rose much more strikingly from 46.8 per cent to 114.7 per cent. Hence, India experienced the knock-on effects of the global crisis, through three distinct channels, viz., the financial sector, exports, and exchange rates. Important issues related to domestic liquidity shortage, exchange rate volatility and reduction in access to foreign currency funds, inadequate credit availability and slowdown in demand and decline in business and investor confidence and optimism.

Apart from these three conventional channels of the transmission of the crisis, India was also adversely affected by the confidence channel leading to varying degrees of stress in all the financial markets—equity, debt, money and foreign exchange markets. Further, the impact on real channel was reflected in a sharp decline in export demand for the goods and services. India's two-way trade (merchandise exports plus imports), as a proportion of GDP, more than doubled from 19.6 per cent in 1998-99 to 40.7 per cent in 2008-09. Financial integration, as measured by the ratio of total external transactions (gross current account flows plus gross capital account flows) to GDP, more than doubled from 44 per cent in 1998-99 to 112 per cent in 2008-09. Thus, the crisis impacted the Indian economy, though on a subdued scale and magnitude vis-à-vis the USA and other developed countries. This is reflected in the fact that output growth, which averaged 9.5 per cent per annum during the period 2005-08, declined perceptibly to 6.8 per cent in 2008-09. Exports, which grew at 25 per cent during 2005-08, decelerated to 12.2 per cent in 2008-09 and declined by 2.2 per cent in 2009-10. Similarly, in sharp contrast to the pre-crisis years, where capital flows far outstripped the current account deficit, net capital flows were significantly short of the current account deficit. Wider current account deficit exacerbated the pressure on the rupee leading to a steep depreciation of the rupee from 39.37 per dollar in January 2008 to 51.23 per dollar in March 2009.

Faltering of India's growth story, slowing of consumption, crippling of infrastructure by a funds crunch and constricting of outsourcing by rising protectionism hampered the country's exports and affected diverse sectors, particularly, textile, real estate, infrastructure, civil aviation, automobile, housing and information technology. Shrinking cash inflows and rising debts increased demand from industry for more reductions in benchmark rates and increased pressure on banks to provide cost-effective prompt services. Alleviating the pain of the comprehensive, macroeconomic slowdown and the whole risk-averse and tight consumer credit environment requires bankers to take decisions faster and more judiciously.

The banking system in India is sound and the financial markets relatively more robust than their Asian counterparts in terms of several critical parameters like capital adequacy ratio, asset quality (net non-performing asset/net advance), efficiency (operating expense/net profit; income (interest and non-interest/average working fund) and profitability (return on assets; operating profit/average working fund; net profit/net worth; profit/employee earnings). There are, however, issues of consolidation, enhanced growth of top and bottom lines, capital raising, expanded financial inclusion and increased global footprints. Despite several limitations, public sector banks (PSBs) out-performed the private banking and financial institutions as also forcefully brought out in the Turner Report.

Indian banks did not have any direct exposure to sub-prime mortgages, failed institutions and had extremely limited off-balance sheet activities or securitized assets. With an overall capital adequacy ratio of 13 per cent for commercial banks, the Indian banking system has not been severely dented and there is no systemic concern. The challenges, however, highlighted the need to raise the bar so as to avoid mismatches in asset pricing, develop proper risk management and capital management, build quality assets, focus strongly on customers, manage costs effectively and administer credit efficiently.

Reduced demand and tighter financial conditions adversely affect liquidity and prospects of the banking and other sectors such as real estate, aviation and information technology. Severe liquidity and credit crunch are seen in lower capital inflows, reduced ability of Indian corporate to raise resources via the equity route, significantly increased risk perception leading to keeping all future investments by institutional investors like pension or endowment funds on hold and cascading effect on private equity (PE) firms. Given difficulties in foreign borrowing and capital markets, the government eased overseas borrowing norms for companies and announced three stimulus packages, while the RBI repeatedly slashed key interest rates.

Global Initiatives for Structural Reforms: Crisis on All Streets

The woeful inadequacies of the global financial system require simultaneous stimulation of the economy to enhance aggregate demand, avoiding of protectionism across countries and strengthening of international financial institutions through a "global monitoring authority to promote global supervision" of cross-border investment, trade and banking with fast-growing economies. The world's financial architecture must change drastically because world unemployment swelled by 20 million with the vulnerable being particularly hit. Since a significant share of the developing world's population continues to be in abysmal and persistent poverty, developing countries needed to understand social outcomes and devise appropriate social protection schemes.

While devising a new global financial system because of IMF's "legitimacy deficit", there is need for a broad spectrum strategy to surmount this crisis and move ahead on the road back to solvency through measures including sustaining liquidity, reducing volatility in foreign exchange rate, allowing capital inflows and keeping domestic and external financing available. This requires designing more effective early warning systems; strengthening transparency and accountability; enhancing regulation and underwriting standards; coordinated actions and reinforcing international cooperation between countries and multilateral institutions; assessment of role of sovereign wealth funds as providers of capital because of inadequacy of financial institutions' capital cushions; examination of role of Standard and Poor's, Moody's and Fitch in structuring and rating securities; good central bank governance and effective public communication; and continuous evaluation and effectiveness of policy tools. Policy prescriptions stemming from regulatory failure in US necessitate a transparent and effective framework, domestic reforms together with prudential norms, efficient regulatory systems and healthy capital adequacy norms with an accent on prudent investments and quality lending. Since institutional resilience can effectively reduce the severity and duration of economic shocks and dislocations, there has to be an emphasis on institutional strengthening.

Besides higher funding for the IMF and use of innovative ways to reshape world's financial and economic order, developed countries must not resort to protectionism and global capital flows must remain unimpeded. Hence, all markets, territories, and actors endangering the global financial system should be continuously monitored with zero tolerance for non-compliance. Streamlined and transparent auditing standards must take effect and the rating agencies must be effectively regulated with stricter rules, a specific rating scale for complex products and regular publication of their returns.

A better understanding of financial stability, role of global cooperation in rejigging international financial architecture and identification of appropriate development rules in minimising financial contagion must constitute important building blocks. Implementation of mechanisms to protect developing countries from the impact of the economic meltdown and the projected slower growth rates do not reduce allocation for the social sector in national budgets is imperative. Almost 90 per cent of developing countries were highly or moderately exposed to the impact of the crisis, as they faced slowing economic growth, high levels of poverty, or both (*Global Monitoring Report*, 2009).

Monetary Policy

Central banks in emerging markets did not adequately monitor developments in credit growth and asset prices because of their obsessive concern with price stability, which proved unsustainable. Professor Stanley Fischer, Governor, Bank of Israel has cogently argued that "flexible inflation targetting is the best way of conducting monetary policy". In accordance with the tripartite set of goals of monetary policy set out in modern central bank laws, the avowed objectives of a central bank ought to be to (i) maintain price stability, (ii) support the other goals of economic policy, particularly growth and employment, so long as medium-term price stability is preserved, and (iii) support and promote the stability and efficiency of the financial system. This is imperative because the meltdown highlighted the complete illogicality of trying to achieve the twin goals of price and financial stability with the single instrument of short-term interest rates and therefore, underscored the need to target inflation flexibly.

The countries that suffered financial sector crises had much deeper output crisis. Thus, the presence of a strong and robust financial system makes the standard anti-cyclical monetary policy response more effective. But the existing financial system is procyclical and prone to bubble-like behaviour. No wonder, then, rapid credit growth increased asset prices well beyond their fundamental values, fuelling a boom in consumption and investment. All crises ranging from the Great Depression in the US in 1930s, Japan in the 1990s to the East Asia in 1997 originated from rapid credit creation that manifested in higher asset prices and higher collateral values, leading to further increases in credit. A possible solution is "shading of the interest policy, termed as 'leaning against the wind'". But Ben Bernanke and Gartler have demonstrated that using interest rate policy in this way may not be strong enough to arrest the upswing of asset prices and leverage. Moreover, asset bubbles are difficult to detect and their impact on the economy difficult to assess. Further, interest rate policy which "leans against the wind is costly as compared with the cost of dealing with the fall-out".

Central banks are now reviewing the role of monetary policy in countering financial imbalances by finding means of bringing in changes in credit, leverage and asset prices. The Federal Reserve and Bank of England have justifiably stressed the need for a closer investigation of macro-prudential tools focused on financial sector and interest rate to respond to the challenges of financial cycles.

The Financial Stability Forum (FSF) and the Basel Committee are ascertaining the appropriateness of capital buffers above Basel minima to the loan growth at each individual firm, introduction of a dynamic provisioning framework, and building up of maximum leverage rates. Such countercyclical measures require balancing the conflicting requirements of countering financial excesses and developing a dynamic financial sector capable of supporting the growth of the economy. Since such policy rules may reduce supervisory discretion and introduce pre-commitment, these rules must be updated periodically so that they are not arbitraged, and are abreast of new developments in the financial sector.

Fiscal Measures

Despite sweeping globalization, the free play of the unfettered market mechanism is fraught with great danger. Since the market on its own is inadequate, the governments must play an important role in shaping economic policies. Given the overarching fiscal stress and predicaments faced, what is needed is not just larger but also smarter and highly selective investment prioritized on national goals and on performance outcomes.

While in normal times countries should maintain fiscal discipline and monetary and financial stability, crisis situation demands a pro-active and responsive monetary policy and fiscal policy with timely, targeted, and temporary measures for the much needed stimulus and mitigate the severity of recession. Indeed this is what both the Government and the RBI have attempted to do in India.

Basel Approaches to Quantifying Capital Requirements

The supervisory approach mainly covers supervision of financial institutions (banks, securities' firms and insurance companies); financial infrastructure (accounting, auditing, corporate governance standards, payment and settlement systems); and transparency (data dissemination, fiscal and monetary policy transparency).

Adequate bank capitalisation cushions losses, checks bank solvency, curbs credit to non-credit worthy borrowers and reduces the incentive of banks to assume excessive risk. Introduction of multiple risk weights with preferential treatment for high rated assets and treatment of credit risk mitigating techniques, i.e. securitisation, derivatives, netting services, equity holdings, venture capital and guarantees, could be offset by increased capital requirement of market risk and operational risk, adequately capitalizing subsidiaries on a standalone basis and meeting group capital adequacy requirement reduces capital charge of banks. While inaccurate capital calculation can cause financial losses both due to poor risk management and regulatory penalties for non-compliance, "calibration" of alternative regimes in calculating regulatory capital requirements encourages banks to implement sophisticated mechanisms to lower capital requirement.

Basel III Methodological and Policy Frame

Post-global crisis, the Basel Committee on Banking Supervision (BCBS) issued far-reaching proposals (December 2010) to effectively modify the policy frame over the long haul by strengthening global capital and liquidity regulations. These reforms, which require banks to hold more and better quality capital and more liquid assets, will limit their leverage and mandate them to build up capital buffers in good times to promote resilient banking. Basel Committee's March 2012 Review stressed that "full, timely and consistent implementation of Basel III will be fundamental to raising the resilience of the global banking system, in maintaining market confidence in regulatory ratios and in providing a level playing field".

While there is an increasing tendency towards convergence in standards across countries, there is also some divergence in the regulatory response in Europe, the US and Asia because of the implications of regulatory reforms for growth, equity and stability in terms of costs and benefits—both temporally and spatially.

A review of the financial stability frameworks and tools of central banks, including monetary policy, facilitated an assessment of the benefits and costs of an enhanced role of central banks in financial regulation; an exploration of objectives and scope of financial regulation; an evaluation of general principles of the existing financial structure and their relative strengths and weaknesses. The crisis led to, at times, a fragmented and uncoordinated response and highlighted the need to balance the pursuit of financial innovation, development of exotic financial products, adroit risk management and supervision and a steady growth of the banking system.

While capital management is inherently linked to risk, managing capital in a dynamic Basel III risk environment requires thrust on the bank level to improve the resilience of individual banking institutions during periods of financial stress; and the macroprudential level to mitigate the procyclical amplification of system-wide risks that build up across the banking sector because of heavy reliance on market price-based assessments of risk and value. Since such assessments encouraged banks to take excessive risks during booms and reinforced constraint during economic downturns, the G20 leaders reduced the reliance of Basel II's market risk framework on value-at-risk (VaR) models and external ratings, endorsed non risk-adjusted leverage ratios, and enforced "a requirement for banks to build buffers of resources in good times that they can draw down when conditions deteriorate". Accordingly, accounting standards have been increased to improve standards for loan-loss provisioning.

Market-based fair value accounting "contributed to an increase in the procyclicality of the system". Hence, attempts have been made to "improve standards for the valuation of financial instruments based on their liquidity and investors' holding horizons" to control market forces, rather than work with them.

The Basel Committee issued the Basel III rules text, which presented the details of global regulatory standards on bank capital adequacy and liquidity agreed by the Governors and Heads of Supervision, and endorsed by the G20 leaders at their November 2010 Seoul summit. The rules text present the details of the Basel III Framework, which covers both microprudential and macroprudential elements.

Key elements of this framework, which are aimed at strengthening both sides of balance sheets of banks, require financial institutions to enhance the quantum of common equity, set out higher and better quality capital and creation of capital buffers to absorb shocks. The framework also stipulated to provide for better risk coverage, strengthen the capital requirements for counterparty credit risk exposures arising from derivatives, repos, and securities financing activities; the introduction of a leverage ratio as a backstop to the risk-based requirement, adoption of countercyclical capital framework; increase transparency, suggest measures to promote the build up of capital that can be drawn down in periods of stress, the introduction of two global liquidity standards, a global minimum liquidity standard for a revised capital framework, greater space for banking supervision by regulators under Pillar II and further transparency and market discipline under Pillar III.

Unlike Basel II, which focused solely on capital requirements, Basel III examines bank regulation more holistically since banks suffered liquidity and leverage induced stresses well beyond the sustainability of their weak capital buffers in 2007-09. Since Basel III necessitates a consistent increase in capital in both qualitative and quantitative terms, several new requirements stipulate that the banks have adequate capital to support its risks beyond the core minimum requirement, take prompt and decisive action to reduce risks and restore capital in case of identification of deficiencies with a broad spectrum of measures for addressing increased risk. Some major changes, however, relate to emphasis on core equity capital (minimum of 7 per cent of RWAs vs 2 per cent currently); introduction of liquidity requirement in the form of liquidity coverage ratio and net stable funding ratio (NSFR); constraints on leverage in form of Leverage ratio; and introduction of counter cyclical capital buffer.

Everything in business is always in flux and flow. Accordingly, bank regulation should have both a strict minimum beneath which the bank is legally bankrupt and a manageable target capital requirement. Unlike Solvency II, which may require a nearly fixed capital requirement, banking regulation should require a buffer amounting to the difference between available and minimum capital.

Some basic issues in India relate to infusion of capital and a sharp increase in the equity component from 2 per cent to 4.5 per cent while the minimum CRAR remains at 8 per cent. Further, there is a capital conservation buffer of 2.5 per cent composed of equity, thereby raising the equity component in capital from 2 per cent to 7 per cent. The RBI has consistently adopted prudent and effective policy in respect of exposure of banks to risky segments, viz. the real estate sector, capital market and NBFCs to increase the resilience of the system. More fundamentally, the thrust on countercyclical capital, countercyclical provisions and the use of truly loss-absorbing buffers (i.e. some buffers above the strict regulatory minimum to a level aligned with the bank's own assessment of the degree of stress faced) moderates the credit and asset price boom and significantly mitigates increased fragility. Developing less pro-cyclical prudential regulations requires fostering risk management practices suitable both for individual banks and the banking sector as a whole.

There are also issues of leverage ratio (ratio of Tier 1 capital to book value of assets including off-balance sheet items), high pool of liquidity, information asymmetry, stress testing, migration to IFRS, asset quality and infrastructure financing.

The international architecture for prudential financial regulation, which evolved in an incremental and ad hoc manner since the mid-1970s, was devastated by the global financial meltdown and necessitated a revisiting of regulation of banks, credit rating agencies, accountancy, hedge funds, derivatives, credit default swaps/obligations and mortgage backed securities. But some basic causative factors such as mis-priced liquidity, weak bank governance, too much leverage and too little loss-absorbing capital, repeatedly occur in almost all financial crises, irrespective of period and geography. Since the solutions suggested by various reviews and assessments were path-dependent and specific to the development of the financial sector in any country, the degree of success of their applications also varied.

The magnitude of global economic meltdown induced a belief about the collective failure caused by the conspicuous absence of the existing regulatory framework to deal with systemic risk because of manifest inability of financial markets to always self-correct, difficulty of detecting the signs of instability on an ongoing real time basis and huge costs of instability. Cataclysmic changes in financial markets, financial products and practices expanded cross-border banking, increased interdependencies between banks in different countries, intensified vulnerabilities and fuelled contagion risk. Many global banks altered their financing strategies, relying more heavily on market funding, and the attendant liquidity disruption and shortfalls further amplified financial system fragility. Several complex financial products were introduced into the markets without either fully understanding the inherent risks or the absence of the regulatory framework necessary to create incentive for proper risk management with an enabling technology and effective tools.

The IMF's Working Paper isolated and identified various deficiencies. Such deficiencies in the functioning of central banks and treasury departments included insufficient thrust of central banks and supervisory agencies on development of macroprudential tools and monetary policy to address consolidation of exposures to aggregate risks; recalcitrance of treasury departments in adjusting the scope of special resolution regimes to mitigate the systemic impact of failure and address moral hazard incentives arising from implicit safety nets; non-application of heightened prudential standards for large and complex institutions; inadequate success in promoting systemically robust procedures for the clearing and settlement of trades. Lack of a robust infrastructure for credit derivatives; and the overall framework was not fully conducive in achieving its objectives, and often left the responsibilities and tools of central banks in their pursuit of financial stability, ill-defined. International regulation, however, increased to include corporate governance, accounting, and auditing standards, strengthening of institutional architecture and regulatory and supervisory responsibilities.

With capital charge for various forms of risk now becoming mandatory, risk also stems from volatility in business cycles, susceptibility to contagions and diversification. Size necessitates greater capital. But bigger size banks leverage this position more effectively than small-sized banks. Size of the banks also guards effectively against any normal risks emanating from business such as credit, market and operational risks.

While the RBI's Report on Currency and Finance (Sept. 2008) placed the requirement of additional capital for the banking sector at ₹ 5,68,744 crore (maintain capital-to-risk-weighted assets ratio-CRAR at 12 per cent) over five-year, ICRA estimates that the new capital requirement would necessitate Indian banks (except foreign banks) raising ₹ 6,00,000 crore in external capital over next nine years, besides lowering their leveraging capacity.

Additional capital is required to meet growth of off-balance sheet activities, sensitivity of banks balance sheet to changes in interest rates, increasing globalization and Basel III compliance. Banking capital could be shored up by public equity offers, venture capital, selling stakes to large foreign banks to meet fluctuations in capital requirements stemming from fluctuating quality of risk exposures and fully meet all elements of expected losses by provisioning and availability of exclusive capital to support unexpected losses. Future estimation of risk-reward matrix must not only consider the amount of available capital, but also incorporate leverage adjustment costs and the duration mismatches of assets and liabilities.

Given the preponderance of the public sector banks (PSBs) in India, these banks require most of this capital. While higher core capital could dilute the return on equity for banks, Indian banks may still find it easier to make the transition to a stricter capital requirement regime than some of their international counterparts since the regulatory norms on capital adequacy are already more stringent, and most Indian banks have historically maintained their core and overall capital way above the regulatory minimum prescribed by the BCBS on bank capital adequacy, liquidity and leverage. The key differences between the RBI's Basel III guidelines and the BIS's Basel III norms are a more stringent minimum common equity Tier I capital of 5.5 per cent (versus BIS's 4.5 per cent); and March 2017 deadline (BIS's deadline-January 2019) for the implementation of a 2.5 per cent capital conservation buffer.

The Government provided ₹ 16,500 crore and ₹ 15,888 crore for capitalization of PSU banks in 2010-11 and 2012-13 budgets, respectively. The capital infusions were in the form of direct equity and hybrid Tier I capital, including perpetual non-cumulative preference shares. Due to October 2011 downgrading of SBI due to shortfall in Tier II capital, GoI is considering infusing capital to the extent of ₹ 4500 – ₹ 6000 crores. Private banks are well capitalized, though some may need equity to fund their growth plans.

At an aggregate level, Indian banks fare well against the Basel III requirement for capital. Considering the stricter deductions from Tier I and some of the existing perpetual debt (around ₹ 25,000 crores) would become ineligible for inclusion under Tier I, some banks may need to infuse superior or core capital (equity capital or Tier I). Additional capital may also be required to support a growth rate in excess of internal capital generation rate.

Systemic Liquidity

Central banks provided liquidity in interbank markets and changed their monetary operations, e.g. reduced penalties on banks not achieving their reserve targets, changed discount rates and terms of open market operations to more illiquid and credit risky securities to remove liquidity stress during the financial crisis. While earlier the aggregate amount of reserves provided to the system was kept constant, the distinction between liquidity position and unconventional monetary policy became increasingly blurred and central banks became "market makers of last resort". But reaching zero interest lower bound is not the end of expansionary monetary policy since the central bank can pursue an expansionary monetary policy through unconventional measures like quantitative easing even when it has cut the central bank interest rate essentially to zero. In fact, this is what the Fed, the Bank of England, the Bank of Japan, and other central banks did during this crisis and the Fed became the market maker of the last resort in this regard.

Mitigating the impact of systemic risk on the financial system and the economy, however, adversely affects the central banks themselves. Providing liquidity in the interbank markets against credit-risky securities weakens the balance sheets of central banks and makes it difficult for the central banks to implement properly the conventional monetary policy. "In small open economies...systemic liquidity provision can lead to a sharp depreciation of the exchange rate and in the longer run, increase inflation" (Jácome, 2008). Hence, central banks attempt to reduce the frequency of systemic liquidity stresses through greater regulation of key private liquidity providers like commercial banks and effective regulation of markets.

Central Banks as Lenders of Last Resort

Banking theory and cross-country empirical evidences unmistakably bring about the imperative need for the central bank to be the lender of last resort in the case of a liquidity crisis arising from a temporary shortage of liquidity, typically in a financial panic. Central banks become involved in the resolution of individual systemically important institutions (SIFI), which are under severe liquidity stress in their extended function of being the lenders of last resort (LOLR), e.g. Bank of England in case of Bear Stearns, Federal Reserve's line of credit to JP Morgan Chase, Federal Reserve's acting as a bridge bank, taking temporary control of American Insurance Group (AIG). This happens to obtain "knowledge that goes beyond what is known by the market" in case of doubtful long run viability of the institution, "broader economy of the failure of a stricken institution", interest in the "prudential liquidity regulation and the effectiveness of supervision" and the reputation of central banks, which "translates into an interest in the capital regulation of SIFI".

Across geographies, viz. the euro zone, the United Kingdom, the United States, the central bank increasingly appears to be the unconditional lender to the whole banking system. This thesis can be substantiated by a recent Bank for International Settlements (BIS) publication (*BIS Quarterly Review*, March 2012). Ireland had to spend almost 40.4 billion euros, while Germany put around 40.2 billion on the table for its financial sector (Eurostat—April 23, 2012).

Contrary to popular perception, the cost of the bank bailout is not closely related to the importance of the financial sector in the economy. For example, the cost of bailing out the German banks is almost three times higher than that of bailing out the British banks. The strong involvement of the public authorities in the governance of Germany's regional banks has a bearing on this exorbitant cost. This conclusion is in line with the findings of earlier studies, e.g. EDHEC professor Florencio Lopez de Silanes et al., who in their cross-sectional study [La Porta, Rafael, Florencio Lopez-De-Silanes, and Andrei Shleifer. 2002. "Government Ownership of Banks" 2002. *Journal of Finance*, 57(1): 265-301] of 92 countries (developed, developing and transitional economies), demonstrated that the countries with a significant State presence in the banking sector also have lower income per habitant and less developed, more unstable and relatively inefficient financial systems.

Central banks are important in the managing oversight of SIFI and reducing counterparty credit risk inherent in these systems. Some success has been achieved in reducing systemic risk in national and international payment and settlement systems. Thus, central banks must have formal powers of oversight over systemically important clearing and settlement systems, apart from a stronger power over users of such systems—much more than the moral suasion usually relied on. But there is mixed evidence about the role of the central bank in the case of solvency crisis. This is why the distinction between liquidity and solvency problems and the attendant policy prescriptive implication assumes significance for the central bank and the government in a crisis.

Costs and Benefits, Central Bank's Role in Financial Regulation

> "This has been a central-banking century.... The number of central banks has risen from 18 in 1900 to 172 in 1998. The world now has almost half a million central bankers."
>
> *The Economist*, 28 November 1998

The role of central banks has increased manifold since this observation was made by *The Economist* some years ago. It has been increasingly realized that the conventional models failed because of their complete inability in aggregating concentrations of subprime mortgage risk across different business areas, insufficiently long data histories of VaR models and use of a point-in-time rather than through-the-cycle methodology necessitating an expanded role of central banks in financial regulation. Covering economic risk creates incentives for central banks to reduce the frequency of systemic crises, and develop tools to reduce macro-systemic risk, and micro-prudential tools to reduce the frequency and impact of crises on individual systemic institutions. While micro-prudential regulation deals with individual risk (i.e. factors affecting the stability of individual institutions), macro-prudential regulation focuses on factors affecting the stability of the financial system as a whole (i.e. common, herd behaviour, and with shifts in generalised attitudes to risk).

A central bank's expertise in financial infrastructure is useful in management of crises and development of micro-prudential tools to reduce the systemic impact of failure by encouraging the use of systems posing far less systemic risk. Central banks' expertise in macro-financial analysis helps in designing macroprudential tools and facilitating the use of monetary policies and macroprudential policies in complementary ways.

However, the regulatory role of the central bank brings potential costs, e.g. sustenance of an insolvent institution under the central bank's supervision, even when unnecessary or undesirable. LOLR support may cause greater uncertainty because when the crisis broke out in the UK in 2007, Bank of England believed Northern Rock to be solvent but immediately made public its LOLR-support of Northern Rock. While emergency lending could benefit from being kept secret, Bank of England believed that a covert operation was likely to be leaked, creating further dislocations in the market. The central bank's decision to place an institution in the public domain leads to great public scrutiny. Hence, LOLR operation to bail-out an insolvent institution may debilitate the balance-sheet of the central bank.

The conflict between supervision and becoming LOLR ignores several aspects that give rise to synergies between supervision and resolution. Supervisory information helps gauge the systemic impact of failure of an institution and the effect of being LOLR on central bank's balance sheet. A role in resolution also induces the central bank to adopt a tough supervisory stance from the beginning because of the impact on its own balance sheet and the reputational costs of mishandling of the crisis. Such a stance by the central bank also attempts to "sharpen their eyes in the supervision of individual systemic institutions".

Micro-prudential objectives may conflict with the macroeconomic objectives of the central bank forcing them to compromise the conduct of monetary policy, particularly when the banking system is under stress. The monetary authority may then hesitate to impose the appropriate degree of tightening through concern for the solvency of the banks. But instead of the concern with bank solvency *per se*, the central bank needs to be more concerned about the impact of strains in the banking sector on the supply of credit, and the outlook for output and inflation. In response to the 2008-09 financial crises, central banks globally reduced interest rates motivated partly to counter the effect on the economy of dried-up credit markets.

The striking difference in the speed of policy easing across advanced economies in response to the financial crises occurred because of differences stemming from the macroeconomic position and the supervisory role of the central bank. But it is unclear whether differences in the decisiveness of monetary easing occurred because of biases either arising from a potential conflict of interest between supervision and monetary policy, or better access to supervisory information and a better understanding of the interaction between financial stresses and the macroeconomic outlook.

While a central bank is responsible for prudential supervision of individual institutions and monetary policy, highly visible failure in the former may undermine people's confidence in the latter. But in the case of the supervision and resolution of an institution, the type of judgement, the people, and the processes followed in formulating policy are different from the course of monetary policy, e.g. Bear Stearns, Northern Rock, Lehman Brothers, and AIG. Accordingly, there are differences, especially when monetary policy is delegated to an institutionally separate monetary policy committee. But even if failures in supervision could create reputational risks for monetary policy, the supervision and monetary control may not be better conducted by separate agencies. A central bank's concern for its reputation in monetary policy can create strong incentives to seek uninhibited implementation of supervisory standards, which may lessen the frequency of crisis events, e.g. the recent recession.

The central bank's role in the supervision and resolution of individual institutions may politicize the central bank. But it neglects central bank's *de facto* involvement, including through being the LOLR to institutions and pro-active role in recession. Hence, a formal role can strengthen the central bank and enable it to reduce systemic risk, thus decreasing the likelihood of political interference in crisis situation.

In case central bank's policy independence is less secure, steps should be taken to increase its policy independence by a clear mandate for both monetary and financial stability, even by reaffirming its policy independence in law, instead of shielding it from a formal responsibility for financial stability. Further, "it can lead to an undue concentration of powers, especially when the central bank also undertakes an independent monetary policy".

Benefits of complementary use of monetary and micro-prudential tools and synergies between supervision and monetary policies include access to valuable information, sounder micro-prudential policies and insulation from outside pressures. A concentration of power has the distinct advantage of benefiting from increasing credibility in formulating macro- and micro-prudential policies, enhancing its ability to withstand the pressure created by politicians and financial industry.

There are major implications of the relative benefits and costs (e.g. when a country is part of a currency union, or operates a currency board) of central bank's role in financial regulation. While some conflicts of interest stem from central bank's supervisory role, better supervision of SIFI brings huge macroeconomic benefits.

Financial Stability Frameworks

Pre-crisis attempts to introduce a new financial regulatory structure include the US Treasury's March 2008 blueprint. This blueprint stressed complex and ineffective regulation of deposit taking institutions, with five coordinating federal agencies in regulation and resolution of national banks and state authorities, particularly in oversight of mortgage markets.

Simplification and consolidation of the existing regulatory structure is "regulation by objectives" of overall market stability, business conduct regulation, market discipline and consumer protection. The US's blueprint vests Federal Reserve with becoming "the overall market stability regulator" with a formal "responsibility for overall financial stability" and "broad powers". There will be a separate Federal prudential regulator to oversee market practices across the financial industry, securities, insurance and banking industries.

The prompt corrective action framework introduced in the US in 1991 excluded investment houses and other financial institutions. The type of financial institutions to be regulated depends largely upon the functions performed, viz. 'banking', 'insurance', and 'securities services'. But because of changing financial services, some financial institutions pose a threat to mitigating systemic risk and responding accordingly.

While actively monitoring and managing risk throughout the investment process is a must, ensuring effective regulation of systemic risk is uneasy because of the difficulty in distinguishing macro-systemic revolving around aggregate risks and micro-systemic risk. The realization of risk manifests itself in changes in asset prices attached to aggregate developments. Usually, the holder of a leveraged position is tempted to increase his/her leverage when the development in prices is favourable. Accordingly, the provision of further leverage may cause a bubble.

With a sudden reversal in asset prices, the leveraged position will default, leading to offloading of the asset, which in turn, creates a downward spiral in asset price—'bubble-bursting', e.g. the Great Depression (1929-33), the Japanese crisis of 1990s. In Iceland, the leveraged exposure to exchange rate, which fell sharply, led to a crisis necessitating regulation of "leveraged providers of leverage".

Role of Central Banks—Emerging Contours

The light-touch banking regulation of the pre-crisis banking era "was basically minimalist in nature, segmented in scope, done in silos displaying undue faith in the market discipline, devoid of any big-picture awareness on the part of the supervisors". Thus, while the build-up of leverage and the underpricing of credit risk were recognized in advance of the turmoil, their impact was not fully realized. Further, there was no globally coordinated approach to assess the implications of these systemic risks and policy options to address them. There was also insufficient recognition of the interconnectedness of risks within both regulated and unregulated markets.

The "lax supervision of the financial markets" in 2008-10 of Federal Reserve and the European Central Bank (ECB)—"the agencies responsible for monetary policies underpinning the world's most important economies and markets" (Horne, 2010)—delayed timely measures like lowering interest rates pre-crisis. Once the rates were slashed to the minimum, the Federal Reserve and ECB erred in the opposite direction and exceeded their statutory authority by using "quantitative monetary easing" facilities to inject massive amounts of liquidity into virtually all financial markets.

The "new normal" marks a paradigm shift both in institutional arrangement for regulation and the nature of regulation itself. Accordingly, considerable international regulatory change, e.g. new capital and liquidity requirements, resolution and recovery planning, tighter constraints on business lines and leverage, changes in market infrastructure and improvements to consumer protection has occurred together with a convergence of regulatory, government and economic forces leading to reinforced role of central banks in maintaining financial stability. The fundamental principles of financial regulation strongly suggest that what is sorely needed "is not more regulation *per se*, though that may well be required in some areas, but better and different regulation". Professor Fischer has stressed the point saying, "in a crisis, central bankers (and no doubt other policymakers) will often find themselves implementing policy actions that they never thought they would have to undertake and...would prefer not to have to undertake". Hence, it is important for central bankers to "never say never".

Capital Requirement under Basel III

The Basel III framework, which is based on the computation of risk-weighted assets (RWAs) up to 2019, monitors and enforces compliance relating to quality, consistency, and transparency of the capital base; the risk coverage of the capital framework (particularly, the capital requirements for trading-book and securitization exposures); formal leverage ratios; and promotion of countercyclical capital buffers. Since RWAs at present in India are based on standardized approach, the shift from standardized approach to risk-based approach would help Indian banking in optimally utilizing risk capital.

This is a difficult task and requires coordinated and concerted action by policymakers, regulators and industry with a sense of urgency to work together to achieve the desired outcomes without the unintended consequences. Towards this end, there is a manifest need to stay vigilant, maintain a robust regulatory framework and market infrastructure, and diligently enforce the rules so that industry participants behave appropriately, help develop the financial sector and safeguard investor interests. With investment products and financial markets getting increasingly complicated, a tight-rope walk requires ingenuity in dealing with complex situations. Viewed therefrom, the tectonic shift in the banking world requires acquiring a deeper insight into the Basel III implications including the effects on credit pricing, liquidity, buffers, netting and securitization; and adroitly managing the country-specific and product-specific risk capital allocation. Calculation of market risk capital and liquidity risk under the new Basel III regime necessitate learning the core areas of Basel III and the recent updates, benchmarking the current risk management against global best practices and master market risk with a greater understanding of value-at-risk (VaR) methodologies.

In an increasingly interconnected and complex world, both the business opportunities and risks have grown manifold. Mismanaged risks could lead to collapse of institutions and can quickly transform into a systemic crisis with quite huge reconstruction costs. The quantitative risk management models, however, do not completely reflect the risks in the real world. It is in this context that the banks are required to conduct stress tests for their requirements of potential capital while considering the impact of stress testing scenario. With worsening credit quality at the macro level, the capital ratio of the banking industry will take a hit because of the interlinkages among macroeconomic indicators and financial performance. This makes it necessary for stress tests to be an integral part of risk management.

Financial Stability Report (FSR) of the RBI

The Financial Stability Report (FSR) of the RBI (June 27, 2012) stressed "Risks to financial stability have worsened since December 2011, primarily due to the global risks and domestic macroeconomic conditions". The RBI identified global sovereign debt problems and risk aversion, domestic fiscal position, widening current account deficit and structural aspect of food inflation that pose as threat to stability. Further, "The downside risks to the global macroeconomic environment are expected to intensify further in the coming months, owing to political uncertainty in the Euro area, the persistence of global imbalances, fiscal stress and sluggish growth prospects." The contagion of Eurozone is spreading to other advanced and emerging economies.

The report pointed out that accommodative monetary policy of advanced economies may create vulnerabilities for the financial system. The domestic economy is constrained by upside risks to inflation, and high fiscal deficit among others remained areas of concern. As the RBI said, "the downside risks to growth may persist given the headwinds from the global economy and moderation in private and government consumption and investment demand".

While banks remain resilient to credit, market and liquidity risks and would be able to withstand macroeconomic shocks, given their comfortable capital adequacy positions, asset quality concerns persist and liquidity pressures have intensified. Credit and deposit growth in the banking sector have decelerated while banks' reliance on borrowed funds has increased. Further, distress dependencies between banks have risen. The analysis of the network of the Indian banking system reveals that the systemic importance of the 'most connected' banks has increased, necessitating a closer monitoring of the banks to mitigate risks. While the stability of the banking sector have deteriorated marginally since September, soundness indicators remain robust. An offshoot of decelerating GDP growth is weakening asset quality of banks and slowdown in credit growth. Further, banks' non-performing assets continue to be elevated. Key risks to banks' balance sheets emerge from persistent asset quality issues, mainly with public sector banks, the central bank said. It noted that rise in non-performing assets (NPAs) has outpaced credit growth for banks. As on March 31, 2012, NPAs grew 43.9 per cent y-o-y, far higher than 16.3 per cent credit growth in that period. Banks' NPAs could continue to remain elevated due to the large restructuring of loans over the last one year.

The FSR has reported stress tests carried out under various scenarios. But, unlike many countries, the Indian banking system in the past did not face severe stress. This makes the task of specifying stress scenarios for Indian banks rather difficult. Attempts have been made to apply the stress scenarios of other countries but there are widespread doubts and skepticism about the contextual significance of such stress scenarios because of the complexity and unpredictability of the models of the financial markets. As

Emanuel Derman stressed, "It's not that physics is better, but rather that finance is harder. In physics you are playing against the God, and he doesn't change His laws very often. In finance, you are playing against God's creatures, agents who value assets based on their ephemeral opinions."

It is also necessary to calculate the regulatory capital using the internal model method for selecting qualitative and quantitative data to back-testing, master the current best practice in liquidity risk, identify and implement capital reduction strategies by applying natural offset/netting, market reset and break clauses, and modelling the credit exposure by use of best practice templates for various scenarios such as presettlement versus settlement risk, derivatives transactions (for both foreign exchange and interest rate swaps), single counterparty risk and a portfolio of counterparties. In sum, it is important to assess how the new global regulatory framework will impact the internal capital base of banks, credit risk management, buffer, leverage ratio and compensation practices. This requires designing a realistic implementation schedule and interacting with regulators.

While an efficient financial intermediation is a prerequisite to economic growth, the financial sector needs to be regulated both quantitatively and qualitatively to keep the system stable. But the crisis drove home the significance of the quantum and quality of regulation. Regulators have to remain balanced and objective, irrespective of the market situation, closely monitor their objectives, maintain healthy skepticism and ensure the effectiveness of the organisational design, structure and governance to achieve the avowed strategic and operational objectives.

Policy Prescriptions

- Thrust on liquidity risk management and risk transmissions and check on credit derivatives.
- Reexamination of instruments of central banks for emergency liquidity support and convergence by central banks to best practices.

- Restricting spread of dislocation and to repair banks' balance sheets through greater capital infusion and recapitalization.
- Rapid and informative disclosure.
- Changed design of regulation of mortgage to prevent recurrence of a supply overhang leading to painfully corrected housing prices.
- Need to desist from imprudent risk, sanction of household loans on the basis of the traditional canons of disposable income, security norms and repayment capacity and strict regulation of mortgage underwriting.
- Interest rate and liquidity measures to ensure timely and reasonably priced credit.
- Macro-prudential supervision relating to the entire financial system and systemic interactions. Professor Stanly Fischer correctly pointed out: "It is very likely that the central bank will play a central role in financial sector supervision, particularly in its macro-prudential aspects, and that there will be transfers of responsibility to the central bank in many countries."

The New Normal

Post-global financial meltdown of 2008, the world economy has changed in important and profound ways. The global economic environment continues to be turbulent despite indications of modest growth. Recent data suggest that global growth prospects are gradually strengthening but the growth in the US economy is weakening and downside risks remain elevated. The International Monetary Fund, in its latest World Economic Outlook, projected global growth at 3.5 per cent for 2012 and 4.1 per cent for 2013.

The European Central Bank (ECB) has infused liquidity of more than one trillion euro through long-term refinancing operations to bring economic and financial stability, improve market functioning and, in turn, boost market confidence. But there are concerns of a sustainable solution to the sovereign debt problem, low growth prospects and the increasing fragility of the banking sector. The yield on Spanish 10-year bond spiked close to 7 per cent. In view of the gravity of the multi-layered issues at work, there is a need to go beyond country-by-country rescues and pursue systemic reforms across the euro region.

While growth has decelerated in Emerging and Developing Economies (EDEs) because of the cumulative impact of monetary tightening and sluggish global growth, there is little doubt that EDEs will continue to spearhead global growth. However, uncertainties persist in the form of volatile crude oil prices and other commodity prices, medium-term sovereign debt concerns, macroeconomic imbalances persisting in many economies, and disruption in global bond and currency markets. These unsavory developments accentuate the uncertainty that clouds the skewed global economic recovery and growth and the assurance of global financial stability, given that balance sheet restructuring after the global financial crisis is incomplete and slow, and leverage remains high. The world still continues to grapple with the sovereign debt crisis in peripheral Eurozone economies and unsustainable sovereign debts and fiscal deficits of larger economies. This has led to heightened risk aversion and flow of funds to safe havens. For, a crisis in the European banking system can stifle trade finance leading to dissipated growth prospects not just in the euro region but also globally. This makes it necessary to address (a) German sensitivities on the Eurozone, Brazilian sensitivities on the Rio+20 Summit, and Chinese sensitivities on the exchange rate; and (b) the lurking dangers of instability in the Eurozone, faltering growth, demand rebalancing and the distinct possibility of disruption of oil supplies.

The slow and protracted recovery in the post-crisis period has been aptly captured in the evocative phrase "the new normal". This phrase of Mr. Mohamad El-Erain, the Chief of Pacific Investment Management Company (PIMCO) basically implies a downward shift in potential growth of advanced economies because of the debilitated financial sectors and capital destruction. While this phrase has been used in various contexts, this recurring theme in global financial lexicon essentially refers to the DDR dynamics of de-leveraging, de-globalization and re-regulation.

While Dodd-Frank in the US and hedge-fund rules in Europe are quite intrusive, considerable international regulatory change, e.g. new capital and liquidity requirements, resolution and recovery planning, tighter constraints on business lines and leverage, changes in market infrastructure and consumer protection, has occurred together with a convergence of regulatory, government and economic forces in Washington, Brussels and London. *The Economist* stressed, "The power of central banks has steadily increased over the past couple of decades.... Never before in history have central banks wielded so much power" (25 September 1999). Since this two-decade old observation, the role of central banks in maintaining financial stability has been reinforced because of "the new normal". Against this overarching backdrop of "the new normal", there is a paradigm shift from weak and ineffective regulations to more comprehensive and robust regulations and supervision. A strong regulatory and supervisory framework is a necessary and not a sufficient condition. In the ultimate analysis, strong, comprehensive rules and regulations must be effectively enforced.

Despite the problem of 'moral hazard' involved in "guarantees given to failed managements", setting the house of world finance in order must have overriding priority. A comprehensive programme to preserve short-term liquidity, remove damaged assets from bank balance sheets, and recapitalization of banks together with a comprehensive approach to liquidity and confidence requires boldness, imagination and infusion of taxpayers' money. In sum, the strategy of banking and financial institutions must be redefined by check on derivatives and other high-risk exposures, thrust on creditworthiness and asset quality, robust risk management systems, strong capital base, transparency, prudence and regulations staying ahead of innovations and with a clear understanding of the financial and regulatory system. The nature of the regulation of an individual financial institution depends crucially on the systemic nature of its activities. This in turn is related, *inter alia*, to its size, degree of leverage and interconnectedness with the rest of the system.

The Basel Committee's Standards Implementation Group closely monitors and coordinates the implementation of rules and recommendations. The current period is particularly challenging with tighter accounting, funding and prudential rules. In such a difficult regulatory context, the Committee's sequential implementation assessment process is based on countries' progress in adopting the Basel regulatory framework; the consistency of national and regional legislations with the agreed Basel III rules; and to determine whether the rules are practically delivering the anticipated outcomes across different countries and result in comparable outcomes at the bank level.

There are, however, practical difficulties in implementation and diverse approaches to well-designed global rules and regulations, e.g. differences in terms of insolvency regimes, permissible banking business, imposition of taxes on financial transactions, arbitrage by the industry and potentially damaging unilateral changes by national regulators to making the global financial system safe and stable. Since such differences can stymie reforms, attempts must be made to achieve a consensus in real-world lessons because of distinctive peculiarities across regions and institutions. This can be achieved by each country having its own unique set of objectives and constraints, based on their size, structure, regulatory framework, funding or solvency level, and investment goals. In strategizing corporate objectives, financial institutions need to develop a robust, three-tier risk management system based on first-level day-to-day controls performed by investment teams; independent, systematic second-level controls performed by operations controllers and risk managers; and third level controls performed by the internal audit team to increase transparency and accountability, both in individual constituents and the industry.

Given the existence of about 60 Acts and multiple rules in India, a Financial Sector Legislative Reforms Commission (FSLRC) has been constituted to overhaul financial sector rules and regulations.

The writing on the wall is that the message of history is unmistakable: the world needs new ways of thinking about finance and the risks it entails. Indian banks and financial institutions can no longer exist in cocoon or adopt an ostrich like attitude in the wake of the inexorable process of globalization. The dangers of progressive across the board liberalization make it necessary not to be oblivious of safeguards in moving ahead with financial reforms and adopting best practices in mapping the future of Indian banking. Failure is not an option.

It needs no clairvoyance to perceive that no discourse of the contemporary financial landscape can ever be complete without discussing the global financial meltdown of 2008. Financial crises have been a recurring theme in the global financial development.

The chapters in this book cover a large ground. But they all coalesce into the central theme of global financial meltdown. While bringing out the elements of commonality in various crises, the book shows how this was a crisis with a difference and, therefore, coordinated and concerted measures with a sense of urgency have to be implemented. Thus an attempt is also made to suggest the way forward by providing meaningful information, critical examination and reflection on various themes of considerable contextual significance. But it is candidly admitted that the book raises several questions about the dynamics of economic crisis and their impact, the causative factors, instruments, and institutions involved, the regulatory architecture, policy response and strategic options and choices. Clearly, these are questions, to which there may not be any easy answers. We do not claim to have all the answers—far from it. But we do maintain that sometimes asking the right questions is even more important than indicating clear answers. This book is a modest attempt to provide a holistic understanding of the myriad complexities of the recent global financial meltdown in a proper historical and comparative perspective. The book also attempts to provide an understanding of the potential risks involved in commercial banks, develop policy measures towards a more stable and vibrant banking system, the emerging role of central banks and the policy prescriptive implications emanating from the financial meltdown.

The authors would be happy if this book provokes some debates and discussions on the financial meltdown with special reference to the policy prescriptive implications for India at this defining moment of history. The book will be highly useful to a wide cross-section of the reading public, including scholars and academics, the government, international institutions, business communities and planners and policymakers. It will be particularly useful to the students and teachers of Economics, development studies, bankers and researchers in this field.

The first author is thankful to his friends and colleagues working in Canara Bank for acting as a sounding board and providing help and assistance at all times. He is deeply thankful to his wife, Archana Choudhary, IRS, Commissioner of Income Tax, Bangalore for her support to him in all his professional and academic endeavours. He is also thankful to his children Utkarsh and Upasana for bearing with him during this stressful period. He acknowledges the guidance received from his family members, for whom academic excellence is a way of life. He would particularly like to mention the role of his father, Professor D.D. Sharma (Ph.D.) (Edinburgh), former Pro Vice-Chancellor, Lucknow University and his mother, late Dayamoyee Sharma, for instilling in him a passion for academic pursuits. He is thankful to his parents-in-law, Professor J.C. Choudhary and Mrs. Usha Choudhary for their constant encouragement and advice.

Manoranjan Sharma

K.R. Gupta

Introduction

"An infectious greed seemed to grip much of our business community.... It is not that humans have become any more greedy than in generations past. It is that the avenues to express greed have grown so enormously".

—Alan Greenspan, testimony before the
Senate Banking Committee, July 16, 2002

The recent global financial imbroglio was initially triggered by the sub-prime crisis. But the crisis subsequently encompassed sub-prime and prime mortgages, home equity loans, commercial real estate, unsecured consumer credit, leveraged loans, municipal bonds, industrial and commercial loans, corporate bonds and derivative markets. The stunning sequence of fast-moving events and developments that began in the United States in the summer of 2007 culminated in the most far-reaching international financial and economic crisis since 1929. The sequence of all-round financial distress included collapse of Fannie Mae, Freddie Mac, American Insurance Group (AIG), Lehman Brothers and Merrill Lynch with revenues aggregating nearly $322 billion in 2007, followed by Washington Mutual (WaMu) and Wachovia. Lehman Brothers' $639 billion bankruptcy heralded more dramatic banking system failure. Over $2 trillion of America's troubled loans and losses stemmed from illiquid, complex and hard-to-price detritus of the mortgage bust, growing delinquencies of non-housing loans and collapse of "securitization". Michael Lewis demonstrated "the very theory underlying all insurance against financial panic falls apart in the face of an actual panic".

In sharp contrast to the case of Bear Stearns and AIG, Lehman Brothers was allowed to go bankrupt. Lehman Brothers was not treated on par with Bear Stearns and AIG for the simple reason that AIG's failure posed a much bigger risk to the entire financial system than the Lehman Brothers because it was leveraged and massively interconnected with key financial institutions around the globe. Had AIG failed, $307 billion of its derivatives written to banks out of $441 billion worth of Credit Default Swaps (CDS) in its portfolio would have brought to the fore the problem of re-capitalisation of the banks primarily in Europe but also to some extent even in the US because of the inextricable linkages.

The ease with which the world's most powerful institutions were brought to the precipice was symptomatic of a larger malaise: the devastating crisis of confidence. Increasing complexity, loss of control and regulation were clearly reflected in debilitated rich world's financial system, plummeting stock markets, stoppage of inter-bank lending, closure of money and credit markets with skyrocketing interest-rates, fear of a generalised run on the banking system and the shadow banking system being particularly vulnerable on short-term liabilities. The collapse devastated ever wider layers of the population with the debris left behind devastating the working class through rapid growth of unemployment, poverty, homelessness and social misery. All the advanced economies were characterized not just by recession and a severe financial and banking crisis but also a severe political crisis, a crisis of leadership for capitalism. The situation was poignantly reminiscent of William Butler Yeats' amazing poem about the dangers confronting the modern man:

> Things fall apart; the centre cannot hold;
> Mere anarchy is loosed upon the world,
> The blood-dimmed tide is loosed, and everywhere
> The ceremony of innocence is drowned;
> The best lack all conviction, while the worst
> Are full of passionate intensity.
> William Butler Yeats ("The Second Coming")

While all markets were adversely impacted, the US mortgage market was particularly susceptible to growing macroeconomic weaknesses. The markedly different institutional settings between the financial landscape in US and elsewhere influenced different responses and interaction between these institutions largely caused different outcomes. The US mortgage market was distinguished by excessive US housing construction, much greater easing in US's lending standards and loans and quick rise in mortgage arrears rates. This set into motion the vicious cycle of low interest rates—enhanced credit access—more people obtained loans, including for homes—increased demand—higher prices of real estate. Mortgage lenders were more at ease offering "creative financing" to risky borrowers through financing mechanisms such as adjustable-rate mortgages (ARMs). Such ARMs allowed some borrowers to tack on unpaid interest to the principal of their home loan. Borrowers and real estate speculators mistakenly believed that home prices would continue to rise. Thus, the super-bubble was caused by increasing credit expansion, globalization of financial markets, progressive removal of financial regulations and accelerating financial innovations.

The approach, which was principally driven by 'elimination of risk' created by 'originate and distribute' model crashed, risk-rating institutions failed to properly rate complex securities and executive compensation structure encouraged absurdly high returns. "Could this be because the financial system was built on an idea that badly underestimates the risk of catastrophes—and so conspires with human nature to create them?" (Michael Lewis).

Most economists, bankers, planners, policymakers and even those at the helm of affairs find it difficult to answer a simple question. Given the magnitude and severity of the crisis widely acknowledged as biggest growth slump since the Great Depression, how come no one saw the crisis coming? For example, Robert Rubin, a former Treasury Secretary and director of Citigroup, who was entrusted with the task of advising clients on "strategic and managerial issues" testified before the Financial Crisis Inquiry Commission that warning signs of a crisis "were not obvious" and that he did not remember learning of the bank's mortgage-linked collateralized debt obligations until the fall of 2007. This missing of some vulnerabilities even from key vantage points was, by no means, a stray case and reflected irrational exuberance and disarticulation.

To be sure, most economists failed to predict the scale and the impact of the worst US financial crisis since the Great Depression after the sub-prime mortgage market in the United States led to banks both in the US and elsewhere going down under. In a refreshingly candid assessment, Michel Camdessus (Managing Director of IMF during 1987-2000 and Honorary Governor of the Bank of France in 2008), Tommaso Padoa-Schioppa (Chairman of the Ministerial Committee of the IMF) (IMFC) during 2007-08, and Alexandre Lamfalussy (Director-General of the Bank for International Settlements during 1985-93) of the Palais Royal Initiative (PRI) admitted: "The crisis that engulfed the global economy in 2008 caught most experts and policymakers by surprise, bringing to light a number of hitherto unnoticed vulnerabilities" (Boorman et al., 2010).

Despite the plethora of reports and monographs in the discourse on the global financial crisis, mention may here be made of the two reports of the Financial Crisis Inquiry Commission (FCIC) appointed by the US Congress and the internal report of the International Monetary Fund (IMF). These reports have examined the issue of the global financial crisis in considerable detail. The FCIC report identified various factors ranging from "widespread failures in financial regulation", "a dramatic failure of corporate governance and risk management" and "excessive borrowing" for the worst financial crisis in the last sixty years. But the report held primarily the regulators and banks within the US for failing abysmally to identify the build up of risk and the gross inability to initiate corrective action. The Federal Reserve, which "neglected its mission by not piecing the housing bubble" did not look at things holistically and comprehensively. Alan Greenspan, the then Chairman of the Federal Reserve, promoted a culture of deregulation, which resulted from the Wall Street/Treasury nexus and the ideology that informed the class. This culture mistakenly promoted the belief that the markets would correct themselves and the market would bring about efficiency and stability.

A leader in *Financial Times* (October 24, 2008) summed up the situation well as follows "The iron faith in markets and deregulation of Mr. Greenspan, given an honorary knighthood by the Queen in 2002 for his 'contribution to global economic stability', has been shaken.... The most powerful chairman of the Federal Reserve, accorded the status of a mystic with unparalleled insight into the inner workings of the American economy as he presided over an ostensibly limitless growth in prosperity, a contrite Mr. Greenspan now confesses to being 'in a state of shocked disbelief' at the present financial turmoil".

The inherent fallacy in the hypothesis of Alan Greenspan, former chairman of the US Federal Reserve, was highlighted by George Soros, Hedge Fund manager, when he said, "The system, as it currently operates, is built on false premises. Unfortunately, we have an idea of market fundamentalism, which is now the dominant ideology, holding that markets are self-correcting; and this is false because it's generally the intervention of the authorities that saves the markets when they get into trouble" (May 15, 2008). In view of the rapidly deteriorating situation and the catastrophic effects of the financial crisis, Alan Greenspan himself admitted on October 23, 2008 "I made a mistake in presuming that the self-interest of organisations, specifically banks and others, was such that they were best capable of protecting their own shareholders.... I had been going for 40 years with considerable evidence that it was working very well. The whole intellectual edifice, however, collapsed in the summer of last year". Similarly, Lord Turner, Chairman of the FSA (Financial Services Authority) wrote on October 17, 2008: "In April of this year (2008) everybody knew that something pretty big had happened to the world's financial system. What we had no idea, bluntly, was how extreme it was going to be.... There has to be a bit of sort of humility that some or other of the things that we've said in the past must be wrong, because otherwise we wouldn't have gone wrong". Against this backdrop of contradictory elements in the contemporary conjuncture, it is not difficult to understand why Joseph Ackermann, CEO of Deutsche Bank came very close to questioning the fundamental values of capitalism in March

2008, i.e. prior to the crisis, "I no longer believe in the market's self-healing power".

The conventional wisdom, as espoused by the Fed, was completely demolished by the spread of the crisis following the bankruptcy of Lehman Brothers in September 2008. Hence, Stephen Roach, Chairman Morgan Stanley Asia highlighted some of the salient features of the modified approach "The Fed will need to replace its ideological convictions with common sense.... Over the past decade, an ideologically driven Fed failed to make the distinction between financial engineering and innovation.... Driven by its ideological convictions, the Fed flew blind on the derivatives front.... This trust in ideology over objective metrics was a fatal mistake" (October 27, 2008). What worsened matters was the fact the US government was "ill prepared" and "inconsistent" in letting Lehman Brothers go under while rescuing Bear Sterns earlier and bailing out AIG subsequently.

On the basis of a close and careful examination of the IMF's pre-crisis role, the report from the Fund's independent evaluation office has castigated the Fund's then doctrinaire belief in the apparent invincibility of the financial system of the West. This mistaken belief, which stemmed from traditional macroeconomic approaches and modelling, made the IMF oblivious to the imminent danger of the huge risks building up in the US financial sector because of a naïve admiration of the US-UK model of 'light touch' regulation and led to all-round financial devastation seriously endangering the livelihood of millions of people, causing untold misery and suffering. Further, the IMF's ability to identify the risks was hampered by a high degree of "groupthink", "intellectual capture" and the inability to detect the inter-linkages and inter-dependencies of various financial systems. And, as the IMF's report succinctly brings out, the IMF failed to think independently on economic surveillance focusing as it did on the US line of exchange rate misalignment and current account imbalances without paying adequate attention to the housing and the financial bubble building up in the US and other advanced economies. This led to a skewed and absolutely inadequate understanding of the gathering storms, which was to devastate the global economy later. But perhaps as a leading article in *Financial Times* put it so well, we need to have a sense of balance and proportion in this economic catastrophe. As this article pointed out "A clean-up is overdue. Yet, in cleaning up, we must remember deeper truths: human beings will always believe what they want to; and so regulation will always fail. We know, too, that nothing better than the market system is on offer, however flawed. Financial markets fail. They are also indispensable" (*Financial Times*, December 27, 2008).

It is commonly observed that this was the big picture, when the global financial meltdown occurred. But it is not so commonly realised that there were, however, some—though by no means many of the media and the syndicated pundits—who indeed saw the double whammy of liquidity and solvency risks coming. On the basis of a close and careful analysis of the advantages and shortcomings of free financial systems in a historical context, Rajan and Zingales in their book *Saving Capitalism from the Capitalists: How Open Financial Markets Challenge the Establishment and Spread Prosperity to Rich and Poor Alike* (Random House, 2003) warned of the global financial crisis before it devastated the world. But what a remarkable alchemy it is, as pointed out by the internal report of the IMF, critical voices from the IMF's own staff and outside were typically ignored. As the IMF's own report says, "Even warnings in 2005 of its own chief economist Raghuram Rajan about the threat of widespread financial instability were not taken into account". Another paragraph in the same report lamented: "It is a telling commentary that as late as the summer of 2008 the IMF's top management believed that the US would avoid a hard landing" and "that the worst news is behind us".

It is widely agreed that that New York University Economics Professor Nouriel "Dr. Doom" Roubini had accurately forecasted in 2006 that the US housing bubble had to burst. But it is not so commonly realised that Professor Roubini was not the only one to do so though he was perhaps one of the most celebrated economists to eloquently argue so.

Table 1: Anticipations of the Housing Crisis and Recession

Analyst	Capacity	Forecast
Dean Baker, US	Co-director, Center for Economic and Policy Research	" ...plunging housing investment will likely push the economy into recession." (2006)
Wynne Godley, US	Distinguished Scholar, Levy Economics Institute of Bard College	"The small slowdown in the rate at which US household debt levels are rising resulting form the house price decline, will immediately lead to a... sustained growth recession... before 2010". (2006) "Unemployment [will] start to rise significantly and does not come down again." (2007)
Fred Harrison, UK	Economic Commentator	"The next property market tipping point is due at end of 2007 or early 2008... The only way prices can be brought back to affordable levels is a slump or recession". (2005)
Michael Hudson, US	Professor, University of Missouri	"Debt deflation will shrink the "real" economy, drive down real wages, and push our debt-ridden economy into Japan-style stagnation or worse." (2006)
Eric Janszen, US	Investor and iTulip commentator	"The US will enter a recession within years" (2006). "US stock markets are likely to begin in 2008 to experience a "Debt Deflation Bear Market." (2007)
Stephen Keen, Australia	Associate professor, University of Western Sydney	"Long before we manage to the current rise in debt, the economy will be in a recession. On current data, we may already be in one." (2006)
Jakob Brøchner Madsen & Jens Kjaer Sørensen, Denmark University	Professor & graduate student, Copenhagen	"We are seeing large bubbles and if they bust, there is no backup. The outlook is very bad." (2005)" The bursting of this housing bubble will have a severe impact on the world economy and may even result in a recession". (2006)
Kurt Richebächer, US	Private consultant and investment newsletter writer	"The new housing bubble—together with the bond and stock bubbles—will invariably implode in the foreseeable future, plunging the U.S. economy into a protracted, deep recession." (2001) "A recession and bear market in asset prices are inevitable for the U.S. economy.... All remaining questions pertain solely to speed, depth and duration of the economy's downturn." (2006)

Nouriel Roubini, US	Professor, New York University	"Real home prices are likely to fall at least 30% over the next 3 years." (2005) "By itself this house price slump is enough to trigger a US recession." (2006)
Peter Schiff , US	Stock broker, investment adviser and commentator	"[t]he United States economy is like the Titanic ...I see a real financial crisis coming for the United States." (2006) "There will be an economic collapse." (2007)
Robert Shiller , US	Professor, Yale University	"There is significant risk of a very bad period, with rising default and foreclosures, serious trouble in financial markets, and a possible recession sooner than most of us expected." (2006)

Source: Federal Reserve Bank of St. Louis

Double Whammy

While the genesis of the US property bubble was old, the basic contributory factor of this credit implosion was the "easy money" policies of government. The need for new innovative investments led to laxity in lending standards, inflation of real estate markets and proliferation of leveraged buyouts. Conversion of loans into tradable securities together with ineffective regulation, dubious credit ratings, large exposures of highly leveraged institutions dependent on wholesale funding, information asymmetries and negative externalities worsened the crisis. In absolute terms, the credit boom on top of the housing bubble was unparalleled. In America private-sector debt soared from $22 trillion in 2000 (or the equivalent of 222 per cent of GDP) to $41 trillion (294 per cent of GDP) in 2007. In hindsight, the rise in house prices in America in an environment of declining real incomes was in no way sustainable over the long haul and had eventually to result in mounting delinquencies in loan service payments of realty assets. And in fact this is what precisely happened. This throws up the question: Did the crisis indicate that the group of "households who had historically been underserved by mortgage lenders" were not underserved at all, but rather had been able to obtain all mortgages which they could not reasonably be expected to repay at appropriately risk-adjusted interest rates?

At the time of the onset of the crisis, finance and insurance accounted for 8 per cent of GDP, more than twice their share in the 1960s. Joseph Stiglitz in his book *The Roaring Nineties* correctly pointed out "unfettered markets, rampant with conflicts of interest, can lead to inefficiency. We can never eliminate the problems; we can, however, mitigate them. In the nineties, we made them worse". Clearly, then, the secular term trends of increased growth of activity in near-banks, more extensive use of wholesale funding markets, and a movement away from a stable deposit base to a larger proportion of funding obtained with short-term maturities influenced the interest rate channel of monetary policy transmission.

A leader in the widely respected *Financial Times* (February 27, 2008) epigrammatically identified the underlying issues as follows: "A more fundamental lesson still concerns the way the financial system works. Outsiders were already aware it was a black box. But they were prepared to assume that those inside it at least knew what was going on. This can hardly be true now. Worse, the institutions that prospered on the upside expect rescue on the downside. They are right to expect this. But this can hardly be a tolerable bargain between financial insiders and wider society. Is such mayhem the best we can expect? If so, how does one sustain broad public support for what appears so one-sided a game?"

There were certainly issues of weak banks, bad management, corrupt officials, heavy indebtedness, excess speculation, and the fragility of the financial markets. But macroeconomic weakness in the US—the declining hegemonic power but still the leading driving force of the global capitalist economy—was marked by growing internal and external financial imbalances. The US economy underwent debt-financed, consumption-led "expansion" with stagnant wages and employment, and enormously large current account deficits. The unsustainable situation was exacerbated by deregulation, low interest rates, surplus funds and lax regulations. Clearly, the situation, as it existed then, transcended the liquidity crunch and set in motion a vicious spiral. Plummeting housing prices led to reduction in household worth and therefore reduced consumer spending; downsizing in terms of fewer employees led to lower wages and salary incomes; higher prices of food and energy caused a further fall in real incomes; and reduced economic activity in the rest of the world lowered demand for US exports. In view thereof, the United States remained at the financial quake's "epicenter". The backwash effect of the American (or global) financial crisis, however, also devastated financial institutions in other countries "reflecting the same overly benign global financial conditions, an inattention to appropriate risk management systems, and lapses in prudential supervision". The highly inflammable mix of low interest rates and easy access to funds, which encouraged reckless lending, the infamous interest only, no-down payment, no-documentation ("liar") sub-prime mortgages (the so-called ninja—no income, no job, and no assets loans), caused a mare's nest.

In the steadily burgeoning literature on the global financial system in general and the global financial meltdown in particular, it is strongly argued that the underlying causes of the meltdown ranged from proliferation of sub-prime housing mortgages, complex securitisation-based instruments and, in general, a conspicuous absence of effective risk management by leading banks. For example, Charles Bean, Deputy Governor for Monetary Policy of the Bank of England said on November 22, 2008, "The present financial crisis has many parents, encompassing both market failures and supervisory shortcomings. A non-exhaustive list would include: inadequate incentives for care in the origination of loans if the risks are to be passed on; extreme opacity in the nature of the risks underlying complex structured finance assets; too much reliance on statistical models of risk based on past behaviour; disproportionate dependence on ratings by end-investors and a failure to observe due diligence; excessive closeness of the ratings agencies to those who were issuing debt; compensation schemes in financial institutions that encouraged excessive risk-taking and a focus on short-term returns; a failure by originating banks to realise the extent to which distributed risks could return to them; excessive reliance on short-term wholesale funding and inadequate attention to the potential liquidity of assets; and a failure by regulatory and supervisory authorities to appreciate fully the risks inherent in the 'originate-to-distribute' model. The ongoing work of the Financial Stability Forum and G20 to address these and related issues and to strengthen the financial system against any future repeat is, of course, extremely welcome".

Against this backdrop of the meltdown of the sub-prime mortgage market in the summer of 2007, Dr. Y.V. Reddy's assessment in his recent book of the causes of the crisis would enjoy a fair measure of consensus. He contended: "Extensive excesses on several fronts, which occurred in a synchronised fashion, precipitated the crisis. These excesses were observed in liquidity, macroeconomic imbalances, and focus on inflation, financialisation, leverage, risk-taking, deregulation, networking, greed, globalisation and concentration" (Reddy, 2010).

Historical Perspective—Countdown to Armageddon

Considered in a proper historical and comparative perspective, the metamorphosis of the US housing crisis into a full-blown financial crisis in the US and Europe was caused by staggering new heights of inequity and avarice. Nassim Nicholas Taleb, Professor of risk engineering at New York University Polytechnic Institute put it well on December 7, 2008, "A crime has been committed. Yes, we insist, a crime. There is a victim (the helpless retirees, taxpayers funding losses, perhaps even capitalism and free society). There were plenty of bystanders. And there was a robbery (overcompensated bankers who got fat bonuses hiding risks; overpaid quantitative risk managers selling patently bogus methods".

It needs no clairvoyance to perceive that this progression did not erupt overnight but was clearly in the making for some time. For, a study of the National Bureau of Economic Research (NBER) demonstrated that this economic downturn began in December 2007. Some of the roots of this crisis, which raised the specter of a global stagflation, however, lay in the remedies for the previous official recession, which occurred in 2001.

The turbulence was exacerbated by soaring oil prices, lower spending by the corporate sector and soaring unemployment.

Some of the signposts in the historic failure of American and world capitalism could be identified as the downgrading of General Motors' bonds by rating agencies from investment grade to non-investment grade or "junk", HSBC sacking head of its US mortgage lending business with losses reaching $10.5 billion (February 22, 2007), suspension of shares in New Century Financial on fears of bankruptcy (March 12, 2007), heavily discounted sale by cash-strapped firm Accredited Home Lenders Holding of $2.7 billion of its sub-prime loan book (March 16, 2007) and filing of bankruptcy by New Century Financial (April 2, 2007).

Other chronological indicators of the implosion of major corporations, the devastating consequences of a greed-driven culture and dubious or illegal corporate accounts and standards of behaviour included heavy losses of GM finance unit on sub-prime mortgages and closure of UBS's US sub-prime lending arm, Dillon Read Capital Management (May 3, 2007), bailout package of $3.2 billion by investment bank Bear Stearns of two of its funds exposed to the sub-prime market (June 22, 2007), announcement by Bear Stearns to its investors to write-off the money invested in two of its hedge funds (July 18, 2007), Bear Stearns ban on cash withdrawal from a third fund because of heavy redemption requests and filing of bankruptcy protection for the two funds bailed out earlier (July 31, 2007). Filing of bankruptcy by American Home Mortgage (August 6, 2007), BNP Paribas' announcement regarding its inability to fairly value the underlying assets in Parvest Dynamic ABS, BNP Paribas ABS Euribor and BNP Paribas ABS Eonia because of exposure to US sub-prime mortgage lending markets (August 9, 2007) were climatic moments in a protracted process and clearly reflected the terrifying rise of financial skullduggery and systemic damage wreaked. A leader in *Financial Times* (October 31, 2008) justifiably ridiculed the complete ignorance about the impending crisis: "In the fraught weekend that preceded Lehman Brothers' slide into bankruptcy, the bankers and regulators huddled in the headquarters of the New York Federal Reserve made a startling discovery. 'We have no idea of the details of our derivatives exposure and neither do you,' a senior Lehman banker told government officials, according to people familiar with last month's events. He was right".

Similarly, an article in *Independent Leader* (September 20, 2008) pithily pointed out the deficiencies of the contemporary world system, "It is no exaggeration to say that, in financial terms, the world changed fundamentally this week. The firestorm that has blown through the global economy in the past seven days has destroyed so many famous names that it is hard to know where to lay the first wreath. Lehman Brothers has gone bankrupt. The 'thundering herd' of Merrill Lynch has been sent to the abattoir. Investors have been desperately ditching shares even in those icons of global capitalism, Goldman Sachs and Morgan Stanley. The sickness in the credit markets has snuffed out HBOS, Britain's largest mortgage lender. Others remain on the critical list".

Privatizing Profits, Socializing Losses!

The obsession with making immediate short-term gains led to disastrous mistakes over the long run. This stark reality check and the outrageous behaviour of the greed-driven private sector prompted the Fed to move troubled assets from the balance sheets of American financial companies into a new institution in a move reminiscent of Greenspan's scathing comments of "privatizing profits, socializing losses". This cronyism and profligacy in flagnant violation of compliance regulations—characterised as "business blockers" profit suckers, who contribute only costs to the company's bottom line—led to a quick operating of the reverberations, where there was a spectacular downfall. Power made top executives stridently assertive and also eroded their ability to see things from a different balanced perspective. The ethical choices depended largely on the choices available at that particular point of time and the heavy concentration of like-minded persons. Compensation for major executives of the seven largest US banks aggregated $95 billion in three years, while banks lost $500 billion because of extremely risky decisions. Hence, guilty persons are accountable for the bankruptcy, sale, restructuring and merger of some of the world's iconic financial institutions because the mighty few are often not "owners" of assets "but only the trustees and managing directors of invested funds".

Real and Worrisome Fault-lines

While the Fed supervised commercial banks, investment banks largely fell under the purview of the Securities and Exchange Commission (SEC). Deficiencies in working of Fed, SEC, absurdly high CEO salaries, collusion of internal and external audit, reckless pursuit of greed and overindulgence, delusion of the "too big to fail" (TBTF) hypothesis and thriving caution, prudence, due diligence and regulation to the winds—all contributed to the global meltdown. At best, the revered institutions like Fed, SEC overlooked the potential calamity inherent in the excessive leveraging of equity to the extent of 30 to 40 times by investment banks, i.e. Bear Stearns, Lehman Brothers and others; at worst, these institutions colluded in the meticulously worked out elaborate farce. The downside effects of financial leveraging (the magnification of results associated with borrowed money) meant that each dollar lost by financial institutions led to reductions in lending of fifteen dollars or more and exposed macroeconomic structural weaknesses.

This patently absurd situation was rightly ridiculed by Michael Lewitt, Investment Advisor, when he observed "Allowing investment banks to be leveraged to the tune of 30 to 1 is the equivalent of playing Russian roulette with 5 of the 6 chambers of the gun loaded. If one adds the off-balance sheet liabilities to this leverage, you might as well fill the 6th chamber with a bullet and pull the trigger" (April 11, 2008. Quoted again in Testimony of Jared Bernstein, Senior Economist Economic Policy Institute, Joint Economic Committee of the United States Senate and the United States House of Representatives, July 23, 2008).

As the tremors of the looming financial crisis ripped through Wall Street, Andrew Lahde of Lahde Capital Management wrote scathingly about the way things were mismanaged in the build-up to this huge crisis "I was in this game for the money. The low-hanging fruit, i.e., idiots whose parents paid for prep school, Yale, and then the Harvard MBA, was there for the taking. These people who were (often) truly not worthy of the education they received (or supposedly received) rose to the top of companies such as AIG, Bear Stearns and Lehman Brothers and all levels of our government. All of this behavior supporting the Aristocracy only ended up making it easier for me to find people stupid enough to take the other side of my trades. God bless America.... I truly do not have a strong opinion about any market right now, other than to say that things will continue to get worse for some time, probably years. I am content sitting on the sidelines and waiting. After all, sitting and waiting is how we made money from the subprime debacle" (Open letter, October 17, 2008). Clearly, it was too good to last, the bubble had to burst, the cookie had to crumble and how! As Sherlock Holmes would have said "elementary, my dear!"

Seven Triggers of Crisis

(i) Reckless sub-prime lending; (ii) originate, securitise and service model, i.e. the origination and distribution (O&D) model; (iii) proliferating credit derivatives market without central counter-party; (iv) excessive leverage, permissive regulatory framework; (v) US housing market downturn; (vi) valuation challenges of complex derivative products; and (vii) low probability extreme events—underestimation versus panic.

Source: Rajendra Chitale, 2008.

In view of divergent opinions and analyses about the origin and spread of the global financial crisis, George Bernard Shaw's classic comment "if all economists were laid end to end, they would not reach a conclusion" has certainly some merit. But there is a fair measure of consensus that the genesis of the financial sector imbroglio lay in the "global imbalance", which was characterized by high savings and large current account surpluses in China and some other countries co-existing with debt financed over-consumption leading to large US deficits the loss of relative power by the United States and the rise of other centers of accumulation. Plainly, the intensification of the adverse feedback loop between the financial system and the real economy, the huge disequilibrium in the American economy because of excessive consumerism, which rose from 2/3 of the GNP to almost 3/4 of the GNP and the benign macroeconomic environment of high global output growth, low inflation and absurdly low interest rates, was unsustainable over the long haul. In the interregnum, it led to a general carelessness or a tendency to under-price risks and the elusive search for beta and progressively rising yield fostered financial innovation. In other words, wealth and income imbalance, current account imbalance, and financial sector imbalance that together with financial innovations made up for the heady mix that caused the crisis. This is why Ben S. Bernanke justifiably maintained in his Speech at the Council on Foreign Relations, Washington, D.C:

> In my view...it is impossible to understand this crisis without reference to the global imbalances in trade and capital flows that began in the latter half of the 1990s.
>
> "Financial Reform to Address Systemic Risk" Speech at the Council on Foreign Relations, Washington, D.C. (March 10, 2009).

The dubious ratings process, which had awarded 'AAA' (Alarm, Assault and Agony) ratings on structured financial products of most of those companies subsequently downgraded to BB ratings (better beware), justifiably evoked concern and consternation on the deplorable rating acquisition practice by payment of huge fees to Moody's, Standard and Poor, and Fitch. The dubious ratings process justifiably evoked consternation on the deplorable rating acquisition practice by payment of huge fees. The repeal of the Glass-Steagall Act, which erected a firewall between the commercial and investment banking parts of the financial system since the 1930s and adoption by the US Congress in 1999 of the Financial Services Modernisation Act, which scrapped all regulatory restraints on financial services, symbolized the almost complete deregulation of a financial sector, which became complex, opaque, and ungovernable. In other words, such moves spawned a deadly banking model of creating and trading mortgage-backed securities. This model together with the Commodities Futures Act, 2000, which produced the "shadow banking system", played a catalytic role in rapidly deteriorating ground realities characterized by deflation, rising unemployment and emergence of Keynes' liquidity trap.

Professor Paul Krugman, Nobel Laureate, characterised the shadow banking system as the "core of what happened" because of "malign neglect". In fact, Krugman (2009) quotes Tim Geithner on the risks of the rise of the shadow banking system to forcefully make the point "Once the investors in these financing arrangements—many conservatively managed money funds—withdrew or threatened to withdraw their funds from these markets, the system became vulnerable to a self-reinforcing cycle of forced liquidation of assets, which further increased volatility and lowered prices across a variety of asset classes. In response, margin requirements were increased, or financing was withdrawn altogether from some customers, forcing more de-leveraging. Capital cushions eroded as assets were sold into distressed markets. The force of this dynamic was exacerbated by the poor quality of assets—particularly mortgage-related assets—that had been spread across the system. This helps explain how a relatively small quantity of risky assets was able to undermine the confidence of investors and other market participants across a much broader range of assets and markets". Hence, Professor Krugman effectively argued that regulation should have been imposed on all banking-like activity.

The predatory corporate practices of derivative instruments like options and futures by investment banks and hedge funds further worsened the situation. An incisive article in *Financial Times* tersely pointed out: "The crisis is partly an epistemological one. Few people outside of the financial industry have ever understood how the new complex derivatives work. Were they hedges or means of multiplying leverage? It turns out that few people inside the industry understood either. The most astonishing stories of the past week have to do with AIG's final weekend, when teams of government analysts and accountants from the world's leading investment banks could not figure out how much cash the company would require in order to collateralise its credit-default swaps. Estimates rose from $20bn to $85bn" (September 19, 2008).

The massive run-up in home prices was driven by the proliferation of new forms of securitized finance that facilitated flow of massive sums of loan capital into the property markets. The sale of 'financial instruments' became the 'engine' of the

US economy and the underwriting and trading of these new forms of engineered debt underwent an extraordinary period of growth little realising that US 'produced' little for itself. This environment was characterized by development of a new magical M–M circuit, in which money could be made solely out of money, without the intervention of actual production. Accordingly, in this new scheme of things of leverage and risk management, debt, speculation, risk, and fear became structurally endemic to finance capitalism, in what Alan Walks called "Ponzi Neoliberalism". Not only the whole investment-banking model was saddled with inherent contradictions but also there were serious deficiencies in risk measurement and management of the entire system of complex financial instruments starting with creation of artificial demand for housing leading to ridiculously high prices, 1.3 million foreclosures in the US during 2007, sale of dubious sub-prime liabilities to hedge funds, insurance companies and foreign banks, who further repackaged them into mortgage-based securities. The "suboptimal, duplicative and out-of-date" regulatory forbearance characterised the ostensibly transparent but actually opaque markets, which are typical of modern finance. In other words, rates, risk, and regulation were the major factors behind this great recession, which exposed all the accumulated weaknesses based on market fundamentalism. This prompted Sir John Gieve, Deputy Governor of the Bank of England to confess: "The instability of the global financial system in recent weeks has been the most severe in living memory" (October 2008). Similarly, other institutions candidly admitted, "In recent weeks, the global banking system has arguably undergone its biggest episode of instability since the start of World War I" (Bank of England Financial Stability Report, October 2008).

Enormously corrosive mistrust became all pervasive in a catastrophic environment ominously described as 'catastrophe', 'end of the world', 'apocalypse', 'epidemic', 'mayhem', 'precipice', 'abyss of ruin', 'death knell of capitalism', 'carnage' and 'contagion'. No wonder, then, that the hemorrhage in liquidity led to such a sorry pass that counterparties no longer trusted each other. The mayhem caused by the evaporation of trust among banks drove home the significance of Walter Bagehot's pithy observation: "Every banker knows that if he has to prove that he is worthy of credit, however good may be his arguments, in fact his credit is gone".

Convulsive Crisis of Capitalism—A Sense of Déjà Vu!

While the precise sequence of events and their intensity inevitably differ across countries, the experience from earlier crises indicates that there is an element of recurrence and continuity in the various crises down through the ages. This is reminiscent of the Spanish American philosopher George Santayana's observation, "Those who cannot remember the past are condemned to repeat it". The history of the financial institutions is replete with instances of miscalculations, wrong gambles, decisions based on erroneous assumptions and throwing to the winds all norms of caution and prudence. Such blunders occur because of endemic risk to finance capitalism and, therefore, emerge as central to addressing the larger, basic malaise of inherent systemic flaws and fault-lines. Consequently, a snarl of human greed in serious corporate frauds, factors like mis-priced liquidity chasing yield, poor underwriting, too much leverage and too little loss absorbing capital, deficient risk management, weak bank governance occur with depressing regularity in almost all banking crises. As T.S. Eliot put it so well decades ago:

> Time present and time past
> Are both perhaps present in time future
> And time future contained in time past.
> If all time is eternally present
> All time is unredeemable.
> ...
> What might have been and what has been
> Point to one end, which is always present.
> Footfalls echo in the memory
> Down the passage which we did not take
> Towards the door we never opened.
>
> T.S. Eliot ("The Four Quartets")

This thesis of the inherent nature of the crisis in the capitalist system, the inevitability of the boom-and-bust cycles can be substantiated both by the incisive analysis of Karl Marx, the immediacy of the internal contradictions of capitalism and the resistance that the system continuously regenerates and the fact that the capitalist system has lurched from one crisis to the other with disruptive effects. In other words, the crisis of capitalism is structural and deeply entrenched as a thoughtful article in *Bloomberg Businessweek*, entitled "Marx to Market" (September 14, 2011) admitted: "The Bearded One has rarely looked better. The current global financial crisis has given rise to a new contingent of unlikely admirers. In 2009 the Vatican's official newspaper, *L'Osservatore Romano*, published an article praising Marx's diagnosis of income inequality.... In Shanghai, the turbo-capitalist hub of Communist-in-name-alone China, audiences flocked to a 2010 musical based on Capital, Marx's most famous work. In Japan, Capital is now out in a manga version.... Consider the particulars.... Marx predicted that companies would need fewer workers as they improved productivity, creating an 'industrial reserve army' of the unemployed whose existence would keep downward pressure on wages for the employed.... It's hard to argue with that these days.... The condition of blue collar workers in the U.S. is still a far cry from the subsistence wage and 'accumulation of misery' that Marx conjured. But it's not morning in America, either". But *Bloomberg Businessweek* is oblivious to the central tenets of Marxian thought, which consider the reserve army of labor as applicable not just to developed countries but also to labor throughout the globe.

Accordingly, we need to be weary of "the reality of global capitalism". In the words of Slavoj Žižek, co-director of the International Centre for Humanities, Birkbeck College, "It is unlikely that the financial meltdown of 2008 will function as a blessing in disguise, the awakening from a dream, the sobering reminder that we live in the reality of global capitalism. It all depends on how it will be symbolised, on what ideological interpretation or story will impose itself and determine the general perception of the crisis. When the normal run of things is traumatically interrupted, the field is open for a 'discursive' ideological competition.... Consequently, to put it in old-fashioned Marxist terms, the main task of the ruling ideology in the present crisis is to impose a narrative that will not put the blame for the meltdown on the global capitalist system as such, but on its deviations—lax regulation, the corruption of big financial institutions etc.... The danger is thus that the predominant narrative of the meltdown won't be the one that awakes us from a dream, but the one that will enable us to continue to dream" (November 14, 2008).

Paul Volcker, former chairman of the US Federal Reserve and chair of the Economic Recovery Panel in President Obama's administration clearly said in his speech to the economic club of New York, April 8, 2008 "Today's financial crisis is the culmination, as I count them, of at least five serious breakdowns of systemic significance in the past 25 years—on the average one every five years. Warning enough that something rather basic is amiss.... Simply stated, the bright new financial system—for all its talented participants, for all its rich rewards—has failed the test of the market place". This is why free markets are often reviled, particularly during economic downturns because of the inherent risks involved and the propensity for some individuals and corporations to corrupt the system. As George Bernard Shaw forcefully said: "If history repeats itself, and the unexpected always happens, how incapable must man be of learning from experience".

Market economies have faced 124 "systemic" banking crises (i.e. episodes in which bad debts soared across the economy and much of the banking sector was insolvent) since 1970. Of the various banking crises, stock market collapses and credit crunches, the collapse of Overend and Gurney in May 1866, the Barings Crisis in 1890, the Wall Street crash of 1929 contributing to the Great Depression of the 1930s, US Savings and Loan Scandal, 1985, the US stock markets crash of 1987, the collapse of hedge fund Long-Term Capital Market (LTCM), which originated in Asia in 1997 and spread to Russia and Brazil in 1998, the Dot.Com Crash, 2000 are noteworthy. This emboldens us to say, a la, Confucius:

Our greatest glory is not in never failing;
But in rising each and every time we fall.

The collapse of the sub-prime market in August 2007 was widely labeled a "Hyman Minsky moment". It has been repeatedly argued that the subsequent implosion of the financial system and deep recession confirm Minsky's "financial instability hypothesis" regarding economic crisis in capitalist economies. With global capital markets, investment banks and derivatives such as credit swaps, currency swaps, credit linked notes, interest rate swaps, etc. becoming more complex than ever, it is important to fit all pieces of the puzzles together for a holistic assessment of the deficiencies in capitalist triumphalism. This is why Basel III and other Basel Committee initiatives developed during the crisis attempt to better prepare supervisors and banks for the next inevitable crisis.

On the basis of an incisive analysis of disruptions to periods of financial stress that rocked the world, the IMF has identified and isolated the following important lessons:

- Globalisation has increased the frequency and spread of financial crises, but not necessarily their severity;
- Early intervention by central banks is more effective in limiting their spread than later moves;
- Difficult to tell at the time whether a financial crisis will have broader economic consequences and regulators often cannot keep up with the pace of financial innovation that may trigger a crisis.

In the overarching context of sweeping globalization, it is important not to be oblivious of the fact that greater financialization and fragility creates new dependencies and therefore new possibilities for global crisis. For, complacency and selective or short memories are particularly corrosive forces, which undermine movement towards a sound financial architecture and need constant vigil for an in-depth understanding of scenario planning and its application, focus on future risks and opportunities instead of focusing on past and present ones, to acceptance of uncertainty instead of holding on to ever diminishing certainty and enhanced planning, investment evaluation and strategic risk management capabilities.

Massive Bailout Packages

The breathtaking scale and speed of the downturn and its broad scope led governments concomitantly in Europe, US and Asia to respond to both the weakening economy and financial instability. While the nature of stimulus took the forms of infrastructure, tax cuts and non-bank bailouts, financial support in G7 and BRIC countries was provided through liquidity provision, capital injection, asset purchases and even nationalization. In assessing the size of the stimulus, countries balanced the cost to their own budgets with the benefits of increased growth and employment for their own economies.

While bailouts are needed in the short run, these bailouts must be targeted at low-income victims. The solution requires eventual revamping of the financial framework to reduce formation of bubbles and limit risks, including better financial information; simplified legal contracts and regulations; expanded markets for managing risks; home equity insurance policies; income-linked home loans; and new measures to protect consumers against hidden inflationary effects. The success of these measures possibly unfroze credit and prevented a serious recession. Economic stimulus is a necessary but not a sufficient condition. Consequently, while injecting economic stimulus, determined efforts must be made to restore confidence and fully overhaul the financial system through a concerted and coordinated approach.

Impact on Developing Economies

While the impact of the global economic meltdown on national economies was diverse and varied, there cannot be any doubt about the susceptibility of local economies to the global market system. The meltdown affected developing countries through financial contagion and stock market spillovers and transmission of economic downturn in developed countries through trade and trade prices, remittances, FDI and equity investment. With robust GDP annual growth of 7.5 per cent over the past decade, two and a half times faster than the rest of the world, Asian Emerging Market Economies (EMEs) have been the engine of world growth. EMEs were considered 'decoupled' from advanced economies because of their substantial foreign exchange reserves, improved policy framework, robust corporate balance sheets and relatively healthy banking sector. But capital flow reversals, sharp widening of spreads on sovereign and corporate debt and abrupt currency depreciations highlighted inherent fallacies of the 'decoupling theory' and brings to the fore the issues of avoiding or compensating the outflow of capital from developing countries and emerging economies to the industrialized countries, development of a strong institution that could compensate the outflow of private capital and need for additional credit lines of the IMF.

ADB reduced growth projections of many Asian economies, including India's because of larger convergence in business cycle in terms of growth of real GDP, inflation, interest rates. Vulnerabilities in Asia increased considerably in terms of several development indicators such as commodity price sensitivity, current account balance, gross reserves to short-term external debt, net external position vis-à-vis BIS reporting banks, growth in credit to the private sector, equities, inflation and real policy rate. All-round devastation was clearly discernible in decline of 20-40 per cent in imports and exports of Japan, Singapore, China and Vietnam. China, India and Korea eased their monetary stance. But the space for monetary maneuverability was extremely limited in countries such as Pakistan, Philippines and Vietnam, which were characterized by macroeconomic difficulties and double-digit inflationary price spiral.

The contagion in the global financial markets was transmitted to Asia and spillage of sub-prime domino affected stability of capital flows, housing and equity markets, banking industry, capital market development, stock markets, inflation, aid and poverty alleviation, construction-led growth and microfinance necessitating immediate synchronised action at national, regional and global levels to stimulate domestic demand by shifting from increasingly capital-intensive manufacturing towards labour-intensive services and thus spurring economic recovery.

The Indian Experience

Despite the turmoil in global financial markets, the Indian growth story remained largely intact because of India's democratic polity, sequential economic reforms, prudential regulations and RBI's calibrated policies. Domestic demand was the key growth driver with merchandise exports contributing less than 15 per cent of GDP and Indian financial market is more circumspect than the Western regulators. While trade to GDP in FY 08 ratio rose from 21.2 per cent in 1997-98 to 34.7 per cent in 2007-08, ratio of trade and capital flows to GDP rose much more strikingly from 46.8 per cent to 114.7 per cent. Hence, India experienced the knock-on effects of the global crisis, through monetary, financial and real channels. Important issues related to domestic liquidity shortage, exchange rate volatility and reduction in access to foreign currency funds, inadequate credit availability and slowdown in demand and decline in business and investor confidence and optimism.

Faltering of India's growth story, slowing of consumption, crippling of infrastructure by a funds crunch and constricting of outsourcing by rising protectionism hampered Indian exports and affected diverse sectors, particularly, textile, real estate, infrastructure, civil aviation, automobile, housing and information technology. Shrinking cash inflows and rising debts increased demand from industry for more reductions in benchmark rates and increased pressure on banks to provide cost-effective prompt services. Alleviating the pain of the comprehensive, macroeconomic slowdown and the whole risk-averse and tight consumer credit environment requires bankers to take decisions faster and more judiciously.

While banks in India are more robust than their Asian counterparts in terms of several critical parameters such as capital adequacy ratio, asset quality and earnings, there are issues of consolidation, enhanced growth of top and bottom lines, capital raising, expanded financial inclusion and increased global footprints. Despite several limitations, PSBs outperformed the private banking and financial institutions.

Indian banks did not have any direct exposure to sub-prime mortgages, failed institutions and have extremely limited off-balance sheet activities or securitized assets. ICICI Bank Ltd's exposure to Lehman Brothers was $83 million (less than 0.1 per cent of its consolidated balance sheet) and State Bank of India, Bank of India, Bank of Baroda, Punjab National Bank, Axis Bank Ltd., etc. also had small exposures. With an overall capital adequacy ratio of 13 per cent for commercial banks, the Indian banking system was not severely dented and there was no systemic concern. The challenges, however, highlighted the need to avoid mismatches in asset pricing, develop proper risk management and capital management, build quality assets, focus strongly on customers, manage costs effectively and administer credit efficiently. The Committee on Financial Sector Assessment (CFSA) Report highlighted the need for introspection in the Indian financial industry and also underscored the relative strengths of the Indian Financial System.

Reduced demand and tighter financial conditions adversely affect liquidity and prospects of the banking and other sectors such as real estate, aviation, information technology. Severe liquidity and credit crunch were seen in lower capital inflows, reduced ability of Indian corporate to raise resources through the equity route, significantly increased risk perception leading to keeping all future investments by institutional investors such as pension or endowment funds on hold and cascading effect on private equity (PE) firms. Given difficulties in foreign borrowing and capital markets, the government eased overseas borrowing norms companies, announced three stimulus packages, while the RBI repeatedly slashed key interest rates.

Supportive Monetary and Fiscal Policy in India

The triad of infusion of cash, low rates and restoration of mutual trust among banks brought some order in inter-bank markets and halted the southward movement of lending rates. India responded through fiscal stimulus and RBI's policy of monetary accommodation and adoption of counter-cyclical regulatory measures to provide ample rupee liquidity, comfortable foreign exchange liquidity and credit flow to productive sectors. RBI adopted both conventional measures, such as, reduction in Repo rate from 9 per cent to 5 per cent, reduction in CRR from 9 per cent to 5 per cent, relaxed norms for external borrowings, raised interest rate ceilings on NRI deposits and unconventional measures such as rupee-dollar swap facility for Indian banks, effective reduction in the SLR from 25 per cent to 21.5 per cent with 1.5 per cent points of the reduction earmarked for liquidity support by banks to mutual funds and NBFCs.

The worst is over but the damage led to a rise in NPAs and the banking sector lost its pricing power. The risk of higher inflation because of excess liquidity increased bond yields and losses on bond portfolios.

Synchronised Global Initiatives for Structural Reforms

The woeful inadequacies of the global financial system required a new balance between state and market, between the economic and the political sphere with financial stability as a global public good. This is a tall order and necessitates, inter alia, simultaneous stimulation of the economy to enhance aggregate demand and avoiding of protectionism across countries because of the complex, global and interconnected nature of the world. Raghuram G. Rajan and Luigi Zingales in their powerful book *Saving Capitalism from the Capitalists* (2003) demonstrated that only unfettered markets, rather than protectionism can provide an environment supporting competition, innovation and economic growth. This move towards a "new economic multilateralism", which provides an accent on full employment and global collective action to advance the cause of "fair globalization", requires changes in accountability and governance, establishment of early warning capacities, a new framework for the management of exchange rates, and a review of regional currency agreements.

There has been a paradigm shift in the relative roles of various countries, particularly the rise of non-Western economic and political players with emerging economies accounting for over 50 per cent of global output. Studies by Price Waterhouse Coopers, Goldman Sachs clearly underscore the watershed changes in the global financial landscape. A 2006 study by Price Waterhouse Coopers projected that in the year 2050, the Chinese economy would be almost as large as that of the United States in dollar terms, and that India would be the third largest. Subsequently in 2007, Goldman Sachs published its "Dreaming with BRICs" report which said India would overtake the world's second largest economy, the Japanese one, by 2032 (in real US dollars, not PPP dollars). The crux of the projections was the likely productivity surge in India due to the "demographic dividend" and the "urbanisation bonus"—essentially a higher educated younger population, increasingly living in urban areas, would be far more productive than the less educated and largely rural population of the past.

While Price Waterhouse Coopers' forecast that the "E-7" (Brazil, China, India, Indonesia, Mexico, Russia, and Turkey) will be about 25 per cent larger than the current G7 and will be driving the growth of the global economy may not find universal acceptability, there is no mistaking that the these emerging economies have acquired their own place in the sun and are poised to play an increasingly important role in the global landscape in future. Accordingly, there has to be a re-examination of the role for the IMF in the light of new realities, including the mandate, resources, operational modalities and governance of the IMF to reduce the vulnerability of EMEs to financial instability and crises while preserving adequate policy autonomy in managing their integration into the international financial system, and capital flows and exchange rates. Together with a reorientation of the IMF, there must be an exploration of the role of the Financial Stability Forum and the G20/30.

It is also important to strengthen international financial institutions through a "global monitoring authority to promote global supervision" of cross-border investment, trade and banking with fast-growing economies. The world's financial architecture must change drastically because world unemployment could swell by 20 million with the vulnerable being particularly hit. Hence, developing countries need to understand social outcomes and devise appropriate social protection schemes.

While devising a new global financial system because of IMF's "legitimacy deficit", a broad spectrum strategy was needed to surmount this crisis and move ahead on the road back to solvency through measures such as sustaining liquidity, reducing volatility in foreign exchange rate, allowing capital inflows and keeping domestic and external financing available. The crisis starkly brought to the fore the imperative necessity of bridging the regulatory gaps.

The new regulatory paradigm holds important lessons for reducing the fissures in the world economic system. The contours of this new regulatory policy frame, which are aimed at checking the disruptive forces, necessitate streamlining financial market regulation; tracking movements in securitization and credit derivatives; tackling financial market's informational asymmetries; designing more effective early warning systems; strengthening transparency and accountability; and enhancing regulation, including underwriting standards and including off-balance sheet items, hedge funds, offshore financial centers and tax havens. To discernibly improve the regulatory framework for the banking system and strengthen anti-cyclical effects, coordinated actions and reinforcing international cooperation between countries and multilateral institutions; assessment of role of sovereign wealth funds as providers of capital because of inadequacy of financial institutions' capital cushions; examination of role of Standard & Poor's, Moody's and Fitch in structuring and rating securities; good central bank governance and effective public communication; and continuous evaluation and effectiveness of policy tools are necessary. In other words, policy prescriptions from failure of regulatory oversight in US necessitate a transparent and effective framework, domestic reforms together with prudential norms, efficient regulatory systems and healthy capital adequacy norms with an accent on prudent investments and quality lending. There has also to be a renewed thrust on a complete institutional revamping, while ensuring that excessive regulation does not stifle innovation.

Besides higher funding for the IMF and use of innovative ways to reshape world's financial and economic order, developed countries must not resort to protectionism and global capital flows must remain unimpeded. Hence, all markets, territories, and actors endangering the global financial system should be continuously monitored with zero tolerance for non-compliance. Streamlined and transparent auditing standards must take effect and the rating agencies must be effectively regulated with stricter rules, a specific rating scale for complex products and regular publication of their returns in the pursuit of the DDR dynamics, i.e. de-leveraging, de-globalization and re-regulation. IMF's *Global Financial Stability Report: Responding to the Financial Crisis and Measuring Systemic Risks* stressed the need to redefine global financial regulation and revamp the financial architecture to secure greater stability and prevent virulent crises with global ramifications.

To be sure, there are important differences in the process and pattern of reforms and in some cases, even the broad contours of reforms in the wake of the seamless progression to the dangerous manipulation of American financial markets have evoked acrimonious debates. Without quibbling over such differences, it can reasonably be maintained that fundamental global reforms necessitate quick response to early detection of strains, coordination within each country, and in many cases across borders, and a framework for decisive action by potentially different sets of authorities. In other words, global reform has to be an inclusive process comprising both industrial and developing countries.

This is imperative for a better understanding of financial stability, role of global cooperation in rejigging international financial architecture and identification of appropriate development rules in minimising financial contagion must constitute important building blocks. Dr. Y.V. Reddy in his recent book vigorously argues that while globalisation of finance is desirable, "the accompanying global cooperation arrangements for efficiency and stability are yet to be agreed upon". Further, "there is no evidence of a fundamental review of the ideological base of the global economy and global finance". This leads us to the fundamental questions of the emerging contours of the new global financial architecture, the role of G20 in this process and implementation of mechanisms to protect developing countries from the impact of the economic meltdown and ensure that the projected slower growth rates do not reduce allocation for the social sector in national budgets. In view of the emerging macroeconomic environment, the dialectics, dilemmas and challenges of global financial system, resolving finance capitalism's dilemmas necessitate state redirection of income distribution, investment and economic development.

Almost 90 per cent of developing countries are highly or moderately exposed to the impact of the crisis, as they face slowing economic growth, high levels of poverty, or both (Global Monitoring Report, 2009). Accordingly, Horst Köhler, German President and former head of the IMF persuasively argued "I am still waiting for a clear, audible mea culpa. The only good thing about this crisis is that it has made clear to any thinking, responsible person in the sector that international financial markets have developed into a monster that must be put back in its place.... Capitalism only has a future if it rises up to its responsibilities, especially its responsibility towards the weak. It is about practising responsibility and solidarity without at the same time switching off market and price mechanisms" (May 14, 2008).

Role of Monetary and Fiscal Measures—"Keep an Eye on the Long-term While Dancing in the Flames" (Sir Philip Hampton, Chairman, Royal Bank of Scotland).

Even in this era of sweeping globalization, the free play of the unfettered market mechanism (laissez faire economic theory) is fraught with great danger and there are inherent limitations to the theory "state intervention is always flawed". Conventional microeconomics and the theory of "market fundamentalism", which have their origins in the work of Adam Smith, would have us believe that the objective relations between supply and demand bring about the desired equilibrium point with regulation being not only unnecessary but also detrimental. But, as the events show, the markets did not oscillate around an equilibrium point but injected an upward trend into the system through speculation and thus brought to the fore the vulnerability of theoretical beliefs in the free market.

In the words of Joseph Stiglitz, "the reason that the invisible hand often seems invisible is that it is not there". Clearly, then, since the market on its own is not enough, the paradigm of "efficient markets" is not flawless and, therefore, the market mystique needs to be examined with caution. Accordingly, the governments must play an important role in shaping the economic policies and the broader frame of reference. The Keynesian thesis of "pump-priming" continued to be relevant contextually and fiscal stimulus had an important part in the route back from the precipice. Given the overarching fiscal stress, the role played by market failures and the kinds of predicaments faced, what is needed is not just larger but also smarter and highly selective investment prioritized on national goals and on performance outcomes. Investments in infrastructure and technology in general and speedy implementation of various components of the National Highways Development Projects power projects and airport privatisation in non-metro cities stimulate the economy in the short run and enhance growth in the long run.

Both economic theory and cross-country experiences strongly suggest that in such turbulent times, a pro-active and responsive monetary policy and fiscal policy with timely, targeted, and temporary measures provide the much needed stimulus to the economy and mitigate the severity of recession. Indeed this is what both the government and the RBI attempted to do in India. While the RBI reversed its earlier stance of a tight monetary policy, the government announced a fiscal stimulus package to push overall economic activity. Banks put in place a constellation of measures both on interest rates and liquidity to ward off the impending crisis. Towards this end, banks must ensure both the timeliness and reasonable pricing of credit, particularly to the SMEs and the housing sectors in India.

Strategic Options and Choices

Cataclysmic events and qualitative changes in the rules of the game have caused a feeling of unease and a sense of concern all around. These are reminiscent of Timothy Findley's observation (*Not Wanted on the Voyage*, Toronto, Viking, 1984), "Well. It wasn't an excursion. It was the end of the world". Things are certainly not easy any more for the banking and financial sector with both the sector and iconic banking and financial institutions being at the crossroads. But this is not the end of the world provided the agenda that is widely known is implemented with alacrity. As Jagdish Bhagwati (*In Defense of Globalization*, Oxford University Press, New Delhi, 2004) firmly argued, "globalization is part of the solution, not part of the problem, but that we do need institutional changes and support mechanisms to smooth out its occasional rough edges". We strongly maintain that the first step towards "smooth(ing) out its occasional rough edges" is to ask the right questions. Is the conventional strategy workable in the present environment, where all elements are critically in ferment? Given the huge socio-economic implications involved, should we perhaps not attempt to modify the strategy in line with the altered ground realities and new growth theoretic? The answers to these questions are obvious. What is not so obvious is how we are going to implement those answers and make them a reality.

The growth and soundness of the global banking system, marginally improved on two major counts since 2008 with modest improvements in profitability of banks in the US and UK in 2010 and a steady effort by global banks to strengthen their capital base, which can prepare them to absorb future losses more effectively.

In sum, the background developmental processes need not be taken as exogenously given, particularly because of the debilities and infirmities of the global banking system starkly highlighted by the global financial meltdown. The overarching environment is characterized by the following aspects:

- The system as a whole and most advanced economies, especially the fiscally strained economies in the Euro zone, still show anemic credit growth.
- Sovereign debt pressures since the early 2010 gave rise to renewed credit, market and funding risks in the Euro zone economies with troubled sovereigns and the peripheral economies.
- Despite attempts at de-leveraging, global banks in most advanced economies, especially in the Euro zone and UK, continue to be highly leveraged with dependence on wholesale funding markets.
- Persistence of credit risks at elevated levels is attributable not just to sovereign credit risks but also risks emanating from unsecured bank credit in many advanced economies.
- Reduced financial inclusion in most advanced economies because of both supply and demand side factors.
- Growing divergence between the performance of banking systems in advanced and emerging economies. While growth of banks in advanced economies has been low, the credit growth in major emerging economies has been high leading to concerns about overheating of these economies. The high levels of inflation coupled with increasing short-term capital flows into these economies have aggravated concerns about financial stability.

Well-defined, meticulously implemented and carefully monitored measures, including a greatly improved fiscal situation could perceptibly alter the ground realities. But such thoughtful measures need to be well supported by a broad spectrum of measures by a partnership of government, banks and financial institutions to realize a high and sustainable growth trajectory. Further, both advanced economies and emerging economies need to work individually and collectively towards strengthening and reviving the global banking system.

Strength and Resilience of Banks in India

Banking, as a sub-sector of the overall economic system, receives its impetus from the economic indicators. Reduced financial repression through statutory pre-emptions and enhanced prudential regulations together with progressive deregulation led to a heightened consciousness of ownership and capital structure, enhanced competition, increased autonomy, technological upgradation and performance change. Despite global concerns, the banking sector in India remains healthy, resilient, profitable and continues to perform well in terms of all identified parameters such as financial position, asset quality, return on assets (RoA), capital to risk weighted asset ratio (CRAR), productivity, profitability, etc.

Table 2: Performance of Banks in India

Performance Parameter	Benchmark	SCBs	
		2009-10	2010-11
Return on Assets	>1%	1.1	1.1
Gross NPA	<3%	2.5	2.3
Net NPA	<1%	1.1	0.9
CRAR	>9%	14.5	14.2
Cost-Income	<40%	45.8	46.0

	Bank credit to GDP	RoA	RoE	Gross NPAs	Net NPAs	Cost Income Ratio	Interest Spread (%)	CRAR
2009-10	49.5	1.1	13.3	2.5	1.1	45.8	2.7	14.5
2010-11	50.0	1.1	13.7	2.3	0.9	46.0	3.1	14.2

SCBs Performance

	2009-10	2010-11
Aggregate Deposits (% change)	17.2	15.9
Time Deposits (% change)	16.2	18.7
Demand Deposits (% change)	23.4	-0.6
Bank Credit (% change)	16.9	21.5
Credit-Deposit Ratio	72.2	75.7

Source: Report on Trends and Progress of Banking in India, RBI.

The Report on Trend and Progress of Banking in India (2011) clearly brought out the financial soundness of the banking sector in terms of capital adequacy, asset quality, leverage ratio, credit boom and liquidity. Let us highlight the strength and resilience of banks in India as highlighted in Report on Trend and Progress of Banking in India.

1. Capital Adequacy

Capital to Risk Weighted Assets Ratio (CRAR)

The CRAR of all bank groups under Basel II remained well above the stipulated regulatory norm of 9 per cent in 2010-11.

Table 3: Capital to Risk Weighted Assets Ratio (%) under Basel II

	2010	2011
Public Sector Banks	13.3	13.1
Private Sector Banks	17.4	16.5
Foreign Banks	17.3	17.0
All SCB's	14.5	14.2

Source: RBI, *op. cit.*

The CRAR of SCB's declined in 2010-11 over the previous year mainly owing to a decline in Tier II CRAR ratio. Among the bank groups, foreign banks registered the highest CRAR, followed by private sector banks and PSBs in 2010-11. In the short- to medium-term, SCB's are not constrained by capital in extending credit. The table below shows the component-wise Capital Adequacy:

Table 4: Component-wise Capital Adequacy Under Basel II

	SCB's	
	2010	2011
(A) Total Capital	567381	670389
(i) Tier I Capital	395100	474581
(ii) Tier II Capital	172281	195808
(B) Risk Weighted Assets	3901395	4724933
(C) CRAR %	14.54%	14.19%
of which Tier I	10.13%	10.04%
Tier II	4.42%	4.14%

Source: *Ibid*.

Indian Banks can Comfortably Cope with the Proposed Basel III Framework

Even with the proposed Basel III framework, which will become operational from January 1, 2013 in a phased manner, Indian banks will not have any problem in adjusting to the new capital rules both in terms of quantum and quality. Quick estimates based on the data furnished by banks in their off-site returns, showed that the CRAR of Indian banks under Basel III will be 11.7 per cent (as on June 30, 2010) as compared with the required CRAR under proposed Basel III at 10.5 per cent.

2. Asset Quality

The asset quality of the banking sector improved in 2010-11 over the previous year. The gross NPAs to gross advances ratio declined to 2.25 per cent in 2010-11 from 2.39 per cent in the previous year.

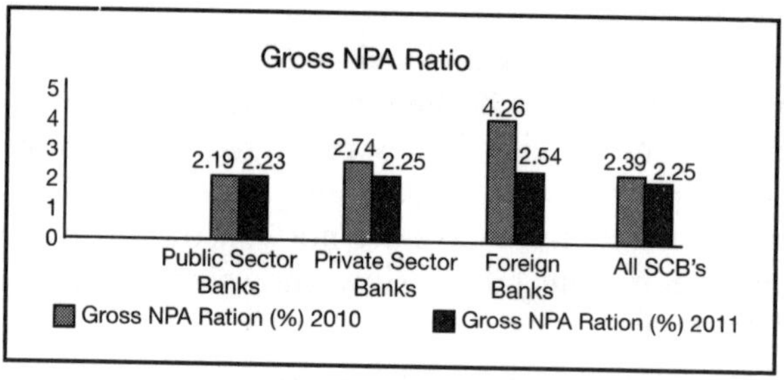

Fig. 1: Gross NPA Ratio

The improvement in asset quality was visible in both private sector banks and foreign banks. Public sector banks, however, witnessed deterioration in asset quality in 2010-11 over the previous year. The percentage of outstanding GNPAs written off to total outstanding GNPAs (as at end-March 2010) is shown below:

During the year 2010-11, the banking sector wrote off almost 10 per cent of the outstanding gross non-performing loans (as at end-March 2010), which helped in limiting the growth of gross non-performing loans. The extent of write off was lower in 2010-11 as compared with the previous year. This indicated that writing off of NPAs was an important factor in maintaining the asset quality of the banking sector at tolerable levels.

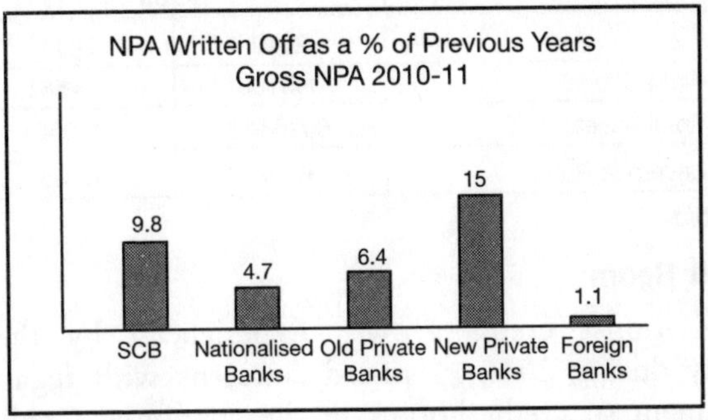

Fig. 2: NPA Written-off as a Per Cent of Previous Year Gross NPA 2010-11

Slippage Ratio

Slippage ratio calculated as addition of gross NPAs during the year as a per cent of outstanding standard assets of the previous year is another important indicator of asset quality. New private sector banks recorded the lowest slippage ratio in 2010-11.

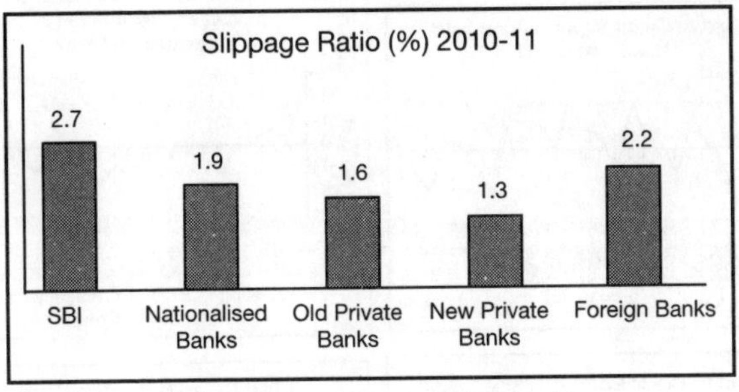

Fig. 3: Slippage Ratio (%) 2010-11

3. Leverage Ratio

Leverage ratio indicates the extent to which the business is relying on debt financing.

Despite the higher growth in balance sheet during 2010-11, the leverage ratio, as in the previous year, remained constant at 6.6 per cent in 2010-11 for SCBs owing to the corresponding growth in the capital base.

Table 5: Leverage Ratio in SCBs

	SCBs	
	2010	**2011**
Tier I Capital	395100	474581
Total Assets	6026444	7183521
Leverage Ratio	6.6%	6.6%

Source: *Ibid*.

4. Credit Boom

The robust credit growth experienced by the Indian economy during 2010-11 raised concerns with regard to the development of credit booms in the economy. Credit booms can seriously undermine the financial soundness of the banking sector owing to deterioration in credit quality. The analysis provided in the following charts indicates that the credit growth during 2010-11 did not lead to development of any credit boom in the economy both at the aggregate and sub-sectoral level. The ceiling given above is based on RBI's statistical study.

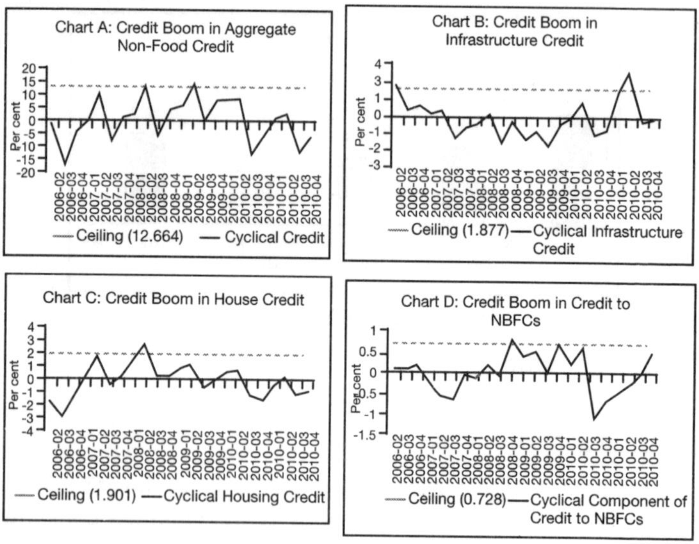

Fig. 4: Credit Growth in Indian Economy

5. Liquidity

During 2010-11, banks operated under tight liquidity conditions. The Liquidity Adjustment Facility (LAF) window of the Reserve Bank, which had remained in surplus mode for nearly 18 months, switched into deficit mode at end-May 2010 and largely remained in deficit for rest of the financial year 2010-11.

Autonomous factors like the centre's surplus balance with the Reserve Bank and currency in circulation were key drivers of liquidity conditions in 2010-11. The liquidity conditions have continued to remain in deficit mode during 2011-12 so far.

The average issuance of certificates of deposit (CDs) remained high during 2010-11 at around ₹ 33,000 crore as compared to around ₹ 17,000 crore during 2009-10. In line with the rise in rates in other money market segments, the effective interest rate in respect of aggregate CD issuances increased to 9.96 per cent at end-March 2011 from 6.07 per cent as at end-March 2010.

Transforming Risk Management Architecture

Victor Hugo stressed long ago "The invasion of armies can be resisted but not an idea, whose time has come". Risk management "is certainly an idea, whose time has come". Risk management begins with an understanding of risk and an assessment of critical systems and processes and how risk mitigation enables an organization to keep risks acceptable and implementing controls to meet expectations of managers, customers, investors, and employees is a common business practice. Irrespective of the method used, the key to risk management lies in timely delivery of risk information to the decision makers, with the time, tools and incentives to act upon it. As Francis Bacon pointed out: "If a man will begin with certainties, he shall end in doubts; but if he will be content to begin with doubts, he shall end in certainties".

The traditional face of banks as mere financial intermediaries has altered because of the paradigm shift from balance sheet to off-balance sheet intermediation, move from capital adequacy to capital efficiency and transition from banking to financial services. Appropriate risk management architecture is a function of the size, complexity of business, risk philosophy, market perception and the level of capital of banks. Irrespective of the method used, the key to risk management lies in timely delivery of risk information to the decision makers, with the time, tools and incentives to act upon it.

Competition needs to foster convergence towards best practice in risk management because of growing role of market forces, need for internationally consistent prudential norms and a high-quality financial infrastructure and interdependence of prudential standards. Hence, risks must be mitigated by developing a process for assessing critical systems and processes, documenting weaknesses, determining potential threats, and effecting value-based changes. Towards this end, there have to be improved risk management mechanisms, Risk Management Framework for Derivatives Trading, Risk Based Supervision and Outsourcing and Risk Management, revitalized IT systems and adopting a service-oriented architecture (SOA) to minimise risk exposure, streamlined systems and procedures and honing the skill set for client selection, industry analysis, concentration, risk ratings, use of benchmarks, etc. Measuring and managing risk across a range of diverse business activities through Integrated Risk Management requires devising a comprehensive Integrated Risk Management framework, enhancing understanding and communication of risk issues internally by establishing Integrated Risk Management and using advanced modelling techniques to manage inherent risks in e-business. This is crucial because risks, which are often inter-related and even transform from one to another, seldom impact an organisation in isolation. A major lesson from the global financial meltdown is the need to recognise these inter-linkages among risks on banks' part. While many institutions had elaborate risk management procedures in place, these systems focused only on specific aspects of risk (such as credit, market, and operational risk) and therefore, did not enable the capability to view risk holistically with disastrous results.

Transparency, Disclosure and Market Discipline

Transparency, disclosure and market discipline has assumed significance in the wake of highly publicized accounts of misleading financial reporting and other improprieties within corporations across countries. Such events have generally surprised executives and board members, who either had no advance warning or were not aware of the risks facing their companies. This makes it imperative for Boards of Directors, CEOs and CFOs to not only design and implement appropriate corporate governance processes, but also to assess the risks their businesses face today and can reasonably expect to face in the future and to manage those risks effectively. Risks can fester and spread anywhere inside an organization. While several risks are industry-specific such as the regulatory concerns, others are common to all industries such as financial reporting reliability and customer relationship integrity. This makes it necessary to identify, prioritise and manage risks to enhance performance and ultimately, business value with thrust on the following areas:

- **Business Process Risk Management**—risk profiling; risk polarization; analysis and management of threat; systems assessment; process and control evaluation; risk assurance (including internal audit services); business continuity planning (including disaster recovery) and corporate governance.
- **Decision Support**—ensuring integrity of information; developing decision rules; structuring management information flows and instituting systems that provide decision makers with early warning signals.
- **Performance Management**—improving delivery and vendor management; optimising supply chain management; rationalising inventory management; achieving cost reductions.
- **Activity Based and Unit Based Costing**—enabling a comprehensive and systematic basis to price for products and services.

Organizations today find themselves struggling to maintain the minimum required controls expected of them in a new, increasingly regulated—even intrusive—business environment. The traditional audit process is intended to provide assurance that control systems are adequately designed, and within a specific time frame, operating effectively. However, the audit process typically occurs significantly after the transactions are completed, and is rarely able to test all transactions in a comprehensive way for controls compliance. Therefore, there is a significant risk to many organizations that errors and fraud occur and remain undetected, negatively impacting their bottom-line. To assist in the efficient capture and evaluation of data, sophisticated software tools need to be used for evaluation of disclosure controls and procedures and internal controls over financial reporting.

International Standards and Codes

International standards and codes have evoked greater interest because of increasing cross-border flows, upscaling of technology and availability of large institutional funds such as pension funds and mutual funds. As the significance of these mutually reinforcing forces rapidly increases, the stake rise higher necessitating minimization of systemic risks by transparent operations and uniform definitions benchmarked against international norms for credible financial statements and other disclosures that are key means for communicating a firm's operating results and its overall health, as well as for making various operating activities more transparent.

Disclosure of reliable information facilitates market discipline, strengthens confidence and reduces the chance for rumors and misleading information that could cause market instability. The sequencing of the structure of reporting is a function not only of constitutional, legal and institutional mechanisms but also the safety and soundness of institutions and systemic soundness and stability. Indian accounting standards lag behind global practices in Consolidation of Accounts, Segment Reporting, Deferred Tax Accounting, International Transactions and Combinations, Joint Ventures and Related Party Transactions. These aspects make it difficult for the central bank to effectively discharge its responsibilities of ensuring financial market stability.

While there are several issues involved here, some of the important issues relate to the valid approach, adequate coverage of issues, symmetrical treatment between participants, linkage between international standards and codes and financial stability and issues of coverage of standards in IMF surveillance. What is basically required is setting of standards domestically with an international character, consultative and participative processes of setting, prioritising, incentivising, monitoring and reorienting and effective implementation.

Without in any way reducing the significance of standards and codes in the emerging landscape, the calibrated Indian approach is predicated on heightened awareness on the part of the official agencies, self-regulating bodies and market participants rather than making it a statutory requirement.

The Internal Capital Adequacy Assessment Process (ICAAP)

The New Capital Adequacy Framework (NCAF), based on the Basel II Framework evolved by the Basel Committee on Banking Supervision (BCBS), has three pillars, viz. Pillar 1—the Minimum Capital Ratio, Pillar 2—the Supervisory Review Process (SRP) and Pillar 3—Market Discipline. The SRP attempts to ensure that the banks have adequate capital to support all risks in their business and fosters development of more effective risk management techniques for monitoring and managing their risks. This would, in turn, require a well-defined internal assessment of the calculation of regulatory capital in relation to credit, market and operational risks. In conformity with Pillar 2, financial institutions are required to demonstrate to the regulator, i.e. the RBI in India that they have robust internal risk assessment and management information systems to efficiently assess their economic capital requirement. The main aspects to be addressed under the SRP, and therefore, under the ICAAP, include: (a) the risks not fully captured by the minimum capital ratio prescribed under Pillar 1; (b) the risks not at all considered by the Pillar 1; and (c) the factors external to the bank.

Under Basel II, the ICAAP requires an assessment of Pillar 1 minimum capital requirements; the extent of total shareholder funds required to meet a bank's strategy and maintain minimum capital requirements; and ensuring that material risks of the firm are understood by its Board of Directors (BoD).

The sufficiency and appropriateness of risk management, as required under ICAAP, needs to transcend regulatory purposes. ICAAP needs to be increasingly used as a core management instrument to make the business more efficient and less risky in the overarching context of rapid reforms, proliferation of new products, adoption of sophisticated technology, increasing exposure to a diverse set of markets and profound changes in regulation while meeting compliance tests and challenges from regulatory supervisors. In view thereof, ICAAP is not an isolated process but is an integral element of an organization's strategy for managing risk to create value. This is why ICAAP must span the unique portfolios and consider all material risks faced by the institution. Accordingly, developing a sound ICAAP goes beyond—much beyond—a set of tools and checklists for implementation; it requires a deep understanding of the sources, nature, and interactions of risk. This is a tall order for banks and requires, inter alia, development, articulation and communication of the vision to manage its capital through economic cycles; establishment of effective policies, practices, and techniques to appropriately identify, measure, aggregate and monitor the risks incurred by the institution; build credible stress tests, early detection tools, and actionable contingency plans; enhance organizational capabilities, knowledge, and skills to manage risk under changing circumstances; creation of documentation embodying the organizational risk strategy and practices; and demonstration of implementation of methods, procedures, processes and information systems to ensure adequate capital. What it is that sets apart banks successful in risk management from other banks in the comity of banking and financial institutions? The distinctiveness of successful banks lies in the capability to price the products/services competitively based on perceived risks and effective utilization of the capital/resources.

Given the multi-layered issues at stake, the ICAAP must be based on proven methodologies and data, including leading edge tools, robust and validated models, transparent frameworks to generate discernible results. Four crucial elements in the ICAAP relate to assessment (identification and measurement) of the risks a bank is, or may be, exposed to; application of mitigation techniques to lower capital requirements; stress-testing techniques; and role of the BoD and management. Viewed thus a multidisciplinary and integrated view of risk management across the value chain is necessary to create innovative solutions customized to organizational needs, from data architecture through advanced portfolio optimization, to support more effective decision-making.

Since the capital adequacy ratio prescribed by the RBI under the Pillar 1 of the Framework is only the regulatory minimum level, addressing only credit, market and operational risks, holding additional capital is necessary for the banks, because of the distinct possibility of some under-estimation of risks under the Pillar 1 and the actual risk exposure of a bank vis-à-vis the quality of its risk management architecture unable to be fully captured in the regulatory CRAR. Such under-estimation could emanate, inter alia, from (a) Interest rate risk in the banking book; (b) Credit concentration risk; (c) Liquidity risk; (d) Settlement risk; (e) Reputational risk; (f) Strategic risk; (g) Risk of under-estimation of credit risk under the standardised approach; (h) 'Model risk', i.e. the risk of under-estimation of credit risk under the IRB approaches; (i) Risk of weakness in the credit-risk mitigants; (j) Residual risk of securitisation, etc.

In view of the size, level of complexity, risk profile, scope of operations, gravity of the issues and the variety of underlying issues at work, including the evolving nature of methodologies and techniques in respect of measurement of non-quantifiable risks such as reputational and strategic risks, it is clear that there cannot be a broad-brush or 'a one-size fits all approach' to the ICAAP. Despite some generic features, it is essential to develop ICAAP requirements, action plan, and roadmap based on unique aspects of bank and portfolio; overall risk strategy, policy, and appetite; and key issues and best practices. In developing this objective and comprehensive assessment, it is important to factor in major risks, assets, and capabilities by identifying and evaluating all areas of material risk; models and analytic tools; departments, teams, roles, and responsibilities; measurement, management, and monitoring processes; and governance and control. Hence, banks must select their own approaches for setting risk appetite, risk assessment (Pillar 2 risk such as reputation risk, concentration risk, etc.), capital planning, capital budgeting and stress testing through a well-defined internal process. The determination by banks of their regulatory capital depends on their own risk management and risk measurement systems to maintain an adequate capital cushion for various risks. While capital plans are usually based on the bank's forecasts for growth, the successful implementation of the plan depends on the cooperation of all departments.

The ICAAP customarily includes executive summary; background of the ICAAP process; statement of firm's attitude to risk; business strategy; risk assessment; capital planning; and stress and scenario testing. The adoption of the ICAAP attempts to bridge the gap between regulatory and economic capital through a comprehensive assessment of all the material risks perceived by the bank, and planning the capital as a cushion against all quantifiable risks. The process consists of the sequential stages of identifying risks; assessing capital; forward capital planning; and conclusion.

The ICAAP incorporates all risks, viz. credit risk; market risk; operational risk; liquidity risk; insurance risk; concentration risk; residual risk; securitization risk; business risk; interest rate risk; pension obligation risk; any other identified risks. In respect of certain risks, which are difficult to quantify, the bank must assess the impact of such risks in the light of various control/mitigation measures. The crux of the issue is that banks in India must demonstrate the maintenance of the capital to risk weighted assets ratio (CRAR) well above the targeted level of 12 per cent on a consolidated (group-wide) basis to maintain buffers for strategic purposes and to meet capital requirement of other risks (other than Pillar 1 risks) in its business. Pillar 2 requires that risks are presented to, and discussed by, the BoD to ensure its acceptance and understanding. Pillar 2 also requires a bank to maintain capital ratios with concurrence of the regulator. While risk models and capital are an integral part of this mechanism, it is also necessary to consider any other internal risks, may result in losses such as fraud, rogue trading, or strategy failure.

There has to be a well-defined risk management structure consisting of Risk Management Committee of the BoD, executive level committees, functional sections both at head office and operating levels for effective management and/or mitigating various risks faced by the bank, in a timely manner.

The risk management process of the Bank must be driven by the BoD, strong organisational culture and sound operating procedures. Risk Management Framework must be supervised by Risk Management Committee, a subcommittee of the BoD and supported by functional committees like Credit Risk Management Committee, Market Risk Management Committee, Operational Risk Management Committee and Asset and Liability Management Committee.

A capital maintenance strategy has to be formulated through creation of contextual economic stress scenarios; development of model inputs and assumptions; selection of optimal testing techniques; sensitivity analysis and stress test execution; and contingency planning. The adequacy of the Risk Management Framework in conformity with ICAAP depends on the comprehensive assessment conducted by the Risk Management Department. The outcomes of such assessments have to be placed to the Risk Management Committee of the BoD on a half-yearly basis. The impact of the stress testing under certain scenarios to optimize the use of capital to create value for the organization and ensure its viability in times of economic stress must also be attempted and major findings placed to the Risk Management Committee of the BoD.

ICAAP, which documents the risk management practices of the bank, helps to assess and identify various risks, viz. interest rate risk in banking book, credit concentration risk, liquidity risk, strategic risk, etc. This is done to ensure that adequate capital is maintained to support the risks faced by the bank by building a schedule of capital under baseline conditions, incorporating systemic quantification and allocation of capital for all material risks; confirmation of granular, consistent, and repeatable results; correlation and diversification effects; and reconciliation of capital calculations.

Major issues, where further analysis and decisions are required, include correlation among various risk assessments using appropriate models, application of RAROC for decision-making to sanction loans and pricing, stabilization of credit risk rating across the bank, fixation of exposure limits for each internal rating grade, hurdle limits and additional capital requirement.

It is also equally important to monitor such exposures, particularly to infrastructure, the power sector, capital market, commercial real estate and systemically important NBFCs on an on-going real-time basis to mitigate concentration risk and diversify credit exposures across activities and regions.

Credit concentration risk can be checked by fixing sectoral caps and exposure limits to individuals, groups, substantial exposure, term loans, exposure to capital markets, real estate sector, unsecured advances, NBFCs, etc. The large borrower is considered to be one to whom the bank's aggregate exposure exceeds 10 per cent of the bank's capital funds. Banks must prudently ensure that exposure to all large borrowers does not exceed 300 per cent of its capital funds. Hirschemen-Herfindahl Index (HHI) is used for determining concentration in its portfolio. If HHI exceeds 0.18, it is considered as a concentration in the portfolio and additional capital charge has to be provided under Pillar 2 assessment. In case of concentration of high risk rated exposure vis-à-vis total rated exposure, bank must provide additional capital charge for concentration of high risk rated exposure, under Grade VI to Grade VIII, if such total high risk exposure is more than 5 per cent of the total risk rated exposure, by stipulating additional risk weight of 50 per cent for the portion exceeding the 5 per cent cut off limit.

The concentration level is assessed under various parameters to ensure that there is no concentration on liabilities side of the balance sheet by formulating a liquidity policy to ensure the ability to meet its financial obligations as and when they fall due. The contingency plan in the areas of assets and liabilities attempts to tide over the imminent or anticipated shortfall in the liquidity position and restricting the mismatches in various buckets within the tolerance limits.

Reputational Risk: Reputation risk is the risk that negative publicity regarding a bank's business practices will lead to a loss of revenue or litigation. Reputational risk is checked by adherence to risk limits/tolerance levels/delegation levels, strengthening corporate governance process, etc. An assessment of reputational risk is based on complaints received from customers and shareholders, average time taken for resolution of customer service related complaints, gravity of adverse publicity in the media during the assessment period and fines or penalties imposed.

Other Risks: The two broad approaches to Interest Rate Risk in the Banking Book (IRRBB) are earnings perspective and economic value perspective/market value approach.

Country Risk: Country risk may stem from deteriorating economic conditions, political and social upheavals, government repudiation of external indebtedness, exchange controls and currency devaluation. The Master Policy for Market Risk Management deals with management of country risk.

Capital Charge for Counter Party Bank Exposure Risk: The policy requires an assessment and mitigation of risk of exposure to counterparty bank with provision of additional capital towards Counterparty Bank Exposure Risk, where the exposure breached the aggregate limit fixed for each bank, during any time from the commencement of financial year till the date of ICAAP calculation. Under Basel III, counterparty credit exposure is to be measured using credit valuation adjustment, which could be viewed as the cost of insuring a portfolio of trades with a specific counterparty against losses due to its default.

Residual Risk: It is the risk faced by the bank in realizing the benefit of credit risk mitigants on application of internal controls. This requires a clear articulation of various aspects of collaterals and periodical review of valuation/audit of securities by professional agencies.

Strategic Risk: Strategic risk is the risk associated with the financial institution's future business plans and strategies. Banks must implement various systems and procedures, viz. policy on outsourcing, specified process for new product approval, Capital Planning Committee for ensuring maintenance of capital required as per the business strategy, periodical stress testing and contingency funding plan to mitigate the strategic risk.

Legal Risk: Legal risk is the risk arising from failure to comply with statutory or regulatory obligation. Banks adopt various measures to ensure compliance with all relevant legislation and regulatory requirements relating to legal risk and establishing proactive legal risk management culture at all levels of business and personnel. Documentation requirements for credit related matters are reviewed on the basis of the experience gained an ongoing basis, to reduce, inter alia, instances of fraud/ misuse there by mitigating the legal risk. Since legal risk is an off shoot of operational risk, it is difficult to quantify on a stand alone basis.

Compliance Risk: Compliance risk is defined as "The risk of legal or regulatory sanctions, material financial loss, or loss to reputation a bank may suffer as a result of its failure to comply with laws, regulations, rules, related self-regulatory organization standards, and codes of conduct applicable to its banking activities". Most banks have a comprehensive compliance policy with well defined roles and responsibilities of the various functionaries and an independent compliance department to monitor compliance matters through a suitable reporting mechanism.

Settlement Risk: Settlement risk is the risk that the counterparty does not deliver a security or its value in cash as per the agreement, when the security was traded. Regulators in India, including RBI and SEBI, have taken various initiatives to minimise the settlement risks prevalent in financial markets across India and globally.

It is important for banks to calculate the capital buffer by using a forecast risk profile instead of simply extrapolating figures from previous events. The ICAAP must clearly distinguish between the bank's regulatory capital, its actual capital, and the capital it needs to hold for business purposes. Using a newly developed ICAAP should provide banks with the best capital buffer required, and the best level of funds from stockholders. While risks are often considered by a bank, they are not always reflected in strategic options and capital planning. Accordingly, ICAAP requires stress and scenario analysis to demonstrate risks at an enterprise level.

While the use of effective risk management techniques is necessary for monitoring and managing the risks, it is equally important to devise suitable quality reporting mechanisms calling for necessary entity-wise feedback at quarterly and annual intervals. Such feedback mechanisms need to be supplemented by use testing, mock SREP and development and execution of training. While possessing the capital coverage determined by internal regulations that is sufficient for the fundamental risks the institution is exposed to, the institutions must develop an adequate risk management system. This risk management system must be refined and fine-tuned on an ongoing basis in accordance with the risk factors identified to leverage the full potential of the ICAAP.

The risk management process must chart out the road map for the future, identify the use of the ICAAP in the transitional journey of the bank, update risk indicators and economic capital indicators/assumptions and present these details to the BoD. In the ultimate analysis, the comprehensive and forward-looking approach, as reflected in the ICAAP, has to be an integral part of the streamlined risk management processes with the full support of the top management to develop long-term solutions to maintain shareholder value through the cycle by ensuring the standards, structure, systems, and skills to effectively manage risks and capital. It is only then that the ICAAP would play a critical role in transforming the Indian banking landscape.

The New Normal—Setting the Agenda

While risk management per se is not alien to banks, Basel II provided a differentiation by making the RM initiatives/ concepts/organization an integral part of the business strategy. This process, which required a thorough review of risk management processes, careful analysis of risks inherent in the business; consolidation because of the relationship between cost and return; and proper documentation by way of ICAAP has gained traction from the proposed Basel III norms making it necessary for banks to think beyond compliance to transform themselves as vibrant and globally competitive entities. This is why risk management is emerging as an important business differentiator.

The effectiveness of policy responses in mitigating the effects of the crisis caused by the meltdown in the financial and credit markets and securing a sustainable recovery highlighted the need for action on various fronts simultaneously. Such action in the pursuit of the medium-term objective of a more sound, competitive, and efficient financial system requires both an orderly resolution of non-viable financial institutions and a strengthening of the international macro-financial stability framework to help improve supervision and regulation at the domestic and global levels; satisfactory resolution of issues such as technology, historical data build-up, manpower skill sets, cost of implementation and mechanisms to improve the effectiveness of market discipline, e.g. strengthening of funding and securitization markets by reducing counterparty risks through centralized clearing organizations.

While sharply focused attempts are needed to tackle the inextricably inter-related areas of de-leveraging: insufficient capital, falling and uncertain asset valuations, and dysfunctional funding markets, some of the basic elements of a contextually significant strategy could be isolated and identified as the following:

- Changed risk framework encompassing risk governance, organisations and processes to mitigate corporate risk in view of the inadequacy of the traditional control techniques to provide reasonable assurance.

- Greater attention to both credit and liquidity risks; re-examination of instruments of central banks for emergency liquidity support and convergence by central banks to best practices.
- Streamline regulations and work towards developing a more proactive regulatory framework that prevents such failures and crises instead of reacting to them. However, all such clear and operationally transparent attempts should focus on effective supervision, regulatory oversight, strong risk management practices, anti-cyclicality and ensure that pro-cyclical effects are in no way exacerbated by building shock absorbers against bad economic and financial outcomes through higher charges on credit, liquidity and other risks; no financial entity should be outside the regulatory framework and regulators should be aware of the leverage and risks outside the regulated entities.
- Foster a risk culture throughout the business-risk is too important to be left to risk managers alone! Accordingly, Board of Directors and senior management should assess the risk appetite of the bank and frame suitable risk management policies and processes to develop best practices to enhance assurance and risk functions for enterprise sustainability. This thesis can be substantiated by the fact that a study by Harald Hau, Associate Professor of Finance at INSEAD, on German banks clearly underscored that financial literacy played a big role in the ability of German banks to weather the crisis—the more financially literate the board, the faster the recovery.
- Create awareness of risks at transaction level/grass-root level. Operationalisation of risk policies and processes and institutionalising risk management

requires development of bank-wide risk management culture.

- Apart from system-wide emphasis on building blocks in terms of people, processes and technology that are required for an effective risk management architecture, there has to be a renewed thrust on missing view points of the current regulatory paradigm for a comprehensive assessment.
- Appropriate Risk Management Architecture necessitates improved integrated risk management mechanisms, capital adequacy, optimum utilization of both quality and quantity of capital, access to sources of capital, sectoral caps, streamlined systems and procedures and honing skill set for client selection, industry analysis, concentration, risk ratings, use of benchmarks, etc.
- Adroit risk management requires both a clear understanding of both the macro-prudential and the micro-prudential risks, loan pricing, capital efficiency and operational efficiency. In view of the multi-layered issues at work, there is a manifest need to combine quantitative and qualitative approaches to actively manage liquidity, valuation, and counterparty risks.
- Technological upgradation. Identification and implementation suitable software solutions, particularly to adopt advanced approaches of risk management. Scope for "Black-Box" approach while adopting the software solutions.
- Historical building up of data—careful assessment of assumptions, stress on assumed correlations and rigourous examination of changes in correlations; documentation, vetting and periodical review of assumptions to ensure that such assumptions are re-calibrated with the market data; robust MIS supported by high quality data amenable to detailed technical analysis; need for abundant caution and prudence in case "no data" exists. An integrated

information system is necessary to provide foundation for forecasting and building up models in respect of various activities; need to take a comprehensive view of operational risk management; creating loss data base, evolving risk matrix, etc.

- Renewed thrust on an incisive evaluation of the borrower's ability and willingness to pay with good quality credit appraisals; prudent underwriting practices and an accent on income proof, asset verification and employment verifications; changed design of regulation of mortgage to prevent recurrence of a supply overhang leading to painfully corrected housing prices.
- Need to desist from imprudent risk, sanction of household loans on the basis of the traditional canons of disposable income, security norms and repayment capacity and strict regulation of mortgage underwriting; reduced use of Direct Sales Agents (DSAs) and other third parties, whose work with multiple lenders reduces the quality of loan; complete and clear documentation; re-evaluation of audit and compliance processes to quickly detect violations and introduce post disbursement quality audit for the loans to ensure adherence to the stipulated norms.
- Adoption of risk based pricing and establishment of risk-reward concepts.
- Risk rating of borrowers through external credit rating agencies (ECAIs) to claim capital leverage.
- Understanding and implementing high standards of Corporate Governance.
- Since fair value accounting (FVA) practices amplify cyclical fluctuations of valuations in highly illiquid markets or in buoyant or dire circumstances, FVA can generate valuations inconsistent with longer term fundamentals and the cash flows and risks necessitating fine-tuning of FVA methodologies to help mitigate the exaggerated effects of some

valuation techniques. This requires a convergence of accounting, prudential, and risk management approaches to valuation to promote a more stable financial system. This is a tall order, and requires, inter alia, supplementing of accounting valuations with additional information such as the expected variation of fair value valuations, modeling techniques, and assumptions; higher capital buffers to the extent of about 30-40 per cent above normal levels in good times and the use of forward-looking provisioning; and shorter reports at higher frequencies rather than longer reports and lower frequencies.

- Focus on business sense for risk monitoring changed risk measures and capital adequacy ratios, redesigned incentive schemes and preparation for the worst.
- Apart from an incisive insight into the complex mechanism of modern finance, a workable knowledge of the modern techniques for analysing the performance and risks of alternative investments, and with qualitative and quantitative insights for optimal portfolio construction and risk management of institutional portfolios containing alternative investments is imperative.
- Appropriateness of disclosures and its validation and its frequency.
- Evolving efficient stress testing framework.
- Extreme hedge fund risk diversification with volatility requires addressing the issues of measurement of extreme risk in the hedge fund universe, extreme hedge fund risk diversification with volatility, importance of the volatility factor in the risk and extreme risk of the main hedge fund strategies and the mechanism of assessment of the quality of extreme risk diversification with volatility for hedge fund portfolios.

- Asset allocators and their advisors need to develop a clear understanding of the sources of performance and risk drivers of alternative investment strategies. Hedge fund managers need to substantiate their claims of value creation with quantitative reports on relative performance and factor exposure while hedge fund administrators and end-investors must be able to perform such analyses independently.
- Manpower skill set—Providing trained and skilled human capital to establish and manage risk management system; reduce attrition and retain trained personnel is also a challenge.
- Rapid and informative disclosure and a streamlined information infrastructure with a greater role of the board and its committees.

Basel II regulations regime implementation exert pressure on capital requirements of banks. The banking sector saw net depletion of 200 basis points in capital adequacy on adoption of Basel II. Given the wide-ranging ramifications of the proposed Base III framework, it is imperative for banks in India to examine the framework and chalk out transition path and initiate steps so as to be prepared for adoption of the new standards in a gradual and calibrated manner.

Pillar 3 is a key challenge to accurately measure and assess the risks in an increasingly uncertain business environment. It is a process where internal risks of systems/initiatives are translated to external disclosures.

Market analysts/rating agencies are likely to place increasing emphasis on bank's response to Pillar 3 requirements. Compliance of the same is likely to be rewarded with strong confidence and improved ratings.

Basel III implementation is likely to accelerate the emerging trend of consolidation to overcome capital constraint, streamlining risk management, maximizing return of capital, greater use of technology for efficiency gains. A winning strategy therefore involves implementing and monitoring best risk management initiatives, capabilities to extend geographical boundaries, expand market/products, going for mergers/acquisitions.

It is widely agreed that weak and ineffective regulations, inter alia, caused global financial meltdown. This necessitates more comprehensive and robust regulations and supervision together with full, timely, consistent and global implementation of the Basel III rules. A consistent global regulatory framework is a necessary and not a sufficient condition to effectively mitigate both individual banking risks and global contagion. In the ultimate analysis, strong, comprehensive rules and regulations must be effectively enforced so that banks, banking systems and supervisors are better prepared to cope with the next crisis, wherever it arises.

The Basel Committee's Standards Implementation Group closely monitors and coordinates the implementation of rules and recommendations. The Committee's sequential implementation assessment process is based on countries' progress in adopting the Basel regulatory framework; the consistency of national and regional legislations with the agreed Basel III rules; and to determine whether the rules are practically delivering the anticipated outcomes across different countries and result in comparable outcomes at the bank level.

There are, however, practical difficulties in implementation and diverse approaches to well-designed global rules and regulations, e.g. differences in terms of insolvency regimes, permissible banking business, imposition of taxes on financial transactions, arbitrage by the industry and potentially damaging unilateral changes by national regulators to making the global financial system safe and stable. Since such differences can stymie reforms, attempts must be made to achieve a consensus because of distinctive peculiarities across regions and institutions.

Road Ahead

The far-reaching nature of the events that unfolded created the problem of 'moral hazard', whereby the institutions causing the financial risk were not the ones to fully bear it and the dilemma involved in "guarantees given to failed managements".

There was, however, a broad consensus that setting the house of world finance in order had overriding priority in moving from recession to recovery. A comprehensive programme to preserve short-term liquidity, remove damaged assets from bank balance sheets, and recapitalization of banks together with a comprehensive approach to liquidity and confidence required boldness, imagination and infusion of taxpayers' money. While few banks are comfortable with the more intrusive regulation that inevitably accompanies greater government involvement in the industry, the need for new and more effective internal approaches to managing risk, including implementing modern quantitative analysis of performance and risks, consolidating an enterprise-wide risk system across a range of risk categories, organizations, and information technology systems with a renewed thrust on soundness and solvency, balanced with generating returns is indisputable because as William Shakespeare observed in his classic work, *Julius Caesar*,

> The fault, dear Brutus, is not in our stars,
> But in ourselves, that we are underlings.

Accordingly, in the quest to achieve high performance by 2012, most commercial banks in developed markets have settled for lower risk and moderate growth. In sum, the strategy of banking and financial institutions has to be redefined by check on derivatives and other high-risk exposures, thrust on creditworthiness and asset quality, robust risk management systems, strong capital base, transparency, prudence and regulations staying ahead of innovations and a clear understanding of the financial system. Socio-economic and technological forces continue to transform the global economy and organizations around the world in a manner, which was even difficult to visualize a few decades ago. The adoption—and what is even more important, the adaptation—of new technologies, the rapid obsolescence of technology, the need for just-in-time learning and the search for cost effective ways to meet the learning needs of a global workforce have redefined the processes governing the design, development and delivery of learning and development of the banking and the financial sector.

The manner in which the banking sector evolves has far reaching implications not only for the sustenance and growth of banks but also on the process and pattern of economic development. In this kind of setting, while a consistent and coherent set of policies across countries to stabilize the global financial system is needed to maximize impact while avoiding adverse effects on other countries, there are no easy one-size fits all solutions. It can, however, justifiably be that what is needed is a paradigm shift from short-term management to a long-term strategic approach. There cannot be any, what F.R. Leavis termed in a different context, "blunting of edge, blurring of focus and muddled misdirection of attention" (Leavis, 1972). This paradigm shift requires a three-pronged strategy of flexibility in areas of finance, operations and product offerings, diversification across products and geographies and prudent cost management to slash costs without reducing competitiveness to be a winning player in the global banking industry. As these changes intensify, the stakes rise higher necessitating a fundamental reorientation of strategies by banks to successfully meet the onslaughts of the progressive across the board liberalization. Banks have overcome trials of adversity in the past; with confidence, dedication and steadfast pursuit of well-defined goals, they would emerge unscathed in the trial of prosperity in the future.

The Chinese character for "crisis" combines the ideas of danger and opportunity. The ramifications of these large scale transformation are significant not only for our banks but also the overall economy. In the context of the steadily rising economy, the dynamics of banking development and the transforming macroeconomic landscape, a new set of policies tailored to the specific needs is called for to foster a virtuous cycle of regenerative, broad-based growth. But there is no cause for alarm as the system is well equipped to meet them. What is needed is the pursuit of competitive advantage by achieving higher levels of efficiency and productivity and attain and maintain global benchmarks in terms of all identified parameters.

This vision for a vibrant and internationally competitive banking sector in India is based on achievement of competitive advantage. Competitive advantage requires continued accent on efficiency, productivity and profitability and upscaling of technological upgradation on a much larger canvas, transition to greater capital account convertibility, while being consistent with continuing obligations under the WTO commitments. This would enable banks to emulate the international best practices and successfully weather the seemingly insurmountable challenges of this volatile era.

The writing on the wall is clear, the message of history unmistakable: the world needs new ways of thinking about finance and the risks it entails. While focusing on the risk management framework through culture change in banks, new technology to capture and analyse data, there has to be a rethink on new ways to organisation. While in view of the conflicts involved in resolving inter-governmental differences in the G20 context, each country will have to devise its own roadmap, Indian banks and financial institutions can no longer exist in cocoon or adopt an ostrich like attitude in the wake of the inexorable process of globalization. The dangers of progressive across the board liberalization in this brave new world make it necessary not to be oblivious of safeguards in moving ahead with financial reforms and adopting best practices in mapping the future of Indian banking. Solutions to the future may not come easily, but we cannot find them unless we keep looking. Failure is not an option.

Mapping the Future of Indian Banking

It is important to explore new opportunities for investment and value creation through an enhanced knowledge of banking M&A strategies, identify the challenges and solutions of creating and increasing value, get the inside track on past, present and future deals and markets, analyse the real progress in removing barriers to cross-border banking consolidation and build business relationships, line up future deals and expand the network.

The process of competition, convergence, consolidation, compliance and cost efficiency needs to be carefully pursued by banks through changes in products, technology, structure, processes, detection and elimination of "cost drivers" and introduction of advanced management concepts and practices to successfully introduce new financial instruments and strategies. The focus has to be on technology, infrastructure and human resources, which provide the cutting edge of development.

Cataclysmic changes cause a widespread feeling of unease and a sense of concern. These are reminiscent of Timothy Findley's poignant observation (*Not Wanted on the Voyage*, Toronto: Viking, 1984), "Well. It wasn't an excursion. It was the end of the world". Things are not easy for banks. But this is not the end of the world provided the agenda that is widely known is implemented with alacrity. Attempts to provide a perspective for future require development of the core competencies of banks while exploring new vistas, continuous development of new products, cultivation of the organisational culture and cooperation. In sum, the background developmental processes need not be taken as exogenously given because as T.S. Eliot famously said

> Where is the wisdom we have lost in knowledge? Where is the knowledge we have lost in information?
>
> —T.S. Eliot, *The Rock* (1934)

What is needed is a comprehensive strategy for defining strategic customer segments and value propositions, establishing enterprise wide customer guiding principles, identifying specific synergies, variations and gaps among business units and creating strategic customer initiatives to enhance the inherent strength and resilience of banks.

While building on the past, we must invest in the future; while strengthening our core competencies, we must explore new vistas of development and seed options for future growth. There has been thrust on volume-led growth to competitive balance sheet size, migration from interest income to non-interest income and capital adequacy to capital efficiency because of increased competition in financial market in general and banking sector in particular, progressively reducing net interest margin, stiff competition for good corporate loans with development of capital market and increased market capitalization and relentless pursuit of the strategy of balance sheet growth to maintain reasonable profit growth.

Banks are implementing strategies to immune their balance sheets from interest rate fluctuation by greater attention on non-interest income segments. Growing services sector and financial market have created new avenues for fee-based income. Merchant banking, international trade, funds transfer, payments and settlements, consultancy services, financial derivatives, utility services, etc. opened up new income sources for banks. But there has to be a transition from branch banking to virtual banking, market segmentation to customer segmentation and product planning to customer profitability.

In pursuit of their "glocalisation" strategy of thinking globally, acting locally, banks must respond quickly to opportunities and threats and embrace change across the development spectrum-change across customer stimuli, competitive threats and technological automation. Success requires a threshold level of performance in terms of three key parameters—customer service, product innovation and operational excellence—and a clear leadership in one dimension. Development strategies must be broadened to incorporate all these three critical dimensions for secular dynamic change and structural transformation.

1

Background and Causes of Meltdown

Introductory

The world is probably at the end of a severe financial crisis triggered by an unprecedented rise in mortgage delinquencies and foreclosures in the United States, with adverse consequences for banks, finance companies and markets around the globe. Unarguably, it was the worst economic slowdown since the Great Depression of 1930s as it slashed global investment, sharply reduced international trade, dried up demand, which led to sharp drops in prices of several commodities, eroded margins and took away profits of big and small companies, exhorting them to resort to mass layoffs.

BACKGROUND

It is believed that the crisis had its roots in the closing years of the 20th century though it did not become apparent before 2007. As a matter of fact, only a few sharp eyes were able to notice the impending slowdown even at that time though some premonitions had appeared in some journals and newspapers.

Since America was the epicenter of this crisis, it is necessary to trace the events that created conditions of downturn in that country, and which turned into a global contagion within a span of a few months. It has been established that 80 per cent of US mortgages issued in recent years to subprime borrowers were adjustable-rate mortgages (ARMs). Subprime lending is mainly in the form of mortgages for the purchase of residences to borrowers who do not meet the usual criteria for borrowing at the lowest prevailing market interest rate. When the house prices began to decline in the US in 2006-07, refinancing became more difficult, and as ARMs began to reset at higher rates, mortgage delinquencies soared. The securities backed with subprime mortgages, widely held by financial firms, lost most of their value. The result was a large decline in the capital of many banks and USA government sponsored enterprises, and a severe credit crunch around the world. The default rates began to rise quickly thereafter. Lax regulation, deregulation of government policies and huge investment from private sector had greatly increased Wall Street's involvement in higher risk lending. It is believed that subprime mortgages increased nearly three times over during the period 2003 to 2007. When the housing prices started to drop in 2006-07 and interest rates began to rise in the US, refinancing became increasingly difficult. As easy initial terms expired, defaults and foreclosures shot up dramatically, and this triggered a financial crisis through 2007 and 2008.

Heavy Investment by Banks and Financial Companies in MBS

The financial agreements called mortgaged-backed securities (MBS) have been issued and traded for decades without any problem. They derive their value from mortgage payments and housing prices. The amount of these financial agreements greatly increased during the initial years of the new millennium as financial institutions and investors around the world started investing heavily in them. The market for MBS comprised subprime loans developed in the US housing boom. Some major banks and financial institutions had borrowed and invested heavily in subprime MBS. They reported losses of approximately US $440 billion in July 2008.

Magnitude of Subprime Mortgage Market

The value of USA subprime mortgages was estimated at $1.3 trillion as of March 2007 with over 7.5 million first-lien subprime mortgages outstanding. Between 2004 and 2006, the share of subprime mortgages relative to total originations ranged from 18 per cent to 21 per cent, as against less than 10 per cent in the years 2001-03 and during 2007. In the third quarter of 2007, subprime ARMs, making up only 6.8 per cent of USA mortgages outstanding, also accounted for 43 per cent of the foreclosures which began during that quarter. By October 2007, approximately 16 per cent of subprime adjustable-rate mortgages were either 90-days delinquent or the lender had begun foreclosure proceedings, roughly three times the rate in 2005. By January 2008, the delinquency rate had risen to 21 per cent and by May 2008 it was nearly 25 per cent.

It is believed that the value of all the residential mortgages owed by households in the US to purchase residences was approximately US $9.9 trillion by the end of 2006, which rose to US $10.6 trillion by July 2008. During 2007, foreclosure proceedings on about 1.3 million properties were started by the lenders, which was nearly 80 per cent increase over 2006.[1] This further increased to 2.3 million in 2008, a further 80 per cent increase over 2007.

It was noticed that subprime borrowers had weakened credit histories and reduced repayment capacity. Subprime loans thus had a higher risk of default than loans to prime borrowers. It is worthy of note that if a borrower is delinquent in making timely mortgage payments to the loan servicer (a bank or other financial firm), the lender may take possession of the property through a process called foreclosure. Between August 2007 and October 2008, close to one million residences completed their foreclosures in the US. This unprecedented magnitude of foreclosures and the failure of large banks like Lehman Brothers and sale of Merrill Lynch & Co. triggered a panic and sharp fall in the stock markets all over the world as people started apprehending a global recession akin to the Great Depression of 1930s.

CAUSES OF MELTDOWN

The crisis can be attributed to several factors pervasive in housing markets and credit systems. The major causes are discussed below.

Repayment Defaults by Homeborrowers

There is a consensus of opinion that the most significant cause of the global financial crisis was the inability of homeborrowers to make their mortgage payments. Various papers, articles and reports on the issue have referred to predatory lending, i.e. the practice of selling financial products by institutions without disclosing the inherent risks. This, coupled with high speculation by the borrowers who involved themselves to excessive debt levels, created conditions full of risk. According to BBC, "Two important catalysts of the subprime crisis were the influx of money from the private sector and banks entering into the mortgage bond market and the predatory lending practices of mortgage brokers, specially the adjustable rate mortgage."[2]

In its "Declaration of the Summit on Financial Markets and the World Economy" (15 November 2008), the G20 leaders cited the following causes of the meltdown:

> During a period of strong global growth, growing capital flows, and prolonged stability earlier this decade, market participants sought higher yields without an adequate appreciation of the risks and failed to exercise proper due diligence. At the same time, weak underwriting standards, unsound risk management practices, increasingly complex and opaque financial products, and consequent excessive leverage combined to create vulnerabilities in the system. Policy-makers, regulators and supervisors, in some advanced countries, did not adequately appreciate and address the risks building up in financial markets, keep pace with financial innovation, or take into account the systemic ramifications of domestic regulatory actions.

The declaration points out to a number of factors that contributed to the building up of the bubble which eventually burst towards the end of the third quarter of 2008. All of the causes of contagion are interrelated and thus, cannot be studied in isolation. Some of them are discussed more elaborately below.

Speculation

Speculation refers to the activity of buying and selling goods or shares in a company in the hope of making a profit, but with the risk of losing money. Speculation in residential real estate proved to be a major contributing factor to the meltdown.

Housing prices nearly doubled between 2000 and 2006—a vastly different trend from the historical appreciation of roughly equivalent to the prevalent rate of inflation. Homes had also not traditionally been treated as investments, being subject to high speculation. But this behaviour dramatically changed during the housing boom.

During 2006, 22 per cent of homes purchased (1.65 million units) were for investment purpose, with an additional 14 per cent (1.07 million units) purchased as vacation homes. During 2005, these figures were 28 per cent and 12 per cent, respectively. In other words, a record level of nearly 40 per cent of homes purchases were not intended as primary residences.

According to David Lereah, chief economist of National Association of Realtors (NAR), the 2006 decline in investment buying was quite expected because, by that time, many speculators who had made good profit left the market, causing the investment sales to fall much faster than the primary market.[3] Some of the mortgage companies had identified the risks inherent in subprime mortgages as the highly leveraged position in multiple properties by several investors was known to them. Nicole Gelinas of the Manhattan Institute had described in "Sheltering Speculation" the negative consequences of not adjusting tax and mortgage policies to the shifting treatment of a home from conservative inflation hedge to speculative investment. Economist Robert Shiller, in "Infectious Exuberance", drew attention to the 'speculative bubbles' that are fueled by contagious optimism seemingly impervious to facts that often takes hold when prices are rising. "Bubbles", he says, "are primarily social phenomena; until we understand and address the psychology that fuels them, they're going to keep forming." Keynesian economist Hyman Minsky has described how speculative borrowing contributed to rising debt and an eventual collapse of asset values. He has cited speculative borrowing as a contributing factor to the subprime mortgage crisis.

Building of Boom on Easy Credit

Low lending rates and large inflows of foreign funds created easy credit conditions in the US for several years prior to the crisis, leading to a housing market boom and even encouraging debt-financial consumption. Home ownership reached an all-time high of just below 70 per cent in the US in 2004. The price of typical American house increased by 140 per cent in 2006. This housing bubble made quite a few homeowners to refinance their homes at lower interest rates or finance consumer spending by taking out second mortgages secured by price appreciation. In the US, the household debt as a percentage of annual disposable personal income was 127 per cent at the end of 2007 as against about 75 per cent in 1990.

The housing prices were increasing, consumers were saving less but borrowing and spending more. There was a culture of consumerism, which according to Christopher Lasch, is a factor "in an economy based on immediate gratification".[4]

Housing debt grew from just around $900 billion in 1990—which constituted about 60 per cent of disposable personal income—to $7.4 trillion by the end of 2000, and to $14.5 trillion by mid-2008, constituting as high as 134 per cent of disposable personal income. It is believed that a typical US household owned 13 credit cards, spending lavishly with 40 per cent of households carrying a debt. This easy credit and housing price increase built a boom, caused the US housing prices to peak and then decline as eventually there was a large surplus of unsold homes. Easy and cheap credit and a belief that house prices would continue to appreciate, encouraged a large number of subprime borrowers to obtain adjustable-rate mortgages which lured borrowers with below market interest rates for the remainder of the mortgage term. However, many borrowers were unable to make higher payments once the initial grace period ended, and tried to refinance their mortgages. But, once house prices began to decline in many parts of US, refinancing became difficult. The borrowers who found it difficult to escape higher monthly payments began to default. As the number of borrowers who stopped making their mortgage payments increased, foreclosures and supply of homes for sales increased, leading to a decline in housing prices and contraction in homeborrowers' equity. The decline in mortgage payments also reduced the value of mortgage-backed securities which eroded the net worth of banks and other financial institutions and adversely impacted their financial health. When they drastically cut down further lending, there was a severe liquidity crunch slowing down economic activities. This vicious cycle, according to Martin Feldstein, was "at the heart of the crisis".

Negative Equity in Homes: The major and unexpected decline in house prices meant that several borrowers, whose homes were worth less than their mortgages, had a negative equity. It has been reported that by September 2008, about nine million borrowers (approximately 11 per cent of total homeowners in the US) had zero or negative equity, and the number crossed 12 billion by December 2008. Since home mortgage is typically 'sans recourse' debt secured against property, the borrowers with negative equity have an obvious advantage in defaulting. It is pertinent to mention here that the situation in America was different from that in India where the banks do not sanction 'without recourse' loan even though backed by security of property, and insist on third party guarantee of a person of substantial means, besides the personal security of the borrower.

Inventory of Unsold Homes: Increasing foreclosures increased the inventory of houses offered for sale. During 2007, the number of new homes sold was just over two-thirds of those in 2006. By January 2008, the ratio of unsold new homes to December 2007 sales volumes was 9.8:1. As many as four million existing homes were for sale by December 2008. This overhang of unsold homes further lowered the house prices and put more homeborrowers at the risk of either default or foreclosure, starting a vicious circle and aggravating the situation further.

Changing Behaviour of Lenders

Some studies have shown that the behaviour of lenders underwent a dramatic change in the years before the crisis. They offered more and more loans to higher-risk borrowers. Subprime mortgages which were $35 billion in 1994, reached $160 billion in 1999 and a whopping $600 billion in 2006. Percentage-wise, subprime mortgages were 5 per cent of total originations in 1994, 9 per cent in 1996, 13 per cent in 1999 and reached 20 per cent in 2006. A study by Federal Reserve found that the average difference between subprime and prime mortgage interest rates decreased significantly during the years 2001 to 2007. According to a working paper series, declining risk premia and credit standards were instrumental in creating boom and bust cycles. Lenders in America offered increasingly risky loan options and the borrowers fell for them.

Prudent bankers and financiers always insist on 20 to 30 per cent margin. China and India have down payment requirements exceeding 20 per cent. In America, down payment requirement for first-time homebuyers was just 2 per cent. Noelle Knox has brought to light the fact that 43 per cent of homebuyers in 2005 made no down payment.[5] Margin money or down payment performs some important functions. It tests the creditworthiness of the prospective borrower. Those in such poor financial condition as cannot arrange margin money get rejected. Secondly, margin money puts the borrower's stake in the goods financed and keeps his/her interest alive. Thirdly, it prevents the financial institution from exposing itself to the maximum extent of cost of project and thus curtails its risk. Finally, there is also less burden on the borrower as the equated monthly instalments (EMIs) of loan taken to the extent of 75-80 per cent of the cost are less than the one availed 100 per cent. Lenders in the US did not follow the prudence of taking down payment and consequently burnt their fingers.

The types of loan offered to homebuyers had extremely lax norms. For example, the "no income, no job and no assets" loan could be availed by anyone. The financial firm's security was the home financed. Any erosion in the value of home would substantially harm the firm's interest. Another example is the interest-only adjustable-rate mortgage which allows the homeowner to pay just the interest during an initial period. Still another is a 'payment option' loan, in which the homeowner can pay a variable amount, but any interest not paid is added to the principal. An estimated one-third of ARMs which originated between 2004 and 2006 had 'teaser' rates below 4 per cent, and these increased significantly after some initial period, as much as doubling the monthly payment.

The proportion of subprime ARM loans made to people with credit scores high enough to qualify for conventional mortgages with better terms increased from 41 per cent in 2000 to 61 per cent by 2006. However, there were many factors other than credit score that affected lending. In addition, mortgage brokers in some cases received incentives from lenders to offer subprime ARMs even to those with credit ratings that merited a conforming loan.

Mortgage underwriting standards declined precipitously during the boom period. The use of automated loan approvals allowed loans to be made without appropriate review and documentation. In 2007, 40 per cent of all subprime loans resulted from automated underwriting. The chairman of the Mortgage Bankers Association claimed that mortgage brokers, while profiting from the home loan boom, did not do enough to examine whether borrowers had the capacity to repay. Mortgage fraud by lenders and borrowers increased enormously around this period.

Securitization Practices

In the traditional mortgage loans, the banks originated the loan and retained the credit risk. This model gave way to distributive model through securitization practices in which the banks sold their mortgages and distributed the credit risk to investors through mortgage-backed securities. Securitization, in simple terms, meant that those issuing mortgages were no longer required to hold them till maturity. By selling the mortgages to investors, the originating banks recovered their funds, enabling them to issue more loans and get transaction fees. There was thus more focus on processing more and more mortgage transactions rather than nurturing the credit and ensuring its success.

Securitization accelerated in the mid-1990s. The total amount of mortgage-backed securities issued almost tripled between 1996 and 2007, from $2.5 trillion to $7.3 trillion. The securitized share of subprime mortgages increased from 54 per cent in 2001, to 75 per cent in 2006. American homeowners, consumers and corporations owed about $25 trillion during 2008. American banks retained approximately $8 trillion of that total directly as traditional mortgage loans. Bondholders and other traditional lenders provided another $7 trillion, while the remaining amount of $10 trillion was provided by the securitization markets. These markets started to close down in the spring of 2007 and nearly shut down in the fall of 2008. More than 30 per cent of the private credit markets thus became unavailable as a source of funds. In February 2009, Ben Bernanke stated that securitization markets remained effectively shut, with the exception of conforming mortgages, which could be sold to Fannie Mae and Freddie Mac.

A more direct connection between securitization and the subprime crisis relates to a fundamental fault in the way that underwriters, rating agencies and investors modeled the correlation of risks among loans in securitization pools. Correlation modeling—determining how the default risk of one loan in a pool is statistically related to the default risk for other loans—was based on a 'Gaussian copula' technique developed by statistician David X. Li. This technique, widely adopted as a means of evaluating the risk associated with securitization transactions, used what turned out to be an overly simplistic approach to correlation. Unfortunately, the flaws in this technique did not become apparent to market participants until after many hundreds of billions of dollars of ABS and CDOs backed by subprime loans had been rated and sold. Felix Salmon called these developments "a recipe for disaster". He stated that by the time the investors stopped buying subprime-based securities, the effects of the crisis had already begun to emerge, foreboding serious consequences.[6] Nobel Laureate

Dr. A. Michael Spence also severely criticized the financial innovation of securitization intended to redistribute and reduce risk, which according to him "appears mainly to have 'hidden' it [the risk] from view".[7]

Faulty Credit Ratings

Credit rating agencies are now under scanner for having given investment grade rating to mortgaged-based securities in risky subprime mortgage loans. During boom, such high ratings set off large-scale sale of MBSs to investors, thereby building a housing bubble. Some people argue that these ratings were accepted as justified because of risk-reducing practices such as credit default insurance and equity investors willing to bear the first losses. However, the US House of Representatives Committee on Government Oversight and Reform stated that there are indications that some involved in rating subprime securities were fully aware that the process was faulty. Some critics have alleged that the rating agencies were paid handsomely by investment banks and other firms that organize and sell structured securities to investors. According to SEC-Rating Agency Rules, "significant weaknesses in rating practices", including conflicts of interest were found.

If giving high rating was effectual in shooting up the sale of MBS to investors, the lowering of credit ratings was instrumental in reducing the value of stock prices of many financial firms. According to the available data, between June 2007 and April 2008, the rating agencies lowered the credit ratings on $1.9 trillion in mortgage-backed securities.

The credit rating industry has been called by critics "a central culprit of the financial crisis". Over the last decade, the rating services have helped Wall Street repackage mortgages into securities, thereby fostering the spread of risky lending that eventually imperilled the economy. Many securities that had been rated AAA became worthless.

Government Policies

It is also believed that absence of proper government regulation and policies like deregulation contributed to crisis. The Securities and Exchange Commission (SEC) and chairman of Fed Reserve conceded failure in allowing the self-regulation of investment banks.

Giving a boost to home ownership has been one of the main objectives of American Government under Presidents Reagan, Clinton and George W. Bush. Way back in 1982, Congress passed the Alternative Mortgage Transactions Parity Act (AMTPA), which permitted non-federally chartered housing creditors to write adjustable-rate mortgages. Under this, new mortgage loan types were created such as adjustable-rate option, balloon-payment and interest-only mortgage. These new loan types replaced the long standing practice of banks making conventional fixed rate, amortising mortgages. Whereas traditional loans were time-tested and had a proven record, new loans were dicey and susceptible to misutilisation. The banking industry deregulation was also criticized for contributing to saving and loan crisis and it was alleged that Congress failed to enact regulations that would have prevented exploitations. Widespread abuse of predatory lending occurred with the use of adjustable-rate mortgages. It is pertinent to mention here that about 80 per cent of subprime mortgages in America were ARMs.

The Government Sponsored Enterprises (GSEs) like Fannie Mae began receiving government tax incentives for purchasing mortgage-backed securities which included loans to low income borrowers. Thus began the involvement of the Fannie Mae and Freddie Mac with the subprime market. In 1996, Housing and Urban Development Department set a goal for Fannie Mae and Freddie Mac that at least 42 per cent of the mortgages they purchase should be issued to borrowers whose household income was less than the median in their area. This target was increased to 52 per cent in 2005. Between 2002 and 2006, as the US subprime market grew nearly 300 per cent over previous years, Fannie Mae's and Freddie Mac's combined purchases of subprime securities rose from $38 billion to around $175 billion per year before dropping to $90 billion per year, which included $350 billion of Alt-A securities. Fannie Mae had stopped buying Alt-A products in the early 1990s because of the high risk of default. By 2008, the Fannie Mae and Freddie Mac owned, either directly or through mortgage pools they sponsored, $5.1 trillion in residential mortgages, about half the total US mortgage market. The GSEs have always been highly leveraged and their net worth as of 30 June 2008 was a mere US $114 billion. When deep concerns arose in September 2008 regarding their ability to honour their guarantees, the government was forced to place the companies into a conservatorship, effectively nationalizing them at the taxpayers' expense (Bloomberg, 2008-09).

The Glass-Steagall Act was enacted after the Great Depression of 1930s. It separated commercial banks and investment banks, in part to avoid potential conflicts of interest between the lending activities of the former and rating activities of the latter. Nobel laureate Joseph Stiglitz criticized the repeal of the Act. He called its repeal the "culmination of a $300 million lobbying effort by the banking and financial services industries...spearheaded in Congress by Senator Phil Gramm".[8] He believed that it contributed to the crisis because the risk-taking culture of investment banking dominated the more conservative commercial banking culture, leading to increased levels of risk-taking and leverage during the boom period. Another economist Eric Weiner expressed the opinion that the Federal government bailout of thrifts during the savings and loan crisis of the late 1980s may have encouraged other lenders to make risky loans, and thus given rise to moral hazard.[9]

Conservatives have also debated the possible effects of the Community Reinvestment Act (CRA), with detractors claiming that the Act encouraged lending to borrowers who were not creditworthy and defenders claiming a thirty year history of lending without increased risk.[10] Detractors also claim that amendments to the CRA in the mid-1990s, raised the amount of mortgages issued to otherwise unqualified low-income borrowers, and allowed the securitization of CRA-regulated mortgages, even though a fair number of them were subprime.[11]

But Federal Reserve Governor Randall Kroszner and FDIC Chairman Sheila Bair stated that the CRA was not to blame for the crisis. According to them, there were a number of factors—

including the boom and bust cycles which are a part of any economic system—which were responsible for the crisis.

Policies of Central Banks

Central banks have been entrusted with the task of keeping inflation within tolerable levels. Although they have some authority over commercial banks and other financial institutions, they do not seem to be concerned with avoiding asset price bubbles like the dot com bubble and the housing bubble. It has also been alleged that the central banks generally react after such bubbles burst rather than ensuring that the bubble does not get formed in the first place. Some people believe that the policymakers are themselves divided on the issue of identifying the asset bubble and determining the required monetary policy to deflate it. Things go out of control before their debate comes to an end and the remedial action gets too delayed to make an impact.

Bill Brown in his market watch commentary has drawn attention to moral hazard involving Federal Reserve actions. Some other observers have also stated that Federal Reserve Bank of New York's rescue of Long-Term Capital Management in 1998 led large financial institutions to believe that it would intervene on their behalf if the risky loans turned bad.

The Federal Reserve's policy of lowering the interest rates in the early years of the new millennium led to a rise in home prices. Between 2000 and 2003, the fund rate targets were lowered from around 5 per cent to 1 per cent. The experts believe that this was done to soften the effects of the bursting of dot com bubble. The Fed believed that since the rate of inflation was low, interest rates could be lowered without any perceived impact on the economy. It ignored some other important factors like increased demand due to more people willing to take credit. True inflation at times was actually higher than measured inflation. Lowering of interest rates spurted home prices, which could not be anticipated by Fed Reserve. Richard Fisher, President and CEO of Federal Reserve

Bank of Dallas stated that Fed's interest rate policy was misguided.[12]

Between 2004 and 2006, the Fed fund rates were raised significantly, which contributed to an increase in one-year and five-year ARM rates. The ARM interest rate resets were more expensive for homeborrowers, and the defaults started increasing. Thus, the policies of Federal Reserve, the central bank in America were also responsible for the financial crisis.

Credit Default Swaps

Credit default swaps (CDS) are financial instruments used as a hedge to protect investors, particularly in mortgaged-based securities, from the risk of default. CDS is a bilateral contract wherein a buyer makes a payment to a seller in exchange for a payoff, if an underlying financial instrument it has is exposed to default. For instance, by buying a CDS, a bank could protect itself against losses on a security such as bond if the bond issuer defaults on a coupon payment. In the US, as the net worth of banks and other financial institutions deteriorated because of the losses suffered due to borrowers' defaults in subprime mortgages, the burden of those providing the insurance to pay their counterparties increased. This not only created an uncertainty in the system, but also ruined many credit insurers.

Credit default swaps, like all other swaps and financial derivatives, may either be used to hedge risks, particularly to insure creditors against default, or to draw profit from speculation. During the period 1998 to 2008, the volume of CDS outstanding almost doubled with the amount of debt covered by CDS contracts in November 2008 being over $40 trillion. Another anomaly was that there was no central clearing house to honour CDS in case a party to a CDS was unable to perform its obligations. The required disclosure of CDS-related obligations has also been criticized as inadequate. Insurance companies such as American International Group (AIG), Michigan Boating Industries Association (MBIA), and Ambac faced sharp rating downgrades because of their potential exposure to CDS losses due to widespread mortgage defaults. AIG's having CDS insuring $440 billion of mortgage-based securities resulted in its seeking and obtaining a Federal government bailout. Stephen Bernard brought an important fact to light. CDSs, according to him, merely reallocated existing wealth, provided that the paying party can perform. But the question is which side of the CDS will have to pay and whether it will be able to do so. He went on to say, "when investment bank Lehman Brothers went bankrupt in September 2008, there was much uncertainty as to which financial firms would be required to honour the CDS contracts on its $600 billion of bonds outstanding".[13] Huge losses to Merrill Lynch in 2008 were attributed to the drop in the value of its "unhedged portfolio of collateralized debt obligations" after AIG ceased offering CDS on Merrill Lynch's debt obligations. According to Gretchen Morgenson, "The loss of confidence of trading partners in Merrill Lynch's solvency and its ability to refinance its short-term debt led to its acquisition by Bank of America. Some banks were so concerned that they considered stopping trading with Merrill Lynch if Lehman Brothers went under."

Financial Institutions' Debt Levels and High Incentives to Executives

During the years 2004 to 2007, many financial institutions, particularly investment banks, issued large amounts of debt, and invested the proceeds in mortgage-backed securities, in the hope that house prices would continue to rise, and that households would continue to make their mortgage payments. Many people resorted to financial leverage of borrowing at a lower rate of interest and investing the proceeds at a higher rate. This was like an individual taking out a second mortgage on his residence to invest in the stock market. During the housing boom, this strategy proved profitable but it resulted in huge losses when house prices began to decline and mortgages began to default in large number. Both financial institutions and individual investors holding mortgage-based securities suffered heavy losses in 2007 and 2008 from these defaults.

From 2005 to 2007 was also the period when all the top five US investment banks significantly increased their financial leverage, which made them more vulnerable to the declining value of mortgage-based securities. These five institutions reported over $4.1 trillion in debt for the year 2007—about 30 per cent of the US nominal GDP for 2007. Due to easy financing by banks, the percentage of subprime mortgages to total originations increased from less than 10 per cent to about 20 per cent.

During the latter half of 2008, three of the largest US investment banks went in deep trouble. Lehman Brothers went bankrupt while Bear Stearns and Merrill Lynch were sold to other banks. These failures brought instability in the global financial system. Morgan Stanley and Goldman Sachs opted to become commercial banks and agreed to subject themselves to more stringent regulation.

The bonuses that the Wall Street executives took home in 2006 amounted to nearly $24 billion. Ben Steverman and David Bogoslaw summed up the position in their article "The Financial Crisis Blame Game", thus:

> Wall Street traders were thinking of the bonus at the end of the year, not the long-term health of their firm. The whole system—from mortgage brokers to Wall Street risk managers—seemed tilted toward taking short-term risks while ignoring long-term obligations. The most damning evidence is that most of the people at the top of the banks didn't really understand how those investments worked.[14]

It has also been alleged that the investment banker incentive compensation was focused on fees generated from selling financial products rather than the performance of those products and the value they generated for the buyer over a period of time. Their bonuses were skewed towards cash rather than stock and were not subject to recourse or claw-back, i.e. there was no provision of recovery of bonus from the recipient by the firm in case the mortgage-based securities and collateralized debt obligations did not perform. Moreover, the increased risk involving financial leverage, taken by major investment banks was not factored while calculating the compensation of senior executives.

High Current Account Deficits in the US

USA's imports exceeded exports in the latter half of the decade leading to the new millennium, resulting in current account deficit which continued to rise even in the ensuing period. Between 1996 and 2004, America's current account deficit rose by $650 billion; in percentage terms it increased from 1.5 per cent to 5.8 per cent of the GDP. In 2005, Federal Reserve's Chairman Ben Bernanke brought the policy of addressing the implications of this high trade deficit by borrowing large sums from abroad, mainly from the countries having trade surpluses, e.g. the emerging economies of Asia, and the oil exporting countries of West Asia. The balance of payments (BoP) identity requires that a country having a current account deficit must also have a capital account (investment) surplus of an equivalent amount. Large amounts of foreign capital were therefore made to flow into the US. Foreign investors had large funds to lend, either because they had very high personal savings rates, which Bernanke called 'saving glut', or because of the high oil prices which benefitted the oil exporting countries. Some economists feel that high amount of capital was 'pulled' into the US by its high consumption levels. Thus, a flood of funds reached the US financial markets. While foreign governments supplied funds by purchasing US Treasury bonds, the households in America used the funds borrowed from foreigners to finance consumption or to bid up the prices of housing and financial assets.[15] Financial institutions invested foreign funds in mortgage-based securities creating the so-called bubble. Thus, Bernanke's policy of addressing the problem of current account deficit through inviting foreign funds, and high consumption levels of American people in general were also responsible for creating conditions ripe for financial crisis.

Shadow Banking System

The US Treasury Secretary Timothy Geithner has blamed the entities in the paralled banking system—also called the shadow banking system for "freezing of credit markets". These entities became critical to the credit markets, supporting the financial system, but suffered from a major drawback of not being subject to same regulatory controls as the main banking and financial institutions. Moreover, these entities were much more vulnerable as they borrowed short-term in liquid markets to purchase long-term, illiquid and rather risky assets. Any disruptions in credit markets were likely to make them subject to rapid deleveraging, forcing them to sell their long-term assets at capitulated prices. In one of his speeches, Geithner summed up the magnitude of involvement of shadow banking, thus:

> In early 2007, asset-backed commercial paper conduits, in structured investment vehicles, in auction-rate preferred securities, tender option bonds and variable rate demand notes, had a combined asset size of roughly $2.2 trillion. Assets financed overnight in triparty repo grew to $2.5 trillion. Assets held in hedge funds grew to roughly $1.8 trillion. The combined balance sheets of the then five major investment banks totaled $4 trillion. In comparison, the total assets of the top five bank holding companies in the United States at that point were just over $6 trillion, and total assets of the entire banking system were about $10 trillion. He stated that the combined effect of these factors was a financial system vulnerable to self-reinforcing asset price and credit cylces.[16]

Noble laureate Paul Krugman also refers to the shadow banking system as the "core of what happened to cause the crisis". He says:

> As the shadow banking system expanded to rival or even surpass conventional banking in importance, politicians and government officials should have realized that they were re-creating the kind of financial vulnerability that made the Great Depression possible—and they should have responded by extending regulations and the financial safety net to cover these new institutions. Influential figures should have proclaimed a simple rule: anything that does what a bank does, anything that has to be rescued in crises the way banks are, should be regulated like a bank.[17]

The Indebted US Economy

There is a unanimity among economists in saying that the ultimate point of origin of financial crisis can be traced to heavily indebted US economy. The collapse of the real estate market in 2006 may be taken as the first warning while sharp decline in rates of subprime mortgages was the first symptom that the boom was going to bust. Some experts believe that large default rates of subprime mortgages could not have accounted for the severity of the crisis. It was low-quality mortgages which caused maximum damage to the entire financial system. According to leading economists, M. Fratianni and F. Marchionne, the financial system had become very fragile due to several factors such as creation of complex and non-transparent assets, transfer of assets from the banks' balance sheets to markets, inability of rating agencies to assess the inherent risks and present fair value of assets/products to the buyers, and "failure of regulators and supervisors in spotting and correcting the emerging weaknesses".[18]

GLOBAL FINANCIAL CRISIS: A CHRONOLOGY

Though the global crisis can be attributed to several causes, the subprime mortgage crisis was unarguably the major among these. What started it was the dramatic rise in mortgage delinquencies and foreclosures in the United States, with major adverse consequences for banks and financial markets around the globe. The crisis, which has its roots in the closing years of the 20th century, became apparent in 2007 and has exposed pervasive weaknesses in financial industry regulation and the global financial system.

The debacle of the hyper-buoyant housing market and the freewheeling attitude of the subprime mortgage industry, illustrated by the collapse of Lehman Brothers resulted in a takedown of giant financial institutions that had successfully weathered the stock market crash of 1929. Lehman Brothers Holdings Inc. was a global financial services firm that, until declaring bankruptcy in September 2008, did business in investment banking, equity and fixed-income sales, research and trading, investment management, private equity, and private banking. It was a primary dealer in the US Treasury securities market. Its primary subsidiaries included Lehman Brothers Inc., Neuberger Berman Inc., Aurora Loan Services Inc., SIB Mortgage Corporation, Lehman Brothers Bank, FSB, Eagle Energy Partners, and the Crossroads Group. The firm's headquarters were in New York City, with regional headquarters in London and Tokyo, as well as offices located throughout the world.

In May 2008, the United States Federal Reserve System auctioned off $24.12 billion in Treasury Securities to help relieve the subprime mortgage crisis. Further, lending standards on home mortgages, some consumer loans and business loans were tightened. In June, premier US banks and insurance companies like Wachovia (the fourth largest bank in the US) and the American International Group (AIG), the world's largest insurance company sacked their CEOs for the losses incurred because of the subprime mortgage crisis. During this time, Ireland's Economic and Social Research Institute declared for the first time that the country was in the grip of recession. However, it predicted that the economy would regain its growth momentum towards the end of 2009 and would be back to normal growth by 2010.

In July 2008, the European Central Bank increased interest rates in the Eurozone to 4.25 per cent to tackle inflation. The US Federal Reserve tightened mortgage regulation in an attempt to stamp out the practices that had led to the subprime mortgage crisis. In response to the subprime mortgage crisis, the then US President George W. Bush signed the Housing and Economic Recovery Act in 2008. The unemployment in the United States rose to 5.7 per cent, the highest in more than four years. The New York Attorney General Andrew Cuomo reached a $7 billion settlement with Citigroup to buyback auction rate securities from about 40,000 clients throughout the United States. The UK home repossessions rose by 48 per cent. The Consumer Price Index in the United States rose by nearly one per cent in July 2008, leading to an annual inflation rate of 5.6 per cent, the highest in 17 years.

In the beginning of September 2008, reserve balances from banks in the Federal Reserve System started increasing over required levels of about $10 billion just before the stock market crash. Gradually, the signs of recession began to appear in other parts of the country as well. In September, the European Commission predicted the fall of UK, Germany and Spain into recession and further added that the outlook for the rest of the Eurozone was gloomy. The Washington Mutual, the largest savings and loan company in the United States, fired its Chief Executive due to heavy losses incurred on account of the subprime mortgage crisis. It was this time that the AIG sought an emergency $40 billion loan from the United States Federal Reserve. The AIG which was not only the largest insurer but also a significant participant in the credit default swaps markets suffered a liquidity crisis following the downgrade of its credit rating. The Federal Reserve took several measures to expand emergency lending to tackle the crisis. At the request of AIG, it agreed to lend it $85 billion in exchange for a 79.9 per cent equity interest and the right to suspend dividends to previously issued common and preferred stock.

On 7 September 2008, the United States Director of the Federal Housing Finance Agency (FHFA) announced the decision to place two United States Government-sponsored enterprises—Fannie Mae (Federal National Mortgage Association) and Freddie Mac (Federal Home Loan Mortgage Corporation)—into conservationship run by FHFA. Conservation was the only form in which taxpayer's money was committed to the GSEs.

On 15 September 2008, Lehman Brothers filed for Chapter 11 bankruptcy protection. The filing marked the largest bankruptcy ever in US history.

The subprime crisis had begun to show its signs in the early 2007 which reached a critical stage during September 2008. It was characterised by substantial decline in liquidity in the global credit markets and insolvency threats to investment banks and other financial institutions. In February 2008, the US Congress approved a $168 billion economic stimulus package and sent it to the then US President George W. Bush for his approval. In March, the US investment bank Bear Stearns got emergency funding from JPMorgan Chase with the backing of Federal Reserve Bank of New York. During this time, JPMorgan Chase announced plans to buy investment bank Bear Stearns for $2 a share following the liquidity problems caused by the crisis. The US Federal Reserve System became lender to various other large investment banks. It cut the Federal funds rate by 75 basis points to 2.25 per cent, which was followed by another cut of quarter percentage points to 2 per cent.

On 16 September, the Reserve Primary Fund, an important money market mutual fund, lowered its share price below $1 as a consequence of exposure to Lehman debt securities. This led to demands from investors to return their funds as the intensity of the financial crisis increased. By 18 September, money market sell orders from institutional investors totalled $500 billion, out of a total market capitalisation of $4 trillion. However, $105 billion liquidity injection from the Federal Reserve averted immediate collapse. On 19 September, the United States Treasury offered temporary insurance, similar to FDIC insurance bank accounts, to money market funds. A few days later, short selling of financial stocks was suspended by the Financial Services Authority in the United Kingdom and by the Securities and Exchange Commission in the United States. The authorities in other countries took similar measures.

On 19 September, Troubled Assets Relief Program (TARP), a plan to combat the subprime mortgage crisis was proposed by the Secretary of the Treasury, which permitted the United States Government to purchase illiquid assets—formally termed toxic assets—from financial institutions. Within a couple of days, the Secretary of the Treasury and President Bush announced a proposal to buy up to $700 billion of illiquid mortgage-backed securities to increase the liquidity of the secondary mortgage markets and reduce potential losses encountered by the financial institutions. This draft proposal of the plan was received favourably by investors in the stock market. US President George W. Bush addressing the nation on prime time television to discuss the crisis warned that the

United States would face a 'long and painful recession' if the package was not passed.

Unemployment in the United States rose to a seven year high, and orders for durable goods fell to their lowest level in 18 months. Home sales during August 2008 fell to a 17 year low. Goldman Sachs and Morgan Stanley, the two last remaining independent investment banks on Wall Street became bank holding companies as a result of subprime mortgage crisis. The US Congressional leader and the George W. Bush administration reached an outline Emergency Economic Stabilisation Act of 2008 for the bailout of financial institutions hit hard by the subprime mortgage.

The Russian Government lent the country's three biggest banks—Sberbank, VTB Bank and Gazprombank—1.13 trillion roubles ($44 billion) to boost liquidity. Trading remained suspended for the third consecutive day in Russia's two main stock exchanges—the MICEX and the dollar-denominated RTS —amidst fears of financial collapse. Russian President Dmitry Medvedev ordered ministers to inject another 500 billion roubles (£10.8 billion, US$20 billion) of funds from the state budget to stabilize the markets.

The key risk indicators became highly volatile during September 2008, which led the US Government to pass the Emergency Economic Stabilisation Act of 2008. Section 128 of the Emergency Economic Stabilisation Act of 2008 permitted the Federal System to pay interest from 6 October onwards, on the excess balances, causing further pressure on international credit markets. By the end of second week of January 2009, excess on the balances reached $870 billion as against the increase in reserve balances of only $65 billion after September 2001 before declining to normal levels within a month.

In the first week of October 2008, a major banking and financial crisis emerged in Iceland with a decline of 30 per cent in its currency, krona, against the euro. An emergency meeting was held the same day and a legislation was passed granting great powers to government to seize and regulate banks. Standard and Poor's cut Iceland's foreign-currency sovereign credit rating. It also lowered Iceland's banking industry country risk assessment from Group 5 to Group 8. Iceland's Financial Supervisory Authority took control of troubled Landsbanki Bank. Iceland's largest bank, Kaupthing Bank, was nationalised by the country's Financial Supervisory Authority. Russia agreed to provide Iceland with emergency loans of €4 billion ($5.4 billion). Significant losses were marked on stock exchanges all across the world. The Dow Jones Industrial Average slipped by as much as 800.06 points which is the biggest intra-day drop ever recorded. The Dow closed below the 10,000 mark for the first time since 26 October 2004. The US Federal Reserve announced plans to buy billions of dollars of short-term commercial paper to restore liquidity to the money market. The Chairman of the Federal Reserve proposed to cut interest rates in the wake of emerging situations. The shares plunged nearly 20 per cent in Russia amid fears of global crisis and fall in oil prices. Trading was suspended in Russia's leading stock exchanges.

Britain also took certain measures to tackle the situation. Britain's Chancellor of Exchequer released details of a rescue package to restore confidence in British banks. As part of the package, the British Government announced to provide £50 billion of investment, a further £200 billion in short-term loan and guarantee up to £250 billion of intra-bank loans. The German Parliament passed a €500 billion ($673.8 billion) bailout package for banks.

The Australian Prime Minister Kevin Rudd announced to guarantee all deposits in all Australian banks for a period of three years to combat the situation emerging from subprime mortgage crisis. The Reserve Bank of Australia pumped $1.5 billion into the banking system to mitigate the severity of crisis. The amount was nearly three times as much as the market's estimated requirements. New Zealand and United Arab Emirates also announced to guarantee all bank deposits in their banks. Greece, as a part of measures to combat the situation, introduced a €100,000 guarantee for the €230 billion bank deposits in the country for three years—well above the EU-wide Ecofin-mandated minimum of €50,000 for one year. It also assured about the stability of its banking system. The US Federal

Reserve Board cut interest rates by half a percentage point to 1.5 per cent as part of a coordinated activity with the European Central Bank and other central banks. It approved the merger of Wells Fargo and Wachovia after Citigroup withdrew the legal case to put on hold a proposed merger. The head of the International Monetary Fund expressed concern over the US financial crises and warned of a global meltdown. The IMF also offered to lend to countries, if required.

In *World Economic Outlook,* the IMF presented a gloomy projection for the global financial system. The Finance Ministers of G7 who met with the IMF Chief and World Bank President in Washington announced a plan to combat the crisis with the help of 'all available tools' to support key institutions. The then US President George W. Bush committed to a collaborative action with G7 Finance Ministers. He announced new measures to attack the current economic crisis including plans for the US Government to buy stakes in major banks. The heads of 45 countries from Asia and Europe met in Beijing to discuss the situation emerging from the financial meltdown. The Reserve Bank of India added almost $1.32 billion, through a refinance operation, to cope with the situation.

On 7 October 2008, the Federal Reserve announced the formation of a Commercial Paper Funding Facility, intended to serve as a funding backstop to facilitate the issuance of term commercial paper by eligible users. Several countries announced new deposit guarantees, while some increased them. Taiwan outlined plans to double the guarantee to NT $3 million ($92,000). European Union agreed to increase guarantees across the EU to at least €50,000 per saver. Several EU states such as Netherlands, Spain, Belgium and Greece announced increases on top of this minimum. They announced to guarantee up to €100,000. On 8 October, the British Government announced £25 billion, available as "Tier 1 capital" preference share capital or PIBS (Permanent Interest Bearing Securities), to various financial institutions such as Abbey, Barclays, HBOS, HSBC Bank, Royal Bank of Scotland, and Standard Chartered as part of a bank rescue package. An additional £25 billion was scheduled for other financial institutions, including British subsidiaries of foreign banks. Besides, the plan included increased ability to borrow from the government, assistance in raising equity and a support for international efforts. The European Central Bank, Bank of England, Federal Reserve, Bank of Canada, Swedish Riksbank, and Swiss National Bank announced simultaneous cuts of 0.5 per cent to their base rates. Following them, the Central Bank of People's Republic of China also cut its interest rates. Stock markets all across the world witnessed a sharp fall which led to suspension of trade in Russia and Indonesia. The Japanese benchmark index Nikkei fell over 9 per cent.

On 9 October, the cost of short-term credit rose, while there were heavy losses in the United States stock market. The Dow plunged to 8600, lowest in the last five years, though the losses were moderate in Europe. The following day, there were heavy losses in Asian and European markets. Russia's stock markets remained closed on 10 October due to falling stock prices. The Russian Parliament passed a plan authorizing lending of $36 billion—gained from global oil sales—to banks that enabled them to meet creditor worthiness requirements. In the US, the government authorized by the Emergency Economic Stabilisation Act, announced plans to infuse funds into banks by purchasing equity interests in them—in effect partial nationalisation like the one done in Britain. Stock markets crashed across Europe and Asia. London, Paris and Frankfurt dropped 10 per cent within an hour of trading. The Wall Street also opened weak for trading and kept on falling further. Global markets experienced their worst week since 1987.

The Dow Jones Industrial Average dropped 697 points within the five minutes of trading session on Wall Street. It fell below 7900 to its lowest level since 17 March 2003, though it improved in the afternoon and experienced a loss of just 128 points or 1.49 per cent at the end of the day. The New York Stock Exchange, with the Dow at 8,451, was trading at 40 per cent down from its record high on 9 October 2007. The day was marked by extreme volatility in US markets. On October 11, the US Government announced a shift in emphasis in its rescue efforts from buying illiquid assets to recapitalising banks, including strong banks, in exchange for preferred equity.

On 12 October, European leaders, meeting in Paris, announced recapitalisation plans for Europe's banks. Plans were also announced to guarantee bank deposits for five years. Mechanisms were also outlined to increase the availability of short-term credit. It was decided that the European countries would finance their own rescue plans and tailor them to local conditions. A rescue plan of €1 trillion was announced. Bank guarantee plans were also announced by Australia and New Zealand. Norway, which is not in the Eurozone, announced in a hastily called press conference, a US$57.4 billion (350 billion Norwegian kroner) plan of offering Norwegian banks new government bonds.

In their meeting in Washington, the G7 nations pledged to support the important financial institutions to prevent their failure. This decision came in the wake of bankruptcy of Lehman Brothers which led to the loss of funds by other financial institutions. It was thought that the losses may have triggered a tightening of the credit crunch as banks ceased to lend to one another. However, no enforceable mechanism was created to support the pledge.

On 13 October, stock markets worldwide rose. The International Monetary Fund offered possible technical and financial aid to Hungary which suffered during the crisis due to the flight of investors to euro, Swiss franc, and dollar-denominated investments. As in the rest of the world, stock prices rose on the Hungarian exchange and pressure on forint, the national currency, eased, which had dropped to 30 per cent against the dollar since July 2008. The Prime Minister of Spain, Jose Luis Rodriguez announced to provide up to €100 billion of guarantees for new debt issued by commercial banks in 2008. The UK Government initiated the process of nationalisation by injecting £37 billion in the three largest banks. The banks, in return for the bailout, agreed to cancel dividend payments until the loans were repaid, had board members appointed by the Treasury and limited the executive pay. The European Central Bank attempted to revive credit market by weekly injecting of unlimited euro funds at an interest rate of 3.75 per cent. Following its European partners, Italy pledged to intervene to prevent any bank failures in its country. Its Finance Minister Giulio Tremonti, announced to guarantee new bank bonds of up to five years until the end of 2009 and the Bank of Italy would provide €40 billion in Treasury bills to banks to refinance inferior assets that could not be used as collateral. Coordinating with the Eurozone countries, the Dutch Government announced to guarantee interbank lending up to €200 billion. It was followed by setting up of a €20 billion Dutch fund in order to help recapitalise banks and insurance companies.

On 14 October, the US announced a plan to take an equity interest of $250 billion in US banks with 25 billion for each of the four largest banks of the country. The plan also included an option allowing the government to purchase common stock according to a formula which could return substantial profit to the taxpayers, should the stock price of the companies substantially appreciate. It was thought that the additional capitalisation and the guarantees will help banks resume a normal lending pattern with each other and borrowers as well. Japan also took many such measures to help its market and to prevent the worse of the credit crisis. It lifted restrictions on companies buying back their shares, strengthened disclosure on short selling and temporarily suspended the sale of government-owned stocks. The Australian Government also released a $10.4 billion stimulus package to support its economy. The Economic Security Strategy was designed to help pensioners, low income families and for the first time, the homebuyers to withstand the impact of global meltdown.

On 15 October, the London Stock Exchange FTSE 100 fell substantially. It slipped down by 7.16 per cent. The decline sparked off more losses in the US, as the Dow Jones Industrial Average suffered the biggest fall in terms of percentage since 1987, dropping over 733 points, while the NASDAQ dipped almost eight and a half per cent and Standard and Poor's plunged over nine per cent.

As a result of various measures taken, there was some improvement in the availability of credit, though stock markets and currencies like British pound and euro continued to decline worldwide during the last few days of the October. Asian markets particularly suffered heavy losses while the losses in the European markets were substantial. The Dow Industrial Index experienced the highest volatility during the week. The dollar and the yen showed particular strength which had a baleful effect on global economies, including the US and Japan. On 22 October, Pakistan along with Hungary, Siberia, Ukraine, etc. approached the IMF for aid in dealing with severe balance of payments difficulties. A great number of countries like Turkey, South Africa, Argentina, Romania, Bulgaria, etc. were facing financial difficulties. Although they had not held securities based on subprime mortgages, yet they were unable to borrow money and hence, were experiencing a severe credit crisis.

On 24 October, stock markets plunged all across the world amidst fears of imminent global recession. This was aggravated by the remarks of Alan Greenspan that the crisis was "a once-in-a-century credit tsunami". It was further fuelled by the comments of Gordon Brown, the UK Prime Minister, who in his speech admitted that Great Britain was already in the grip of recession. Following the trends, the US stock markets also fell sharply on opening and closed with the Dow Industrial Index down 312 points. On 24 and 25 October, the 7th Asia-Europe Meeting was held in Beijing with the European Union meeting Asian states to draw out a common approach ahead of the Emergency International Meeting which was scheduled to be held on 15 November in Washington.

On 26 October, Hungary and Ukraine made tentative arrangements with the International Monetary Fund for emergency aid packages. In Poland, the value of stocks dropped 50 per cent for the year, and the Polish currency, zloty, fell against both the dollar and the euro. South Africa was badly affected by the crisis, as there was dramatic decline in the price of platinum which is widely used in automobile industry. Various countries of the world were engaged in emergency discussions with the IMF. The Gulf Cooperation Council met in Riyadh in the wake of falling prices of oil and a 40 per cent drop in equity prices to formulate a coordinated response to the crisis.

In the second round of recapitalisation, the US Treasury funded 20 banks with 38 billion dollars. Criteria for funding was based on the strength of the bank. The stronger the banks with higher CAMELS ratings, the greater the chance of being offered aid.

On 28 October, stocks rose dramatically worldwide in anticipation of rate cuts by central banks. In the US, the Dow Industrial Average rose 10.8 per cent and closed above 9000. On 29 October, the US markets closed slightly down despite the announcement of a reduction in the federal funds by the Federal Open Market Committee. The US markets were up on 30 and 31 October—cutting losses to the Dow Industrial Average during October to 17 per cent—down 30 per cent for the year upto that period. In Russia, stock markets had crashed down 70 per cent. Despite significant foreign reserves, Russia was faced with sharply reduced commodity prices.

In Asia, Japan announced its second economic stimulus plan of $51 billion on 30 October. Hong Kong and Taiwan cut interest rates while Japan announced an interest cut to 0.3 per cent. The Federal Reserve established a $30 billion currency swap line with South Korea, Singapore, Brazil and Mexico.

JPMorgan Chase, the largest bank in the United States, announced to work with those home owners who were ready to pay their mortgages by reducing interest payment or principal. Counselling centres were planned for the affected areas. Bank of America and Countrywide Financial also announced similar programs.

The United States Government announced a second bailout of AIG. The total value of the new plan, roughly amounting to $150 billion, was the largest government support package extended to a private company in US history. Employment data released by the Labour Department on 7 November showed that about 500,000 jobs were lost in the United States during September and October 2008 with unemployment rising to 6.5 per cent in October. There was an anticipation that unemployment will rise to 8 per cent by the middle of 2009. On 6 November, amidst predictions of deep recession in the UK and the Eurozone, the Bank of England, in anticipation of the danger of inflation, lowered its base rates by 1.5 percentage points, from 4.5 to 3 per cent. It was accompanied by a 50 basis point drop in the base rate to 3.25 per cent by the European Central Bank. The IMF predicted for 2009, a worldwide –0.3 per cent decrease of the BIP for the developed economies (–0.7 per cent for the USA and –0.8 per cent for Germany).

On 9 November, the People's Republic of China announced a domestic stimulus package of $586 billion to finance programs in 10 major domestic areas in the next two years. Economic growth declined in China with sharp drops in property and stock values. Some Chinese factories engaged in low-end export manufacturing were badly affected by the emerging situation. On 12 November, the US Treasury Secretary Henry Paulson scrapped the original Troubled Asset Relief Program and announced a shift in focus to consumer lending. The remaining portion of the TARP budget was to be used to help relieve pressure on consumer credits like car loans, student loans, credit cards, etc. On 13 November, the Dow Jones Industrial Average marked another dramatic session, opening at 8,282.66, with sharp fluctuations, eventually closing at 8,835.25 with a net gain of more than 550 points. On 15 November, the leaders of the G20, at the invitation of the then US President George W. Bush, held the initial session of the Summit on Financial Markets and the World Economy. They agreed to cooperate with respect to global financial crisis and issued a statement regarding immediate and medium-term goals and actions, required to be taken to reform the international economy.

The Eurozone entered the first recession during November as the combined Gross Domestic Product of the 15 members dropped 0.2 per cent in the second and third quarters of 2008. In the third quarter, the GDP of Japan fell 0.4 per cent, following a 3.7 per cent drop in the second quarter. The

Japanese economy posted consecutive second quarter contraction for the first time since 2001, officially putting the country in a recession. On 19 November, proposed bailouts of US automakers, were rejected. Automobile sales declined sharply in Europe and bailouts were under consideration. On November 19, the Dow Jones Industrial Average fell sharply by 427.47 points or 5.07 per cent, closing below 8,000 points for the first time since March 2003. The US financial stocks led the way with Citigroup and showed a 23 per cent drop. The UK FTSE 100 fell by about the same percentage, closing just above 4000. The BBC Global 30, combining Europe, Asia and North America in a single index, fell by 5.1 per cent.

On 20 November, the Dow Jones Industrial Average dropped 445 points, closing at 7,552, the lowest point in six years. Shares of Citigroup plummeted another 26 per cent and shares of other major US financial institutions dropped by more than 10 per cent. On 21 November, the Dow Jones Industrial Average recovered slightly, closing above 8,000. However, stocks of Citibank, Bank of America and JPMorgan Chase continued to decline. As of the week ended on 16 November, stock losses in United States markets during 2008, as measured by S&P 500, were equivalent to those suffered in 1931, i.e. over 50 per cent. Total losses during the Great Depression exceeded 80 per cent but that was over a period of three years.

21 and 22 November marked the largest two session gain in Dow Jones Industrial Average since October 1987. The Dow gained 891.10 points, i.e. 11.8 per cent and closed at 8,443.39 points. On 23 November, the United States Government agreed to a rescue plan for Citigroup. It was announced in a joint statement by the Treasury Department, the Federal Reserve and the Federal Deposit Insurance Corp that in exchange for preferred stock valued at $27 billion paying 8 per cent interest, a further $20 billion would be invested into the company and that the government would limit loss on $306 billion in risky loans and securities to $29 billion plus 10 per cent of any remaining losses. Citigroup received US$32 billion under the United States Emergency Economic Stabilisation Act. The company

announced to cut 75,000 jobs by early 2009. The US Federal Reserve announced a new stimulus package of US$800 billion to buy debt and mortgage-backed securities and make loans to holders of consumer debts. During the month of November, the IMF approved a US$2.1 billion reserve package for Iceland to combat the financial crisis. The European Union proposed a €200 billion stimulus package which included already spent money.

On 1 December, the National Bureau of Economic Research officially declared that the US economy had entered recession in December 2007. The Labour Department reported that the US lost 533,000 jobs in November 2008, the biggest monthly loss since 1974. The unemployment rate rose from 6.5 per cent to 6.7 per cent. After experiencing a positive trend in the last week of November 2008, the S&P fell 80 points to 816, down 9 per cent. Financial stocks in the S&P 500 declined 17 per cent. The Dow Jones Industrial Average dropped 679 points and closed at 8149 with a fall of 7.7 per cent. Oil prices fell below $50 a barrel in New York trading.

On 9 December, the Bank of Canada lowered its key interest rate by 0.75 to 1.5 per cent, the lowest since 1958. The bank officially announced that the economy of Canada was in recession. Canada lost 70,600 jobs in the month of November, the highest since 1982. The US Government announced a proposal for a US$17.4 billion bailout package for three major US automakers—Chrysler, General Motors, and Ford—to avoid bankruptcy. The money was proposed to be taken from the $700 billion bailout package originally intended to rescue the US banks. President George W. Bush said that it would not be a "responsible course of action" to allow the companies to collapse. In the third week of December, the US industry leader asked the Federal Reserve for assistance unfreezing the commercial real estate market, which had not securitized any loans in the last six months of 2008. The US consumer price index had fallen in November by 1.91 per cent on a non-seasonally adjusted basis, the biggest decline since the Great Depression of 1930s. Bernard Madoff, former chairman of the NASDAQ exchange market, was arrested on a single securities fraud charge for operating a $50 billion Ponzi scheme which was found affecting banks, individuals and charities in the US and Europe.

The Central Bank of America spent US$30 billion in currency market interventions in November 2008. Canada announced a US$3.3 billion bailout for its troubled automotive industry. In December, Toyota Motor Corporation, the world's largest automaker, forecast its first operating loss in 70 years caused by the automotive crisis.

In the second week of January 2009, Sony announced $1.1 billion operating loss. On 18 January, the Danish Parliament agreed to a financial package worth 100,000,000,000 Danish krone (US$17,596,339,961). On January 20, Philippines expressed fears of 60,000 IT job losses due to Intel shutdown. On 19 January, the Royal Bank of Scotland (RBS) lost around 70 per cent of its share price after the news of a GB£28 billion loss for 2008 and the UK Government's increased stake of 70 per cent in the company. The Royal Bank of Scotland's shares fell by more than 10 per cent both in London and New York stock exchanges.

American International Group (AIG) reported a record $61.7 billion quarterly loss and received a new dollop of US taxpayer aid as part of a plan to break the company into smaller, easier-to-manage units. The struggling insurance company received $30 billion in new federal assistance, indicating that the policymakers still believe that AIG is too big to fail. Chief Executive Edward Liddy said the company had become "too complicated, too unwieldy and opaque" to be run as a single business.

The decision came as AIG announced that it lost $61.7 billion during its fourth quarter, surpassing the $54.2 billion record set by Time Warner in the first quarter of 2002. Edward Liddy said that his company was in a much dire condition than expected. He also stated that the deal with the government keeps a difficult economic situation from deteriorating further by making sure the company survives, but he could not guarantee that AIG would not need more federal aid.

Despite the loss, the company's credit rating remained intact, at least for some time. Fitch Ratings said the government's support overrided the quarter's loss for most of the parameters for company's ratings. AIG's stock rose 16.7 per cent, or 7 cents to 49 cents in morning trading. Ironically, the report sent the rest of the stock market tumbling, finally pushing the Dow Jones Industrial Average below 7,000 points. It was alarming to note that AIG had lost almost all of its market value over the year, falling an extraordinary 99 per cent. In the last three months of 2008, the New York-based firm lost $22.95 per share. It lost $5.3 billion, or $2.08 per share, in the previous year's corresponding period. Sales fell to negative $23.8 billion, as the company had to reverse gains it had recorded from investments in past quarters.

The dramatic reshaping of AIG was similar to drastic steps being taken at Citigroup to shore up its operations. In early 2009, Citi announced plans to hive off a mountain of bad loans, shed non-critical businesses like US mortgage lending, and refocus on its traditional commercial, retail, and private banking operations globally. It even decided to change its name back to Citicorp.

The US Government agreed to convert $25 billion of its preferred equity stake in Citigroup to common shares, giving it a 36 per cent stake in Citi and helping the bank restructure its capital base in the face of mounting losses from bad loans and other assets. Citi also took $45.0 billion in new capital from the government's Troubled Asset Relief Program and obtained federal guarantees on $300 billion of assets.

Seeing some stability in the stock market, America's Financial Services Authority lifted the ban on short-selling in January 2009. However, layoffs continued due to weak economic climate. The US aluminium group Alcoa cut 13,500 jobs and curbed production to reduce costs. Marks and Spencer also announced plans to close 25 of its small food stores, two regular stores and cut 1,230 jobs. The Federal Reserve forecast that the US recession will likely continue in 2009 with moderate recovery in 2010.

Germany's second biggest bank Commerzbank said that it was to be partly nationalised, with the German Government taking its 25 per cent plus one share for €10 billion. This announcement led many people to say that capitalism was going to die, or at least see a radical change in its features. The Bank of England cut interest rates to 1.5 per cent, the lowest level in its history. The UK Government said it will own 43 per cent of the combined HBOS/Lloyds TSB after a dearth of interest from institutional shareholders in the two banks' capital raising left the Treasury take up to 99 per cent of the unsubscribed new shares. It was a measure of government's efforts to boost investor confidence in the difficult time of economic meltdown.

In line with many other banks, the European Central Bank also cut interest by 2 per cent on 15 January 2009. Barack Obama took over as US President on 20 January, and the Democrats' $825 billion economic rescue plan was announced. Obama said that 80 per cent of the spending of his recovery package will take place within the next 18 months.

On 26 January, Standard and Poor's announced that the jump in the number of US bankruptcies was accompanied by a drying up of the sources of financing which allow companies to reorganize under US' Bankruptcy Code Chapter 11, leading to US companies facing a greater risk of liquidation. Caterpillar, the world's biggest maker of construction equipment and heavy duty engines announced that it may cut up to 20,000 jobs as the orders fell. Nissan Motors also announced to cut the same number of jobs worldwide in the near future.

On 11 February 2009, the US Congress said that the stimulus package will be worth $789 billion as against $825 billion announced earlier. German Government on 18 February considered law to allow the nationalisation of Hypo Real Estate which it described as a "systematically relevant institution that could not be allowed to fail". It was to be the first bank nationalisation in Germany since the Great Depression of 1930s.

European leaders met in Berlin on 22 February to discuss adopting a common approach to the global economic downturn. The measures considered included toughening up on tax havens and doubling of IMF fund. On 24 February 2009, the UK Government announced that it was preparing to convert its £4 billion of preference shares in Lloyds Banking Group into non-voting equity in return for a pledge that the bank will make billions of pounds of credit available to the economy. This will free Lloyds from making interest payments to the government. Nomura announced its plans to raise over 290 billion yen in a discounted share sale in order to arrange capital after losses for four successive quarters.

The Purchasing Manager's Index (PMI), which is a composite index maintained by the Institute for Supply Management (ISM) extracting data from over 400 purchasing managers, indicated that the Eurozone was falling further into recession after a plunge in private sector economic activity. The Index, which is regarded as offering a good up to date guide to trends in economic activity fell to 36.2 in February from 38.3 in the previous month. Russia reported an 8.8 per cent contraction in its GDP. Japan seemed to be severely hit by the meltdown as its exports fell 45.7 per cent in January. On 26 February, President Barack Obama released a headline budget which included a $250 billion provision for future bailout funds.

On 5 February 2009, Bank of England and other European banks cut interest rates to 0.5 per cent. On 6 March, it was announced that the Bank of England will provide £150 billion through a scheme of quantitative easing to help the economy in this difficult period. The data in the US showed a decrease in business spending. The homeowners fell further behind on their mortgages, and the unemployment situation worsened. In February alone, 650,000 jobs were lost in the US, taking the country's unemployment rate to 7.9 per cent.

On 10 March, the European Union published an assessment that stated that the recession may last until 2010. The assessment document painted a darker picture of the EU outlook than previous forecasts by European Commission. The UK, France and Sweden reported sharp falls in industrial production, while Germany reported a drastic decline in exports. The country's industrial production, orders and profits seemed to have collapsed. On 16 March, President Barack Obama's advisors severely criticized AIG group for its plans to pay $165 million in bonuses. The insurance company had received a bailout of $173 billion.

In a landmark decision, the US, on 23 March 2009, announced a plan to buy up to US $1 trillion worth of toxic assets to help repair banks' balance sheets. The plan called 'Public-Private Investment Programme' was to purchase the troubled mortgages and securities that had been at the root of financial crisis. In the UK, Lord Turner, Chairman of the Financial Services Authority released a comprehensive report to set out a detailed blueprint for regulatory reform in the wake of global financial crisis. The IMF warned that the UK economy was likely to keep shrinking in 2010. In 2009, it was predicted to shrink by 3.8 per cent. Bank of Japan announced that it will offer $10.2 billion in subordinated loans to help its banks and prevent the drying up of lending. The European Commission proposed binding roles on hedge funds and private equity groups. This was supposed to tighten financial regulation.

The figures released on 24 March 2009 showed the UK unemployment rising above 2 million. A UK Government bond auction failed for the first time in several years as investors refused to buy securities because of increasing worries over the country's deteriorating public finance. The auction for the long dated bonds fell short of the £1.75 million target.

On 1 April 2009, the protestors gathered outside the Bank of England on the opening day of the G20 summit to campaign against the recent actions of banks, which they blamed for the current financial crisis. The leaders of world's largest economies reached landmark agreements at the G20 summit as to how to tackle the global financial crisis. They agreed to take measures to bring strong financial regulation, enhance the role of financial institutions to tackle such situations and proposed to arrange funds worth US $1.1 trillion to put the world economy back on track.

On 7 April, Japan announced a fiscal stimulus package of $100 billion to fight recession. In Europe, it was announced that hedge funds and private equity managers will need to be registered, hold a minimum level of capital and disclose relevant information on borrowings to regulators under a draft EU proposal. This measure was suggested with the objective of avoiding a repeat of the 1998 collapse of Long Term Capital Fund Management. The Royal Bank of Scotland said it was slashing 9,000 jobs to save £2.5 billion by the year 2011.

On 10 April 2009, Germany revealed plans for its first nationalisation of a bank in the post-war era. It was alleged that the recent nationalisation of Fortis' Dutch banking unit and the Dutch Government's acquisition of an interest in ABN-Amro was in breach of the European Union rules on the state aid to troubled banks. On 14 April, Goldman Sachs announced details of a US $6 billion rights issue in an attempt to repay part of its US Government loan. On 15 April, Singapore's central bank devalued the city state's currency amidst warnings of worst economic plunge on record. Its GDP shrank by 11.5 per cent in the first quarter of 2009 as compared to the same period of 2008. On 21 April, the IMF declared that the deteriorating global economy meant that the financial institutions faced total losses of $4,100 billion on loans and other assets and it urged governments to take bolder steps to shore up institutions.

In its budget presented on 22 April, the UK Chancellor stated that Britain's public finances faced their toughest times since World War II as the country was in its worst peacetime recession. A slew of measures were taken including increase of income tax to 50 per cent for those earning £1,50,000 or over, increase in duties on beer, tobacco and fuel. Besides, a cash for scrappage incentive scheme was launched, offering people £2000 to trade in old cars for new ones in an effort to stimulate the troubled automobile industry.

On 27 April, the US Treasury Secretary Tim Geithner assured World Bank and the IMF that the US would take whatever policy steps were necessary to ensure economic recovery, on both national and international levels.

On 30 April 2009, the Federal Reserve left the interest rates unchanged and stated that the US economy was showing signs of improvement. This was the first time that a positive statement came from any quarter since the start of meltdown in 2008. However, the Bank for International Settlements revealed that global cross-border lending by banks shrank by almost $5 trillion in the nine-month period ending 31 December 2008, the sharpest fall ever recorded.

On 1 May 2009, Chrysler filed for bankruptcy, but the company would still receive up to $7.5 billion in state aid to restructure itself. Its partnership with Fiat was still stated to go ahead. In UK, the stock market FTSE 100 saw a rise of 8.1 per cent during April 2009, the biggest one month rise since 2003. On 5 May, the IMF approved a US $17 billion standby loan for Romania to help its economy in the financial crisis. On 7 May, the Bank of England announced that it will keep interest rates at historically low level of 0.5 per cent. It also announced that it will pump an additional £50 billion into the UK economy through the existing qualitative easing programme. The European Central Bank announced that it will cut interest rates to a record low of 1 per cent.

On 15 May, the UK Treasury Select Committee released a report on remuneration saying that the banking crisis had exposed serious flaws and shortcomings in remuneration practices. The report stated that the bonus-driven remuneration structures encouraged reckless and excessive risk-taking and exposed companies to financial risks. The design of bonus schemes was not conducive to the interests of shareholders and the long-term sustainability of the banks. The report proposed a number of reforms including enhanced disclosure requirements about remuneration structures, and a code of ethics on remuneration consultants.

On 19 May, the World Bank President Robert Zoellick said that the global economy may return to growth by late 2009 or in 2010. European banking officials also reported some signs of growth. It was reported that Bank of England had made record profits as a result of increased activities attributable to the financial crisis. The decision to provide finance at the then prevailing base rate of 5.5 per cent to institutions during 2008 resulted in pre-tax profit of

£995 million. The Treasury was likely to receive half of the profits through dividends. President Obama's administration indicated that a pool of institutions would be allowed to start repaying funds lent under the Troubled Assets Relief Program.

The slowdown had spread not only to capitalist countries but also communist economics. It was reported that Russian banks were suffering due to rising number of bad loans and could need a minimum of £10 billion to repair the damage. Meanwhile, Moody's downgraded four of South Korea's major banks.

On 20 May 2009, a stress test was conducted on some major banks in America. It was stated that ten of the nation's largest banks will need to raise a total of $74.6 billion of extra funds to increase their cash reserves. The US Government signalled that its financial rescue efforts may have reached their high watermark as the much anticipated 'stress tests' conducted by regulators showed that the banks can withstand an adverse economic scenario though they will be required to raise fresh capital to boost their reserves against losses. Federal Reserve Chairman Ben Bernanke said that the Treasury stood ready to provide whatever additional capital may be necessary to ensure that the banking system was able to navigate a challenging economic downturn. Treasury Secretary Geithner said that the tests will help clear the clouds of uncertainty hanging over the banking system with an unprecedented level of transparency and clarity.

On 2 June 2009, car giant General Motors filed for bankruptcy protection marking the biggest failure of an industrial company in US history. The move was backed by the US Government which was expected to take 60 per cent share in the company. On 3 June, Latvia became the first EU country to face a sovereign debt crisis after failing to sell a single bill worth $100 million at a treasury auction prompting fears of a fresh storm in Eastern Europe due to flight of capital. On 17 June, the US Government announced a major reform of banking regulation to prevent future financial crisis. It will require big banks to put more money aside against future losses to curb excessive risk-taking. It was proposed that a special agency be created to protect the interests of consumers and regulate the provision of mortgages and credit cards. It was also proposed that the US central bank, Federal Reserve, should also be given the authority to monitor major financial institutions.

On 24 June, the Organisation for Economics Cooperation and Development (OECD) said that the world economy was near the bottom of the worst recession in post-war history. It predicted zero growth in the UK economy in 2010 and said that the budget deficit of the country would reach 14 per cent. On 25 June, the US Government figures showed that the country's economy shrank at an annualized rate of 5.5 per cent in the first three months of 2009, better than previous estimates. The Federal Reserve said that the latest economic data suggested that the pace of economic contraction was slowing.

On 26 June, Russia disclosed that it was issuing OFZ treasury bills to strengthen its large banks, in return for preference shares. Only banks with a capitalisation of above $1.6 billion would qualify. The access was thus limited to Russia's top 55 banks.

The Mergers and Acquisitions volumes for the first half of the year 2009 were the lowest since the first half of 2004, despite the increased levels of activity in the capital markets during the said period and notwithstanding the fact that in the first six months of 2009, non-financial groups raised $887 billion in bond markets, 64 per cent more than in the same period of previous year.

On 30 June, the office for National Statistics showed that the UK economy suffered a 2.4 per cent fall in GDP in the first quarter of 2009 as compared to the same quarter of previous year.

On 1 July 2009, a survey indicated that UK manufacturing activity shrank at its lowest place for a year in June, raising hopes that the worst of downturn was over. According to Bank of Japan's quarterly survey, business confidence in the country had improved for the first time in two and a half years. India's exports fell for the eighth month in succession in May, as overseas demand for goods continued to decrease. The number of jobs lost in the US in June 2009 were 4,67,000 which has much more than had been expected. Retail sales in countries that use euro fell more than what was expected in May. It was taken as a sign that the consumers were still curtailing their spending.

On 4 July 2009, the Venezuela Government took formal control of its third largest bank, Banco de Venezuela.

On 5 July, it was reported that some investment banks are seeking ways to reduce the impact of potentially increased capital requirements through 'smart securitization'—a process which is claimed to enable banks to substantially reduce the amount of capital they hold in relation to an asset. However, several banks criticized this as arbitrage 'capital' and it remained to be seen whether it will adequately address the underlying risk.

On 6 July 2009, the Indian Government unveiled its annual budget and stated that its first challenge was to return to an annual growth rate of 9 per cent at the earliest. The UK Government decided to give more power to Bank of England to control the amount of money that banks and building societies lend. It was a step to strengthen financial regulation.

On 7 July 2009, it was reported that the level of people falling behind with consumer loans in the US hit a new high in the first quarter of financial year 2009-10. This led the US Government to consider yet another stimulus package. Experts however felt that of will but more burden in the country's already high fiscal deficit. According to the British Chambers of Commerce (BCC), the worst of recession was over in UK but to talk of a recovery was premature. European finance ministers concurred with a proposal aimed at forcing banks to put aside more money in good time that would half their in tough periods.

On 8 July 2009, the IMF said that worldwide economic growth was expected to recover to 2.5 per cent in 2010. Industrial output in Germany rose by a surprising 3.7 per cent in May compared with April. It was a sign that the country's recession was easing. As per reforms proposed by the Chancellor, the UK banks will face tougher regulation and consumers get more protection. This was another step towards financial regulation. In an interesting development, China's finance ministry failed to sell all 28 billion yuan (4.1 billion dollar; 2.55 billion pound) one year government bonds it offered at an auction.

On 9 July 2009, Bank of England kept the cost of borrowing unchanged at 0.5 per cent for the fourth month in a row. Boosted by government incentives and continuing resilience of the country's economy, car sales in China shot up 48 per cent in June from a year ago.

On 10 July 2009, General Motors stated that it had emerged from bankruptcy protection after creating a "new GM" made up of the company's best assets.

On 15 July, it was made known that China's GDP growth was 7.9 per cent as the country almost achieved its target of 8 per cent for the year for 2008-09. The surge came in the second half on the back of increased government spending and a boost in lending by banks.

On 16 July 2009, the Walker review proposals on financial sector corporate governance were released. David Walker, former Chairman of Morgan Stanley International, recommended that financial institutions should establish board risk committees, separate from audit committees to ensure that the executives were properly monitored.

That the then existing systems of regulation were being reviewed after global financial turmoil is evidenced by the fact that the Financial Services Authority (FSA) on 30 July 2009 called a meeting between the major participants in the oil and commodities market in order to review the current system of regulation. The FSA was adopting a more proactive stance so that there should not be a repeat of the speculations that drove oil prices in excess of $150 a barrel in 2008.

On 3 August 2009, Hongkong and Shanghai Banking Corporation (HSBC) reported interim pre-tax profits of $5 billion for the first half of 2009-10. It represented a 51 per cent decline in profits as compared to previous year, but the figure was quite in line with analysts' predictions. Some experts markets had probably passed the low point the cycle.

The consumer spending in US also climbed for the second consecutive month in June, despite growing unemployment.

On 5 August, Lloyds Banking Group reported an interim pre-tax loss of £4 billion, which included £13.4 million of impairment charges made by the group to its loan portfolio in the first half of the year. The disparity between these figures and those of HSBC and Barclays was said to be due to Lloyds' lack of large scale investment banking arm to cushion the losses from its combined loan portfolio.

On 6 August, Bank of England decided to increase its quantitative easing program by an additional £50 billion, to a total of £175 billion, and announced that the recession was deeper than expected, but that the decline was slowing.

The German exports however rose by 7 per cent in June, the fastest pace in three years. It was the latest sign of recovery in Europe's biggest economy. Royal Bank of Scotland Group which is 70 per cent owned by texpayers reported a pre-tax profit of £15 million for the first six months of 2009-10.

On 10 August, it was reported that car sales in India rose by over 30 per cent in the first six months of 2009-10 over the corresponding period of the previous year, as a result of some new launches and lower interest rates. Annual growth rates of China's industrial output and retail sales were reported to have risen in July 2009, which was a sure sign the country's economy was improving. However, Russia's economy was stated to have shrunk at an annualized pace of 10.9 per cent in the first quarter of 2009-10.

According to lenders in UK, the number of mortgages for homebuyers granted in June 2009 rose by 23 per cent over May. The US productivity also rose at a fast annual pace during the quarter April to June 2009.

On 13 August, it was reported that there were signs that the eurozone was emerging from the recession, as figures showed that the French and German economies grew by 0.3 per cent in April, May and June 2009, belying the economists' fears that they would continue to shrink. The economy of Hong Kong was also stated to be emerging from recession, posting a growth of 3.3 per cent in the first quarter of 2009-10.

The International Energy Agency (IEA) remained cautious about the prospects of recovery in the energy demand in 2010. Its Oil Market Report that came in August 2009 said that while there had been an improvement in some economic indicators in a few countries, the global economy was at best stabilizing, and the market was still fundamentally weak.

It was reported that Japan showed a 0.9 per cent growth in GDP in the second quarter of June 2009, and was said to have come out of recession. However, the South African economy contracted for the third quarter in succession, i.e. April-June 2009.

On 21 August, the US central bank chief Ben Bernanke said that the world's biggest economy was nearing the start of recovery. The stock markets worldwide rose sharply following this statement. The US consumer confidence also rose in July—the latest sign that the economy was recovering. However, the Congress warned on 25 August that the US budget deficit will soar to almost \$1.6 trillion (£978 billion) during 2009. The data released on 27 August showed that the US GDP fell by 1 per cent in the second quarter of June 2009.

The world's second biggest retailer, Carrefour, of Italy reported a loss for the first half of the year after writing down the value of assets. The eurozone's annual rate of inflation was negative in August, for the third consecutive month.

India's economy grew 6.1 per cent in the second quarter of 2009-10, as compared with the corresponding period of the previous year. It was slightly better than expected.

On 1 September 2009, the impact of recession continued to be felt, as unemployment levels across 16 countries that use the euro, hit a 10 year high in July, it was reported.

As Germany and France were keen to discuss 'exit-strategies' from the measures designed to stimulate their economies at G20 meeting in London, the UK's Chancellor of the Exchequer warned them on 3 September 2009 that the growth would be stifled if they withdrew anti-recession measures too soon. Jean-

Claude Trichet, the President of the European Central Bank (ECB) also spoke against calls to reduce fiscal stimulus plans. He expected the economic recovery to be "uneven, both inside and outside the Euro area".

There were some positive news from the British services sector, which was stated to have registered its fastest growth for nearly two years. The figures released on 4 September raised hopes that the UK economy was on the road to recovery.

Finance ministers from the world's most powerful economies on 5 September 2009 agreed to take a series of measures to regulate the global banking system.

On 5 September, it was reported that the Iceland's economy contracted 2 per cent in the quarter ending 30 June 2009. Its GDP also shrank 6.5 per cent as compared to the corresponding period previous year. This showed that the economies of Scandinavian countries are still not recovering from recession.

On 7 September, the Basel Committee of central bank governors was reported to have agreed provisionally on a set of rules based on the principles highlighted during the London G20 meeting of August 2009. The key proposals included increases in the size of capital reserves that banks are required to hold, together with much stricter guidelines on the quality of reserves, and a limit on bank borrowings of 25 times the assets. Since the European banks will be required to hold a larger proportion of their reserves in cash and simple equity, rather than the current equity debt mix allowed under the current rules, they will be hit particularly hard.

On 8 September, JPMorgan released a study into the effect of the proposed capital adequacy reforms on investment banks, saying that the long-term profit levels will fall by around 30 per cent—leading to lower bonuses and more redundancies. The report however predicted that the traditional lending banks will not be as much affected by the reforms in capital adequacy requirements, because of the relatively low risk nature of their business model. It will not be out of place to mention here that India has not been as much affected by the global recession as most of other countries because of its sound financial system well regulated by the Reserve Bank of India. Our banks' way of lending is traditional and less prone to risks.

In an interesting observation, Lloyd Blankfein, the chief executive of Goldman Sachs stated at a banking conference on 9 September 2009 that the big banks had lost control of some of the exotic instruments that they were creating in the run up to the credit crisis. It can be pointed out in this regard that in their excitement to expand their businesses, these banks had forgotten to evolve a mechanism whereby the inherent risks could have been detected well in time and remedial measures be taken before the situation blew out of proportion. The central banks did not develop framework to keep the activities of banks within proper control.

On 10 September, it was reported that US President Barack Obama's massive stimulus package had created 1.1 million jobs. According to another report, the world's largest economies have spent $10,000 per person in an effort to get the better of the financial meltdown.

The European Commission on 14 September forecast that the eurozone was emerging from recession. Federal Reserve Chairman Ben Bernanke said that the US recession was probably over but the economy will remain weak for some time due to unemployment. The Organisation for Economic Co-operation and Development (OECD) said the global recession could cost 25 million people their jobs. It was reported that the UK retail sales were unchanged in August as compared with the previous month, casting doubt on the strength of the recovery in consumer spending.

On 18 September, the Bank of Japan (BOJ) gave an upbeat assessment of the Japanese economy and hinted that it may soon withdraw some emergency support measures. The US credit rating agencies will face tighter supervision under new rules adopted by the Federal Reserve.

On 21 September, Robert Zoellick, President of the World Bank called on the G20 leaders to set an ambitious agenda for 'responsible globalisation' that links efforts to promote more balanced growth with financial stability. The World Bank President also called for global unity of efforts to counter climate change. Zoellick also predicted that growth for the remainder of 2009 could beat expectations but added a cautionary note stating that there wont be a double dip, "but we are not out of woods yet".

The Royal Bank of Scotland (RBS) was reported to be planning a £3-4 billion rights issue in order to both reduce the stake it would give the government for RBS's participation in the asset protection scheme and to improve the bank's balance sheet.

It was reported on 23 September that the Federal Reserve is developing plans for future interest rate increases, although these were not expected until the second half of 2010. The Federal Reserve is looking at ways of reducing $800 billion of bank reserves created during the financial crisis by entering into 'reverse repo' trades with mutual money market funds who they expect could refinance around $500 billion of Federal Reserve assets.

The European Commission proposed the creation of a new European Systemic Risk Board (ESRB), to assess and warn about threats to financial stability in the region. This would be a new body made up of central bank governors for all the member states in the 27-country bloc, and chaired by the President of the European Central Bank, which will also provide working support. The ESRB will have the power to make recommendations and warnings to member states who will in turn be answerable to the ESRB for non-compliance. Also there will be a new European System of Financial Supervisors, which will oversee the banking, securities, insurance and occupational pensions sector. Its role will be to develop harmonised rules and common approaches to supervision.

On 25 September, the G20 leaders agreed to support new global standards on remuneration practices produced by the Financial Stability Board (FSB). The principles agreed to reward long-term success over short-term risk taking and include measures such as deferral of bonuses over a three year period and the ability to clawback pay in the event of non-performance.

Goldman Sachs on 28 September announced a wide ranging recruitment drive across all regions in order to develop the bank's asset management business at a time when many other financial institutions are resorting to lay-offs and putting recruitment on hold. The Organisation for Economic Co-operation and Development also called for innovative policies to tackle high global unemployment. US consumer confidence fell unexpectedly in September, suggesting Americans are not as convinced as US policymakers of an economic recovery.

Japan's core consumer prices dropped 2.4 per cent in August year-on-year, the fourth successive month of record falls. The yen was reported to have weakened from the previous day's eight-month high against the US dollar following comments from Japanese Finance Minister Hirohisa Fujii. The collective wealth of the richest 400 Americans fell by $300 billion (£187 billion) over the past year, according to the Forbes 400 rich list. This showed the impact of global meltdown on individual wealth. It was reported that the prices in the eurozone fell in September at a faster rate than they had in August. The International Monetary Fund (IMF) cut its forecast for the amount likely to be written-off globally in bad loans and investments by 15 per cent.

On 30 September 2009, the International Monetary Fund revised their initial estimate of the total loss to the global economic system as a result of the credit crisis from $4 trillion to $3.4 trillion. However, the IMF's Global Financial Stability Report warned that many financial institutions had so far only declared approximately half of their likely total losses.

The UK Government published a statement that HSBC, Lloyds Banking Group, Royal Bank of Scotland, Standard Chartered and Barclays had agreed to fully implement the Pittsburgh G20 bonus reform proposals in the 2009 bonus round. Questions were raised as to whether the US would follow suit, following the concerns expressed by the US regulators as to whether the strictly drafted rules could be applied to a variety institutions in such a blanket fashion.

The global economy was expanding again and financial conditions had improved significantly, the International Monetary Fund said on 1 October 2009. The unemployment rate across the 16 countries that used the euro had risen again as the effects of the recession continued to be felt. But the activity in the UK manufacturing sector continued to decline in September, a survey indicated.

On 2 October 2009, Japan's jobless rate unexpectedly fell to 5.5 per cent in August from July's record high of 5.7 per cent, official figures showed.

In contrast, the US economy lost 263,000 jobs in September, which was more than had been expected, according to official non-farm payrolls figures.

The President of the World Bank, Robert Zoellick pleaded to the rich nations to inject more capital into the bank, following warnings that serious cash flow problems will be faced during 2010-11. He estimated that between $3-5 billion would be required, in order to fund on-going and new projects, although he accepted that raising such a figure would be difficult in the current climate.

On 5 October 2009, the financial firms may be recovering, with business volumes growing for the first time in two years, survey that shown. The US services industry expanded in September for the first time in a year, a survey has shown.

Sales of new cars rose 11.4 per cent in September compared with the same month last year, according to the Society of Motor Manufacturers and Traders (SMMT). However, UK industrial output fell unexpectedly in August, confounding analysts' expectations of an increase and casting doubt on the strength of the economy.

On 6 October 2009, Australia raised its main interest rate to 3.25 per cent from 3 per cent, becoming the first G20 nation to do so as the global economy begins to recover. The US aluminium-maker Alcoa announced a surprise profit after three consecutive quarterly losses.

The Brazilian unit of Spanish banking giant Santander raised 14.1 billion reais (£5.1 billion; $8.1 billion) in the country's biggest share offering. The increasing budget deficit continued to be a major worry for the US. According to Congress estimates, it had trebled to a record $1.4 trillion (£877 billion) in the year from 1 October 2008 to 30 September 2009. The US dollar index also dropped to a 14-month low in the first week of September raising concerns about the dollar's reserve currency status. With dollar declining against other major currencies there was a sharp rise in the prices of precious metals, particularly gold.

It was reported that Germany's trade surplus fell 43 per cent in August after a drop in exports from Europe's biggest economy, according to the national statistics office.

On 11 October 2009, President Dmitry Medvedev said Russia's economy will shrink by 7.5 per cent in 2009, but claimed that Kremlin intervention had prevented a worse decline. The Centre for Economics and Business Research predicted that UK interest rates will remain at their historic low of 0.5 per cent through 2010, and will remain below 2 per cent until 2014. If proved true, this is likely to leave sterling the lowest-yielding major currency at a time when interest rates outside the UK look set to start rising. The Organisation for Economic Co-operation and Development said unemployment in its member countries had edged higher.

On 14 October 2009, Chinese official export figures for September suggested improvements in economies in the rest of the world.

On 15 October 2009, the European Union and South Korea signed a trade deal that could be worth up to 19 billion euros ($28 billion; £17 billion) to European exporters. The Dow Jones Industrial Average topped thc 10,000 mark for the first time in a year. Eurostar reported a rise in sales between July and September, with "some signs of an upturn in business travel".

On 16 October 2009, Google reported its highest quarterly profit, suggesting that the Internet advertising market is bouncing back from the recession. US industrial production also rose more than expected in September, growing for the third straight month.

But the eurozone trade balance with the rest of the world slipped into deficit in August after a big surplus in July, as exports fell by more than imports. The European Commission warned that Germany's planned state aid for Opel may breach competition rules, raising the prospect of its sale being halted. Bank of America reported a $1 billion (£612 million) net loss for the three months from July to September, which was worse than had been expected.

On 19 October, a Dutch court declared DSB bankrupt after last-ditch attempts to find a buyer for the bank failed. It was considered premature to talk about the beginnings of a recovery despite growing optimism, according to the influential Ernst & Young Item Club. The New York Stock Exchange planned to create a technology service centre in Belfast, creating up to 400 jobs. The number of new houses being built in the US edged up in September, but by less than expected, raising concerns about the strength of the US recovery. Caterpillar, the world's largest maker of construction and mining equipment, said it saw 'encouraging signs' of economic recovery. Workers at Opel's factory in Spain announced four days of strikes starting the following week after failing to reach an agreement with Magna on job cuts. Chinese annual car production topped 10 million for the first time as carmakers boosted output to meet growing demand, state media said. The UK's public sector net borrowing reached £14.8 billion last month—a high for September, official figures showed. US bank Morgan Stanley agreed to sell its retail asset management business to investment manager Invesco in a deal worth $1.5 billion (£913 million).

More UK companies faced the threat of insolvency next year, a report said, even though the number of firms failing had fallen in the past three months.

On 21 October 2009, the Governor of the Bank of England called for banks to be split into utility companies for their deposit taking and payments systems and risky ventures, a view sharply at odds with the Treasury, the Financial Services Authority and the G20 proposals. The British Bankers Association warned that the hasty implementation of new rules governing capital and liquidity requirements risks damaging economic recovery.

On 22 October 2009, President Barack Obama welcomed plans to force some companies which accepted government aid during the financial crisis to cut executive pay. China said it was on track to hit its growth target of 8 per cent in 2009, after the economy grew 8.9 per cent from a year ago in the third quarter.

On 23 October 2009, the UK economy unexpectedly contracted by 0.4 per cent between July and September, according to official figures, meaning the country was still in recession. It was announced that the Federal Reserve had drawn some rules under which the top 28 financial institutions in the US must demonstrate strong risk management and corporate governance, and show that their pay schemes did not encourage excessive risk taking.

It was reported that the number of US bank failures in 2009 had topped more than 100 after US federal regulators shut down a trio of small Florida banks. Caterpillar, the world's largest construction and mining equipment maker, said it will permanently cut 2,500 jobs in the US. Magna's takeover of Opel moved a step closer after Spanish workers voted to accept plans that would save their factory from closure and saw fewer jobs cut. India's largest carmaker, Tata Motors, beat expectations for its quarterly profit. South Korea's economy grew between July and September at its fastest quarterly rate since the first quarter of 2002.

On 26 October 2009, the European Commission ordered ING to sell off its insurance and investment management business in a radical break-up for the financial services group. The dismantling of ING reflect the concerns of the competition authorities that their decision to wave through state aid pumped into the group during the crisis was too generous. The 'back to basics' restructuring plan announced by the group earlier in 2009 had envisaged separate management of insurance and banking but had focused on the sale of individual assets rather than the tearing up of its business model.

On 27 October 2009, oil giant BP reported third-quarter profits well ahead of expectations, sending its share price up 5 per cent. But India's leading shares slipped more than 2 per cent after the country's central bank said it was time to roll back some of its economic support measures.

On 28 October 2009, the steel giant ArcelorMittal reported a profit for the July to September quarter, ending a run of three consecutive quarterly losses. Spanish banking giant Santander announced a profit of 2.2 billion euros ($3.3 billion; £2 billion) for July to September, almost unchanged from a year ago. Nomura Holdings, Japan's biggest brokerage, reported its second straight quarterly profit after trading activity increased. Norway became the first European country to raise its interest rates since the beginning of the global financial crisis. The fall in the number of people paying into private sector final-salary pension schemes had slowed, despite a trend for these benefits to be closed.

On 29 October 2009, official data due later was expected to indicate that the US economy had started to grow, but analysts warn the continuing recovery would be slow. Anglo-Dutch oil giant Royal Dutch Shell reported that its quarterly profit had fallen sharply, and warned that the outlook remained 'very uncertain'. Loss-making carrier Japan Airlines (JAL) confirmed it was to apply for financial assistance from a newly-formed state-backed turnaround agency. The US economy grew at an annual pace of 3.5 per cent between July and September, its first expansion in more than a year.

Official figures confirmed on 29 October that the US economy had returned to growth in the third quarter after the longest period of economic contraction since the Great Depression. US consumer spending on durable goods saw an upturn, boosted by the 'cash-for-clunkers' car-buying subsidy. Residential investment experienced a similar increase for the first time in more than three years.

It was reported on 30 October that the unemployment levels across the 16 countries that use the euro rose to 9.7 per cent in September, had reached the highest rate since January 1999. US consumer spending fell for the first time in five months in September, coinciding with the end of the government's car scrappage scheme. China's manufacturing sector grew in October at its fastest rate in 18 months, a survey suggested. Chancellor Alistair Darling confirmed early November that Lloyds, RBS and Northern Rock would be broken up and parts sold to new entrants to the banking sector.

The UK Treasury announced in the beginning of November that a further £33.5 billion would be injected into Royal Bank of Scotland in order to ensure that the bank survives the crisis, bringing the total government investment in the institution up to 84 per cent. Of the headline amount, £25.5 billion was to be directly invested into the bank while the remaining £8 billion was to be set aside in an emergency liquidity fund. The bank had also been forced into selling its RBS branded branches, the Scottish Natwest branch network, the Churchill and Direct Line Insurance businesses and parts of the bank's investment banking arm, in order to satisfy state aid rules.

The Federal Reserve announced on 4 November amendments to their policy statement which indicate that the federal funds rate, currently targeted to be between 0-0.25 per cent, will remain at exceptionally low levels for an extended period.

The World Bank upped its 2009 growth forecast for China from 7.2 per cent to 8.4 per cent, but said that the nation needed to encourage more consumer spending. The European Central Bank (ECB) kept interest rates on hold at a record low of 1 per cent for the sixth month in a row. The Financial Services Authority (FSA) fined Swiss banking giant UBS £8 million for failing to stop its employees making unauthorized transactions.

General Motors (GM) confirmed that it planned to cut 10,000 jobs across its European car unit Opel, which included the Vauxhall brand in the UK. It pointed to the fact that the company had not recovered from the onslaught of recession.

The Bank of England announced on 5 November that a further £25 billion would be injected into the economy, bringing the total amount expended under the quantitative easing programme to £200 billion. However, the announcement made clear that the bank would be following the moves made by the European Central Bank and the Federal Reserve by slowing the payments into the economy over the next three months, in an effort to return to pre-crisis policy.

The unemployment rate in the US rose to 10.2 per cent in October, which was its highest rate since April 1983, according to figures from the US Labor Department. Major economies across the world were showing strong signs of recovery, but it did not seem to be the case of America. A Moody's study showed that banks worldwide faced increases in funding costs that could cut profits and increase costs to the customer. A short-term debt amounting to more than $7,000 billion expiring in the next three years will need to be refinanced with longer-dated bonds.

Russia's central bank announced on 10 November that investors in the rouble should be wary that appreciation was not guaranteed in a bid to stem an advance in the currency sparked by rising oil prices and a falling US dollar. The rouble had indeed become the best performing major currency against the US dollar since the first week of September and had largely recovered from the financial crisis when the central bank had to utilise foreign exchange reserves to prevent a slide in the currency.

A US Senate committee proposed a major overhaul of the US regulatory system that would cut the powers of the Federal Reserve and create a single banking regulator. The draft legislation created an agency to oversee systemic risk, which could call for banks to be broken up and impose more stringent capital requirements. Lloyds Banking Group said it was to cut 5,000 more jobs by the end of 2010 as it continued to reduce overlap following its merger with HBOS in 2008.

The economic data from China suggested that industrial production grew year-on-year at a level faster than expected.

The number of people unemployed in the UK rose again in the three months to September, although the increase was the smallest since May 2008.

Mervyn King announced that Britain was "facing a prolonged period of balance sheet adjustment" as households, businesses and government reined in spending to affordable levels. The Bank of England forecast growth rates of 2.1 per cent for 2010 and 4 per cent for 2011 in its quarterly inflation report.

The eurozone economy has emerged from recession after growing between July and September, figures showed. Asia is leading the world out of recession, the region's leaders said. Figures released by the Japanese Government show that the country's economy had grown for a second successive quarter.

The deputy governor of the Bank of England spelt out a number of regulatory measures mid November needed for oversight of complex international financial institutions that stopped short of requiring the break-up of banks that were considered "too big to fail". The Bank of England's forecast, made on 18 November, for medium- to long-term growth was the strongest it had made since it was granted independence in 1997. The central growth forecast for 2010 and 2011 was 2.2 and 4.1 per cent respectively—the highest in 12 years. The bank also made upward revisions to its inflation forecasts with consumer price inflation in the first quarter of 2010 expected to rise to 2.7 per cent.

It was announced on 19 November that October's UK public borrowing figures reflected a deterioration in public finances, taking the rolling 12-month total of debt to £138 billion, nearly triple the level a year ago. The Organisation for Economic Co-operation and Development said on 19 November that growth and recovery were expected in 2010 in just about all world regions.

The Dutch state announced plans to provide ABN-Amro and Fortis Bank Nederland with a further €4.4 billion in capital to keep their merger on track. FBN and the Dutch assets of ABN were nationalised 2008 when Fortis, their former owner, collapsed. The capital injection must be approved by parliament but Wouter Bos, Finance Minister, argued that there was no practical alternative to pressing ahead with the merger to form a new bank that could eventually be floated or sold.

The economies of the 30 members of the Organisation for Economic Co-operation and Development grew by 0.8 per cent in July to September, the group said. Sales of previously-owned US homes jumped by 10.1 per cent in October as buyers rushed to take advantage of tax credits, which had then been extended. It was reported that the US economy grew by far less than originally forecast between July and September, according to revised official figures.

Japan's exports fell at their slowest annual rate in a year in October, providing further evidence of the country's emergence from recession. US consumer spending rose more than expected in October, raising hopes that the economic recovery is continuing despite stubbornly high unemployment. The UK economy also contracted at a slower pace than originally estimated between July and September, figures showed.

European shares were hit by concerns over Dubai's financial health, after a government-owned company asked for an extension on repaying its debts. US shares also fell on worries about Dubai's debt problems.

The Dubai Government said on 30 November that it will not guarantee the debt of Dubai World, which caused global panic because it could not pay back creditors immediately. India's economy grew at a faster-than-expected rate of 7.9 per cent in the three months to September, compared to the same period last year. Australia's central bank raised interest rates for the third month in a row, as the country's economy continued to recover from the downturn. The Bank of Japan announced new measures to boost the economy and tackle deflation. UK manufacturing activity slowed in November as new orders fell sharply, a survey indicated, casting doubts on the strength of the sector's recovery. The Venezuelan Government shut down four private banks, accusing them of financial irregularities.

On 2 December 2009, Germany's Economy Minister Rainer Bruederle warned that German firms would face another credit crunch if the country's banks did not lend more. European Union finance ministers agreed plans for a new Europe-wide system of financial regulation. The ratings agency

Standard & Poor's cut the credit ratings of four Dubai-based banks because of their exposure to the debt-laden Dubai World. Although the US economy was improving, it was too early to say that the recovery will last, Federal Reserve Chairman Ben Bernanke said.

Dubai's stock market fell by 6 per cent on 7 December on new worries about the size of the emirate's debt burden.

Japan agreed a 7.2 trillion yen ($81 billion; £48 billion) stimulus plan designed to prevent the country's economy from slipping back into recession. US President Obama set forward a number of proposals aimed at boosting employment, including calling for tax cuts for small businesses. In a major reversal, the rating agency Standard & Poor's cut Spain's credit outlook from stable to negative. Another negative news came from Greece whose debt reached the highest level in its modern history, as stated by the country's Deputy Finance Minister Phillippos Sachinidis. However, Australia's unemployment rate fell unexpectedly in November, as the country's economic recovery continued.

The US House of Representatives on 11 December approved the most sweeping changes to the country's financial sector since the Great Depression of the 1930s. Dubai Government announced that it had been given a $10 billion (£6.13 billion) handout from United Arab Emirates neighbour Abu Dhabi to help it pay off its debts.

The Federal Reserve decided to keep US interest rates on hold between zero and 0.25 per cent, as had been widely expected.

The number of people unemployed in the UK rose by 21,000 between August and October to 2.49 million.

Citigroup said the Abu Dhabi Investment Authority (ADIA) had filed a claim against it seeking to stop a 2007 deal to buy $7.5 billion (£4.6 billion) worth of stock.

November's eurozone annual inflation figure was the first positive rate for seven months, the figures confirmed.

Official figures showed that China overtook Germany in 2009 to become number one exporting nation. Export of

German goods fell by 18.4 per cent in 2009 compared with the previous year—the biggest year-on-year fall since 1950, according to the Federal Statistics Office. Overall, German exports last year were equivalent to $1,121.3 billion, which compared with the $1,201.7 billion exported by China. It accentuated the view that China was rising fast as an economic superpower, and that Asian countries like China and India had not been as much affected by global economic meltdown as Europe and America.

For the first time since 1993, the UK Treasury found itself facing a deficit in January 2010. Despite public sector net borrowing totalling $4.3 billion for January, the Treasury maintained that this figure was expected as was covered self-assessment income and capital gains tax for the period 2008-09 which spanned the height of recession. It expressed confidence that the total deficit for the financial year would fall well below its target of £170 billion, resulting in spare funds for the government. However, this in turn sparked a political debate as to whether any excess cash should be directed towards cutting the deficit or increasing spending.

US consumer confidence fell to the lowest level in ten months on fears about a slow labour market recovery. US house prices meanwhile continued to straddle along, showing a small monthly fall in December 2009 while recording slowing annual declines.

Germany recorded a budget deficit of 3.3 per cent of GDP in 2009, which was well below the level for most of Europe's larger economies. It was the first year since 2005 that Germany had breached the Maatricht stability and growth targets, of keeping deficit spending by European Union members below 3 per cent.

Ben Bernanke, Chairman of the US Federal Reserve revealed on 24 February that the US central bank was looking into a number of questions relating to Greek currency transactions structured by Goldman Sachs and other companies. Lloyd's Banking Group reported a £6.3 billion underlying pre-tax loss for 2009, a slight improvement on the £6.7 billion deficit recorded a year earlier.

Hector Sants resigned as head of Financial Services Authority on 8 February, 2010 after working for three years as chief executive. He advocated banking reform, both in the UK and internationally but criticised the conservatives' plans to give the FSA's supervisory role to the Bank of England and spin out consumer protection responsibilities to a new agency.

According to the UK Prime Minister Gordon Brown, the world's leading economies were close to agreeing to a globally coordinated bank tax after President Barack Obama's move in January 2010 to raise $90 billion (£57.7 billion) from a US bank levy. He believed that the IMF will endorse a global levy before its April meeting in Washington in a move that could cost the financial services sector tens of billions of pounds a year.

It was reported on 12 February that Goldman Sachs and other banks may have to give up their bank status if they wish to avoid Obama's proposal to separate proprietary trading from commercial banking, known as the "Volcker Rule". Markets were not sure how the rule would affect groups like JPMorgan Chase, which had proprietary trading desks and private equity units. Executives at Goldman said that if the Volcker Rule was passed, it would perhaps sell its deposit-taking bank, which though was an insignificant part of Goldman's $900 billion plus balance sheet.

Germany's Chancellor, Angela Merkel condemned investment banks for causing the financial crisis and for their suspected involvement in the debt crisis in Greece. In the meantime, there was continuing civil unrest and turmoil throughout Greece with further industrial action planned for the fourth week of February 2010 with no sign that an EU rescue package was forthcoming. This followed Germany's insistence that Greece must reduce its public spending before other EU countries stepped in.

It was decided that in the first week of March 2010, the 23 largest banks in the US that had over $100 billion of assets would be overseen by the US Federal Reserve rather than being supervised by a single regulator. This proposal was put forward in an attempt to prevent a repeat of the Lehman bankruptcy and the burdensome bailout of AIG. Mr Geithner the US Treasury Secretary told senators that only the central bank was capable of fully supervising these large institutions. Many senators, however, were reluctant to allow the US Federal Reserve to retain its supervisory powers.

Due to concerns that the draft EU directive could adversely affect the hedge fund and private equity sectors, Gordon Brown and Nicolas Sarkozy met in the second week of March 2010 to find a compromise solution. The EU directive was aimed at tightening regulatory controls and both the UK and US were apprehensive that this would negatively impact the industries. Mr Geithner, expressed concerns that the regulatory controls would "discriminate against US firms" but EU officials responded that the proposed directive was a measure taken in response to the G20 decision to enhance transparency in the financial system.

Speaking at the National People's Congress on 14 March 2010, the Chinese Premier, Wen Jiabao, warned other countries not to press China on its currency policy and described such pressure as an attempt at protectionism. The statement came in the light of accusations that the renminbi had been deliberately undervalued.

Moody's projections indicated in the middle of March that the extent of federal borrowing was so high that interest payments on government debt would be 15 per cent greater than government revenues by the end of the decade (2001-10).

UK Chancellor, Alistair Darling on 24 March delivered an extremely political budget at the expense of the rich and banks. Darling's budget was strongly criticised by the economists who felt that apart from tax increases and £9 billion in spending cuts, the budget was vague.

Towards the end of March 2010, a survey conducted in UK showed that the country was losing its competitiveness as a financial centre. However, many firms predicted that the financial services sector would see a rise in business volumes during the quarter April-June 2010, though they felt that tighter regulations and new taxes on financial institutions would weigh negatively on such rise.

The German Government brought a scheme through which future bailouts would be funded by banks themselves. Financial institutions would contribute towards a fund that may be drawn upon whenever there is a threat to financial stability. The scheme was expected to raise £1 billion. It was learnt that UK and France may also launch such a scheme as both these countries were thinking of imposing a levy on banks.

The Bank of England issued a report stating that during April-June, banks would continue to make personal loans and overdrafts available only to 'better quality' borrowers. This was in contrast to the banks' willingness to provide mortgages and credit to businesses and was considered an important step towards financial regulation.

It was reported in the first week of April 2010 that the financial reform legislation proposed by the US President was starting to gain momentum. Negotiations were continuing and a bill was expected to be signed by Barack Obama on the second anniversary of the collapse of Lehman Brothers. Within the House of Representatives and the Senate and between Republicans and Democrats there was a growing recognition that there was an urgent need to enact legislation to address the underlying issues of the financial crisis.

The British Chambers of Commerce published the results of its survey of 5,500 companies. The most prominent result showed that the economy had evaded a "double-dip recession" in the first quarter of the calendar year 2010. Following the loss of investor confidence on the bond markets, it seemed inevitable that Greece would have to seek a rescue package from the EU and International Monetary Fund (IMF). The eurozone members agreed to provide up to €30 billion in loans to Greece over the next year. During a teleconference of eurozone finance ministers, the loans will be supplemented by contributions from IMF that could yield an additional €15 billion according to European officials.

US President Barack Obama pushed President Hu Jintao of China to allow the renminbi to appreciate, as new figures showed that China's foreign exchange reserves were growing at a slower rate than before. The analysts were studying the effect of a stronger renminbi on other Asian currencies as well as the wider consequences for currency markets as a whole.

The International Monetary Fund urged US and European regulators to consider imposing higher customised capital requirements on "systemically important" banks deemed "too big to fail". However, the experts felt that the decision of capital surcharges for big banks was controversial, with bankers arguing that large institutions should not be penalised by regulators because of their size. US and European governments pledged to overhaul regulation to avoid a repeat of the huge public bailouts of troubled financial institutions seen during the financial crisis.

Brazil's central bank attempted to tackle rising inflation by raising interest rates by three-quarters of a percentage point from 8.75 per cent to 9.5 per cent which was the first time since 10 September 2008 that the bank had increased its rates. Brazil, like other rapidly developing economies, China and India, was reported to have weathered the credit crisis admirably and only experienced a brief recession from which it has said to have already recovered and its economy was growing.

The European Central Bank bought €16.5 billion of eurozone government bonds as part of an international rescue plan, amid widespread investor apprehension that the intervention was not sufficient to stabilise debt markets. The euro fell to its weakest level against the US dollar since April 2006 in spite of the €750 billion international support package and central bank intervention. The euro had fallen 14 per cent against the dollar upto mid-May 2010.

New rules for hedge funds and private equity funds operating in Europe won the backing of European Union finance ministers. The move followed a similar endorsement by a group of EU lawmakers earlier and meant that regulation of the industry in the region had moved much closer.

Towards the end of May 2010, the Qatar Investment Authority, a sovereign wealth fund, expressed interest in buying some of the US Treasury's 27 per cent stake in

Citigroup. The wealth fund's interest in Citi came as other wealth funds were shying away from banks, largely because of big losses on such investments in the past.

It was made known in the last week of May 2010 that Prudential Financial Inc. was trying to renegotiate the $35.5 billion price tag Asian Insurance Arm (AIA) of American Insurance Group. Prudential hoped to strike a deal at around $30 billion. The takeover would make Prudential the biggest foreign insurer in the fast-growing Asian markets and the largest life assurer outside of China.

In the second week of June 2010, the Institute of International Finance warned that economic growth in the eurozone, the US and Japan would be cut by 3 per cent between now and 2015, if current proposals to force banks to hold more capital and liquid assets go forward unchanged.

It was reported on 15 June that the Spanish banks were borrowing record amounts from the European Central Bank as the country's financial institutions struggled to gain funding from capital markets.

Spanish banks borrowed €85.6 billion from the ECB in May 2010, the highest amount since the launch of the eurozone in 1999.

It was reported that the US banks second-quarter results would be weighed down by a £1.35 billion bill to pay for the UK tax on bankers. The tax forced banks to pay a one-off 50 per cent levy on UK bonuses above £25,000, including those awarded in shares to employees of US banks working in the UK. Unlike some European rivals, most US banks paid the full amount, shielding bankers from the effects of the levy.

In an emergency budget designed to seize control of public finances strained by the biggest financial crisis in decades, UK Chancellor George Osborne outlined, in the third week of June 2010, cuts for most government departments of 25 per cent by 2014-15. This represented one of the most drastic spending squeezes in any advanced economy in recent times.

On 25 June, it was made known that plans by global regulators for banks to set aside billions of dollars in extra capital to cope with future crises were to be pared back after intense lobbying by the industry. However, the proposed short-term emergency funding measures were to go ahead. The French Government announced a further €3.5 billion of tax rises for 2011 as it sought to bolster confidence in its commitment to reduce its budget deficit. The latest announcement brought the amount France aimed to raise from tax in 2010 to €13.2 billion.

US lawmakers scrapped a proposed $19 billion bank fee as Democrats struggled to secure sufficient votes to pass the Wall Street reform bill. The new proposal involved ending early the $700 billion Troubled Asset Relief Programme and increasing the revenue raised by the Federal Deposit Insurance Corporation.

In the first week of July, apprehensions grew that the global recovery was faltering after a slew of data pointed to weaker global demand led by slower growth in China. Figures showed manufacturing output slowing across large parts of the world, posing further challenges to leading economies as they endeavoured to address shaky fiscal positions without falling back into recession. China was considering stripping its $200 billion sovereign wealth fund of the country's banking stakes, in a move that could free it of some restrictions when it invested in the US. Under the proposal, China Investment Corporation would no longer be responsible for holding the state's majority stakes in the country's biggest banks such as Bank of China.

European commercial banks began using their holdings of gold to raise cash with the Bank for International Settlements, in a further sign of strains in the money markets on which many relied for funding.

The Bank of England made nearly £10 billion in paper profits by buying UK Government bonds as part of emergency efforts to pump money into the British economy. The buy-back programme that began in March 2009 and involved purchasing nearly £200 billion in gilts—generated gains of £9.7 billion for the Bank, according to analysis for the *Financial Times*.

On 8 July 2010, new rules restricting bankers' bonuses were approved by European Union lawmakers. As a result, bankers would only be able to receive between 20 and 30 per cent of any bonus in upfront cash. It was said to be the toughest restriction worldwide of this kind.

On 15 July, the US Senate passed a landmark reform of Wall Street, delivering President Barack Obama's second big legislative victory and imposing some restrictions on banks. Goldman Sachs agreed to pay a $550 million fine to settle US regulators' accusations that it misled investors in a mortgage-backed security—a move that ended the highest profile regulatory case since the crisis.

Italian Prime Minister Silvio Berlusconi's government won senate approval for its €25 billion austerity programme, overcoming dissent from the prime minister's allies as well as opposition parties.

On 18 July, the International Monetary Fund sought commitments by as early as November to boost its lending resources to $1,000 billion from $750 billion to build safety nets that could prevent financial crises. South Korea, as the president of the Group of 20 leading economies for 2010 was helping craft the plan.

Global banking regulators, on 27 July reached a breakthrough agreement to tighten capital requirements and impose new worldwide liquidity and leverage standards, but they softened some of their proposals and delayed others to at least 2018. The Basel Committee on Banking Supervision stated that all except one of the 27 member countries had signed up to the new principles, which limited what banks could count as so-called tier-one capital—the only kind that could be counted on to absorb losses.

It was make known on 28 July that India was planning to start conducting twice-yearly stress tests on its banks, following in the footsteps of financial regulators in the US and Europe.

Portugal became the first eurozone country to agree to set aside cash—or other assets—against derivative transactions in a decision intended to reduce its funding costs.

On 30 July, the US public's hope of getting repaid for the bailouts of Bear Stearns and AIG in the financial crisis increased after the Federal Reserve reported a paper profit for the first time on all the holdings of securities bought from the companies.

Citigroup agreed to pay $75 million to settle Securities and Exchange Commission charges that it failed to disclose to investors more than $40 billion in exposure to subprime mortgages.

Goldman Sachs said on 4 August that it was preparing to shut down the unit that traded with the bank's funds and move its traders to either an independent hedge fund or its asset management arm to comply with new US law and prevent an exodus of star employees.

On 5 August 2010, Barclays launched a spirited defence of its approach of combining retail and investment banking under one roof. John Varley, chief executive, said Barclays' so-called universal model had proved its resilience and profitability through the financial crisis.

Meanwhile, the eurozone's economic recovery was exceeding expectations but it was too early "to declare victory", stated the European Central Bank. Evidence was mounting that the next few months would see stronger growth than originally forecast, according to Jean-Claude Trichet, ECB president.

European and US banks appeared to have won some 'breathing' space after earnings reports brought on 8 August suggested that recovery was well underway. The banks had been under severe pressure over their exposure to faltering eurozone economies, their own financing difficulties and the regulations set to come into force in Europe and America.

On 10 August, the US Federal Reserve took a first step towards extending its crisis-era monetary policy regime, as it downgraded its view of the economic outlook amid rising fears of a "double-dip" recession. The officials agreed to begin reinvesting more than $150 billion (£95 billion) in annual proceeds from maturing mortgage-backed and agency securities into Treasury debt, halting plans to allow a natural shrinkage of the $2,300 billion balance sheet the US central bank built up during the recession.

US regulators increased their scrutiny of the country's largest banks, digging deeper into riskier activities and pushing institutions to conduct more rigorous "stress tests" of their financial health.

It was stated mid-August that China was on track to officially eclipse Japan as the world's second largest economy by the end of 2010, which would symbolise Beijing's rise and the shift in global economic and political power. New figures released on 16 August showed that China's economy had Japan's in the second quarter after Japanese gross domestic product fell unexpectedly.

Angela Merkel, Chancellor of Germany, was sticking with plans to cut public spending and hold off tax cuts even as the country's recent growth spurt suggested that the economy overtaken could expand in 2010 at twice the rate prevously forecast by Berlin.

The United Kingdom Listing Authority (UKLA) said on 18 August that it had loosened requirements on financial data so that a listed company must provide a target in order to avoid suspension of the acquirer's shares. It also said it would not allow listed companies to attempt to avoid the information provisions of the rules by creating a new holding company, or "topco", used to take over both acquirer and target.

Ireland accused Standard & Poor's on 25 August of a "flawed" analysis of the country's debt position after its credit rating downgrade to AA– sparked a sell-off in Dublin's bond markets.

Postponing cuts in public and private sector debts would be "very dangerous" and risk a Japanese-style "lost decade", Jean-Claude Trichet, European Central Bank president warned on 27 August.

The European Central Bank was expected in the last week of August 2010 to extend emergency support for eurozone banks until early next year as it would gauge how well the

16-country region might withstand a big US or global slowdown.

Irish banks were gearing up to repay more than €25 billion of debt in September in what could prove an important test of investor sentiment towards the broader eurozone financial sector.

It was reported on 31st August that the healing of the US banking sector had picked up pace in the second quarter with lenders' profits rebounding to pre-crisis levels amid falling loan losses. However, according to official data released, the earnings performance masked the wide gap between resurgent large banks and their struggling smaller rivals.

The Securities and Exchange Commission warned credit rating agencies of their authority to bring fraud cases over conduct outside the US that had "foreseeable effects" in the country.

Europe must "accelerate the pace of structural reform over the next year to consolidate an uneven economic recovery", José Manuel Barroso, President of the European Commission, told the European parliament in his first "state of the union" address on 7 September.

Barclays confirmed Bob Diamond, head of its fast-growing investment bank, as its next chief executive.

On 12 September global banking regulators sealed a deal to effectively triple the size of the capital reserves that the world's banks must hold against losses, in one of the most important reforms to emerge from the financial crisis, known as Basel III.

In mid-November, the Government's Independent Commission on Banking (ICB) was reported to have begun meeting top regulators and central bankers from around the world to hear the views of the world's most senior policy-makers for its report on the UK's finance industry. Sir John Vickers, chairman of the ICB, met Paul Volcker, former US Federal Reserve chairman, and its head, Ben Bernanke, as well as held talks with the top European Union officials in charge of regulating the financial sector.

It was reported on 15 November that global takeover activity was likely to pick up in 2011, according to some of Europe's top deal-makers, but it will take until 2014 at least before it returned to the levels of the pre-crisis boom. A survey of 100 senior executives, personally involved in about a tenth of the $2 trillion (£1.25 trillion) worth of deals carried out in 2009, found that just over half of them believed the gradual improvement in the world economy would see a further rebound in mergers and acquisitions (M&A) activity.

On 16 November, a group of economists launched a campaign against the Federal Reserve's decision to increase its quantitative easing programme by $600 billion (£375 billion). They warned that QE2, as it was known, will simply exacerbate America's economic woes.

Argentina won the green light from western governments to negotiate repayment of some $7 billion in defaulted debt without an International Monetary Fund review of its accounts, but ruled out settling its bill in one year.

It was reported on 22 November that capital raisings for growth outstripped efforts by UK companies to repair balance sheets for the first time since the financial crisis began, in a sign that companies could be regaining confidence. According to research by Trowers & Hamlins, the City law firm, more than four-fifths of the money raised through secondary offerings in the third quarter of 2010 were earmarked for growth-related activities rather than bolstering shaky finances as compared with just 17 per cent in the same period a year ago.

China lambasted the US for its decision to launch another $600 billion in monetary easing, fearing that this round of "quantitative easing" may feed the flood of money rushing into mainland China from overseas. Asia's primary convertible bond market was said to be powering ahead. Good news was coming out of the region (apart from the prospect of further fiscal tightening in China), with strong economic growth and relatively stable capital markets.

A monthly index released on 24 November showed global goods trade slowing to a quarterly growth rate of just 0.9 per cent in the third quarter, the smallest expansion rate since the precipitous drop in trade in the second quarter of 2009.

On 27 November, income-seeking investors were increasingly turning to emerging market bond funds offering strong yields and exposure to currency movements but advisers warned that these funds could be much more volatile than traditional fixed-interest investments. Net inflows to emerging market bond funds totalled almost $40 billion in the first nine months of 2010, according to EPFR Global, the data provider.

On a day when Ireland's crippled banks were subjected to downgrades by ratings agencies and its borrowing costs hit record levels of above 9 per cent, the Euro traded at two-month lows of $1.32 and bank shares across Europe tumbled.

Comparisons to the weekend of September 13-14, 2008 have been made frequently in 2009 and 2010, two years since the US investment bank Lehman Brothers was allowed to go bust. They were made again on 29 November before Ireland agreed last night's €85 billion (£72 billion) bailout. But despite hopes that this will be the beginning of the end of Europe's financial crisis, many thought there were more jittery weekends to come.

It was reported that India's economy grew close to 9 per cent in the three months to the end of September, putting pressure on the Reserve Bank of India to continue its aggressive campaign of raising interest rates over the next two months. The economy's acceleration by 8.9 per cent in the third quarter, considerably surpassed analysts' expectations that growth would fall short of the 8.8 per cent year-on-year recorded in April to June.

Spain and Ireland were set to launch large-scale privatisation programs, it was made known. The Spanish government was looking at auctioning stakes in its national lottery operator and airports and Ireland was thinking of privatisations in its electricity and gas sectors as part of a joint European Union and IMF bailout package agreed towards the end of November 2010.

The International Monetary Fund warned on 3 December that the fast-growing Indian economy could overheat, with high inflation and asset bubbles, but also praised the government's economic policies to date. Dominique Strauss-Kahn, IMF managing director, said that some emerging economies, including India, were reaching the limits of "overpotential" as they recovered strongly from the global financial crisis.

Investors will increasingly switch to buying "risktargeting" funds that seek to primarily manage their level of risk, rather than their return, according to industry figures. A survey of 40 fund management groups, with $2,000 billion of assets, conducted by Skandia Investment Group, found that 62 per cent believed demand for risk-targeting funds, often fund of funds vehicles designed to provide a given standard deviation of returns, would rise in 2010.

The amount raised in stock market flotations around the world in 2010 was expected to break the 2007 record of $300 billion (£190 billion), according to research from accountants Ernst & Young. Asian companies were behind a surge in the number of floats. Britain and Europe did better than last year, but accounted for only a tiny proportion of new activity because of fears about the future of the euro and the sovereign debt crisis.

The FTSE 100 rose more than 10 per cent as the end of 2010 approached, helped by the international nature of most of its constituents. Leading shares were poised for another bumper year in 2011 and could even test their record highs, according to City analysts, despite the continuing global financial problems and government austerity measures.

It was reported that banks could be forced to publish details of guaranteed bonuses after a group of global regulators said rewards at financial firms must be more transparent to help prevent another banking crash. City workers should also have their pay and bonuses linked to the longer-term performance, according to a consultative document issued by the Basel committee for banking supervision.

Data released on 29 December by the European Central Bank showed banks in the eurozone increased their lending to companies in November, reversing a drop in the previous month and spurring hopes that the ongoing economic recovery will be buttressed by an extension of credit. Loans to companies in the 16-member eurozone rose by 0.2 per cent, or €11 billion month-on-month.

In 2010, companies raised £10.1 billion through initial public offerings on the London Stock Exchange more than six times 2009's £1.5 billion, but still it was nowhere near the record of almost £30 billion in 2006.

It was a good year for private equity. The debt market for buyouts was frothier than it had been since the global financial crisis wiped out collateralised loan obligations and other toxic fixed income products in 2008. The demand for yield in a low interest environment carved out a whole new market for high-yield bonds issued by companies that were raising an average of three to five times their annual earnings for buyouts.

Conclusion

The dominant explanation of the crisis is that the fundamental cause was "greed and corruption on Wall Street". The crisis did not happen suddenly. It had its roots in key policy decisions stretching back more than three decades.

At the domestic level, the key decisions in the US were to deregulate commissions for stock trading in the 1970s and then to eliminate the Glass-Steagall restrictions on mixing commercial and investment banking in the 1990s. In the days of fixed commissions, investment banks could make a comfortable living, booking stock trades for their customers. Deregulation meant greater competition, entry by low-cost brokers such as Charles Schwab, and thinner margins. The elimination of Glass-Steagall restrictions then allowed commercial banks to encroach on the investment banks' other traditional preserves.

In response, investment banks were forced to branch into new lines of business such as originating and distributing complex derivative securities. They were forced to use more leverage, funding themselves through the money market to sustain their profitability. Thus, arose the first set of causes of the crisis: the originate-and-distribute model of securitization and the extensive use of leverage.

It is pertinent to mention here that these were unintended consequences of basically sensible policy decisions, though it is hard to defend rules allowing price fixing in stock trading. Eliminating Glass-Steagall restraints may well have been a sensible choice as conglomeratization allows financial institutions to diversify their business and develop qualitatively as well as quantitatively. For example, combining with commercial banking allows investment banks to fund their operations. Actually, this model had proved its viability in many European countries.

What created problems was that other policies were not changed as per the demands of the new environment. Conglomeratization takes time before yielding dividends. Those who were hasty in leveraging their business found themselves in trouble. For example, Merrill Lynch, like many other investment banks, was allowed to lever up its bets. It remained outside the purview of the regulators. As a self-standing entity, it was then vulnerable to inevitable swings in housing and securities markets.

The other key element in the crisis was the set of policies giving rise to global imbalances. The Bush administration cut taxes, causing government dissaving. The Federal Reserve cut interest rates in response to the recession. All the while, the financial innovations described above worked to make credit even cheaper and more widely available to households. The result was increased US consumer spending and the decline of measured household savings into negative territory.

Another important factor was the rise of China and the decline of investment in much of Asia following the 1997-98 crisis, with China saving nearly 50 per cent of its Gross National Product. All that money had to go somewhere. Much of it went into US treasury and the obligations of Fannie Mae and Freddie Mac. This propped up the dollar and reduced the cost of borrowings for US households by, on some estimates,

100 basis points, encouraging them to live beyond their means.

These were not outright policy mistakes. The emergence of China is a positive development. Lifting a billion Chinese out of poverty is arguably an important endeavour. The fact that the Fed responded quickly to the collapse of the hi-tech bubble prevented the 2001 recession from becoming worse. But there were unintended consequences. Those adverse consequences were aggravated by the failure of US regulators to tighten capital and lending standards when abundant capital inflows combined with loose Fed policies to ignite a ferocious credit boom. They were aggravated by the failure of China to move more quickly to encourage higher domestic spending commensurate with its higher incomes.

We all had to pay the price of recession. As financial problems surfaced, a bloated financial sector was being forced to retrench. Foreign central banks suffered immense capital losses for their mindless investment. As the People's Bank and other foreign central banks absorbed their loses on US treasury and agency securities, capital flows towards the US diminished. The US current account deficit and Asian surplus shrank. The US households are said to be beginning to save.

Emphasizing greed and corruption as causes of the crisis leads to a bleak prognosis. We cannot make investors less greedy or prevent them from cutting corners when they see doing so as in their interest. But emphasizing policy decisions as the mechanism amplifying these problems into a threat to the entire financial system suggests a more optimistic outlook. Policy mistakes may not always be avoidable. Unintended consequences cannot always be prevented. But they at least can be corrected. Correcting them, however, requires looking more deeply into the root causes of the problem. That is what the entire comity of nations and the set of international financial institutions did and were able to overcome most of the major problems caused by the crisis.

Notes

1. *Realty Trace* Press Release. January 29, 2008.
2. "The downturn in facts and figures", BBC. 2007 http://news.bbc.co.uk
3. "Speculation Statistics", http://mone.cnn.com
4. Christopher Lasch, "The Culture of Consumerism". Consumerism Smithsonian Center for Education.
5. Noalle Know, "43 per cent, of first-time home buyers put no money down." *USA Today*.
6. Felix Salmon, "Recipe for Disaster: The Formula that Killed Wall Street". *Wired*.
7. A. Michael Spence, "Lessons from the Crisis". *PIMCO*. November 26, 2008.
8. Joseph Stiglitz, "Capitalist Fools", *Vanity Fair*, 2009-01.
9. Eric Weiner, "Subprime Bailout: Good Idea or Moral Hazard", NPR. org.
10. Robert England, "Assault on the Mortgage Lenders". *National Review*.
11. "Congress Tries to Fix What It Broke". *Investor's Business Daily*. September 17, 2008.
12. Richard W. Fisher, "Confessions of a Data Dependent: Remarks before the New York Association for Business Economics". http.org
13. Stephen Bernard, "AP-Lehamn Debt Auction Gives, due to Potential Losses", *The Associated Press*, October 10, 2008.
14. *Business Week*, October 2008.
15. "When a Flow Becomes a Flood". *Economist*, January 2009.
16. Gaithner, "Reducing Systemic Risk in a Dynamic Financial System." (Speech).
17. Paul Krugman (2009). *The Return of Depression Economics and the Crisis of 2008*. W.W. Norton Co. Ltd.
18. M. Fratianni and F. Morchionne, (2009). *The Role of Banks in the Subprime Financial Crisis*. SSRN.

2

Spread and Worldwide Impact of Financial Turmoil

Major Impacts of Meltdown

Meltdown that started in America snowballed into a global crisis in September 2008. But the impact on the US was particularly severe, as can be seen from the following facts.

In the one and a half year period of June 2007 to December 2008, Americans lost over 25 per cent of their net worth. In November 2007 itself, the US stock market indexes S&P 500, NASDAQ and Dow Jones went down over 40 per cent from their 2007 highs. Housing prices dropped by more than a quarter, and futures markets signalled a 30-35 per cent drop. Total home equity which was estimated at 13 trillion in 2006, dropped to less than $9 trillion by mid-2008. It was alleged that during the said period, savings and investment assets (except from retirement savings) lost $1.2 trillion while pension assets lost even more at $1.3 trillion. Total losses reached a staggering $8.4 trillion.

It is widely believed that the crisis began to adversely impact the financial sector in February 2007 when Hongkong and Shanghai Banking Corporation (HSBC), the world's then largest bank, wrote down its holdings of subprime-related mortgage-based securities by $10.5 billion, said to be the first major subprime-related loss to be reported. During the year 2007, more than hundred mortgage companies "either shut down, suspended operations or were sold". The CEOs of Merrill Lynch and Citigroup resigned in late 2007. As the crisis became severe, many financial firms either merged or started "seeking merger partners". According to a BBC report, the crisis caused a sort of panic in 2007 in financial markets and forced the investors to take their money out of risky mortgage bonds and shaky equities and put it into commodities as "stores of value". *Sunday Herald* pronounced that financial speculation in commodity futures following the collapse of the financial derivatives markets contributed to the world food price crisis and oil price increases due to what it called a "commodities super-cycle". *New Statesman* also echoed similar views when it stated: "Financial speculators seeking quick returns have removed trillions of dollars from equities and mortgage bonds, some of which have been invested into food and raw materials."[1]

The profits of over 8,500 depository institutions in America insured by the FDIC declined from $35.2 billion in the fourth quarter of 2006 to just $646 million in the corresponding quarter of 2007, which was a decline of 98 per cent. The banks' performance during the 4th quarter of 2007 was the worst since 1990. The trend continued in 2008. Profits declined in the first quarter of 2008 to $19.3 billion from $35.6 billion in the first quarter of 2007, a decline of 46 per cent.

Financial Markets Impacts, 2008

By August 2008, the financial firms around the world were in deep trouble. They had to write down their holdings of subprime-related securities by US$501 billion. The International Monetary Fund (IMF) estimated that the financial institutions worldwide will ultimately have to write off $1.5 trillion of their subprime mortgage-based securities. As of November 2008, about $750 billion in such losses had been recognized. These losses eroded much of the capital of the world banking system. There was thus a massive reduction in the credit available for lending to business and households.[2]

Failure of Lehman Brothers

Lehman Brothers, which built the nation's railroads and survived the Great Depression of 1930s, filed for bankruptcy protection in September 2008. Its failure sank banks and stocks, in America but the fallout reverberated far beyond Wall Street. In Florida, Lehman Brothers was an icon of finance and real estate, managing public assets, selling securities, underwriting bond deals and handling residential and commercial mortgages.

In the past decade, Florida paid Lehman at least $27 million in fees for managing public investments and brokering and underwriting bond deals. The bank hired former governor Jeb Bush as a consultant in June 2007, five months after he left office. As governor, Bush also served as a trustee for the State Board of Administration, which invests public money.

Lehman was the dominant Wall Street broker that sold the state board $1.4 billion of risky, mortgage-related securities that started tanking in August 2007. The risky investments Lehman sold to the state board meant losses to the budgets of almost 1,000 state and local governments.

In its complaint, Florida says Lehman Brothers sold it securities that were not registered with the Securities and Exchange Commission. Such securities are meant only for qualified, sophisticated buyers that understand the risks. But documents show that the state board's managers were made aware of the risks all along. Before they bought the securities, they received confidential memos, e-mails and investor reports from brokers and sponsors that warned of the risks. Florida lost more than $400 million in sales of Lehman stocks and bonds. That squeezed dozens of state organizations—from the Division of Blind Services to the Chiles Tobacco endowment—to a health insurance subsidy for retirees. The biggest casualty was Florida's giant public pension fund. It took a $230 million hit on Lehman stocks and bonds. The pension fund held another $53 million in Lehman bonds that lost most of their value and had $323 million tied up in tarnished mortgage-related securities purchased from Lehman.

Almost one million public employees and retirees—from teachers and firefighters to social workers and police officers—had participated in Florida's plan. They all suffered heavy losses on their investments.

The State Board of Administration, which manages the pension fund, downplayed the long-term effect of the Lehman bankruptcy. Spokesman Dennis MacKee said that benefits paid to retirees won't be affected. Government employers would have to pay more to plug any pension fund but it was considered "very unlikely" the losses would result in higher costs.

The housing market boom had turned Lehman Brothers from a modest firm into the world's fourth largest investment bank. But as the housing market started to shrink, the assumptions that the experts made began to break down one by one. The investment became a mistake, resulting in a stunning loss of $613 billion. On 15 September 2008, Lehman Brothers collapsed. It was the largest bankruptcy in the US history. The participation of the subprime borrowers made lending much riskier than before.

Lehman Brothers, unaware of the hidden risks, decided to invest big on Collateralized Debt Obligations (CDOs). It even had a 35 to 1 debt to equity ratio, that is, it only owned $1 out of every $36 in its bank account—the other $35 were borrowed from somewhere. This meant that a loss of just 3 per cent of the money on its balance sheet, would have meant the loss of all the money it owned. After suffering heavy losses (more than 3 per cent of the money in its balance) from CDOs, borrowers began to lose confidence and called back the loans. As Lehman had always relied on short-term loans, its lenders were able to pull their cash back quickly. Now the bank was in trouble. It borrowed much more than it was able to return and soon found itself unable to pay back.

The failure of Lehman Brothers was in fact a catalyst for a massive sell-off in the credit and stock markets and a general flight to safety from which the markets found it nearly impossible to recover. Standford economist John Taylor stated that the credit markets did not react all that badly to Lehman going under, and that the crisis was really the product of market uncertainty about the effects of government action.

Although Lehman's failure alone was not responsible for investors' flight from the stock market, yet it was the first and crucial moment in the market panic. Paul Krugman went as far as saying that "the collapse of Lehman Brothers almost destroyed the world financial system...."

Sale of Merrill Lynch

Merrill Lynch & Co. spent decades building one of Wall Street's premier investment banks. But the recession took just a few months to undo the efforts as it was struck with huge toxic debt—much of it related to mortgage—which had destroyed Lehman's balance sheet. Due to severe credit crisis Merrill had to write down more than $40 billion during 2008. According to Morgenson, "Merill Lynch's large losses...were attributed in part to the drop in value of its unhedged portfolio of CDOs after American Insurance Group (AIG) ceased offering credit default swaps on Merrill's CDOs. The loss of confidence of trading partners in Merrill Lynch's solvency and its ability to refinance its short-term debt led to its acquisition by the Bank of America."[3]

The United States' financial chieftains arrived at a consensus to protect Merrill from failure after investor confidence in the bank was completely shaken. A safety valve was created by Merrill by forcing it to turn to Bank of America for buy out.

Bank of America, the US' second largest bank by asset size, and Merrill Lynch entered into a deal that valued the latter at US$29 per share. Merrill's shares had lost around 80 per cent of their value to trade at $17. The deal with Bank of America was worth $50 billion. For Bank of America, which had acquired many other companies, the deal meant that it would be able to forage into investment business. The deal created one of the dominant institutions on Wall Street and was perhaps one of the most significant corporate combinations to emerge from the crisis.

The collapse of Lehman Brothers was the key point of the financial crisis. Within a span of just two days, $150 billion were withdrawn from the US money funds against the average two day outflow of $5 billion. The money market which was subject to normal functioning of the banks was in jeopardy. As the credit for banks CDs and non-financial firms, i.e.

commercial paper depended on the money market, there was a severe credit crunch. The TED spread, which is an indicator of credit risk and a measure of the risk of interbank lending, went four-fold shortly after the collapse of Lehman Brothers. And this credit freeze brought the global financial system to the edge of collapse.

As a result of the crisis, several major financial institutions either failed or were bailed out by the respective governments. Some of them merged voluntarily with other institutions while others were forced to do so. The specific circumstances varied in each case, but in general, the value of mortgage-backed securities held by these companies, resulted in their insolvency—as investors pulled funds from them—or they were simply unable to secure new funding in the market as credit dried up. According to Blackburn, "These firms had typically borrowed and invested large sums of money relative to their cash or equity capital, meaning they were highly leveraged and vulnerable to unanticipated credit market disruptions."[4]

America's five largest banks had combined liabilities or debts of $4 trillion. As said earlier, Lehman Brothers went bankrupt, Bear Stearns and Merrill Lynch were taken over by other companies, while Goldman Sachs and Morgan Stanley were bailed out by the US government during 2008. Government Sponsored Enterprises (GSEs) Fannie Mae and Freddie Mac either directly owed or guaranteed nearly $5 trillion in mortgage obligations, with a similarly weak capital base, when they were placed into receivership in September 2008. Other notable global failures included Northern Rook, which was nationalised at a cost of $150 billion.[5] In the US, Washington Mutual was seized by USA Office of Thrift Supervision (OTS) in September 2008. Several US banks received funds as part of the Troubled Asset Relief Programme (TARP) or $700 billion bailout.

Impact on India 2009-10

The global economic slowdown impacted both developed and developing economies. The Gross Domestic Product (GDP) slackened, and the employment opportunities fell sharply.

Instead, there were large lay-offs. According to the Report by Ministry of Labour & Employment, the sectors which were adversely impacted included Real Estate, Textile, Metals, Automobiles, Gems & Jewellery, Transport, IT/BPO and Mining. During the quarter October-December 2008, half a million workers lost their jobs in about 4,000 units visited across these sectors. However, in the next quarter, a quarter million jobs were added in the 4,000 units surveyed from 21 centres spread across 11 States/UTs. This recovery, though modest, was attributed to the stimulus measures of the government. The survey for April-June 2009 showed a decline of employment by 1.31 lakh in these centres. Overall, there is an atmosphere of uncertainty, deceleration in industrial production, decrease in profits for most of the year 2009. It was observed that there was a marginal increase in employment in the exporting units.

The overall quarter-wise picture of changes in employment in eight major sectors for the calendar year 2009 is shown the Table 3.1 below:

Table 3.1: Sector-wise Changes in Employment 2009

(in lakhs)

Sl. No.	Industry/Group	Changes in employment during				
		Dec, 08 over Sep, 08	Mar, 09 over Dec, 08	Jun, 09 over Mar, 09	Sep, 09 over June, 09	Oct, 08 to Dec, 09
1	Mining	–0.11	NC	NC	NC	–0.11
2	Textiles	–1.72	2.08	–1.54	3.18	2.00
3	Leather	NC	–0.33	0.07	–0.08	–0.34
4	Metals	–1.06	–0.29	–0.01	0.65	–0.71
5	Automobiles	–0.83	0.02	0.23	0.24	–0.34
6	Gems & Jewellery	–0.99	0.33	–0.20	0.58	–0.28
7	Transport	–0.96	–0.04	–0.01	0.00	–1.01
8	IT/BPO	0.76	0.92	–0.34	0.26	1.60
9	Handloom / Powerloom	NC	0.07	0.49	0.15	0.71
	Overall	–4.91	2.76	–1.31	4.97	1.51

Source: Ministry of Labour & Employment

Table 3.1 shows that transport and leather industries were adversely affected by the slowdown. Most of other industries were affected by decrease in one quarter or the other. Overall, the picture in India was not as discouraging as in many other countries. Towards the end of the year, textiles showed a remarkable increase in employment, while IT/BPO saw sizeable employment increase in the latter half of the year.

A lot has been said about India and China as the fastest emerging economies in the world. The common characteristics of both these countries, viz. sustained periods of high economic growth, a large pool of skilled workers, a big domestic market, reliable financial system, etc. have provided these countries an environment for developing fast, particularly during the last two decades. It is believed that, by and large, the global economic crisis made three major effects on the advanced economies: (i) the breakdown of financial system, including their lending systems and mortgage; (ii) negative growth of output and consumption; and (iii) larger unemployment. If we have to assess how India has fared during the economic crisis, we must see its performance on the above three fundamental factors. A fair observation in this regard would be as outlined below.

There has been no big impact on India's financial system. In fact, our regulatory framework—with RBI as the apex bank, the nationalised banks, private banks, both Indian as well as foreign banks operating in India—has stood very well in these trying times. In terms of output and consumption, Indian economy slowed down a little, still its performance was quite satisfactory in 2009, and is expected to improve further by the end of financial year 2010-11. On the third front, viz. unemployment, we have already seen that though there has been rise in unemployment, yet a large number of sectors like IT/BPO, Textile and even Housing have come up very well since the start of calendar year 2010. India's GDP growth has been moderate during the meltdown, but an overall major slump was avoided because of a respectable growth in the services sector.

It has been observed that the Indian economy has sustained a higher growth rate than most other economies of the world because it had the advantage of being driven by high levels of aggregate domestic demand, rather than being largely dependent upon exports, which would obviously have fallen sharply as they did, because other countries' demand for various types of goods and services was under severe pressure during the global meltdown. It is pertinent to mention here that India's rural areas which are developing fast with the spread of infrastructure, connectivity and education, has supplemented India's economy with a sharp rise in demand for various types of goods. The impact of slowdown was therefore less on India than many other countries.

Three countries—Brazil, India and China fared well during the economic crisis mainly because of inherent strengths of their economies, a US Congressional oversight panel said recently. The panel in its report for the month of August 2010 said, "Because the financial crisis originated in domestic housing bubbles, and was transmitted by highly leveraged multinational financial firms, countries that were shielded from those forces fared comparatively well.... Brazil, India, China, Australia and Canada, for example, generally avoided the banking crises that plagued US and much of Europe; nonetheless their economies felt many of the aftereffects of the global financial crisis."

While ruling party ministers in the govt. had rooted for the RBI to relax rules in India to allow banks here and other financial institutions to take more risky bets, the RBI stood firm, thereby saving the day for the country. "India's highly regulated banking sector had limited operations outside India, and therefore very little exposure to subprime lending in the US," the report said, adding that India only felt the follow-on effects of the crisis. The country's export-driven economy suffered when global demand dropped; its financial sector suffered from the global liquidity squeeze, which led to a fall in lending; and its stock market lost roughly 50 per cent of its value between June and December 2008.

"Although the Indian government did not provide capital to Indian banks, it did respond to the crisis with fiscal stimulus equal to about two per cent of GDP, and it shifted from a tightening monetary policy to an expansionary one," the report said. Talking of China, the report stated that China maintained capital controls that limit foreign investment by individuals and businesses. These controls had beneficial effects during the crisis, since Chinese investors had little exposure to troubled parts of the US and European financial systems.

India's capacity to withstand the global economic crisis and report one of the quickest turnarounds have been commended, as the country's GDP growth rate picked up from 5.3 per cent and 5.8 per cent in the third and fourth quarters of the financial year 2008-09 to 6.1 per cent in the first quarter of 2009-10.

It is believed that India enjoys an advantage of favourable age distribution of population as compared to many developed as well as other developing countries of the world. It is learning to increasingly use its manpower resources for a fast development of the economy, which has helped the country fight the economic crisis. The dynamics of India's large informal sector is such that it is absorbing the lion's share of the country's growing labour force, leaving little scope for unemployment to grow substantially, contrary to what happened in other countries where the economic crisis was marked by large lay-offs and rising unemployment. The Manpower Employment Outlook Survey conducted in early 2009 showed that at least 25 per cent of the employers surveyed had positive plans of hiring people, which was quite optimistic, considering the tough economic conditions.

The share of service sector and some manufacturing activities in GDP has grown so rapidly during the last decade or so in India, that the global slowdown could not impact it very substantially. Though there was a rise in unemployment, there was no alarm, so to speak.

There were apprehensions that the economic crisis would increase poverty, because the flow of remittances from non-resident Indians (NRIs) gainfully employed in foreign countries will decline. Such remittances represent a major source of foreign exchange as a percentage of GDP in several developing countries, and an important support for many households. But in case of India these remittances do not form a significant part of GDP. Its GDP growth therefore did not contract much. The return of a section of migrants from abroad reduced outflow of workers from India and thus increased unemployment. But the difference was that those coming from abroad brought in investment capital and created self-employment opportunities as well as some employment for others, which is turning to India's advantage. Moreover, post-2009 when things started becoming better as partial recovery started and was predicted to be full in the near future, many migrant workers went back abroad. Unemployment therefore eased out.

Impact on World Economy

According to World Bank estimates, GDP growth in the developing world was to slow to a projected 2.1 per cent in 2009 from 5.8 per cent in 2008. The Bank had more than halved its November 2008 projection of 4.4 per cent growth in developing countries in 2009, reflecting the rapid deterioration of global financial and economic conditions. The new "Global Economic Prospects" update also stated that global growth was expected to contract by 1.7 per cent in 2009. This was to be the first decline in world output since World War II. GDP was projected to decline by 3 per cent in OECD countries and by 2 per cent in other high-income economies.

The World Bank's baseline forecast predicted growth momentum to turn weakly positive in 2010 as financial-sector consolidation, lost wealth and knock-on effects from the financial crisis were likely to continue to dampen economic activity. But the pace and timing of the recovery were still uncertain:

> Across the developing world, we see that conditions of recession are affecting the poorest people, making them even more vulnerable than before to sudden shocks—but also reducing opportunities available to them, and frustrating their hopes.

According to Justin Yifu Lin, World Bank Chief Economist and Senior Vice President, Development Economics, this could reverse years of progress, and was nothing less than an emergency for development.

In the update, the World Bank emphasized that even though growth should rebound, although slowly, economic activity will remain depressed, with unemployment and significant sectoral adjustment persisting for the next two years. "Even if global growth turned positive again in 2010, output levels would remain depressed, fiscal pressures will mount, and unemployment levels would rise further in virtually every country well into 2011," explained Hans Timmer, Manager, Global Trends, in the World Bank's Development Prospects Group.

World trade in goods and services fell 6.1 per cent in 2009, a historic decline. At $47/bbl in 2009, oil prices were more than 50 per cent below their 2008 levels. Non-oil prices also remained low, some 30 per cent lower than in 2008. However, in 2010 the oil prices recovered to be around $80/bbl, while non-oil prices also went up from their 2009 levels. It is pertinent to mention here that the rise of oil prices beyond US$100 per barrel was due to different reasons, including social unrest in some Arab countries.

Fiscal balances also deteriorated sharply in developing countries because of weaker revenues, higher borrowing costs, and larger transfers to maintain social safety nets. This could be particularly worrisome in developing Europe and Central Asia, where trade and production contracted, the private sector was quite vulnerable, and social safety nets have broad coverage.

Signs of Recovery

According to International Monetary Fund (IMF), the risks to global financial system have subsided due to various policy actions taken by respective governments, central banks and help rendered by international institutions. A lot of liquidity was injected into the market by means of stimulus packages. The balance sheets of many banks and financial institutions have been stabilized. The credit market has recovered a lot of lost ground and is functioning well nigh smoothly. The "stability in core markets has helped reduce risks in the emerging market economies, especially in Asia and Latin

America."[6] Besides, "...the augmented resources of the IMF have helped lessen tail risks (those that are unlikely but with potentially devastating consequences in vulnerable countries."[7]

The banking systems have recovered from the point of collapse with the reopening of capital and funding markets to banks; profits have returned to banks. By September 2009, the write downs from bad loans and securities had fallen by US$ 600 billion over the previous six months, i.e. "from $4 trillion to $3.4 trillion, as a lessening in financial stress narrowed spreads."[8] However, there is a consensus of opinion that road to recovery will not be smooth and that financial rehabilitation is unlikely to be straight. The risks have not disappeared yet. In this regard, the words of Jose Vinals, IMF Director are very appropriate:

> If we fail to meet the challenges still being faced by the financial system in the...crisis, we risk reigniting systemic risks and even derailing the economic recovery now in train...that is simply we cannot afford.[9]

Recovery is indeed a good sign, but there is an inherent danger in it, i.e. it may kill the urge of governments, world bodies and other forces which have so far put their best foot forward in combating the recession and retrieved the situation to a large extent. If the world loses that urgency of effort, things could become complicated.

Although the banks' earnings looked up, these were still not big enough to meet the write downs anticipated upto at least March 2011. The banks' balance sheets had more or less stabilized, largely because of the stimulus packages of the respective governments. If there are further pressures on balance sheets, there could be a financing gap, defined by the Global Financial Stability Report of the IMF as the "projected credit capacity...sufficient relative to the demands of sovereign borrowers and the private nonfinancial sector". When the effect and tenure of stimulus packages ends, some banks, etc. may not be able to withstand the pressures after being on their own. If the situation demands more or further stimulus packages, which was still the case in America in mid-2010, the fiscal deficit could increase with its attending consequences. It has been observed by experts that one per cent increase in fiscal deficit leads to 10 to 60 basis points increase in long-term interest rates.

Owing to pressures on the balance sheets of banks, they are left with a capitulated capacity for lending to companies which has affected the latters' recovery from recession. The average growth of banks lending capacity, which went beyond 8 per cent during the period the period 2002-07, came down to around 2 per cent by the end of 2009, and turned negative in 2009 and 2010. It is not expected to reach its precious levels any time soon, though the situation is likely to improve further by the end of calendar year 2011.

Another adverse impact of the global economic slowdown as pointed out by IMF, was that "many private sector financial risks were transferred to the public sector during government rescue operations, leaving the government vulnerable to future shocks."[10] According to IMF, the countries having a high debt/GDP ratio and large contingent liabilities are particularly vulnerable. Such countries were advised to "reduce their exposure to systemic risks by designing and implementing medium term consolidation plans that take into account the unwinding of the actual and contingent interventions in the financial sector".[11]

Although the emerging markets, e.g. China, India, Brazil, etc. stood well against the crisis, yet they have their weak points. Foreign portfolio investment dried up in 2009, though the situation improved in 2010 and 2011. The countries which were heavily dependent on bank credit, especially in the emerging economies of Europe, suffered the most when the flow of such credit decreased considerably. But in Asia, as the recovery of portfolio flows picked up, the property and equity prices started increasing.

The Global Financial Stability Report examined the need to reform financial regulation to ensure that the risks that caused global economic crisis, like the "riskly lending to subprime US home buyers" were not repeated.

Signs of Uncertainty

According to WTO's half-yearly review report on trade and trade-related developments for the period 1 November 2009 to mid-May 2010, the governments worldwide should strive to preserve the level of trade openers and remove the trade restrictive measures. The main observations made in the review report as briefly discussed below.

Accumulating Trade Restrictions

It was observed that some governments were imposing new trade restrictions. However, the overall pattern of trade restrictions was indicating a decline. This declining trend was welcome, and the attention should be focused on the "growing risk of a potential accumulation of trade restricting measures implemented since the break of the global financial crisis. The risk is compounded by a relatively slow pace of removal of previously adopted restrictive measures."[12] The information collected by WTO regarding trade-related measures implemented between the review period revealed that many countries had taken restrictive measures that could adversely impact trade.

However, what was encouraging was that some countries took measures to facilitate trade. Such measures included reducing or temporarily exempting import tariffs, and putting an end to a few trade-restrictive actions initiated in the preceding periods. But the trade-restrictive measures outnumbered those that facilitate trade.

Also observed in the report was an increasing trend in the use of export restrictions, affecting food products and commodities. The measures included increases in exempt duties, introduction of new duties, export prohibitions and export quotas. Some countries, on the other hand, took measures to facilitate export by reducing restrictions, but such measures were far from adequate to bring the export trade to the previous Devels.

The review report stated that even as a successful conclusion of Doha Development Agenda was awaited, it was important for governments to recommit that they will "refrain from raising trade barriers as a means of overcoming the effects of global financial crisis, and to roll-back those trade restricting measures already in place...."

Since the stimulus measures and programs will end in the near future, the governments need to be vigilant. They need to be on guard against protectionism because, poor economic conditions around the world, and the resultant high unemployment, low demand and mounting pressure on finances may force the governments to resort to protectionist actions following strong calls in this regard from various quarters.

In some countries, the stimulus measures including packages are still in force. But the new programs for dealing with the crisis and the situation that developed after its impact on businesses, exports, markets, etc. are being less frequent than immediately after the crisis. This tends to slow down the pace as well as magnitude of recovery. It needs to be understood that this is an extraordinary situation in the global economy which needs exceptional responses in all earnestness.

The review report states that the global recession impacted the car industry, iron and steel industry, and textile industry the hardest. The governments have taken a number of trade-related measures to boost these sectors, but many challenges are still being faced by these industries. These have been called sensitive sectors as they are characterized by high employment and huge capacity. Thus, trade restriction, put in these industries have to be limited.

Impact on Public Finances

The global financial crisis impacted the public finances of most countries. Fiscal revenues declined due to low commodity prices. The governments worldwide provided direct fiscal support to the financial sector, which cushioned the global economy from the adverse effects of the crisis. According to IMF, there has been "a fiscal deterioration that is particularly strong for advanced countries, where the increase in both government debt and contingent liabilities is unprecedented in scale and pervasiveness...."[13]

The fiscal balances of G-20 countries weakened by about 8 percentage points of GDP on average, the government debt rose by around 20 percentage points of GDP in 2008-09. According to David Bevan, the GDP did not experience a general fall in the low income countries as a result of the economic crisis, but the growth reduced (in 2009) to less than half the pre-crisis level of 5 per cent. Besides, there was a decline in exports, remittances and foreign direct investment (FDI).

Fiscal policy encompasses actions which affect the balance between government revenue and expenditure, viz. budget surplus or deficit, and the evolution of government debt. Though some low-income countries have been able to stabilize their economies, yet they have found it difficult to maintain fiscal discipline.

The paper by David Bevan draws attention to the fact that "fiscal policy in developing countries is highly pro-cyclical in contrast with the high-income countries where it is often found to be countercyclical. Making and implementing fiscal policies is usually very difficult. However, as per IMF, "countries with output gaps and sustainable debt and financing options have scope to implement expansionary policies, other countries will simply have to adjust...."[14] The automatic stabilizers, the paper suggests, offer only a modest stimulus, and the discretionary policy will have a small and temporary effect. It has also been suggested that a short-term fiscal stimulus if applied on the expenditure side, proves more rewarding than in the revenue side of the budget. It was also felt that we need "a more countercyclical response than shown in previous downturns".

Some experts restrict fiscal policy to budget surplus or deficit, but is may be stated in this regard that it is not possible to focus on these net effects or consequences thereof without paying attention to the "scale of government activities". It is also not appropriate to discuss fiscal implications of shocks, or fiscal responses to them, without some framework within which to think about fiscal policy in general (Gupta et al., 2004b). Bevan's paper argues that some complicated dynamics is going on, recession or no recession, in each country's fiscal policy and position. Fiscal shock "does not take place against a neutral background." Therefore, it is not possible to gauge precisely what was the impact of global economic slowdown on the fiscal position of the countries. The impact has to be different in different countries. "The key point", argues Bevan, "is that fiscal policy design must be forward looking, but rooted in the country's initial conditions...."[15]

So far as fiscal responses to the crisis are concerned, the governments employed macroeconomic policy instruments like monetary policy and exchange rate policy in an attempt to put their economies back on track. However, what type of policy mix was to be adopted depended on the perceived nature of shock as well as on conventional wisdom about policy efficacy. There was a time (before 1970s) when discretionary fiscal policy was considered a central element in giving a direction to a nation's economy. But in the period that followed, this policy fell into disrepute as it was believed to "impart an inflationary bias to the system;...have perverse effects, exacerbating rather than damping the deviations; to interfere with rational private responses...."[16] The role of fiscal policy has thus considerably reduced, and the nations relied largely on what are unknown in modern parlance as "built in stabilizers—anything that increases government's budget deficit, or reduces its budget surplus during a recession, and increases its budget surplus or reduces its budget deficits during inflation, without requiring explicit action by policymakers."[17]

The governments in the advanced countries like USA, UK, France and Japan engineered substantial discretionary fiscal stimuluses. Countries with output gaps and sustainable debt and financing options have scope to implement expansionary policies.... The main focus of fiscal stimulus should be on the expenditure side (IMF). Other countries simply have to make adjustments. Expanding social safety nets is very important even in normal circumstances and more so during difficult times such as recession.

Such safety nets are non-contributory transfer programs seeking to prevent the most vulnerable sections of society from shocks. These programs are largely provided by the government, but private sector may also make contribution through NGOs, private firms, charitable institutions.

AusAID's Response to the Global Recession

According to AusAID, the global recession slowed development and progress towards achieving the Millennium Development Goals (MDGs). The International Monetary Fund estimates that the global economy contracted by 0.6 per cent in 2009[18] and the implications of this have been severe for many. Economic growth in developing countries was only 1.7 per cent in 2009 compared with 8.1 per cent in 2007.[19] However, if China and India are excluded, the economies of developing countries actually contracted by 1.8 per cent.[20] The World Bank has estimated that an additional 64 million people will be living in extreme poverty on less than US$1.25 a day by the end of 2010 as a result of the global recession.[21]

The capacity of developing countries to respond to the crisis varied considerably. Countries with a heavy reliance on export revenue and foreign investment were most exposed to the impacts of the downturn. Those with stronger economies and more financial resources were able to implement effective policy responses to support the economy. They weathered the global recession relatively well. Others, including many of the Pacific Island countries, had less capacity to respond.

Although uncertainty remains, the global recovery is underway, with major developing economies such as China, India, Indonesia and Vietnam leading the way. The World Bank estimates that developing economies will expand by 6.2 per cent and 6.0 per cent in 2010 and 2011 respectively.[22] The key challenge now for the Australian aid program is to help the developing country partners build long-term economic resilience and regain momentum towards achieving the MDGs.

Shared and sustained economic growth remains the most powerful long-term solution to reducing poverty and is a central theme of Australia's aid program. Economic growth creates jobs and income, and generates government revenues which can be invested back into communities, schools and health facilities. This is important because health and education are themselves critical drivers of sustained economic growth. The Australian Government is committed to helping developing countries ensure that the benefits of economic growth are equitably distributed, environmentally sustainable and contribute to progress towards the MDGs.

Although recovery from the global recession is underway, there continue to be significant challenges to progressing growth in-developed countries. The Australian Government therefore providing a range of growth-enhancing initiatives in such areas as infrastructure investment ($562 million in 2010-11), rural development ($292 million in 2010-11), and recently doubled support for microfinance and financial services to $18-20 million per year (compared to 2007-08). These initiatives were designed to assist the developing country partners to achieve inclusive growth, build economic resilience and accelerate progress towards achieving the MDGs.

Future Outlook of World Trade

The World Trade Organisation (WTO) revised upwards to 13.5 per cent, its world trade growth in 2010 following a faster than expected recovery in global trade flows in 2009-10. According to WTO Director General, Pascal Lamy, the surge in trade flows "provided the means to climb out of...economic recession. It underscored, as well, the wisdom governments have shown in rejecting protectionism".

The merchandise exports of developed economies were expected to increase by 11.5 per cent in volume terms, while those of the rest of the world, including developing countries and the Commonwealth of Independent States, will experience a growth of 16.5 per cent. The real GDP of the world, at market exchange rates of 2005, which turned negative at –2.2 in 2009 recovered well to be 3.0 in 2010. The developed economies had a real GDP of –3.5 in 2009, which was 2.1 in 2010, while the developing countries and CIS had a real GDP of 5.9 in 2010 as compared to 2.0 in 2009. This should be studied in the light of the fact that in 2009, the level of world trade was very depressed.

Driven by sizeable recovery of GDP in both developed and developing countries, the world merchandise trade showed a good growth in the first two quarters of 2010. But it was not likely to grow at that pace in the last two quarters of the year because the "fiscal stimulus measures will expire and the inventory cycle wind down" (WTO).

Growth in Specific Regions

South Asia

The growth of GDP of South Asian region rose from 5.4 per cent in 2009 to 7.6 in 2010. In India, it was expected to grow from 5.7 per cent to 8.3 per cent in the calendar year 2010, and to 8.4 per cent in 2011. The growth of the South Asian region, excluding India was likely to expand by 4.1 per cent in 2010.

The increase in output in South Asia in 2010 bore testimony to "growth of private consumption and investment, improvement in consumer and business sentiment and easing credit conditions".[23] Capital flows to the region are also likely to increase to US$87.2 billion in 2011, as the conditions in the developed countries are likely to improve further. According to World Bank, "Increased foreign currency flows from remittances and international capital sources, together with the region's reduced current account balance suggest that the region should not face any serious financing challenges." Sustained inflows are likely to support growth in countries like India "which are attracting...rising shares of total capital inflows...due to their relatively strong growth performance". But this could have the fall-out of inflationary pressures as was seen in most of the calendar year 2010, and could pose a few challenges for those entrusted with the task of managing monetary policy. This does not mean, however, that there are no risks for the region. The World Bank itself has drawn attention to the possibility that the "debt sustainability issues in high-income Europe cause countries in the region to default or impose a major restructuring of debt.... A major default or restructuring could inflict serious damage on their balance sheets, with...large repercussions on the global financial system",[24] including South Asia.

East Asia and the Pacific Region

Led by 9.5 per cent GDP growth in China, the region's GDP growth expanded by more than 85 per cent in 2010. If we exclude China's growth, GDP in the remaining countries of East Asia increased by 5.8 per cent. In case of China, the growth in demand was responsible for 95 per cent increase in its GDP, and 85 per cent increase in the rest of the developing countries of East Asia and the Pacific. World Bank's "Global Economic Prospects, 2010" predicted that due to strengthening of demand in high income countries of Europe, America and elsewhere, exports from East Asia and the Pacific would get a boost. Further, increase in inflows to the region will make up for the decrease in local demand, expected because of winding up of stimulus measures around 2011-12. Since import prices are likely to increase more rapidly than export prices, the region's current account surplus is expected to be relatively steady around 4 per cent of GDP.

The major risks to the global economy, as per World Bank may be due to debt sustainability issues in the Eurozone. If the problems related to it linger on, the global GDP could become much weaker, and the GDP level may remain between 2 and 5 per cent. The effects of such a situation on entire East Asia, according to World Bank, may be quite serious, mainly because both exports and investment constitute a large share of economies of this region and its growth is directly related to the situation obtaining in high-income European countries. The sovereign debt difficulties in some European countries like Greece, Spain and Portugal in 2010 dampened "the emerging trends of importance for the East Asian region". In fact, the economic outlook of entire Europe remained dim in 2010. The adjustments that the European nations made and are still making, have slowed down the economic actively throughout the world, including East Asia and the Pacific, because of low import demand. The region therefore should introduce macroeconomic policies and limit its dependence on the advanced countries of Europe for growth.

Europe and Central Asia

In 2010, the GDP growth in Europe and Central Asia was expected to be 4.1 per cent and is likely to remain between 4.2 and 4.5 in 2011 and 2012, though there may be sub-regional variations. Thus, the recovery in this region will be slow as compared to other regions of the world. The major reasons for this low momentum were outlined by the World Bank as large foreign currency debt obligations; negative wealth effects because of setbacks to real estate and equity markets; restructuring in countries having current account deficits; and weak recovery in high-income countries of Europe. Yet another reason is that the whole region is moving towards fiscal consolidation which arrests growth momentum.

There are also some positive factors which are likely to narrow down the region's financing gap such as flows of private capital into the region. The inflationary pressure in most of the region is likely to remain subdued except in case of Russia and Turkey, giving much needed support to growth.

Notwithstanding above, the private sector debt is likely to remain a major concern and a drag on growth. The average share of total public and private sector in the region as a whole rose to 60.5 per cent, of which the Central and Eastern Europe's share rose to 82 per cent in 2009 and around 87 per cent in 2010. Some experts have pointed to the bounce back factors which may bring better growth during 2011 and beyond, particularly in Russia. Rising wages and "oil incomes would also reduce the drag from the financial sector".

Only Poland among the countries of European Union recorded a positive growth in 2009, as its economy did not decline as sharply as those of others, and thus its recovery will not be as well marked. However, its unemployment rose to 9 per cent in 2010 which affected consumer demand. The Poland government also scaled back on spending which will negatively impact growth. Turkey, which resorted to tax cuts as part of fiscal stimulus measures saw a firming up of consumer and business demand. Its economy is expected to grow steadily during 2011 and 2012 because of tightening of monetary and fiscal policies.

Many smaller regional economies of Europe and Central Asia will experience a slow recovery in household consumption due to weak employment and general policy of fiscal tightening by the governments. According to World Bank, "...the debt crisis in high income Europe will shape conditions globally, but particularly in Europe and Central Asia.... The most vulnerable countries in the region include Albania and Azerbaijan for which Greece, Italy, Portugal and Spain represent more than 20 per cent of their total exports."[25]

Medium-term Prospects

Growth prospects are very uncertain because of the situation in Europe. Nevertheless, developing countries are projected to lead the recovery with growth rates around six per cent. High-income countries, growth will accelerate from about 2-2.3 per cent in 2010 to between 2.3 and 2.7 per cent in 2012.

Risks and Policy Impacts

Should the crisis in Europe worsen, global growth could be, lower by as much as 0.7 percentage points, and in the case of a crisis, a double-dip recession in high-income countries may not be avoided. Long-term growth and poverty reduction in low-income countries could be affected if bilateral aid flows fall as they have during previous recessions.

Conclusion

The economic slowdown which started in America and Europe spread to the entire world by the end of 2008, with adverse consequences for economic growth. Countries like India, China and Brazil were not as much affected but felt the aftereffects of the global financial crisis. It was hastening to note that there was a great sense of urgency by respective government to put their economies back on hack. A large number of measures, including giving stimulus packages, were taken as a result of which the end of 2009 and early 2010 saw signs of recovery. Most of the corporate sector covered much of the lost ground, but there is no room for relating the efforts as uncertainty remains in many areas of economic activity.

Things are expected to improve future by the end of calendar year 2011.

Notes

1. "The trading frenzy that sent prices soaring," *New Statesman.*
2. Roger C. Altman (2008). "The Great Crash." *Foreign Affairs.*
3. Gretchen Mortgenson. "The Reckoning: How the Thundering Herd Faltered and Fell." *New York Times*, November 8, 2008.
4. Blackburn, "New Left Review—Subprime Crisis."
5. Robert Chote, "Financial Crisis: Someone will have to dig us out of all this debt." *The Daily Telegraph.*
6. Global Financial Stability Report: IMF.
7. *Ibid.*
8. *Ibid.*
9. *Ibid.*
10. *Ibid.*
11. *Ibid.*
12. "Recovery in Global Economy with Signs of Uncertainty." *The Stitch Times*, July 2010.
13. Fiscal Implications of Global Economic and Financial Crisis: IMF Staff Team.
14. *Ibid.*
15. David Bevan. *Fiscal Implications of Global Economic and Financial Crisis for Low-Income Countries*, March 2010.
16. *Ibid.*
17. Stanley L. Rue and Campbell R. McConnell. *Essentials of Economics.* Tata McGraw Hill, 208, p. 316.
18. World Economic Outlook. *International Monetary Fund (2010).*
19. Global Economic Prospects: Fiscal Headwinds and Recovery. *World Bank (2010).*
20. *Ibid.*
21. *Ibid.*
22. *Ibid.*
23. Global Economic Prospects. *World Bank* (2010).
24. *Ibid.*
25. *Ibid.*

3

Impact of Economic Slowdown on India

The economic slowdown started in the USA, primarily due to highly leveraged position of a large number of financial institutions including banks who had lent to many borrowers on what is called subprime mortgage, principally involving housing finance. Soon, the meltdown snowballed into a big financial crisis and engulfed the entire world by the end of calendar year 2008. Nations across America, Europe, Asia, Africa and Australia were directly impacted by it. The situation was marked by bank failures, large lay-off of employees, shares plumetting at the bourses, very low demand for goods and services, credit crunch, repayment defaults, substantial erosion of profits of a large number of companies, and even incurring of losses.

Indian economy is said to be decoupled, to some extent, from what is happening internationally as it draws strength from indigenous resources and local demand. Prior to the crisis, India's economy was acknowledged as one of the stars of global economies, growing at 9.6 per cent in 2006 and 9.2 per cent in 2007. In fact, the first decade of the new millennium was the decade of 7 per cent plus growth. In 2006-07 and 2007-08, the country registered the second highest GDP growth in the world after China. All the major indicators of economic development showed positive signs: The industrial growth was strong; services sector remained robust; exports to various countries increased in volume; though infrastructure was not adequate, yet a large number of projects to build it, particularly in power generation, transportation and communication, gathered momentum; foreign direct investment (FDI) increased in percentage terms; and share market looked up. This high growth was supported by market reforms, rising foreign exchange reserves, and Information Technology (IT) and real estate boom.

The pre-crisis period was marked by surging assets prices in America and some parts of Europe. Such prices proved unsustainable, A few new type of financial instruments emerged, but the regulators failed to keep up with them. There was a prolonged credit expansion, leading to accumulation of huge debts. Experts were well aware of the dangerous developments and had even warned of some impending disaster, but the institutions and governments did nothing to keep the situation under control. The inevitable happened in the second quarter of financial year 2008-09.

The immediate trigger of the global economic crisis was the bursting of the housing bubble in the US, also known as the subprime crisis. It is pertinent to mention here that subprime lending is the practice of extending credit to borrowers with certain credit characteristics. A Fico score of less than 620 disqualifies them from obtaining loans at prime rate. Hence, they get it at subprime rate. Fico, which is an acronym for Fair Isaac Corporation, the creators of Fico score, is a type of credit score that makes up a substantial portion of the credit report that lenders often use to assess an applicant's credit risk, and decide whether to extend a loan or not.[1]

Subprime lending covers various types of credit such as mortgages, loans for automobiles, e.g. cars, and loans through credit cards. Subprime borrowers are considered riskier because they usually have poor credit histories. Thus, they are made to pay higher interest rates, but they get access to credit, which otherwise would have been denied to them. Subprime lending became popular in the US in the mid-1990s, with outstanding debt increasing more than ten times, from $33 billion in 1993, to $332 billion in 2003. In December 2007, it reached as high as $1.3 trillion.[2] It was estimated that about 20 per cent of all mortgages which originated in 2006 were considered to be subprime—a rate unthinkable just a decade ago. Perhaps the banks and other financial institutions became overenthusiastic when they discovered that they could make heavy profits from origination fees, making lots of mortgages held as securities by them to sell them to investors. Little did they know that the bubble so being formed would bust in no distant a future, leading to widespread failures and bankruptcies.

In March 2007, the US subprime mortgage industry collapsed "to higher-than-expected home foreclosure rates, with more than 25 subprime lenders declaring bankruptcy, announcing significant losses or putting themselves up for sale."[3] It was considered to be a local crisis. When Federal Reserve injected capital into the financial markets it appeared as if the crisis will soon be controlled. But in the latter half of calendar year 2008, when a large numbers of financial institutions started reporting bankruptcies one after the other, the seriousness of the situation was realized. When Lehman Brothers which was considered an icon of finance and real estate, engaged in managing public assets, selling securities and underwriting bond deals, etc. filed for bankruptcy protection in September 2008, there were shock waves in the entire world financial markets.

Initially, it was thought that most other economies including India would not be significantly affected, but soon the crisis of the US became a global problem (UNCTAD, 2009), affecting major economies worldwide directly or indirectly. It started being called, and rightly so, the most serious financial crisis since the Great Depression of 1930s, with its global effects characterized by the failure of key businesses, decline in consumer wealth, estimated in trillions of US dollars, rapid decrease in international trade, dwindling of foreign investments, steep fall in industrial production, rising unemployment and large lay-offs, erosion of foreign exchange reserves, skyrocketing of oil prices, share markets experiencing unprecedented falls, and sharp decline in economic activities across America, Europe, Asia, Australia and Africa.

The global financial crisis initially impacted different economies (advanced or developing) differently. According to D.K. Nanto, "Advanced countries were first hit mainly by systemic banking crisis in the US and Europe."[4] But the "emerging markets with well-developed financial systems were mostly affected by cross-border financial linkages through capital flows, stock market investors and exchange rates."[5]

Coming back to India, which had shown remarkable growth after the turn of the previous century, as stated earlier, started feeling the effect of global economic crisis immediately after the course of events took a dramatic turn for the worse in America and Europe, viz. in September-October 2008. As a matter of fact, a tough situation developed in the middle of 2008, when substantial price increases of commodities, especially oil and metals took a toll on India. The crisis which shook the entire world in September 2008 started a difficult phase for India too, which was endeavouring to grow at a fast rate to lift its large masses out of poverty.

Was India Insulated from Global Impacts

Initially, it was argued that India will not be as much affected by the global economic crisis as other countries, and would remain immune to it because of the strong fundamentals of its economy, supported by well-regulated banking and financial system with Reserve Bank of India at the helm, supervising financial affairs, taking important monetary decisions and keeping a tight vigil over the activities of banks and other financial institutions.

India's Banking/Financial System and Global Economic Slowdown

It is widely believed that the global economic slowdown did not impact India as severely as it did many other countries. One of the main reasons was that the country has a sound banking and financial system. Reserve Bank of India (RBI) which is India's central bank is not only the banker to the government, banker's bank, lender of the last resort, but also controller of credit and custodian of foreign reserves.

The scheduled banks can borrow from the RBI on the basis of eligible securities or get financial accommodation in times of need or stringency by rediscounting bills of exchange. The commercial banks can always expect the RBI to come to their help in times of banking crisis.

As controller of credit, RBI has the power to influence the volume of credit created by banks in India. It can do so through changing the bank rate or through open market operations. According to the Banking Regulation Act of 1949, the RBI can ask any particular bank or the whole banking system not to lend to particular groups or persons on the basis of certain types of securities. This has helped in keeping India's financial system well under control. Over the years, Indian banks and financial institutions have developed the habit of taking extra precautions while lending. As such they are not exposed to big risks.

The RBI is armed with many more powers to control the Indian money market. Every bank has to get a license from the RBI to do banking business within India. The license can be cancelled by the apex bank if certain stipulated conditions are not fulfilled. Every bank has to get RBI's permission before it can open a new branch. Each scheduled bank must send a weekly return to the RBI showing, in detail, its assets and liabilities. This power of the apex bank to call for information is also intended to give it effective control of the credit system. It has also the power to inspect the accounts of any commercial bank.

As supreme banking authority in the country, the RBI, therefore, has the following powers:

(a) It holds the cash reserves of all the scheduled banks.

(b) It controls the credit operations of banks through quantitative and qualitative controls.

(c) It controls the banking system through the system of licensing, inspection and calling for information.

(d) It acts as the lender of the last resort by providing rediscount facilities to scheduled banks.

Under RBI, India has thus a well-controlled credit system. Banks and other financial institutions are well aware that they have to do their business and confine their activities under the framework of guidelines provided in the law and as per stipulations made by RBI from time to time.

RBI also performs certain non-monetary functions of the nature of supervision of banks and promotion of sound banking in India, besides traditional functions as the central bank of the country. The Reserve Bank of India Act, 1934, and the Banking Regulation Act, 1949 have given the RBI wide powers of supervision and control over commercial and co-operative banks, relating to licensing and establishments, branch expansion, liquidity of their assets, management and methods of working, amalgamation, reconstruction, and liquidation. The RBI is authorized to carry out periodical inspections of the banks and to call for returns and necessary information from them. The supervisory functions of the RBI have helped a great deal in improving the standard of banking in India to develop on sound lines and to improve the methods of their operation.

RBI also has the responsibility of maintaining the official rate of exchange. According to the Reserve Bank of India Act, 1934, the Bank was required to buy and sell at fixed rates any amount of sterling in lots of not less than ₹ 10,000. Since 1935 the Bank was able to maintain the exchange rate fixed though there were periods of extreme pressure in favour of or against the rupee. After India became a member of the International Monetary Fund in 1946, the Reserve Bank has the responsibility of maintaining fixed exchange rates with all other member countries of the IMF.

Besides maintaining the rate of exchange of the rupee, the RBI has to act as the custodian of India's reserve of international currencies. The vast sterling balances were acquired and managed by the Bank. Further, the RBI has the responsibility of administering the exchange controls of the country.

Promotional Functions

With economic growth assuming a new urgency since Independence, the range of the Reserve Bank's functions has steadily widened. The Bank now performs a variety of developmental and promotional functions, which, at one time, were regarded as outside the normal scope of central banking. The Reserve Bank was asked to promote banking habit, extend banking facilities to rural and semi-urban areas, and establish and promote new specialized financing agencies. Accordingly, the Reserve Bank has helped in the setting up of the IFCI and the SFC. It set up the Deposit Insurance Corporation in 1962, the Unit Trust of India in 1964, the Industrial Development Bank of India also in 1964, the Agricultural Refinance Corporation of India in 1963 and the Industrial Reconstruction Corporation of India in 1972. These institutions were set up directly or indirectly by the RBI to promote saving habit and to mobilize savings, and to provide industrial finance as well as agricultural finance. As a result of this well-regulated banking and financial system, the Indian banks and other financial institutions did not have much risky exposure. It is necessary to mention here that Indian people's saving habits played an important role in strengthening the banks in terms of high deposits. In contrast, the American people's lavish style and poor saving habits came in for severe criticism in the after math of financial crisis.

Although there was a real estate boom in the country, especially since the turn of the century, yet it was due to rapid growth of infrastructure which led to building up of a large number of residential properties and commercial complexes around big cities like New Delhi, Mumbai, Kolkata, Bangalore, Pune, Gurgaon and many others cities, because of increasing connectivity through roads and speedier traffic with the building of flyovers, mass transit system like metro (in New Delhi), rather than because of baseless escalation of real estate prices based on extra demand due to subprime lending. As a matter of fact, subprime lending, as it was resorted to by financial institutions including banks in the US, did not exist in India. The banks in India were quite safe and sound to deal with even such a severe crisis as global recession. There may be some clandestine practices by a few unscrupulous builders and real estate companies, but these were too insignificant to make any adverse impact on the market in general.

The effects of financial turmoil which started in America were felt all over the world including India. The unprecedented collapse of financial giants Lehman Brothers, Merill Lynch, Bear Stearns and AIG shook the entire financial market round the globe. India however was fortunate in having only a ripple effect on its economy. Besides the strong banking and financial system, the other factors responsible for India faring rather resolutely during the time of crisis included the slow pace of financial reforms in India, which did not introduce some fast but riskier financial instruments; a cautious approach towards allowing foreign investment in India's business sectors, which insulated a large number of local industries from stiff competition of international companies; and even bureaucratic hurdles and constraints which proved advantageous for India.

Indian financial system had negligible exposure to foreign assets and their derivative products. Some of the systems prevailing in Europe and America such as futures and options have been adopted but with great caution and subject to many conditions so that the situation remained under control even in adverse circumstances.

The important components of financial sector in India can be broadly divided into (i) commercial banks, including public sector and private banks, and Indian and foreign banks operating in India; (ii) co-operative banks, operating largely in towns and small cities under respective states; (iii) non-banking financial companies (NBFCs); (iv) the insurance companies, including Life Insurance Corporation (LIC) of India, General Insurance Corporation (GIC), and (v) market-related companies like mutual funds, etc.

Banking Trends Internationally and in India

The Reserve Bank of India has pointed out two important points of contrast between banking trends prevailing internationally, and in India, which contributed towards a rather muted effect of crisis on Indian banking: (i) Whereas subprime mortage lending was in full swing and formed a sizeable part of total lending in the real estate sector, Indian banks had little exposure to such risky lending. A few Indian banks with overseas branches though had invested in collateralized debt obligations (CDOs) or bonds which had a few underlying entities with subprime exposures, due to which they suffered on account of market-to-market losses caused by widening of credit spreads. However, the additional provisions made to cover these market-to-market losses were not significant enough to impact the overall picture of their balance sheets or the size of their profits.[6] (ii) In India, the prudential limits on banks' exposure to capital markets are in place. With the rationalized norms on capital market, applicable from April 2007, there is a regulatory limit on individual banks' total exposure to capital market, which is now capped at 40 per cent of banks' net worth as at the end of March of the previous year. There are no such caps in banks in America and Europe. Further, the banks' direct investment in shares, convertible bonds/debentures, units of equity-oriented mutual funds and all exposures to venture capital funds must not exceed 20 per cent of its net worth.[7] In contrast, the participation of banks in Europe and America, in these channels is not as regulated as in India.

There had been a high credit growth as the credit deployment by the banks grew rapidly at the average rate of nearly 30 per cent during the three years preceding the global financial crisis. RBI had initiated a remarkable combination of monetary and counter-cyclical measures to moderate credit growth and rule out the possibility of building up the asset bubbles in any segment. The Indian banking system has therefore remained relatively in good health. The balance sheets of banks have shown a healthy picture, and not much affected by the turbulence in the financial markets.

Impact on India—An Assessment

Notwithstanding the factors stated above, India was not without effect by the recession. The financial position of commercial banks towards the end of 2008 and first half of

2009 showed that the global financial meltdown led to a crisis of confidence in the global markets which echoed in the Indian financial system. Contrary to the trends observed during 2007-08 and even the earlier period, there was a reversal in capital flows to India during 2008-09, which led to some disturbance in the Indian financial markets, share market as well as foreign exchange market. Table 3.1 below shows the monthly trends in foreign investment in India from April 2008 to March 2009.

Table 3.1: Monthly Trends in Foreign Investments in 2008-09

(US$ Million)

Months	Foreign Direct Investment	Foreign Portfolio Investment	Total Investment
April	3749	–880	2869
May	3932	–288	3644
June	2392	–3010	–618
July	2247	–492	1755
August	2328	593	2921
September	2562	–1403	1159
October	1497	–5423	–3746
November	1083	–574	509
December	1362	30	1392
January	2733	–614	2119
February	1466	–1085	381
March	1956	–889	1067
March-April	35146	–13855	21291

Source: Reserve Bank of India

Table 4.1 shows that foreign investment in India during 2008-09 was volatile. Foreign Direct Investment (FDI) started declining from June 2008, and there was a steady decline almost each month upto March 2009. From the highest level of US$3932 million in May 2008, it reached its less than one-third at US$1083 million in November 2008. It picked up in January 2009 to US$2733 because of allotment of funds, only to tumble to US$1466 million and US$1956 million in February and March 2009 respectively. Foreign portfolio investment decreased for every month during the period except August and December 2008.

The financial crisis also created a shortage of money supply, whereby India too faced a credit crunch, particularly in terms of foreign exchange. Foreign Institutional Investors (FIIs) offloaded sizeable lots of shares held by them as a result of which foreign currencies, particularly US dollar and British pound firmed up, and Indian rupee weakened to ₹ 40 per US dollar from 47 per dollar. FIIs outflow also had a negative effect on domestic investment. With the fall in the share market due to heavy selling by foreign investors, the sentiment turned so weak that a large number of individual investors also withdrew from the market because of panic and uncertainty. When small investors who had invested through mutual funds also started calling back their investment, the mutual funds also had to sell shares to pay back to the investors, which brought the share pieces down further. Bombay Stock Exchange (BSE) index fell from the peak of around 21,000 in January 2008 to close to 10,000 in December 2008. Many of the stocks, including heavyweights like Reliance Industries Ltd (RIL), Larsen & Tuebro (L&T), Infosys, etc. lost 50 to 70 per cent of their value.

Impact on Growth Rate and Industrial Output

Global financial crisis and the resultant credit crunch slowed down India's economic growth. Actually, the Gross Domestic Product (GDP) started decelerating nearly six months before the US financial crisis started to spread worldwide. India's GDP growth, as compared to 9.2 per cent registered during 2007-08, came down to 6.7 per cent in 2008-09 and marginally recovered to 7.4 per cent in 2009-10. The growth of agriculture and allied sector fell from 4.7 per cent in 2007-08 to meager 1.6 per cent and 0.2 per cent in 2008-09 and 2009-10 respectively. The growth of industry came down from 9.5 per cent in 2007-08 to 3.9 per cent in 2008-09 before recovering to 8.5 per cent in 2009-10. Similarly, growth of services sector decreased from 10.5 per cent in 2007-08 to 9.8 per cent and 9.3 per cent in 2008-09 and 2009-10. It is pertinent to mention here that the sectional share as per cent of GDP is: agriculture & allied = 18.1; industry = 2.7; and services = 53.9.

Other Impacts

Although Indian economy was said to be insulated from external effects and pressures, yet the magnitude of global economic crisis was so big that the country's macroeconomic indicators showed a decelerating trend. Fiscal deficit as percentage of GDP, which was 2.7 in 2007-08, shot up to 6.0 and 6.7 in 2008-09 and 2009-10. As already stated, rupee turned weak against US dollar from ₹ 40.2 per dollar in 2007-08 to 45.9 and 47.4 on average in 2008-09 and 2009-10 respectively. Exports which grew at 29 per cent from the previous year in 2007-08, grew only 13.6 per cent in 2008-09, and experienced a negative growth, i.e. –3.6 in 2009-10. Imports too declined, though trade deficit increased, which was not a good sign for Indian economy. Initially, the software exports were not impacted and they grew at 46.3 per cent in 2008-09 against the growth of 40.3 per during the previous year, i.e. 2007-08. They continued to show good growth in 2009-10, i.e. 49.7 per cent over the previous year.

The impact of global recession on India's services exports was quite visible as growth thereof declined to –21.4 per cent in the first half of 2009-10 as compared to high growth of 27.6 per cent in the corresponding period of the previous year, i.e. 2008-09. All items except insurance witnessed a negative growth. A fall in transportation business was indicative of the fall in merchandise trade, while a fall in travel services was a reflection of the decline in tourist arrivals, which declined by 1.8 per cent in the first quarter of 2009-10. As compared to growth of 4 per cent in tourist arrivals, there was a negative growth of –3.3 per cent in 2009. Foreign Exchange Earnings (FEE) at US$11.39 billion in 2009 also experienced a negative growth of –3 per cent in 2009 as compared to a growth of 9.5 per cent in calendar year 2008.[8]

Over the years India's foreign exchange reserves have shown a steady increase, i.e. from US$151.6 billion in 2005-06, to US$199.2 billion in 2006-07 and US$309.7 billion in 2007-08. But after the onset of recession they decreased to US$252 billion in 2008-09. However, forex reserves increased to US$277 billion of in 2009-10. As on 13 August 2010 they were US$282.08 billion and as on 5 November 2010, US$300.21 billion. The overall picture of India's macro-economic indicators from 2005-06 to 2009-10 is given in Table 3.2.

Impact of the Financial Crisis on Developing Economies

The degree and nature of impact of the financial crisis differed in the developing countries depending on the degree of financial markets integration in the global market (greater impact on countries such as Brazil, China, India); the strength of sectors like tourism and mining and the informal sector; extent of dependence on remittances; level of dependency on food and fuel imports; pressure on government budget expenditure due to falling revenue as a result of the economic slowdown; and vulnerabilities of particular social groups and/or populations (PR-Net, Consolidating Online Discussion on *Impact of Financial Crisis on Developing Countries*, 14 January 2009). While the combination of mounting losses, falling asset prices, and a deepening economic downturn adversely affected the viability of the financial system, the financial crisis affects developing countries through (a) financial contagion and spillovers for stock markets, and (b) transmission of the economic downturn in developed countries through trade and trade prices, remittances and foreign direct investment (FDI) and equity investment. India's plan to fund $495 billion infrastructure development spread over five years till 2012 faced financing gaps. According to the World Bank estimate, $500 billion are required over a period of 2001-10. The annual financing gap during 2001-10 is estimated at close to $14 billion. For the entire period, it worked out to be about $140 billion.

Impact of the US Financial Crisis on Asian Emerging Market Economies (EMEs)—"Exploding the Myth of Uncoupling"

With robust GDP annual growth of 7.5 per cent over the past decade, two and a half times faster than the rest of the world, Asian EMEs have been the engine of recent world growth. EMEs were considered to be 'decoupled' from the travails of advanced economies because of their substantial

Table 3.2: India's Macroeconomic Indicators 2005-06 to 2009-10

INDICATORS	2005-06	2006-07	2007-08	2008-09	2009-10
GDP (at current prices, US$ bn)	**837.2**	**947.0**	**1231.0**	**1222.0**	**1317.0**
GDP Growth (at constant prices, %)	**9.5**	**9.7**	**9.2**	**6.7**	**7.4**
Agriculture & allied	5.2	3.7	4.7	1.6	0.2
Industry	9.3	12.7	9.5	3.9	8.5
Services	11.1	10.2	10.5	9.8	9.3
Sectoral Share in GDP (%)					
Agriculture & allied	18.1	17.2	16.4	15.7	14.6
Industry	27.9	28.7	28.8	28.0	28.5
Services	53.9	54.2	54.8	56.3	56.9
Inflation rate (WPI, annual avg. %)	4.4	5.4	4.7	8.3	9.9(Mar '10)
Gross Fiscal Deficit (% of GDP)	**4.1**	**3.5**	**2.7**	**6.0**	**6.7**
Exchange Rate (Rs/US$, avg.)	44.3	45.3	40.2	45.9	47.4
Exchange Rate (Rs/Euro, avg.)	53.9	58.1	57.0	65.1	67.1
Exports (US$ bn)	**103.1**	**126.4**	**163.1**	**185.3**	**178.7**
% change	23.4	22.6	29.0	13.6	–3.6
Imports (US$ bn)	**149.2**	**185.7**	**251.7**	**303.7**	**286.8**
% change	33.8	24.5	35.5	20.7	–5.6
Trade Balance (US$ bn)	**–46.1**	**–59.3**	**–88.5**	**–118.4**	**–108.2**
Services Exports (US$ bn)	**57.7**	**73.8**	**90.3**	**101.7**	**93.8**
Software Exports (US$ bn)	23.6	31.3	40.3	46.3	49.7
Services Imports (US$ bn)	**34.5**	**44.3**	**51.5**	**52.0**	**59.6**
Services Balance (US$ bn)	23.2	29.5	38.9	49.6	34.2
Current Account Balance (US$ bn)	**–9.9**	**–9.6**	**–15.7**	**–28.7**	**–38.4**
CAB as percentage of GDP (%)	–1.2	–1.1	–1.3	–2.4	–2.9
Forex Reserves (US$ bn)	**151.6**	**199.2**	**309.7**	**252.0**	**277.0**
External Debt (US$ bn)	139.1	172.4	224.4	224.5	261.5
External Debt to GDP Ratio (%)	17.3	18.2	18.1	20.5	18.9
Short-term Debt/Total Debt (%)	14.1	16.3	20.4	19.3	20.1
Total Debt Service Ratio (%)	10.1	4.7	4.8	4.6	5.5
Foreign Investment Inflows (US$ bn)	**21.5**	**29.8**	**62.1**	**21.3**	**69.6**
FDI (US$ bn)	**9.0**	**22.8**	**34.8**	**35.2**	**37.2**
GDRs/ADRs (US$ bn)	2.6	3.8	6.6	1.2	3.3
FIIs (net) (US$ bn)	9.9	3.2	20.3	–15.0	29.0
FDI Outflows (US$ bn) (Actual)	**6.1**	**13.1**	**18.7**	**16.2**	**10.3**
Memo Items:	**2006**	**2007**	**2008**	**2009**	**2010**
Global GDP (% change)	5.1	5.2	3.0	–0.6	4.6
World Merch. Trade (Vol., % change)	8.8	6.5	2.4	–11.8	8.0

Source: Economic Survey, Various issues; Union Budget, RBI Monthly Bulletin, Annual Report & Weekly Statistical Supplement; Ministry of Finance; Ministry of Commerce & Industry; CSO; Institute of International Finance (IIF); EIU; NASSCOM; WEO, IMF.

Notes: (a) Debt-service ratio is the proportion of gross debt service payments to External Current Receipts (net of official transfers).

(b) Short-term debt coverage increased beginning with the quarter ended March 2005, with the inclusion of (i) suppliers' credits up to 180 days and (ii) investment by Foreign Institutional Investors (FII) in short-term debt instruments.

foreign exchange reserves, improved policy framework, robust corporate balance sheets, relatively healthy banking sector and no large direct exposure to securitized assets linked to high-risk lending.

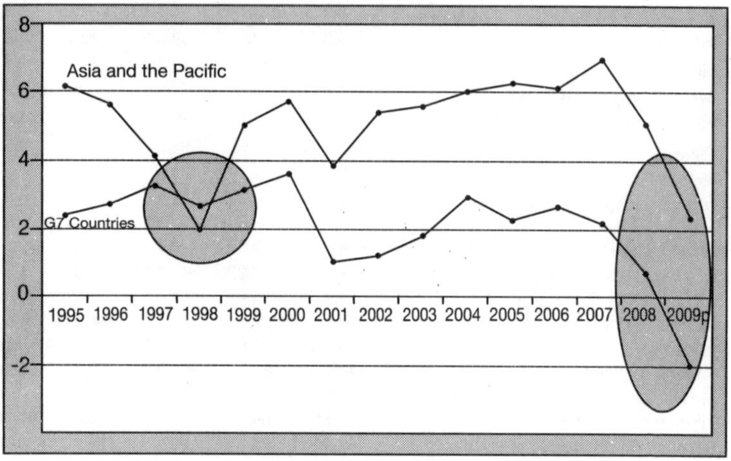

Fig. 3.1: Annual GDP Growth Per Cent—Asia Versus G7 Countries

Source: ILO Calculations, Responding to Economic Crisis 18-20 February 2009

But events and developments such as capital flow reversals, sharp widening of spreads on sovereign and corporate debt and abrupt currency depreciations starkly brought to the fore the inherent fallacies of the 'decoupling theory' (Subbarao, 2009) and the transmission mechanism to Asian economies hurt the growth process through massive reversal of private capital flows, which has been more severe in emerging markets than lower income countries; declining trade volume, i.e. decreasing demand in industrialized economies for Asian exports and lowered industrial output; remittances at risk, depending on remittance share of GDP: Nepal (17 per cent), Philippines (11.7 per cent), Bangladesh (9.7 per cent), Sri Lanka (8.3 per cent); and pressure on domestic investment (UNDP Working Paper, "The Financial Crisis and Its Impact on Developing Countries", 18 January 2009).

While for various historical and other reasons, the process and the pattern of economic development, various countries were differently affected, no country was impervious to the toxic winds of change sweeping the world. The Asian Development Bank (ADB) reduced the growth projections of many Asian economies, including India's, in its half yearly report: *Asian Development Outlook 2008* because of the worsening conditions in major industrial economies that will weaken demand for goods and services.

Most macro and financial indicators deteriorated in the wake of the financial crisis and the vulnerability of emerging Asia increased substantially. In this overarching setting of rising emerging market risk, institutional investors reduced positions, particularly in equities. More than $100 billion in foreign capital flowed out of the Asia's top stock markets, stock markets fell drastically with market capitalization plummeting by 40 to 60 per cent and significant depreciation of most currencies.

The global financial crisis has remarkable parallels with the Asian crisis in that abundant liquidity and excessive, imprudent credit expansion together with the rapid increases in property asset prices (Khor Hoe Ee and Kee Rui Xiong, 2008) preceded investor panic. Widespread investor alarm led to uncertainty in security and valuation of assets, a liquidity run and rising insolvency in the banking system. While most debt in the earlier Asian crisis was sovereign, in the globally synchronized global downturn, most debt was corporate, taken out by Indian, Chinese and other EMEs. Economic growth in all Asian economies, including China and India, was weakened by this globally inter-connected crisis through the spillovers of a rise in the price of risk, a reduction in international bond issuance, a sell-off in equity markets, and some unwinding of carry-trade positions (Mohan, 2009).

ADB reduced growth projections of many Asian economies, including India's because of larger convergence in business cycle in terms of growth of real GDP, inflation and interest rates. Vulnerabilities in Asia increased considerably in terms of several development indicators such as commodity price sensitivity, current account balance, gross reserves to short-term external debt, net external position vis-a-vis BIS reporting banks, growth in credit to the private sector, equities, inflation and real policy rate. There was a decline of 20 to 40 per cent in imports and exports of Japan, Singapore, China and Vietnam. Consequently, China, India, Korea, all repeatedly slashed policy rates and eased their monetary stance. But the space for monetary maneuverability was extremely limited in countries like Pakistan, Philippines and Vietnam, which were characterized by macroeconomic difficulties and double-digit inflationary price spiral.

With the intensification of the global financial imbroglio, the pressure on Asia's economic and financial systems was exacerbated. While Asia was well-placed in terms of large foreign exchange reserves, improved fiscal positions, credit policy reforms, better structuring of banking sector debt and relatively small direct exposure to US subprime mortgages and structured credit products and prudent policies in most Asian economies since the 1997/98 crisis, average GDP growth moderated from 9 per cent in 2007 to 7.5 per cent in 2008 with the impact being clearly perceptible in China and India.

The contagion in the global financial markets was transmitted to Asia and spillage of subprime domino affected stability of capital flows, housing and equity markets, banking industry, capital market development, stock markets, inflation, aid and poverty alleviation, construction-led growth and microfinance. Overriding structural changes underway necessitated a coherent and powerful policy response at national, regional and global levels to stimulate domestic demand by shifting from increasingly capital-intensive manufacturing towards labour-intensive services and thus spurring economic recovery.

India—Bucking the Trend

Global financial crisis affected credit and confidence of the banking and financial markets. In case of the capital market, capital became more expensive as banks lent to one another at higher rates. The stock market witnessed a fall in value of stocks and real estate as a result of credit, assets and investment bubbles. The reversal of portfolio flows in India was large and immediately impacted the services sector, particularly the IT sector. Companies in the IT and financial sectors downsized, slashed costs and did not expand employment.

The three key aspects of the impact on India's social and development sectors were the debilitating impact on employment and poverty; reduced funding for development or development expenditure; and the achievement of the Millennium Development Goals (MDGs) rendered more difficult. Although the main transmission channels primarily affected urban labour markets, the consequential impact on rural economy, employment and household income was not insignificant.

Job losses in export manufacturing often affect the rural-to-urban migrants and their income support to their rural families. Workers unable to find new urban employment, whether in formal or informal sector, seek rural work opportunities leading to a process of distress reverse migration, which often coincides with reduced wages and household income.

During the years 2009 and 2010, an estimated 20.3 million additional jobs were needed to absorb India's growing labour force but the growth in the number of new jobs created was grossly inadequate to keep up with expected labour force growth (ILO, "The fallout in Asia: Assessing labour market impacts and national policy responses to the global financial crisis", 18-20 February 2009).

The most vulnerable social groups during this crisis, as indeed any crisis, were marginalized and vulnerable populations comprising migrants and migrant workers, workers in the informal sector, youth and women and children are among the most vulnerable social groups. There were also increasing concerns of school dropouts and rise in child labour. Indian workers in globally influenced sectors, e.g. civil aviation, textiles, leather, gems, and jewellery, which employ a significant proportion of women workers, faced job cuts.

There was a major concern that the global financial meltdown led to a decline in financing for development through public channels, e.g. reduction in ODA and domestic resources, fundraising possibilities of private channels like NGOs and development organizations were adversely affected. Government budgets were also under constraints on the revenue side as the economies decelerated.

Despite the turmoil in global financial markets, the Indian growth story remained largely intact and the macroeconomic fundamentals of the economy continued to remain strong. The Indian macroeconomic scene was characterised by conspicuous absence of subprime lending, toxic derivatives, bank losses eroding capital, bank credit crunch and mistrust between banks. This was largely attributable to India's democratic polity, sequential process of economic reforms, adoption of prudential regulations and the RBI's carefully calibrated policies. Unlike the devastation wrought elsewhere, the financial sector continued to be robust, monetary policy had sufficient and flexible instruments, the corporate sector not excessively leveraged with some productivity gains, foreign direct investment not deleteriously impacted and largely domestic financing of growth. Against this backdrop, the Prime Minister Dr. Manmohan Singh justifiably assured parliamentarians and the nation that "there is no place for fear. This is the time for unity of purpose and resolute action". Certainly the Indian economy became more resilient, domestic demand continued to be its key growth driver with merchandise exports contributing less than 15 per cent of GDP and the Indian financial market has been more circumspect than the western regulators. While the conventional measure of integration, i.e. the trade to GDP ratio, rose from 21.2 per cent in 1997-98 to 34.7 per cent in 2007-08, the ratio of total external transactions, i.e. trade and capital flows, to GDP rose much more strikingly from 46.8 per cent to 114.7 per cent.

The crisis had both economic and socio-developmental implications for India. The economic impact in India was seen on the growth and employment situation, particularly in services sector, including banking, finance and IT sectors; and the real sector such as manufacturing and exports. The employment and poverty reduction effort, particularly development expenditure, was constrained because of the

Government's difficult fiscal position and the achievement of the Millennium Development Goals (MDGs) was rendered difficult. As economic growth contracted, demand for labour fell, large-scale job losses rose in some sectors, unemployment and underemployment rose, wages took a hit, SMEs were adversely affected and reverse migration increased (ILO, "The fallout in Asia: Assessing labour market impacts and national policy responses to the global financial crisis", 18-20 February 2009).

The trillion-dollar Indian economy experienced the knock-on effects of the global crisis, through the monetary, financial and real channels. Important issues, which emerged related to domestic liquidity shortage, exchange rate volatility and reduction in access to foreign currency funds, inadequate credit availability and slowdown in demand and decline in business and investor confidence and optimism. Despite these disquieting features, the Indian economy in the financial year 2008-09 recorded a 6.7 per cent growth in GDP as against 8.8 per cent reached during the high growth phase of 2003-04 to 2007-08.

Multiple distress indicators needed to be seen in the context of a depreciating rupee, falling total net capital flows from US$17.3 billion in April-June 2007 to US$13.2 billion in April-June 2008, pressure on balance of payments (BoP), faltering growth momentum, domestic credit stringency together with drying up of external liquidity, slowdown of exports of both goods and services and a merchandise trade deficit of 7.7 per cent and a current account deficit of 1.5 per cent of GDP in financial year 2007-08. The Indian stock markets were badgered and there was a severe impact on mutual funds/non-banking financial companies (MFs/NBFCs) because of reduction in flow from non-banks and a heightened perceptions of credit crunch. This is why in the overarching context of the crisis in the financial and credit markets, global and domestic economic policy are influenced by exigencies and not just by macroeconomic growth.

Faltering of India's spectacular growth story, slowing of consumption, crippling of infrastructure by a funds crunch and constricting of outsourcing by rising protectionism hampered Indian exports and the slowing down of the Indian economy affected diverse sectors, particularly, textile, real estate, infrastructure, civil aviation, automobile, housing and information technology. Shrinking cash inflows and rising debts led to rising demands from industry for progressive reductions in benchmark rates and the pressure on banks to provide cost-effective prompt services to its existing and potential customers has increased. What was prognostically disconcerting is that foreign branches of Indian banks had a balance sheet size of almost $50 billion. With these entities facing a severe liquidity crunch, domestic liquidity was required to support the external liquidity needs. Apart from this squeeze on domestic liquidity, India had short-term debt of $89 billion (by residual maturity).

Risk aversion and heightened uncertainty in the international financial markets to EMEs led to a decline in external commercial borrowings (ECBs) of the corporate sector from US$7.0 billion in April-June 2007 to US$1.6 billion in April-June 2008, thereby impeding investment growth. India is not exposed to the new and innovative financial instruments that brought about this financial tsunami and there are large foreign exchange reserves making it possible to tide over any short-term disruption in capital inflows.

It has, however, to be realized that even before the recent crisis, the combined fiscal deficit in India was high by international standards. Since such deficits contribute to the persistence of an interest rate differential with the rest of the world and hamper progress towards full capital account convertibility, a self-imposed, rule-based fiscal correction needs to be consolidated and carried forward. The sustained interest rate differential is also connected with the existence of a persistent inflation differential with the rest of the world. Hence, it is important to further reduce inflation expectations towards international levels. Clearly, while there are reasons for concern because of the sheer magnitude of the crisis and the overarching environment, there is no cause for alarm.

The global financial crisis hampered progress in poverty reduction and MDG achievement. There were also the medium-term challenges of continuously adapting monetary management to the emerging needs of a fast growing and increasingly open economy, promoting financial deepening and increasing monetization with expansion of monetary aggregates departs from their traditional relationship with real GDP growth. In this kind of a setting, the task of monetary management was to manage such growth without endangering price or financial stability and foster further development of financial markets.

There has been large capital inflows in recent years, which have brought to the fore the issue of managing the "impossible trinity" and the role of the RBI in maintaining this delicate balance. Professor Robert Mundell's theory of the "impossible trinity" demonstrates that a country cannot have highly mobile capital flows, a fixed exchange rate and its own domestic monetary policy simultaneously. The operating procedure of the central bank comprises the sequential steps of identifying the tools for liquidity management; selection of operational target and money market corridor influence; stipulation of economic and monetary indicators for strategic policy adjustment; and fixing of final target prescription and quantitative definition.

An efficient and effective monetary policy through various transmission channels such as financial market prices (interest rates, exchange rates, yield, asset prices, etc.) and financial market aggregates (money supply, credit volumes, volume of government bonds, etc.) impacts its final targets in the form of output, employment and inflation. There was a paradigm shift in the role of monetary policy from a predominantly financial market mechanism to an all encompassing role, with a much extended policy domain, including an accent on various segments of the real sector, the external sector and the impact of global market movements.

Interest rate, credit aggregates, asset prices and exchange rate are four traditional channels of monetary policy transmission. Interest rate channel provided the dominant transmission mechanism, influencing an expansionary or tight policy stance, aggregate demand through availability of loanable funds (credit channel) and movement in asset prices to generate wealth effects.

An effective response to the large and volatile capital flows depends on sound macroeconomic policies, prudent debt management, exchange rate flexibility, effective management of the capital account, accumulation of appropriate levels of reserves as self-insurance and development of resilient domestic financial markets. Clearly, then, there cannot be any one-size-fits-all approach to the issue of large and volatile capital flows, and individual approaches have to factor in country-specific considerations and requirements. The Indian approach to capital accounts liberalization was based on the distinction between debt and equity flows, higher inflation and interest rates in India vis-a-vis advanced economies, impact of the liberalisation of debt flows on arbitrage flows and an appropriate ceiling on debt flows.

The global financial architecture was rocked by a series of banking distress and even failure of iconic banking and financial institutions. But it is remarkable that even in the present world of global interconnectedness and inter-linkages, banks in India did not face any crisis of the kind witnessed in the US and other developed countries. The strength and soundness of the banks in India stems from India's democratic polity, sound financial performance, prudential regulations put in place by the regulator calibrated approach to the process of financial reforms, both by the RBI and the Government of India and very limited exposure to exotic products. India's approach to managing financial stability was governed by full, but gradual opening up of the current account, a calibrated approach towards opening up of the capital account and financial sector with thrust on greater equity flows; debt flows subject to ceilings and some end-use restrictions; and progressive liberalization of capital outflows. The financial sector, particularly banks, has been subject to prudential regulation of both liquidity and capital; prudential limits set on banks' inter-bank liabilities in relation to their net worth; and asset-liability management guidelines to factor in both on and off balance sheet items. They have to move towards the Basle II framework, dynamic provisioning, and tightened regulation and supervision for NBFCs to reduce regulatory arbitrage.

The current Indian banking landscape is sound, well capitalized and well regulated. Indian banks did not have any direct exposure to subprime mortgages, the failed institutions and had extremely limited off-balance sheet activities or securitized assets. The exposure of ICICI Bank Ltd. to Lehman Brothers was \$83 million (less than 0.1 per cent of its consolidated balance sheet) and State Bank of India, Bank of India, Bank of Baroda, Punjab National Bank, Axis Bank Ltd., etc. also had small exposures. With an overall capital adequacy ratio of 13 per cent for commercial banks, the Indian banking system was not severely dented and there was no systemic concern. An RBI study (September 2007) brought out absence of any direct impact on account of direct exposure to the subprime markets. However, some banks suffered some losses on account of the market-to-market (MTM) losses caused by widening of the credit spreads emanating from the subprime crisis on term liquidity in the market. The challenges, however, highlighted the need to avoid mismatches in asset pricing, develop proper risk management and capital management, build quality assets, focus strongly on customers, manage costs effectively and administer credit efficiently. The Committee on Financial Sector Assessment (CFSA) Report highlighted the need for introspection in the Indian financial industry and also underscored the relative strengths of the Indian financial system. The thesis of a strong and resilient Indian banking sector was also substantiated by stability assessment and stress testing and muted concerns of credit risk.

Capital Adequacy under Basel I and Basel II: Indian Experience

Traditionally, banks held capital as a buffer against insolvency, and liquid assets—cash and securities—to guard against unexpected withdrawals by depositors or drawdowns by borrowers (Saidenberg and Strahan, 1999). Traditional approaches to bank regulation emphasise the positive features of capital adequacy requirements (Dewatripont and Tirole, 1994). On the other hand, it has been argued that capital requirements may increase risk taking behaviour. If equity capital is more expensive to raise than deposits, then an increase in risk-based capital requirements tends to reduce banks' willingness to screen and lend (Thakor, 1996). It has also been found that raising capital requirements forces banks to supply fewer deposits, which reduces the liquidity providing role of banks. Given these pros and cons, it is now argued that capital that needs to be maintained should be consistent with the risk profile and operating environment. The Basel II framework is a step in this direction as these norms aim at aligning minimum capital requirements to banks' underlying risk profiles.

The Basel I framework was confined to the minimum capital requirements for banks, and largely focussed on the credit risk. The Basel II framework, on the other hand expands this approach to include, inter alia, a largely new, risk-adequate calculation of capital requirements which (for the first time) explicitly includes operational risk in addition to market and credit risk. While Basel I required lenders to calculate a minimum level of capital based on a single risk weight for each of the limited number of asset classes, under Basel II, the capital requirements are more risk sensitive. Basel II capital adequacy rules are based on a 'menu' approach that allows differences in approaches in relationship in the nature of banks and the nature of markets in which they operate. Thus, Basel II prescriptions have ushered in a transition from capital adequacy to capital efficiency which implies that banks adopt a more dynamic use of capital, in which capital will flow quickly to its most efficient use. These elements of Basel II take the regulatory framework closer to the business models employed in several large banks.

All the SCBs in India have adopted the Standardised Approach (SA) for credit risk, Basic Indicator Approach (BIA) for operational risk and Standardised Duration approach for market risk for computing their capital requirements under the revised framework as at end-March 2009. Banks are required to maintain a minimum Capital to Risk-weighted Assets Ratio (CRAR) of 9 per cent on an ongoing basis. The Reserve Bank will take into account the relevant risk factors and the internal capital adequacy assessments of each bank to ensure that the capital held by a bank is commensurate with the bank's overall risk profile. This would include, among other things the effectiveness of the bank's risk management systems in identifying, assessing/measuring, monitoring and managing various risks including interest rate risk in the banking book, liquidity risk, concentration risk and residual risk. Accordingly, the Reserve Bank will consider prescribing a higher level of minimum capital ratio for each bank under the Pillar 2 framework on the basis of their respective risk profiles and their risk management systems. Further, in terms of the Pillar 2 requirements of the New Capital Adequacy Framework, banks are expected to operate at a level well above the minimum requirement.

Furthermore, the minimum capital maintained by banks on implementation of the revised framework will be subjected to a prudential floor, which shall be higher of the following amounts: (a) Minimum capital required to be maintained as per the Revised Framework; (b) A specified per cent of the minimum capital required to be maintained as per the Basel I framework for credit and market risks. The specified per cent will progressively decline as indicated in Table 3.3.

Table 3.3: Prudential Floor

Financial Year Ending*	March 2009	March 2010	March 2011
Prudential Floor (as % of minimum capital requirement computed as per current (Basel I) framework for credit and market risks)	100	90	80

* The relevant periods were March 2009, March 2010 and March 2011 for banks implementing the revised framework with effect from March 31, 2009.

Out of 80 banks, all banks except Bank International Indonesia and Sonali Bank have reported CRAR under Basel II and 14 banks have not reported CRAR under Basel I. A frequency distribution based on data of 64 banks, which have reported CRAR under both Basel I and Basel II, suggests that

12 per cent to 15 per cent is the modal range of CRAR (Table 3.4).

Table 3.4: Distribution of Banks Based on CRAR

CRAR (%)	No. of banks as on March 31, 2009					
	Basel I			Basel II		
	Indian	Foreign	Total	Indian	Foreign	Total
9-12	12	0	12	6	0	6
12-15 (Modal range)	**26**	**4**	**30**	**29**	**4**	**33**
15-18	2	2	4	5	4	9
18-21	2	2	4	2	0	2
21-24	1	0	1	1	1	2
24-27	0	0	0	0	3	3
27-30	0	2	2	0	0	0
30-33	0	2	2	0	0	0
33 & above	1	8	9	1	8	9
Total	**44**	**20**	**64**	**44**	**20**	**64**

A bank-group wise analysis reveals that for the State Bank of India and all its associates, the CRAR under Basel II was higher than that under Basel I for the year 2008-09. Same trend was also observed in case of majority of nationalised banks. On the other hand, majority of the foreign sector banks reported higher CRAR under Basel I than that under Basel II. The private sector banks, however reported a mixed trend.

Source: Report on Trend and Progress of Banking in India 2008-09, RBI

Banks in India are better-placed than their Asian counterparts in terms of several critical parameters such as capital adequacy ratio, asset quality and earnings, low NPA ratio, absence of complex financial products, regular intervention by the central bank and proactive adjustment of monetary policy. What is important is that unlike the banking industries in western countries, banks in India were not dependent upon government bailout and stimulus packages. There are, however, issues of consolidation in the banking space, enhanced growth of top and bottom lines, capital raising, expanded financial inclusion and increased global footprints.

Despite several limitations, Public Sector Banks (PSBs) outperformed the private banking and financial institutions. What is particularly important is the fact that, of late, the PSBs have acquired their own place in the sun and faced the onslaughts of the global financial crisis far more effectively than the more prominent players of the Indian banking space.

Supply	Liquidity is controlled by the Reserve Bank of India (RBI).
Demand	India is a growing economy with high though cyclical demand for credit.
Barriers to entry	Licensing requirement, investment in technology and branch network.
Bargaining power of suppliers	High during periods of tight liquidity. Trade unions in public sector banks can stall reforms. Depositors may switch to other avenues in the event of a sharp fall in interest rates.
Bargaining power of customers	High bargaining power leveraged by good creditworthy borrowers because of the presence of large number of banks.
Competition	Intense competition between PSBs, private sector and foreign banks together with non-banking finance companies competing in similar business space.

While the vastly improved performance of PSBs is certainly welcome, this is not enough in view of the magnitude of the challenges. There is a need to repeatedly raise the bar so that the Indian banking system is in a position to fully meet the challenges of today and the expectations of tomorrow, particularly because everything in business is always in flux and flow. But "we stand on the threshold of a new age—the age of revolution.... For the first time in history we can work backward from our imagination rather than forward from our past" (Gary Hamel). While the world needs new ways of thinking about finance and the risks it entails, it would not be proper to underestimate the strength and resilience of the Indian banking system as brought out in the report of Lord Adair Turner, who is the Chairman of the UK's Financial Services Authority. This report written at the request of the British Prime Minister, Gordon Brown hinted at the merits of India's careful approach followed under the former Governor Y.V. Reddy.

With the RBI estimating additional capital requirement of ₹ 5,68,744 crore in the next five years for 12 per cent capital adequacy, capital raising has emerged a crucial issue. The total capital requirement for the banking sector will increase to

₹ 8,64,935 crore by March 2012 from ₹ 2,96,191 crore in March 2007.

The renewed emphasis of Indian banks on streamlining the delivery mechanism and improving the credit quality to cover the risk of defaults and delinquencies led to a northward movement of the rate of interest on loans. Reduced demand and tighter financial conditions adversely affected liquidity and prospects of the banking and other sectors such as real estate, aviation, information technology. Real estate prices in India dropped sharply because of the cash crunch of US companies, which had invested in Indian real estate companies; no fresh inflow of funds to Indian real estate, given the non-accessibility of easy and cheap dollars and at a cheaper rate; difficulties in finishing ongoing projects because of reduced inflow of such money making project completion difficult; and absence of buyers. While commercial real estate and NBFC loans remained vulnerable, housing loans in India were largely for non-speculative purposes and remained highly granular. Hence, the downside was limited with absolutely no danger of the despicable housing loan saga being replicated here.

Some of the ramifications of the severe liquidity and credit crunch were seen in lower capital inflows, reduced ability of Indian corporate to raise resources via the equity route, significantly increased risk perception leading to keeping all future investments by institutional investors such as pension or endowment funds on hold and cascading effect on private equity (PE) firms. Given difficulties in foreign borrowing and capital markets, the government eased overseas borrowing norms companies, announced three stimulus packages, while the RBI repeatedly slashed key interest rates.

Dr. Montek Singh Ahluwalia, Deputy Chairman of the Planning Commission, has tabled a draft Bill intended to set up and reform regulatory authorities across a dozen key economic sectors, laying down a set of common principles to which all regulatory authorities would have to adhere. It would also establish a "commission of commissions" to oversee their implementation. In the first instance, its remit would cover electricity, telecoms, broadcasting, postal services, airports,

ports, railways, highways, water, and oil and gas. Ahluwalia was seeking expert comment before moving to the legislative stage. While some overlap and conflicts of interest persist, the Bill attempts to remove serious bottlenecks in existing systems of regulation hampering private investment by addressing the issues of the legacy of the command economy, regulatory reform across sectors, PSU interests and accountability. Dr. Ahluwalia recommended that the commission of commissions would sit between the Supreme Court and regulatory authorities, enforcing general rules with both it and the authorities themselves answering directly to Parliament; a more clear definition of the jurisdictions of the different authorities; legally enforceable rules of service for appointees; introduction of a new party to the regulatory process with direct representation of consumers and implementation of minimum service standards.

Any attempt to address unsettled issues and unfolding scenarios has to be based on a clear understanding of the macroeconomic frame of reference. There are, however, still emerging challenges and cognisable dilemmas in guarding the guardians. Such dilemmas relate to the difficulty in the non-appointment of former PSU and ministry staff because of their rare expertise, especially in technical matters; and the distribution of powers between ministries and the regulatory authorities.

The global financial turmoil, which caused all round havoc, posed a danger not only to the US economy but also to the world economy. The magnitude and severity of this widespread crisis, which could lead to a total loss in region of US$3 trillion globally (Gopinath, 2009), hurt India's IT industry because the US and UK, which were worst hit by the global crisis, accounted for 81 per cent of India's exports of computer software and IT enabled services (ITES). Further, the largest chunk of Indian IT exports were to the banking financial, and insurance sectors (BFIS), which were the worst hit globally. Since IT is a multi-geography and multi-industry enabler, events and developments in any major economy or industry have a cascading effect.

In line with the projections of the National Association of Software and Service Companies (Nasscom) while exports reached the $60 billion target in 2010, the software export growth target were reduced by some percentage points for 2008-09. Further incremental pricing weakened and required downwards renegotiation; there were weaker YoY growth rates; contracts took longer to be awarded; start dates were deferred and no major deals occurred in the BFIS space for at least a year. There were also issues of consolidation and mergers of banks leading to reduced IT spends; limited benefits from fall in rupee by over-hedging; backlash to off-shoring to India as firms issued pink slips to US employees and small-cap Indian IT firms' weaker offshore models suffered most. The relative resilience of IT exports occurred because the global credit crunch damaged manufacturers much more than service providers, no reduction in trade credit for IT exports was affected and sales by Indian branches/subsidiaries of MNCs to their parent firms continued.

The global economic environment continues to remain uncertain, although the rate of contraction in economic activities and the extent of pressures on financial systems has certainly eased. The Indian financial markets rebounded from their historic lows and continue to function efficiently and exhibit stability with lower volatility. The growth outlook for financial year 2010-11 is well supported by the high domestic saving rate, sound financial system and conducive macroeconomic policy environment.

The Challenge and the Response—Calibrated Policy Moves for Close Performance Monitoring

The US central bank and the Bank of Japan slashed their policy rates to zero and the British and European central banks also followed similar paths. Central banks also bought back large quantities of bonds from banks. This triad of infusion of cash, low rates and the fact that banks began to trust each other again restored a modicum of order a thaw in inter-bank markets and halted the southward movement of lending rates. In line with such global policy initiatives, India responded to the challenge through fiscal stimulus injected by the government and the RBI's policy of monetary accommodation and adoption of counter-cyclical regulatory measures to provide ample rupee liquidity, comfortable foreign exchange liquidity and credit flow to productive sectors.

The government's strategic options and choices were constrained because of heavy fiscal stress emanating from oil, fertiliser, food subsidies; pay commission, debt waiver and the stimulus packages implemented in the face of a GFD/GDP ratio 5.5-6.0 per cent. There were also large increases in market borrowings.

The RBI adopted both conventional measures such as reduction in the Repo rate from 9 per cent to 5 per cent, reduction in Cash Reserve Ratio from 9 per cent to 5 per cent, relaxed norms for external borrowings, raised interest rate ceilings on NRI deposits and unconventional measures such as Rupee-dollar swap facility for Indian banks, the effective reduction in the SLR from 25 per cent to 21.5 per cent with 1.5 per cent points of the reduction earmarked for liquidity support by banks to mutual funds and NBFCs. But these measures were not good enough. In an extremely insightful paper, Jahangir Aziz, Ajaya Shah and Ila Patnaik made wide-ranging suggestions such as cutting CRR to 5 per cent and SLR to 20 per cent, making oil and fertiliser bonds SLR-eligible, increasing the range of repo-eligible assets and even providing insurance against counterparty risk in interbank transactions, setting up a weekly dollar-swap facility against rupee-denominated assets and investing part of the foreign exchange reserves in one-year deposits in foreign branches of Indian banks. While these suggestions did not find universal acceptance, there is no doubt that given the enormity of the crisis, innovative and 'out-of-box' solutions were seriously considered to shore up the financial system. The success of the monetary stimuli was reflected in growth in advances and deposits by 24 per cent, year on year and 22 per cent year on year, respectively in financial year 2008-09 because of a sharp expansion in term deposits and growth in agricultural and large corporate credit.

Table 3.5: Indian Banks: Marginal Signs of Stress

	Financial Year 2007-08	Financial Year 2008-09	Change
No. of banks (nos.)	79	78	–1.3%
Branches (nos.)	776	825	6.3%
Employees (nos.)	11,588	12,039	3.9%
Networth (Rs m)	39,940	47,080	17.9%
Deposits (Rs m)	420,260	519,700	23.7%
Advances (Rs m)	313,540	383,890	22.4%
NIM (%)	4.1	4.4	7.3%
RoA (%)	1.1	1.1	0.0%
CAR (%)	13.0	14.0	7.7%
Net NPA/advances (%)	1.0	1.1	5.0%
Bus./employee (Rs m)	63.3	75.0	18.5%
Profit/employee (Rs m)	0.5	0.6	20.0%

Source: Profile of banks financial year 2008-09

It is widely agreed that the worst is over but the damage was done leading to debt restructuring, a rise in delinquency levels in retail credit and higher NPAs. Consequently, the banks in India perforce became more risk-averse, which had implications for credit disbursement and a focus on analyzing borrower financial health rather than capability. The banking sector also lost its pricing power. The risk of higher inflation because of excess liquidity led to higher bond yields and losses on bond portfolios.

Gross NPAs to gross advances ratio of SCBs declined from the high of 14 per cent in financial year 1999-2000 to 2.3 per cent in financial year 2007-08. Foreign banks and the private sector banks grew faster than the industry from financial year 2002-03 to financial year 2007-08 primarily due to lower base effect and the rapid growth of these banks. In financial year 2008-09, the total growth in lending and deposits was led by the PSBs. However, the growth of private and foreign banks was significantly lower in financial year 2008-09 because of their high exposure to sensitive sectors and stressed parent level problem for foreign banks.

Unsecured bank credit increased over the years, reaching 23.3 per cent of bank lending in financial year 2007-08, compared with only 10.9 per cent in financial year 1999-2000. Lending to sensitive sector also grew by 46.1 per cent CAGR over financial year 2004-05 to 2007-08. Against this backdrop, it is expected that future credit growth will be led by spending on infrastructure, while the retail credit will grow moderately.

The significance of retail lending, particularly housing loans, which constituted a significant portion of the portfolio for most banks, reduced because of higher risk weightage and provisioning requirements. The banks, however, mobilised a higher proportion of low cost deposits with a greater outreach in the semi-urban and rural areas. This helped them to reduce the cost of funds. Apart from streamlining their processes through technology initiatives such as ATMs, telephone banking, online banking and web based products, banks also resorted to greater cross selling of financial products such as credit cards, mutual funds and insurance policies to augment their fee based income.

Indian banks benefitted from higher levels of money supply, credit and deposits as a proportion of GDP in financial year 2008-09 as compared to that in the preceding year.

The net interest margins (NIMs) of Indian banks rose, despite poor pricing power, because of lower cost of funds in financial year 2008-09. While some banks, e.g. ICICI Bank stressed profits and profitability in the trade-off between profits and balance sheet size, most banks chose to reasonably grow both their branch network and assets. PSBs outperformed their private sector counterparts in terms of growth and franchise expansion in the last fiscal. Improved capital adequacy also helped banks to comfortably comply with the requirements of Basle II. While Indian banks last year were characterized by improved performance, the interest income of most banks took a hit because of the restructuring of loans effected across banks. Further the PSU banks also had to provide for the loss of interest on the agri-loans waived by the government.

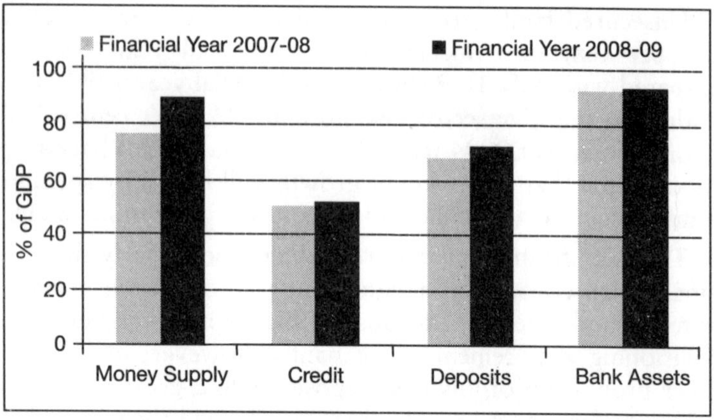

Fig. 3.2: Benefits of Financial Inclusion

Reduced avenues of credit disbursement, moderate credit off-take and greater risk aversion because of the danger of ballooning NPAs, induced banks to keep their surplus funds with the RBI. Consequently, at the end of financial year 2008-09, banks' investment in SLR securities increased to 28.1 per cent of total deposits from 27.8 per cent in financial year 2007-08 much higher than the RBI prescribed level of 24 per cent.

In line with the RBI's direction, all foreign banks operating in India and Indian banks with operational presence outside India migrated to the Basel II norms in financial year 2008-09. All other commercial banks were also encouraged to migrate to these approaches not later than financial year 2009-10.

Tracking Growth Stimulants

In bracing for tomorrow, a paradigm shift in bank financing through innovative mechanisms such as templates for assessing customer risk and pricing product offerings, credit scoring, availability and use of information is manifestly needed. Retail banking requires product development and differentiation, innovation and business process re-engineering, micro planning, marketing, prudent pricing, customisation, technological upgradation, home/electronic/mobile banking, cost reduction and cross-selling.

Profits and Profitability

There is greater need to drive profitability because of inexorable pressures to maintain growth with dissipated treasury profits and constricted net interest margins. There is an imperative need to benchmark branch, product, customer and staff performance to identify and leverage best practices. Performance metric, risk-adjusted customer profitability requires an integrated, enterprise-wide profitability and performance management system, paradigm shift from a departmental focus to an integrated, enterprise-wide framework. Apart from restricting NPAs, enhancing income and reducing expenditure are simultaneously needed with each unit working as a profit centre.

Strengthening of core competencies and exploring new businesses to achieve long-term sustainable growth requires enhanced growth, particularly in income, profits, networth and quality of assets and a paradigm shift in the business mix. Holistic profitability and performance management requires implementation of an enterprise-wide profitability system and integration of important elements of profitability, e.g. micro management, risk management and ABC data into the decision-making matrix.

Growth Triggers

Banking success requires imaginative strategic planning, organisational restructuring, streamlining of human resources and significant changes in the legal, regulatory and supervisory framework. The process of convergence, compliance and cost efficiency needs to be carefully pursued by banks through changes in products, technology, structure, processes, elimination of "cost drivers" and introduction of advanced management concepts, resource-mix, investment opportunities, demanding standards of customers, patterns of shifting value and practices to successfully introduce new financial instruments and strategies and new and cheaper delivery, trading and settlement mechanisms. Banks must become 'one-stop financial shops' and integrate Lean with Six Sigma to deliver Six Sigma quality with Lean speed and maximum value.

Accelerating Growth Beyond Technologies and Geographies

Innovation, which transcends invention, represents the point of convergence of invention and insight. Organizational ethos needs to stress innovation as a key driver of growth that surprises and delights the customer with new, differentiated and relevant benefits—"innovate or perish".

Indian banks will be able to weather the competition and emerge as a key financial hub provided they are relevant to consumers in terms of technology, quality, reliability, pricing, performance and support. Convergence of the information and communication technologies (ICT), "technological evangelisation" and narrowing of "digital gap" require focus on innovation to accelerate growth of both top and bottom lines. Hence, there has to be an accent on product innovation as an integral part of the retail banking revolution; competency building and investment in human capital as a catalyst for transformation with flexible compensation packages, recognition and reward, suitable training; consolidation within the financial system; opportunity to increase size and scale to gain dominances in the local market and penetrate into the global market; transparency, disclosure and market discipline.

Efficient and effective IT management can help in ensuring that critical applications supporting business are optimized, interconnected and seamlessly integrated because of the move from product-society banking to knowledge-society banking and introduction of innovative business models and financial technologies, e.g. ATMs, Internet and Mobile Banking, 'Virtual' Banking, Home Banking, Electronic Funds Transfer at Point of Sale (EFTPOS), Image Processing, decision support systems (DSS) for credit risk appraisal, forecasting loan delinquencies, investment decisions, etc.

Complacency could well be misplaced because the present scenario does not necessarily mean the beginnings of a strong recovery but may merely indicate a slowing rate of decline and concerns of a double-dip recession. The financial crisis is yet to fully peter out because action taken for the short-term was the opposite of the right action for the long-term, raising the risk of a double-dip recession and financial markets are beginning to lose confidence in the credibility of sovereigns. While the precarious financial position in Portugal, Ireland, Greece and Germany evoked most concerns, the effects of this crisis were felt worldwide.

There is also the danger that complacency that the world economy is returning to normal could hamper recovery and block policies to protect against a further slide into abyss. Hence, the jury is still out on whether the worst is over or there is still more pain left in the system and there is a concern that things could get much worse before they get better. In conformity with a confluence of macro-economic environment, industry developments, increasing sophistication and technological automation, a significant modification of the conventional strategy for growth and structural transformation is required. Alleviating the pain of the comprehensive, macroeconomic slowdown and the whole risk-averse and tight consumer credit environment requires bankers to be more fleet-footed, to take decisions faster and more judiciously.

The traditional face of banks as mere financial intermediaries has altered because of the paradigm shift from balance sheet to off-balance sheet intermediation, move from capital adequacy to capital efficiency and transition from banking to financial services. In the rapidly evolving macro-economic environment of intensified competition and increased business complexities, there has to be a renewed thrust on efficiency, productivity and cost reduction; higher credit penetration; greater geographic diversification of bank credit; strengthening service quality and delivery and cross-selling of products/services (fee-income, wealth management, bancassurance, mutual funds, capital markets, structured products, credit/debit cards); rise in non-interest income; reduced intermediation cost and much higher productivity.

Competition needs to foster convergence towards best practice in risk management because of growing role of market forces, need for internationally consistent prudential norms and a high-quality financial infrastructure and interdependence of prudential standards. Hence, adroit risk management systems and practices necessitate improved integrated risk management mechanisms, streamlined systems and procedures and honing the skill set for client selection, industry analysis, concentration, risk ratings, use of benchmarks, etc.

Going Forward

While building on the past, we must invest in the future, while strengthening our core competencies, we must explore new vistas of development and seed options for future growth. As the world economics head for change, India's place in the world economic equation will never be the same. With its huge diversity, India offers vast opportunities. But, in order to capitalise on this vast opportunity, there has to be thrust on volume-led growth to competitive balance sheet size, migration from interest income to non-interest income and capital adequacy to capital efficiency because of increased competition in financial market in general and banking sector in particular, progressively reducing net interest margin, stiff competition for good corporate loans with development of capital market and increased market capitalization and relentless pursuit of the strategy of balance sheet growth to maintain reasonable profit growth.

Banks are implementing strategies to immune their balance sheets from interest rate fluctuation by providing more attention on non-interest income segments. Growing services sector and financial market have created new avenues for fee-based income. Merchant banking, international trade, funds transfer, payments and settlements, consultancy services, financial derivatives, utility services, etc., opened up new income sources for banks. But there has to be a transition from branch banking to virtual banking, market segmentation to customer segmentation and product planning to customer profitability.

Success requires a threshold level of performance in terms of three key parameters—customer service, product innovation and operational excellence—and a clear leadership in one dimension. Development strategies must be broadened to incorporate all these three critical dimensions for secular dynamic change and structural transformation. With a paradigm shift of the Indian economy from a highly controlled economy to one structured on competitive principles, the issues of regulation of markets, of simplification and balancing of the business climate have increasingly come to the fore.

While banks in India are more robust than their Asian counterparts in terms of several critical parameters such as capital adequacy ratio, asset quality and earnings, there are issues of consolidation in the banking space, enhanced growth of top and bottom lines, capital raising, expanded financial inclusion and increased global footprints. Despite several limitations, PSBs outperformed the private banking and financial institutions. The renewed emphasis of Indian banks on streamlining the delivery mechanism and improving the credit quality to cover the risk of defaults and delinquencies led to a northward movement of the rate of interest on loans. Reduced demand and tighter financial conditions adversely affected liquidity and prospects of the banking and other sectors, such as real estate, aviation, information technology. Real estate prices in India dropped sharply because of the cash crunch of US companies, which had invested in Indian real estate companies; no fresh inflow of funds to Indian real estate given the non-accessibility of easy and cheap dollars and at a cheaper rate; difficulties in finishing ongoing projects because of reduced inflow of such money making project completion difficult; and absence of buyers. While commercial real estate and NBFC loans remained vulnerable, housing loans in India have been largely for non-speculative purposes and were highly granular. Hence, the downside was limited with absolutely no danger of the despicable housing loan saga being replicated here.

Observations of CFSA Regarding the Commercial Banking System in India

Based on the stability assessment and stress testing of the financial institutions, the CFSA has found that commercial banking system in India is broadly sound. While the banks were generally in a position to absorb significant shocks due to credit, liquidity and market risks, there were some concerns relating to liquidity risk due to increasing illiquidity in banks' balance sheets. There is, therefore, a need to strengthen liquidity management. Looking forward, the stress tests needed to be conducted on a more systemic basis, to capture second round and contagion risks.

The government ownership of commercial banks posed dilemmas as it has been argued that this could have led to a conflict of roles and regulatory forbearance. The possibility of conflicts of interest could be minimised through evenhanded regulation which had been the case in India. Also, the cost of recapitalisation of Indian PSBs was relatively low.

The government has, in the past, consistently shown willingness to contribute capital and the growth of PSBs was not been constrained because of lack of capital. But, capital augmentation of these banks in future could be a challenge. This could be managed through a variety of ways such as amalgamation where commercial synergies exist, raising capital through newer instruments (such as issuance of perpetual preference shares in foreign currency).

There should now be a focus on capacity building in the commercial banking sector with accent on training, succession planning, lateral recruitment and improved remuneration (particularly for public sector banks) while at the same time discouraging excessive risk-taking through an appropriate and balanced incentives structure. A well considered approach for entry of foreign banks in India needs to be followed, while adhering to the WTO commitment and norms. Recommending that competition must be encouraged, CFSA has advised encouraging market-based consolidation of banks.[9]

Some of the ramifications of the severe liquidity and credit crunch were seen in lower capital inflows, reduced ability of Indian corporate to raise resources through the equity route, significantly increased risk perception leading to keeping all future investments by institutional investors such as pension or endowment funds on hold and cascading effect on private equity (PE) firms. Given difficulties in foreign borrowing and capital markets, the government eased overseas borrowing norms companies, announced three stimulus packages, while the RBI repeatedly slashed key interest rates.

Crisis on All Streets—Global Initiatives Imperative for Structural Reforms of the World's Financial System

The global financial system proved to be woefully inadequate, particularly in view of the manifest structural deficiencies in meeting the regulatory requirements of the present-day international financial system of the Bretton Woods architecture, which led to the establishment of the International Monetary Fund in 1945. The crisis drove home the significance of broad multilateral collaboration and cooperation in economic and financial policymaking and thus brought to the fore the imperative necessity of coordinated and concerted efforts by all countries to make the financial systems healthier and more resilient to global financial sector risks. Cross-country analysis clearly brought out the need for the international financial institutions to be made more robust in order to enable them to address the financial constraints of poor developing countries badly affected by the crisis. It was feared that world's financial architecture must change drastically because world unemployment could swell by 20 million by the year end as the vulnerable were particularly hit. Hence, while highlighting the key challenges and variables that needed to be addressed, developing countries had to understand social outcomes and devise appropriate social protection schemes.

The extraordinarily synchronized nature of the subprime crisis made it necessary to launch the creation of a "global monitoring authority to promote global supervision" of cross-border investment, trade and banking with the fast-growing economies such as China, India and Brazil playing a far more important role in the new global financial architecture and ensuring that the results trickle down to the grassroots level. The world's financial architecture must change drastically in conformity with the transformed realities, particularly because, as cogently argued by Juan Somavia, world unemployment could increase by 20 million in the process surpassing the 200-million-mark for the first time. What lends urgency to the need to devise effective remedies is the near certainty that the poor, the deprived and the vulnerable are affected much more severely than the better-off and the crisis could throw 200 million additional people into poverty. Hence, the developing countries needed to understand the social outcomes and provide appropriate social protection schemes to reduce the devastating impact of the crisis.

While devising a new global financial system because of the IMF's "legitimacy deficit" stressed in a Task Force Report of the Singapore-based Lee Kuan Yew School of Public Policy, the country of nations needed a broad spectrum strategy to surmount the crisis and move ahead on the road back to solvency by initiating a series of developmental measures such as sustaining liquidity, reducing volatility in foreign exchange rate, allowing capital inflows and keeping domestic and external financing available. Towards this end of providing a long-term solution, the contours of the new regulatory paradigm necessitated designing more effective early warning systems; strengthening transparency and accountability; enhancing regulation including underwriting standards; coordinated actions and reinforcing international cooperation between countries and multilateral institutions, e.g. G8, IMF, IBRD, WTO; reinforced international institutions; assessment of the role of sovereign wealth funds as providers of capital in the context of inadequacy of financial institutions' capital cushions; examination of the role of the big three rating agencies, particularly Standard & Poor's, Moody's and Fitch in structuring and rating securities; good central bank governance and effective public communication; and continuous evaluation and effectiveness of policy tools.

The financial stability process needs to grapple with the challenges of regulatory failure in the US, draw lessons from this regulatory failure and implement a transparent and effective framework in conformity with the growth and diversification of our economy and financial sector. But financial stability, particularly in the wake of technological innovation, structural changes in banking, and the evolution of central bank policies is a process, not a one-off miracle to be attained by sudden policy shifts and operational measures. Domestic reforms must be accompanied by prudential norms, efficient regulatory systems and healthy capital adequacy norms with a focus on prudent investments and quality lending. Since institutional resilience can effectively reduce the severity and duration of economic shocks and dislocations, it is well recognized that there has to be an accent on institutional strengthening to ensure that exercise regulation does not stifle innovation.

Juan Somavia, Director-General of the International Labour Organisation correctly stressed "the...search for better financial regulation and a global surveillance mechanism of checks and balances is a welcome step. But we must reach beyond the financial system". Given this overarching crisis, building a post-crisis global economy needs creation of an effective multilateral agency, including a new global regulatory agency. In view of the inherent limitations of unilateralism in a world of economic interdependence, support from a truly global polity with a focus on internationally coherent and decisive policy measures is sorely needed to restore confidence in the global financial system. As the G-7 Summit stressed, what is needed is "a coherent framework that will direct our individual and collective policy steps to provide liquidity to markets, strengthen financial institutions, protect savers, and enforce investor protection".

Apart from concrete steps to revive growth, a boost in funding for the International IMF, longer-lasting changes in the character of banking and investment banking and an exploration of the ways to reshape the world's financial and economic order to restore trust in the financial system, developed countries were asked not resort to protectionism and global capital flows were asked remain unimpeded. A paradigm shift of the system must be based on the realization that the unprecedented budgets for structural policies are neither economically efficient nor politically acceptable. Hence, all markets, all territories, and all actors putting the global financial system at risk should be continuously monitored with zero tolerance for non-compliance with the rules of finance. Streamlined and transparent auditing standards must come into force and the rating agencies must be effectively regulated with stricter rules, a specific rating scale for complex products and regular publication of their returns.

The World Bank and the IMF identified measures to strengthen economic and financial stability, improve market functioning and, in turn, boost market confidence in the pursuit of sustained global recovery. The IMF in its "Global Financial Stability Report: Responding to the Financial Crisis and Measuring Systemic Risks" stressed the need to redefine global financial regulation and revamp the financial architecture.

The basic challenge in financial stability, from a diagnostic viewpoint, related to breaking what the IMF described as the "downward spiral between the financial system and the global economy". Central to this will be the effectiveness of the multilateral bodies in redesigning the financial system, specifically the monitoring and regulatory functions, with the IMF estimating the worldwide losses for financial institutions at $4.1 trillion. As lax regulation contributed significantly to the crisis, the IMF report's call for bolder steps by governments, including nationalization, where necessary, needs serious consideration.

A well-informed understanding of the various aspects that go into the making of financial stability, the role of global cooperation in rejigging the international financial rules and systems, the identification of the most appropriate development rules and the role of developing countries in minimising financial contagion must constitute important building blocks in the road back from precipice. Implementation of mechanisms to protect developing countries from the impact of the economic meltdown and ensure that the projected slower growth rates do not mean reduced allocation for the social sector in national budgets. The World Bank's decision to triple its investment in social protection programmes for 2009-10 from about $4 billion two years before the economic crisis is welcome. The Bank estimated in the *Global Monitoring Report, 2009* that close to 90 per cent of the developing countries were highly or moderately exposed to the impact of the crisis, as they faced slowing economic growth, high levels of poverty, or both.

Experience from the Latin American countries brought out the effectiveness of well-designed social protection programmes in stimulating public spending, apart from boosting human development through better education and health care. The vulnerable sections in the developing world, e.g. those without any form of social safety nets, have to be the focus of such programmes. India was not without impact of global economic meltdown, but not to the extent most other countries like the US, UK, Germany, Greece where the impact was severe. During 2009-10 there were signs of recovery which strengthened in 2010-11. There is used to further strengthen our financial system to ensure that such recessions do not occur in India, mild slowdowns do not affect our country and other economic shocks do not create roadblocks in the way of its march towards rapid progress.

Notes

1. Investopedia, accessed on 15 November 2010.
2. John M. Berry. "Subprime Losses Are Big, Exaggerated by Some." www.bloomberg.com
3. Sumanjeet Singh. "Global Financial Crisis and Indian Economy: Impact Assessment, Policy Responses and Recovery." http://www.aercafrica.org
4. D.K. Nanto. "The Global Financial Crisis: The Analysis and Policy Implications." CRS Report for Congress.
5. Arvind Panagariya. *India: The Emerging Giant*. Oxford University Press, New York.
6. http://www.rbi.org.in/scripts/publications views.aspx?id = 11860.
7. *Ibid.*
8. *Economic Survey 2009-10.*
9. Report on Trend and Progress of Banking in India 2008-09, RBI.

4

Remedial Measures—Stimulus Packages, Monetary Steps and Policy Changes

The breathtaking scale and speed of the downturn and its broad scope led governments concomitantly in Europe, the United States, and some large Asian countries to respond to both the weakening economy and financial instability with a sense of immediacy. The nature of stimulus took the forms of tax cuts and non-bank bailouts, financial support in G7 and BRIC countries through liquidity provision, capital injection, asset purchases and even nationalization to repair the economic machinery quickly. The individual policy prescriptions differed because of historical factors and the distinctive socio-economic milieu which influenced the design of the stimulus package to maximize the impact. In assessing the size of the stimulus, countries balanced the cost to their own budgets with the benefits in terms of increased growth and employment for their own economies. Since some of the benefit (much of it in the case of small, open economies) accrue to others, stimulus packages were likely to be smaller and more poorly designed than they otherwise would be. This is what provided the basic justification for a globally coordinated stimulus package.

When the crisis gripped the world, all countries were in complete agreement about the compelling need to put in place coordinated and concerted measures aimed at shoring up the tottering financial system in conformity with their individual constellation of circumstances. While the impact of automatic stabilizers, which enable the government to mobilize more or less fiscal resources, depending on economic conditions, was more powerful in Western Europe than in most of the Anglo-Saxon countries, America's overall economic landscape was worse than Europe's in terms of consumption, banking, or employment and housing markets. Subsequently, the situation in Europe also deteriorated significantly.

Governments all over the world took stimulus measures to mitigate the adverse effects of financial crisis and put their respective economies back on track. These measures are briefly discussed below.

India

In October 2008, the supplementary demand for grants provided for a gross expenditure amounting to ₹ 2,37,286 crore with net cash outgo of ₹ 1,05,613 crore mainly to finance schemes/plans announced in the Union Budget for 2008-09. However, no provisions were made for the same.

On 7 December 2008, the three major *ad valorem* rates of central excise duty, viz. 14 per cent, 12 per cent and 8 per cent applicable to non-petroleum products were reduced by 4 percentage points each.

For promoting exports, pre-shipment and post-shipment export credit for labour intensive exports, viz. textiles (including handlooms, carpets and handicrafts), leather, gems and jewellery, marine products and Small & Medium Enterprise (SME) sector was made more attractive by providing an interest subvention of 2 per cent up to March 31, 2009 subject to minimum rate of interest of 7 per cent per annum. An additional fund of ₹ 1,100 crore to ensure full refund of terminal excise duty/central sales tax (CST) was announced. Furthermore, an additional allocation of ₹ 350 crore for export incentive schemes was announced.

In order to provide a contra-cyclical stimulus via Plan expenditure, an additional Plan expenditure of up to ₹ 20,000 crore in the current 2008-09 was allocated. In the textile sector, an additional allocation of ₹ 1,400 crore was made to clear the entire backlog of Technology Up-gradation Fund (TUF) scheme. In order to support the infrastructure schemes under Public Private Partnership mode, India Infrastructure Finance Company Limited (IIFCL) was authorised to raise ₹ 10,000 crore through tax-free bonds by March 31, 2009.

On 19 December 2008, the second supplementary demand for grants provided for a gross expenditure amounting to ₹ 55,605 crore with net cash outgo of ₹ 42,480 crore.

In December 2008, the Government announced an economic stimulus package of $4 billion to shield its economy from recession. A substantial increase in Government expenditure coupled with a cut in interest rates by Reserve Bank of India aimed towards raising aggregate demand.

A number of incentives were announced in economic stimulus package of India. These were drawn up by Government to infuse a sense of optimism in the minds of investors as well as industrialists. Incentive schemes in Indian economic stimulus package amounting to $70 million were allocated to boost exports. Measures were taken to boost exports of labor intensive commodities like textiles and handicrafts to provide stimulus to Indian economic revival. Lending rates on housing loans for low- and middle-income segments were also reduced. Medium and small businesses were provided tax exemptions and tax holidays. Value Added Tax was cut at different levels and across products to increase spending. Reserve Bank of India reduced its lending rate to 6.5 per cent and its borrowing rate to 5 per cent on 4 March 2009.

Central Value Added Tax (CENVAT) reduced by 4 per cent, brought down prices of cement, textiles, and cars. CENVAT on non-petroleum products was slashed by up to ten per cent to bring economic recovery. Customs duty on naphtha—an intermediary product for power industry—was completely revoked. To provide an impetus to export, duty on export of iron ore fines was removed and levy on iron lump exports has been cut from 15 per cent to 5 per cent.

A 10-point India economic stimulus package program, charted by the Prime Minister targeted at reviving most badly affected sectors of Indian economy like housing, automobiles, infrastructure, power and medium and small industries. A funding of ₹ 300 billion was earmarked for this. An additional funding of ₹ 100 billion in the form of tax free bonds was earmarked for India Infrastructure Finance Company Limited. Deputy Chairman of Planning Commission commented that this 10-point package was set to force manufacturers to operate in a competitive environment and pass on the benefits to end users.

Three stimulus packages in three months were announced with fanfare. In the quarter ended 31 March 2009, the Pay Commission award boosted community services growth by a whopping 17 per cent. Before this, stimulus to expenditure was provided by farm loan waiver and spiraling subsidies for petroleum products, fertilizers and food. Despite this illusory boost, overall GDP growth only touched 5.3 per cent. Agriculture declined by an unexpected 2.2 per cent in this period as poor harvests of sugarcane, cotton, pulses and oilseeds overwhelmed gains in rice, horticulture and animal husbandry.

India's 9 per cent growth in the preceding five years was due to an unprecedented global boom, not great reforms or efforts by the Government. A sharp global boom raised growth rates in many countries; even Africa grew at an unprecedented 6 per cent.

The experts felt that we must accept that we are part and parcel of the global economy. The global boom drove up our growth to 9 per cent and the global slump has lowered it to 5 per cent. We must abandon the illusion that we can somehow grow fast again while the rest of the world stagnates. We must learn to live with the global downswing. I was believed that we probably cannot end or mitigate the recession in isolation by our own efforts. At best the so-called stimulus packages are actually pain relievers.

India's Interim Budget 2009-10

Pranab Mukherjee presented United Progressive Alliance (UPA) Government's interim budget 2009-10 on 16 February 2009. Apart from highlighting the initiatives taken by the Government and achievements made in agriculture, rural development, education, social sector and public sector enterprises, the Finance Minister drew attention to the global financial crisis. A few excepts from his speech, pertinent to the issue are reproduced below:

> The global financial crisis which began in 2007 took a turn for the worse in September 2008 with the collapse of several international financial institutions, including investment banks, mortgage lenders and insurance companies. There has been a severe choking of credit since then and a global crash in stock markets. The slowdown intensified with the US, Europe and Japan sliding into recession. Current indications of the global situation are not encouraging. Forecasts indicate that the World economy in 2009 may fare worse than in 2008.
>
> A crisis of such magnitude in developed countries is bound to have an impact around the world. Most emerging market economies have slowed down significantly. India too has been affected. For the first nine months of the current year, the growth rate of exports has come down to 17.1 per cent. According to the latest figures available, the industrial production has fallen by 2 per cent year-on-year basis in December 2008. In these difficult times, when most economies are struggling to stay afloat, a healthy 7.1 per cent rate of GDP growth still makes India the second fastest growing economy in the world.
>
> To counter the negative fallout of the global slowdown on the Indian economy, our Government took prompt action by providing substantial fiscal stimulus. The two packages announced on 7 December 2008 and 2 January 2009, provide tax relief to boost demand and aim at increasing expenditure on public projects to create

employment and public assets. In this context, the Government renewed its efforts to increase infrastructure investments. In the period from August 2008 to January 2009 alone, the Government accorded approval for 37 infrastructure projects worth ₹ 70,000 crore.

In addition to expanding public sector investment in infrastructure, our Government has also taken steps to encourage private investment in infrastructure through Public Private Partnership (PPP). I am happy to say that the Government of India has been successful in attracting private investment in infrastructure sectors such as telecommunications, power generation, airports, ports, roads and railways. Under the PPP mode, 54 Central Sector infrastructure projects with a total project cost of ₹ 67,700 crore have been given in-principle or final approval by the PPP Appraisal Committee and 23 projects amounting to Rs. 27,900 crore have been approved for viability gap funding in 2008-09.

To ensure that such projects do not face financing difficulties arising from the current downturn, we have taken a new initiative for providing refinance to the banks for long term credit extended to these projects. Accordingly, the Government has decided that India Infrastructure Finance Company Ltd. (IIFCL) will refinance 60 per cent of commercial bank loans for PPP projects in critical sectors over the next eighteen months or so. For this purpose, IIFCL has been authorized to raise ₹ 10,000 crore in the market by the end of March 2009. An additional ₹ 30,000 crore can be raised if required. With this, IIFCL and banks will be able to support projects involving a total investment of ₹ 100,000 crore in infrastructure. Combined with the steps we are taking to increase public investment in infrastructure, this will provide a big boost to such investment.

The RBI took a number of monetary easing and liquidity enhancing measures including reduction in cash reserve ratio, statutory liquidity ratio and key policy rates. The objective was to facilitate flow of funds from the financial system to meet the needs of productive sectors. Our Government has also announced specific measures to address the impact of global slowdown on India's exports. These include extension of export credit for labour intensive exports, improving the pre- and post-shipment credit availability, additional allocations for refund of Terminal Excise Duty/CST and export incentive schemes, and removal of export duty and export ban on certain items. A Committee of Secretaries has been set up to address, on continuing basis, procedural problems being faced by exporters.

The budget provided 2 per cent cut in excise duty and service tax to give boost to the country's economy. Starting December 2008, this was the third stimulus package announced by the Government to counter the crisis faced due to the global economic downturn.

Industry chambers welcomed the move. "It is another stimulus," Pranab Mukherjee told reporters after the passage of the Interim Budget in the Lok Sabha. The tax concessions meant a revenue sacrifice of about ₹ 30,000 crore. Mukherjee said, "It will have its desired impact because we have given some concessions to the export sector, particularly those which are employment-generating ones, like gems and jewellery, garments and handicraft." "With the strong export linkages India has with these economies it is unlikely India will not feel the impact. Despite the constitutional constraints, I have some flexibility which I want to use to provide a further stimulus to the economy," he added.

The announcements in the budget included 4 per cent across-the-board excise duty cut to be continued beyond 31 March 2009, an additional 2 per cent cut in excise duty, 2 per cent cut in service tax, while excise duty on bulk cement was to be 8 per cent (instead of 10 per cent) or ₹ 230 per metric tonne, whichever is higher. Naptha was exempted from customs duty to provide relief to the power sector. These duty reductions were likely to cost the Treasury nearly ₹ 30,000 crore. This was above the 4 per cent cut in CENVAT announced in December 2008, which was extended to beyond 31 March 2009.

The Government expected the Indian economy to grow nearly 7 per cent in the financial year ending 31 March 2009, the slowest pace in six years. It announced two stimulus packages, one on 7 December 2008 and the other on 2 January 2009 besides the several monetary policy measures undertaken by the Reserve Bank of India, like reductions in repo rate and reverse repo rate. However, it was felt that these reductions were far too little considering the magnitude of the economic slowdown. Moreover, most of the banks were too hesitant to pass on the benefit of reduced RBI rates to the customers. The offtake of bank credit was showing a continuous declining trend since January 2009, which was not a healthy sign for the economy.

Job Creation

There was a plan to make huge investments for petroleum, chemicals & petrochem investment regions (PCPIRs). A PCPIR is a specifically delineated investment region of approximately 250 sq kms for manufacturing facilities for domestic and export led production. The cabinet approval to set up the first three petroleum, chemicals and petrochemical investment regions (PCPIR) in the country would bring in investments to the tune of ₹ 4,86,180 crore while generating employment for 30 lakh people.

The regions spread over 1,307 sq kms in Andhra Pradesh, Gujarat and West Bengal were being anchored by companies like Indian Oil Corporation, Hindustan Petroleum Corporation, GMR, CALS Refinery and ONGC Petro Additions Ltd.

"The Government will provide necessary viability gap funding through existing schemes to ensure availability of external physical infrastructure linkages including rail, road, ports, airports and telecom in a time-bound manner", said Ramvilas Paswan, Minister for Chemicals and Fertilisers. "States will be required to identify and select developers to build and develop internal infrastructure," he continued.

Table 4.1: Proposed PCPIRs at Andhra Pradesh, Gujarat and West Bengal

Projects	State	Cumulative Investment (Rs. crore)	Committed Investment (Rs. crore)	Employment (lakh)	Area (sq kms)
Vizag-Kakinada-Rajahmundry	AP	3,43,000	1,63,890	11.98	603.58
Vagra-Bharuch	Gujarat	50,000	22,930	8.0	453.00
Haidia	W. Bengal	93,180	48,180		250.19
Total		4,86,180	235,000		13,06.77

Source: Ministry of Chemicals and Fertilisers

The policy was notified in April 2007. PCPIR includes SEZs, free trade and warehousing zones and industrial parks and the state Government is required not to acquire but notify the area. The developers will then negotiate and buy land at existing rates.

Union Budget 2010-2011

The main points of the Union Budget 2010-11 are briefly given below.

The Indian economy during the financial year 2008-09 until around the end of 2009-10 was facing uncertainties. Growth had started decelerating and the business sentiment was weak. The economy's capacity to sustain high growth was under serious threat from the widespread economic slowdown in the developed world.

It was not clear to us, as also to the policymakers in many other countries, how this crisis would eventually unfold. What would be its impact on the growth momentum of the Indian economy? How soon will we be able to turnaround the fortunes of our economy? The short term global outlook was bleak and the consensus was that year 2009 would face the brunt of this crisis across the world.

At home, there was added uncertainty on account of the delayed and sub-normal south-west monsoon, which had undermined the kharif crop in the country. There were concerns about production and prices of food items and its possible repercussions on the growth of rural demand.

Today, we have weathered these crises well. Indian economy now is in a far better position than it was a year ago. That is not to say that the challenges today are any less than what they were about a year ago.

The three challenges and the medium term perspective that had been outlined in my last Budget Speech remain relevant, even today. These would continue to engage the Indian policy-planners for the next few years.

The *first* challenge before us is to quickly revert to the high GDP growth path of 9 per cent and then find the means to cross the 'double digit growth barrier'. This calls for imparting a fresh momentum to the impressive recovery in growth witnessed in the past few months....

The *third* challenge relates to the weaknesses in government systems, structures and institutions at different levels of governance. Indeed, in the coming years, if there is one factor that can hold us back in realising our potential as a modern nation, it is the bottleneck of our public delivery mechanisms. There have been many initiatives in this regard, in different sectors, at different points of time. Some of them have been effective in reforming the way the Government works in those areas. But we have a long way to go before we can rest on this count.

Overview of the Economy

The fiscal year 2009-10 was a challenging year for the Indian economy. The significant deceleration in the second half of 2008-09, brought the real GDP growth down to 6.7 per cent, from an average of over 9 per cent in the preceding three years. We were among the first few countries in the world to implement a broad-based counter-cyclic policy package to respond to the negative fallout of the global slowdown. It included a substantial fiscal expansion along with liberal monetary policy support.

The effectiveness of these policy measures became evident with fast paced recovery. The economy stabilised in the first quarter of 2009-10 itself, when it clocked a GDP growth of 6.1 per cent, as against 5.8 per cent in the fourth quarter of the preceding year. It registered a strong rebound in the second quarter, when the growth rate rose to 7.9 per cent. With the Advance Estimates placing the likely growth for 2009-10 at 7.2 per cent, we are indeed vindicated in our policy stand. The final figure may well turn out to be higher when the third and fourth quarter GDP estimates for 2009-10 become available.

This recovery is very encouraging for it has come about despite a negative growth in the agriculture sector. More importantly, it is the result of a renewed momentum in the manufacturing sector and marks the rise of this sector as the growth driver of the economy. The growth rate in manufacturing in December 2009 was 18.5 per cent—the highest in the past two decades. There are also signs of a turnaround in the merchandise exports with a positive growth in November and December 2009 after a decline of about twelve successive months.

Consolidating Growth

Managing a complex economy is a difficult task, more so when it is a growing economy in a globalised world. And yet, choices have to be made and they have to be well timed.

After successfully managing the effects of the global slowdown, we need to strengthen the domestic macroeconomic environment to help consolidate the rebound in growth and sustain it over the medium term. We need to review the stimulus imparted to the economy and move towards the preferred path of fiscal consolidation that facilitated the remarkable growth in the pre-crisis five year period. We need to make growth more broad-based and ensure that supply-demand imbalances are better managed.

The success of the fiscal stimulus in supporting domestic demand could be traced to its composition. The approach of the Government was to increase the disposable income in the hands of the people by effecting reductions in indirect taxes and by expanding public expenditure on programmes like the Mahatma Gandhi National Rural Employment Guarantee Scheme and rural infrastructure. Now that the recovery has taken root, there is a need to review public spending, mobilise resources and gear them towards building the productivity of the economy.

Tax Reforms

The process for building a simple tax system with minimum exemptions and low rates designed to promote voluntary compliance, is now nearing completion. On the Direct Tax Code the wide-ranging discussions with stakeholders have been concluded.

On Goods and Services Tax, we have been focusing on generating a wide consensus on its design. In November, 2009 the Empowered Committee of the State Finance Ministers placed the first discussion paper on GST in the public domain. The Thirteenth Finance Commission has also made a number of significant recommendations relating to GST, which will contribute to the ongoing discussions. We are actively engaged with the Empowered Committee to finalise the structure of GST as well as the modalities of its expeditious implementation. It will be my earnest endeavour to introduce GST along with the DTC in April, 2011.

Financial Stability and Development Council

The financial crisis of 2008-09 has fundamentally changed the structure of banking and financial markets the world over. With a view to strengthen and institutionalise the mechanism for maintaining financial stability, Government has decided to setup an apex-level Financial Stability and Development Council. Without prejudice to the autonomy of regulators, this Council would monitor macro prudential supervision of the economy, including the functioning of large financial conglomerates, and address inter-regulatory coordination issues. It will also focus on financial literacy and financial inclusion.

Union Budget 2011-12

The growth of Indian economy in 2010-11 has been swift and broad-based. The economy is back to its pre-crisis growth trajectory. While agriculture has shown a rebound, industry is regaining its earlier momentum. Services sector continues its near double digit run. Fiscal consolidation has been impressive. The year 2011-12 has also seen significant progress in those critical institutional reforms that would set the pace for double-digit growth in the near future.

While we succeeded in making good progress in addressing many areas of concern, we could have done better in some others. The total food inflation declined from 20.2 per cent in February 2010 to less than half at 9.3 per cent in January 2011, but it still remains a concern. In the medium term perspective, our three priorities of sustaining a high growth trajectory; making development more inclusive; and improving our institutions, public delivery and governance practices, remain relevant. These would continue to engage the Indian policyplanners for some time. However, there are some manifestations of these challenges that need urgent attention in the short term.

Though we have regained the pre-crisis growth momentum, there is a need to effect adjustments in the composition of growth on demand and supply side. We have to ensure that along with private consumption, the revival in private investment is sustained and matches pre-crisis growth rates at the earliest. This requires a stronger fiscal consolidation to enlarge the resource space for private enterprise and for addressing some policy constraints. We also have to improve the supply response of agriculture to the expanding domestic demand. Determined measures on both these issues will help address the structural concerns on inflation management. It will also ensure a more stable macroeconomic environment for continued high growth.

The Government has significantly scaled up the flow of resources to rural areas to give a more inclusive thrust to the development process. The impact is visible in the new dynamism of our rural economy. It has helped India navigate itself rapidly out of the quagmire of global economic slowdown. Yet, there is much that still needs to be done, especially in rural India. We have to reconcile legitimate environmental concerns with necessary developmental needs. Budget for 2011-12 can be seen as a transition towards a more transparent and result oriented economic management system in India. We are taking major steps in simplifying and placing the administrative procedures concerning taxation, trade and tariffs and social transfers on electronic interface, free of discretion and bureaucratic delays. This will set the tone for a newer, vibrant and more efficient economy.

In the budget 2010-11 the Finance Minister had talked about the rolling back of fiscal stimulus implemented over 2008-09 and 2009-10 to mitigate the impact of the global financial crisis on economic slowdown in India. A counter cyclical fiscal policy is our best insurance against external shocks and localised domestic factors.

Tax Reforms

The introduction of the Direct Taxes Code (DTC) and the proposed Goods and Services Tax (GST) will mark a watershed. These reforms will result in the moderation of rates, simplification of laws and better compliance. The Direct Taxes Code Bill was introduced in Parliament in August, 2010. After receiving the report of the Standing Committee, we shall be able to finalise the Code for its enactment during 2011-12. This has been a pioneering effort in participative legislation. The Code is proposed to be effective from April 1, 2012 to allow taxpayers, practitioners and administrators to fully understand the legislation and adjust to the revised procedures.

Unlike DTC, decisions on the GST have to be taken in concert with the States with whom our dialogue has made considerable progress in the last four years. Areas of divergence have been narrowed. As a step towards the roll-out of GST, the Finance Minister proposed to introduce the Constitution Amendment Bill. Work was also underway on drafting of the model legislation for the Central and State GST 24. The other steps that were being taken for the introduction of GST included the establishment of a strong IT infrastructure. Significant progress on the GST Network (GSTN) has been weak. The key business processes of registration, returns and payments were in advanced stages of finalisation. The National Securities Depository Limited (NSDL) was selected as technology partner for incubating the National Information

Utility that will establish and operate the IT backbone for GST. By June 2011, NSDL was to set up a Pilot portal in collaboration with eleven States prior to its roll out across the country.

Foreign Direct Investment

To make the FDI policy more user-friendly, all prior regulations and guidelines have been consolidated into one comprehensive document, which is reviewed every six months. The last review was released in September 2010. This has been done with the specific intent of enhancing clarity and predictability of our FDI policy to foreign investors. Discussions are underway to further liberalise the FDI policy.

Foreign Institutional Investors

Until a few years ago, only FIIs and sub-accounts registered with the SEBI and NRIs were allowed to invest in mutual fund schemes. To liberalise the portfolio investment route, it was decided to permit SEBI registered Mutual Funds to accept subscriptions from foreign investors who meet the KYC requirements for equity schemes. This would enable Indian Mutual Funds to have direct access to foreign investors and widen the class of foreign investors in Indian equity market.

To enhance the flow of funds to the infrastructure sector, the FII limit for investment in corporate bonds, with residual maturity of over five years issued by companies in infrastructure sector, was raised by an additional limit of US Dollar 20 billion taking the limit to US Dollar 25 billion. This raised the total limit available to the FIIs for investment in corporate bonds to US Dollar 40 billion. Since most of the infrastructure companies were organised in the form of SPVs, FIIs would also be permitted to invest in unlisted bonds with a minimum lock-in period of three years. However, the FIIs were allowed to trade amongst themselves during the lock-in period.

Measures in the United States

The Federal Reserve, Treasury, and Securities and Exchange Commission took several steps on 19 September 2008 to intervene in the crisis. To stop the potential run on money market mutual funds, the Treasury also announced a new $50 billion program to insure the investments, similar to the Federal Deposit Insurance Corporation (FDIC) program. Part of the announcements included temporary exceptions to section 23A and 23B (Regulation W), allowing financial groups to more easily share funds within their group. The exceptions were to expire on 30 January 2009, but many of them have been further extended by the Federal Reserve Board. The Securities and Exchange Commission announced termination of short-selling of 799 financial stocks, as well as action against naked short-selling, as part of its reaction to the mortgage crisis.

In the United States of America, economic stimulus package was given the shape of a legislation by making it an act. World financial crisis affected United States most and a number of reputed financial organizations like Lehman Brothers went out of business. In a nutshell, American economy was in poor shape and a radical economic overhaul was necessary in order to bring things back to order.

Stimulus Package—I

In September 2008, the then Secretary of the United States Treasury, Henry Paulson and then President George W. Bush proposed legislation for the Government to purchase up to US$700 billion of "troubled mortgage-related assets" from financial firms in hopes of improving confidence in the mortgage-backed securities markets and the financial firms participating in it. Discussions, hearings and meetings among legislative leaders were held, and the administration made clear that the proposal would undergo significant change before it could be approved by Congress. On 1 October 2008, a revised compromise version was approved by the Senate with a 74-25 vote. The bill, HR1424, was passed by the House on 3 October 2008 and signed into law. The first half of the bailout money was primarily used to buy preferred stock in banks instead of troubled mortgage assets.

Federal Reserve Response

In an effort to increase available funds for commercial banks and lower the fed funds rate, the US Federal Reserve announced on 29 September 2008, plans to double its Term Auction Facility to $300 billion. Because there appeared to be a shortage of US dollars in Europe at that time, the Federal Reserve also announced it would increase its swap facilities with foreign central banks from $290 billion to $620 billion.

As of 24 December 2008, the Federal Reserve had used its independent authority to spend $1.2 trillion on purchasing various financial assets and making emergency loans to address the financial crisis, above and beyond the $700 billion authorized by Congress from the federal budget. This included emergency loans to banks, credit card companies, and general businesses, temporary swaps of Treasury bills for mortgage-backed securities, the sale of Bear Stearns, and the bailouts of American International Group (AIG), Fannie Mae and Freddie Mac, and Citigroup.

Stimulus Package—II

Members of both houses of Congress reached a deal in February 2009 over US President Barack Obama's economic stimulus plan.

Senate majority leader Harry Reid said the deal "bridged differences" between an $820 billion House version of the bill and a $838 billion Senate version. "The package, worth $789 billion (£549 billion), includes tax cuts and spending aimed at rescuing the US economy. The middle ground we have reached creates more jobs than the original Senate bill and costs less than the original House bill," said Senate majority leader Harry Reid. He said the stimulus bill should create 3.5 million jobs. He added that more than one-third of it would be dedicated to tax cuts and incentives for middle-class Americans.

The House approved its $825 billion version of the package without any Republican support. The Senate voted 61-37 to approve a different $838 billion version with few Republicans opting to back it. The bill included help for victims of the recession in the form of unemployment benefits, food stamps, health coverage as well as billions for states that face the prospect of making deep cuts in their own public spending.

The BBC's Richard Lister, in Washington, said it is one of the most expensive pieces of legislation ever to come before the US Congress and it has caused bitter partisan divisions.

Vice President Joe Biden said the passage of the bill would be an important psychological moment for the country as it grapples with the economic downturn. "It is the thing that will kick-start the confidence, the psychology that we can climb out of this," he said. Senator Max Baucus, a Democrat from Montana and one of the negotiators, said that 35 per cent of the total would be in the form of tax cuts.

Provisions of the Final Bill

The final $787 billion version signed by President Obama on February 17, 2009 specifies that 34 per cent of the package is to be devoted to tax cuts equaling $286 billion, and a further $120 billion will be used to fund infrastructure projects. Sixty-four per cent of the package will be allocated for money for social programs and spending. The following details some of the spending:

Department of Defense Facilities

Total: $7.03 billion

$4.2 billion to repair and modernize Department of Defense facilities;

$1.3 billion for medical care for service members and their families;

$890 million to improve housing for service members;

$240 million for new child development centers;

$150 million for the construction of state extended-care facilities;

$150 million for an increase of claims processing staff;

$100 million to improve facilities of the National Guard.

Education

Total: $92 billion

$15.6 billion to increase Pell Grants by $4,731 to $5,350;

$13 billion for low-income public schoolchildren;

$12.2 billion for IDEA special education;

$2.1 billion for Head Start;

$2 billion for childcare services;

$650 million for educational technology;

$300 million for increased teacher salaries;

$250 million for states to analyze student performance;

$200 million to support working college students;

$70 million for the education of homeless children;

$45 billion minimum for education under the State Equalization Fund [35].

Energy

Total: $40.75 billion

$11 billion funding for an electric smart grid;

$6.3 billion for state and local Governments to make investments in energy efficiency;

$6 billion for renewable energy power generation loans;

$5 billion for weatherizing modest-income homes;

$4.5 billion for state and local Governments to increase energy efficiency in federal buildings;

$3.4 billion for carbon capture experiments;

$2.5 billion for energy efficiency research;

$2 billion for car battery (traction) research;

$500 million for training of green-collar workers;

$400 million for electric vehicle technologies;

$300 million to buy energy efficient appliances;

$300 million for reducing diesel fuel emissions;

$300 million for state and local Governments to purchase energy efficient vehicles;

$250 million to increase energy efficiency in low-income housing.

Environmental Cleanup

Total: $6.9 billion

$6 billion for the cleanup of radioactive waste;

$600 million to cleanup hazardous waste that threatens health and the environment;

$200 million to cleanup petroleum leaks from underground storage tanks;

$100 million to evaluate and cleanup brownfield land.

Government Technology Improvements

Total: $864 million

$500 million to update the computer center at the Social Security Administration;

$290 million to upgrade IT platforms at the State Department;

$50 million for IT improvements at the Farm Service Agency;

$24 million to improve security systems at the Department of Agriculture headquarters.

Healthcare

Total: $24.1 billion

$19 billion for health information technology;

$2 billion for Community Health Centers;

$1.1 billion to research the effectiveness of certain healthcare treatments;

$1 billion to fight preventable chronic diseases;

$500 million to train healthcare personnel;

$500 million for healthcare services on Indian reservations.

Housing

Total: $12.69 billion

$4 billion for repairing and modernizing public housing;

$2.25 billion in tax credits for financing low-income housing construction;

$2 billion for Section 8 housing rental assistance;

$2 billion to help communities purchase and repair foreclosed housing;

$1.5 billion for rental assistance and housing relocation;

$510 million for the rehabilitation of Native American housing;

$200 million for helping rural Americans buy homes;

$130 million for rural community facilities;

$100 million to help remove lead paint from public housing.

Hunger Assistance

Total: $20.25 billion

$19.9 billion for the Food Stamp Program;

$150 million to help refill food banks;

$100 million for meals programs for seniors, such as Meals on Wheels;

$100 million for free school lunch programs.

Job Assistance

Total: $4.97 billion

$3.95 billion for job training;

$500 million for vocational training for the disabled;

$400 million for employment services;

$120 million for subsidized community service jobs for older Americans.

Other Infrastructure Projects

Total: $17.355 billion

$4.6 billion for the Army Corps of Engineers for environmental restoration, flood protection, hydropower, and navigation infrastructure projects;

$4 billion for the Clean Water State Revolving Fund (wastewater treatment infrastructure improvements);

$2 billion for the Drinking Water State Revolving Fund (drinking water infrastructure improvements);

$1.38 billion for rural drinking water and waste disposal projects;

$1 billion to the Bureau of Reclamation for drinking water projects for rural or drought-likely areas;

$750 million to the National Park Service;

$650 million to the Forest Service;

$515 million for wildfire prevention projects;

$500 million for Bureau of Indian Affairs infrastructure projects;

$340 million to the Natural Resources Conservation Service for watershed infrastructure projects;

$320 million to the Bureau of Land Management;

$280 million for National Wildlife Refuges;

$280 million for the National Fish Hatchery System;

$250 million to improve Job Corps training facilities;

$220 million to the International Boundary and Water Commission to repair flood control systems along the Rio Grande;

$220 million for other public lands management agencies;

$50 million for the National Endowment for the Arts to support artists.

Other Job Programs

Total: $5.51 billion

$4 billion for state and local law enforcement agencies;

$1 billion in preparation for the 2010 census;

$210 million to build and upgrade fire stations;

$150 million for the security of transit systems;

$150 million for the security of ports.

Other Worker Assistance Programs

Total: $7.27 billion

$4.2 billion to provide an additional Supplemental Security Income and Social Security Disability Insurance payment in 2009;

$1 billion to community action agencies;

$1 billion for community and economic development projects;

$500 million to help the Social Security Administration process, disability and retirement claims;

$200 million for AmeriCorps programs;

$140 million for independent living communities;

$100 million for food, shelter and support services;

$80 million to the Department of Labor Worker Protection and Oversight agency to enforce worker protection laws;

$50 million in grants for community "safety net" organizations.

Scientific Research

Total: $17.55 billion

$8.7 billion to the National Institutes of Health;

$3 billion to the National Science Foundation;

$2 billion to the United States Department of Energy;

$1.3 billion for university research facilities;

$1 billion to NASA;

$600 million to the National Oceanic and Atmospheric Administration (NOAA);

$580 million to the National Institute of Standards and Technology;

$230 million for NOAA operations, research and facilities;

$140 million to the United States Geological Survey.

Telecommunications and Digital TV

Total: $7.85 billion

$7.2 billion for complete broadband and wireless Internet access;

$650 million for DTV conversion coupons and DTV education.

Transportation Projects

Total: $48.76 billion

$27.5 billion for highway and bridge construction projects

$8 billion for high-speed rail projects;

$6.9 billion for new equipment for public transportation projects;

$1.5 billion for competitive grants to state and local Governments for transportation investments;

$1.3 billion for Amtrak;

$1.1 billion for improving airport security;

$750 million for the construction of new public rail transportation systems;

$750 million for the maintenance of existing public transportation systems;

$720 million for improving security at the border and ports of entry;

$240 million for the maintenance of United States Coast Guard facilities.

Veterans Affairs Facilities

Total: $1.05 billion

$1 billion for the Veterans Health Administration;

$50 million for the National Cemetery Administration.

Criticism of Stimulus Plan

Lynn Jenkins, a Republican, said that the economic stimulus bill that President Barack Obama signed into law did not do enough to help states and local Governments with infrastructure improvements. "Less than 3.5 per cent will be spent on roads and bridges, and I think that's unfortunate," Jenkins said, "It looks just like a big spending bill to me, and I'm thinking that's not the direction we should be going right now, given the national debt is already $12 trillion," he added.

Jenkins, the former state treasurer said she supported a bill by the Republican leadership that included deeper tax cuts and more spending on roads and bridges. The Kansas Democratic Party sent out a statement criticizing Jenkins and calling her the "Herbert Hoover of 2009." "By opposing the economic recovery act, Lynn Jenkins voted against creating 33,000 Kansas jobs," said Chris Harris, communications director for the Kansas Democratic Party. "It doesn't take a Certified Public Accountant to understand the beneficial impact it will have on our Kansas economy," Harrio added.

President Obama had not ruled out a second stimulus package, his Press Secretary, Robert Gibbs, said just before Mr Obama signed his $787 billion recovery package into law with a statement that it would "set our economy on a firmer foundation." The President said he would not pretend "that today marks the end of our economic problems. Nor does it constitute all of what we have to do to turn our economy around," Mr Obama said at the signing ceremony in the Denver Museum of Nature and Science. "But today does mark the beginning of the end, the beginning of what we need to do to create jobs for Americans scrambling in the way of layoffs," he added.

Mr Gibbs, speaking to reporters aboard Air Force One on the way to Denver, said, "I think the President is going to do what's necessary to grow this economy." While "there are no particular plans at this point for a second stimulus package," he added, "I wouldn't foreclose it."

Stopping Stimulus Waste

Lawmakers passed a nearly $800 billion stimulus plan—roughly the equivalent of an entire year's discretionary Government spending—in just over a month. When signing the bill, President Obama made big promises. "It's a plan that will be implemented with an unprecedented level of transparency and accountability," Obama told a crowd in Denver. "With a recovery package of this size comes a responsibility to assure every taxpayer that we are being careful with the money they worked so hard to earn." While nearly everyone acknowledged there will be some waste, others were maintaining a cautious if skeptical approach as they wait to see how the spending unfolds.

Perhaps the most novel idea put forth by the White House is a website that is supposed to show where all the money is being spent. The White House, again leveraging an online savvy that helped get them elected, created http://www.recovery.gov/—a site where anyone could go and supposedly see exactly who was getting what. The site contained an overview of the stimulus plan, a chart breaking down where the money was going in broad terms and a handy timeline tracking stimulus milestones and alerting users to upcoming announcements, among other things.

The site promised that "within days after the signing of the legislation, Federal agencies will start distributing funds and you will be able to see which states, Congressional districts, and even Federal contractors are receiving them. As soon as we are able to, we'll display that information visually, through maps, charts and graphics." It went on to say: "You'll be able to send in comments, thoughts, ideas, questions and any responses you have to what you find."

The stimulus plan also increased the budget for the Office of Inspector General in the various federal departments responsible for distributing stimulus money. Each department had an Office of Inspector General charged with investigating and auditing various federal programs. The bill allocated an additional $253 million for these offices to do their work, according to a spokesperson for Senator Claire McCaskill, a Democrat from Missouri, who fought to secure the increased funding.

The administration also created a special board to oversee stimulus spending. The board was supposed to be headed by the Deputy Director for Management of the Office of

Management and Budget and included various Inspector Generals. It was slated to get $84 million in funding, had the power to subpoena and was charged with issuing periodic reports on the stimulus spending.

Republicans in Congress, who generally wanted a much smaller stimulus package (if any at all), criticized the oversight provisions for giving too much power to the President. Mike Steel, a spokesman for House Minority Leader John Boehner, a Republican form Ohio, called the website "a great way of displaying whatever information is put into it." Steel said Congress had very little oversight capacity now that the bill has become law. "We can't rely solely on the administration to self-police," he said. But others dismissed the idea that Congress would actually do anything even if it was given the tools for the job. "Generally, Congress had no record of ever actually doing anything with the oversight reports they get," said Brian Riedl, a federal budget analyst at the conservative Heritage Foundation. Riedl said there will likely be lots of waste in the bill and recommended making all contract awards subject to competitive bidding. Audits, he said, were ineffective because they are done after the fact. But others said audits are an effective tool for deterring waste. "The knowledge that somebody could be checking will increase accountability," said Maya MacGuineas, President of the Committee for a Responsible Federal Budget, a non-partisan watchdog group.

MacGuineas said there's bound to be waste, but also acknowledged the difficult balancing act between passing a robust bill with lots of oversight protections and passing a bill quickly—a requirement most economists say is essential if stimulus is to actually help the economy. "We're striving for as good as we can get," she said.

Critical Evaluation of Stimulus Package

Professor Porter conceded that America did need something to stimulate its ailing economy. But he was not impressed with the shape of the package presented to the US Congress—leaving aside the controversy over the "Buy America" clause.

The initial package included almost $300 billion (£205 billion) of tax-cuts and twice that in extra Government spending, which would extend unemployment benefits, and increase spending in some areas of health care, education and transport. It was all meant to give a short-term jolt to the economy and set in motion projects that will create jobs over the longer term.

The plan left Professor Porter frustrated. In his opinion, much of it displayed "the usual pork-barrel, favourite projects" and he insisted that America ought to be identifying the fundamental challenges facing its economy and the country and investing in those. The country, he said, ought to focus on "issues which would be critical constraints to our future". He accepted that some parts of the stimulus package addressed those subjects, but not enough. He believed that much of it was about the politics of local self-interest. In Professor Porter's view, those included the problem of access to higher education, and a dearth of spending on research and development.

Asked why the plan from the Obama team was being rushed through, Professor Porter considered for a moment, before saying: "I don't think it's so much their plan. "It's a plan that's come out of the political process in Washington," he added. In his view "Washington was broken" and was "good at strategic thinking and had become a circus that jumped from issue to issue and soundbite to soundbite." Professor Porter believed the US had never dealt with any of the real issues that affected its competitiveness such as health care and public education. Any suggestion that these were major problems that needed time and thought for wholesale reform—time that America's economy did not have—were met with a reminder that there were short-term things that could be done immediately. One example would be providing better access to higher education. Increasingly, Professor Porter insisted, university is unaffordable. America's educational attainment in terms of university education had "not gone anywhere in 20 years". The stimulus could provide student loans and grants to support kids going to college, and grants to allow people to re-train, he suggests. "This kind of activity does put money into the economy. It helps the short-term problem, but it's investing behind a fundamental priority, and if we don't address that priority, the country's not going anywhere," he said.

Professor Porter's was not the only voice raised in criticism of the existing stimulus package. Any number of politicians and economists had expressed a range of concerns, but his centred on America's long-term competitiveness. He hoped though, that the plan may yet be adjusted. "President Obama has an ability to break the pattern", he said. "It will be interesting to see if he can use his tremendous, amazing popularity to start to nip and tuck on this stimulus package and get more of it aligned with the nation's real agenda."

But could the United States manage to re-invent itself? Professor Porter expressed his tremendous faith in the resiliency and dynamism of the US economy "which over and over again, takes its hits and moves on". People across the world should not be pessimistic about the US, he insisted, though there was a "but".

With the current stimulus plan, he says, "we're falling into the trap of taking an enormous amount of money that we really don't have right now, and not necessarily spending it well".

The Obama stimulus plan was certainly more ambitious and costlier than many expected, especially in its use of Fannie Mae and Freddie Mac to influence the mortgage market. An analysis by IHS Global Insight concluded that it would help prevent some number of "preventable" foreclosures. But between 10 million and 15 million homeowners were in default and that number was growing at that time.

But it was certainly debatable whether a savior-based plan to prevent foreclosures was necessary. Did America need to "save" homeowners who had sinned against the gods of financial prudence? According to Weiss Research, "Foreclosures are actually resulting in overpriced homes burdened with too much debt being moved into the hands of new buyers, who are paying drastically reduced prices. They can therefore purchase using a traditional mortgage....

Delaying and dragging out the downturn by artificially propping up home prices would arguably work against the market healing."

In the same vein, former Bush economic adviser Lawrence Lindsey suggested an immigration program that would give a provisional green card to anyone who invested at least $10 million in residential property and held it for five years. And bond guru David Goldman of the Inner Workings blog said that he had been getting inquiries from Chinese investors interested in the US housing market. He also highlighted what was easily the worst aspect of the Obama plan, the "cramdown" provision which would allow judges to modify mortgages. "Allowing judges to show generosity to homeowners...and keep them in their homes makes the core assets of the banking system uncertain.... Cramdown probably was responsible for the deterioration of subprime...." That's what happens when you toss 1,000 years of contract law out of the window in the middle of a global financial crisis.

But the plan fell short of what some experts were pushing for, in both elegance and scope. For instance, Alan Blinder, the former Fed vice chairman, wanted a $400 billion, 21st-century version of the New Deal-era Home Owners' Loan Corp, which bought mortgages from banks and then issued more affordable new loans to struggling homeowners. Then there were Glenn Hubbard and Christopher Mayer of the Columbia Business School who advocated a $338 billion plan to allow all mortgages on primary residences to be refinanced into low 30-year, fixed-rate mortgages. And independent investment strategist Ed Yardeni and Carl Goldsmith of Delta Asset Management proposed fully nationalizing Fannie Mae and Freddie Mac and then offering a trillion bucks worth of 30-year, fixed-rate mortgages at 4 per cent to all qualified borrowers to buy a new or existing home.

Maybe one of these pricey plans could have turned around the housing, the market and the economy. Maybe not. But Obama's surely won't. And that's not really the intent, apparently. It's all about stabilization. As the President himself said, "If we act boldly and swiftly to arrest this downward spiral, then every American will benefit. It will prevent the worst consequences of this crisis from wreaking even greater havoc on the economy.... And by bringing down the foreclosure rate, it will help to shore up housing prices for everybody."

"Arresting downward spirals." "Preventing the worst." "Shoring up prices." These were the statements and there was some overhyping the benefits of stimulus packages. The Fed thought that the unemployment rate could climb to over 9 per cent in and 2010 and still be above 8 per cent in 2011—some four years after the recession began. And the Philadelphia Fed surveyed 43 forecasters who predicted that the unemployment rate will be 8.9 per cent in the fourth quarter of 2009. Unemployment was expected to average 8.4 per cent in 2009 and 8.8 per cent in 2010.

AMERICA'S SECTOR-SPECIFIC BAILOUT PLANS

Auto Bailout

GM and Chrysler said they needed $21.6 billion more in loans. But that won't be enough to save Detroit.

General Motors and Chrysler LLC asked the Government for $21.6 billion in additional loans, but the final cost of a bailout of the auto industry was significantly higher. The two struggling auto giants had already received a total of $17.4 billion in loans.

Funds amounting to $7.5 billion in loans had already been approved for the financing arms of GM and Chrysler. Congress also approved in 2008, a funding of $25 billion in loans to help automakers convert their plants to produce more fuel efficient cars. But dealers and suppliers were also asking for federal aid. And consumers may eventually get further incentives from the Government to buy new cars. It was believed it could take up to $130 billion to save Detroit. A breakdown of the rest of the money that was needed is explained below.

Loan guarantees requested by auto parts suppliers was $18.5 billion. The trade groups for parts suppliers were asking loan guarantees for the amount that domestic automakers owed to them. They were also seeking guarantees on other types of commercial loans and help so that General Motors and Chrysler pay their suppliers more quickly. Loan guarantees requested by auto dealers amounted between $5 billion and $20 billion. But the National Automobile Dealers Association was working on a request for federal loan guarantees to make sure they could get the cash they needed to finance their inventories. NADA Vice President and general counsel Andrew Koblenz said it was likely to be in the range of $5 billion to $20 billion.

Line of credit requested by Ford was $9 billion. Ford Motor continued to insist that it shouldn't need federal help, primarily because it locked up financing years before the credit markets dried up. But in December 2008, the automaker had asked Congress to approve a $9 billion line of credit for the company in case sales were worse than expected or a rival's bankruptcy caused widespread failures in its own supplier or dealership base. Since that request, car sales had plunged further and forecasts for 2009 had grown increasingly bleak.

Tax credit for "Cash for Clunkers" program was $16 billion. There were a couple of different proposals floating around Capitol Hill to have the federal Government give buyers of new, fuel-efficient vehicles a tax credit of up to $10,000 if they turned in an old, fuel-inefficient vehicle to be scrapped. One version of the proposal, which would have been available for 1.6 million buyers, was briefly included in the economic stimulus package before it was stripped out. But stand-alone versions of the bill were still being discussed in the Congress, and they had support of both the auto industry and environmentalists.

Allowing car buyers to deduct interest on auto loans amounted to $9 billion. This proposal from Senator Barbara Mikulski, easily passed the Senate during debate on the stimulus bill. But it was stripped out of the final version, leaving a far more modest tax credit that allowed buyers to deduct only the sales and excise tax they paid on a new car purchase. Auto dealers and automakers were strong supporters of making interest deductible as a way to spur demand.

If the Obama administration had decided to move ahead with additional loans for GM and Chrysler, it may have wrapped various proposals into one auto bailout bill. Still, there would be questions about where future funding will come from. Much of the money for Detroit thus far had come from the Troubled Asset Relief Program, the $700 bailout of the nation's financial system approved in 2008.

But much, if not all, of the additional money would was to be approved by Congress, rather than just Treasury. The House passed a $34 billion bailout for GM, Chrysler and Ford in December 2008 but it failed to win approval from enough Republicans in the Senate. But the Democratic majority of both houses had grown significantly since then. So it was likely that a similar bailout measure would find the 60 votes needed to advance in the Senate, assuming all Democrats supported it as they did the stimulus bill passed earlier. The automakers' strongest argument for getting the help to get the industry back on its feet was that it could cost the Government far more if they fail. GM and Chrysler both included estimates in viability plans submitted to the Treasury about how much they would need to fund their operations if they went through a bankruptcy reorganization. GM said it could cost up to $100 billion in loans over two years, while Chrysler estimated it would cost between $20 billion and $25 billion. Both companies said that if they went bankrupt, they would be forced to halt operations and liquidate if they did not receive the loans. And if they were to go out of business, lost federal tax revenue would reach hundreds of billions of dollars, according to company estimates.

Experts agreed that a bankruptcy at either company would be far more expensive for taxpayers than the amount of money they were asking for. "There would be nothing standard about a bankruptcy filing at GM," said Michigan bankruptcy attorney Douglas Bernstein. "You don't normally have the Government as your lender. And I don't think anybody has been through a bankruptcy of this magnitude."

Obama Housing Plan

The Obama administration's housing rescue plan committed up to $275 billion in funds to help reduce mortgage payments for up to 9 million families and arrest the devastating fall in US home prices. According to the plan, $50 billion to modify mortgages were to come from the $700 billion financial bailout fund approved by Congress in 2008; up to $25 billion in direct costs to finance firms Fannie Mae and Freddie Mac to modify mortgages. Up to $200 billion from the US Treasury to increase capital for Fannie and Freddie if necessary, authorized under a housing bill passed in 2008.

The plan enabled refinancing for 4 million to 5 million "responsible" homeowners who took out conforming 30-year fixed mortgages with a down payment of 20 per cent or more and were current on payments. The decline in home values meant many of these families couldn't qualify for conventional refinancing because their loan-to-value ratio then exceeded 80 per cent. The program would allow mortgages owned or guaranteed by Fannie Mae and Freddie Mac to be refinanced through private lenders, reducing monthly payments, as long as the amount owed on a first mortgage did not exceed 105 per cent of the property's current market value. Refinancing rates were to be based on market rates in effect at the time of the refinance plus any associated points and fees quoted by the lender. All of the refinanced loans under the plan were to be in 30-year or 15-year fixed-rate notes. Mortgage lenders started accepting applications after program details were announced on 4 March 2009.

The initiative intended to reach 3 million to 4 million "at risk" homeowners who were struggling to meet their mortgage payments. It aimed to bring payments down to 31 per cent of a borrower's monthly income through modifications at no cost to the borrower. Program targeted owner-occupants with high mortgage debt compared to income or those with "underwater" mortgages that exceeded the value of their homes. Borrowers did not have to miss payments to qualify. Borrowers with high total debt obligations exceeding 55 per cent of their income had to enter consumer debt counseling to help reduce car, credit card and other debt to receive mortgage modifications. The US Treasury was to share the cost of reducing payments with mortgage lenders and servicers. Lenders were to agree to cut interest rates so that monthly payments are no more than 38 per cent of a borrower's income. The Treasury was to match those reductions dollar-for-dollar to bring down payments to 31 per cent of income. Lenders had to agree to keep the modified payments in place for five years. The Obama administration was to seek "careful" changes to bankruptcy law to allow judges to rewrite mortgage terms on loans originated in the past few years. This would apply only to existing mortgages under the GSE conforming loan limits "so that millionaire homes don't clog the bankruptcy courts."

Lenders were to participate in the "at risk" loan modifications on a voluntary basis, but were to receive substantial incentives to do so. The administration anticipated that most major lenders would participate. Mortgage servicers were to get $1,000 for each successful modification under the program, and up to $3,000 over three years if the borrowers stayed current on payments. Mortgage holders also were to receive $1,500 and servicers would receive $500 if the modifications were made before a borrower defaults. Borrowers were to receive up to $5,000 in loan principal reductions over five years if they stayed current on payments. The Treasury was to fund a $10 billion insurance fund to protect lenders against home value declines as a means to discourage foreclosures based on anticipation of falling home prices. Holders of modified mortgages could receive payments from the fund if a home price index fell more than expected, and these could be used as reserves to offset potential increases in foreclosure losses.

The Treasury was to double its capital funding commitments to Fannie Mae and Freddie Mac to $200 billion each under a preferred stock purchase mechanism launched in 2008. The increased backstop did not anticipate increased cash draws or a change in financial position, but was aimed at strengthening investor confidence in the two firms, helping to lower their funding costs and reduce mortgage rates. Fannie's and Freddie's retained mortgage portfolios were to be allowed to increase under the agreements by $50 billion each to $900 billion each. This would be accompanied by corresponding increases in allowable outstanding debt. The Obama administration was also to work with Fannie and Freddie to support state housing finance agencies to help homebuyers.

Financial Sector Rescue Programme—An Assessment

The magnitude of the actions taken to support the banking system as a fallout of the global financial crisis had been unprecedented. As per a BIS estimate, the overall amount of resources committed to the various packages by eleven countries (namely, Australia, Canada, France, Germany, Italy, Japan, the Netherlands, Spain, Switzerland, the United Kingdom and the United States) totalled around euro 5 trillion or 18.8 per cent of GDP; and the outlays were euro 2 trillion or 7.6 per cent of GDP.

The size of the interventions varied greatly across countries. It was higher in countries such as the United Kingdom and the Netherlands, where outlays had reached 44.1 per cent and 16.6 per cent of GDP, respectively. In these countries the banking system is large relative to the real economy and is dominated by large institutions that had been severely hit by the crisis. It was lower in countries such as Japan (0.1 per cent of GDP) and Italy (0.6 per cent) where banks are more focused on traditional credit activities and had been less affected by the crisis. Actions for addressing capital shortages and funding difficulties had been widespread and had mostly taken the form of systemwide programmes.

Measures for improving the quality of bank assets had been less common and had mainly targeted individual large institutions. However, some of the initiatives included comprehensive schemes for dealing with illiquid or bad assets. Among banks that participated in both recapitalisation and debt guarantee programmes, the intermediaries that had received more capital in relation to shareholder equity had also issued more liabilities under guarantee, in relation to total liabilities.

Moreover, most instances of asset purchase/guarantee occurred after earlier capital injections, suggesting that this option was used after a first phase of Government support failed to fully restore confidence in troubled institutions. The average uptake rate by eligible institutions (i.e., the ratio of outlays under a given programme to total commitments) was higher for capital injections (around 50 per cent) than for debt guarantees (less than 20 per cent). The United Kingdom had the highest participation rate for both capital injections and debt guarantees, possibly reflecting the relatively small number of major banks and the tailoring of Government programmes to their needs.

Governments around the globe had to intervene to prevent a wholesale collapse of the financial system. They had injected more than US$ 200 billion in fresh capital into the top 20 banks alone besides the much larger asset and debt guarantees. It was clear that the developed countries' banking sectors to a large extent now depended at that time on massive Government support. If the immediate value destruction in the global banking industry seemed large, the scale of the challenges was even bigger in terms of loss in GDP. The effects of the financial sector rescue measures can be summarised as follows:

- Government interventions were effective in reducing banks' default risk, particularly over a short time horizon. On an average, the announcement of systemwide rescue packages was followed by a fall in CDS premia, especially for announcements of capital injections.
- There seem to be positive spillover effects across countries in terms of CDS spreads showing "early declines" after the announcements of packages by others.
- Some important perceptions emerged from these developments. First, Government intervention had not been sufficient, at least so far, to trigger a

> "virtuous circle" for banks such as a mutually reinforcing increase in capital and borrowing on the one hand and lending and profits on the other. For example, between the first and the second quarter of 2009, the portion of overall bank funding provided or guaranteed by Governments sharply declined. Secondly, the rescue measures had been effective in stabilising the financial system, but this came at a price, represented by distortions and inefficiencies. This was an example of the trade-off that existed between the stability and the efficiency of the financial system.[1]

While bailouts are needed in the short run, these bailouts, as cogently argued by Professor Shiller, must be targeted at low-income victims of subprime deals. In the longer term, the subprime solution requires revamping of the financial framework by a slew of initiatives to reduce the formation of bubbles and limit risks, including better financial information; simplified legal contracts and regulations; expanded markets for managing risks; home equity insurance policies; income-linked home loans; and new measures to protect consumers against hidden inflationary effects. The success of these measures possibly unfroze credit and prevented a serious recession. This is why economic stimulus is a necessary but not a sufficient condition. Consequently, while injecting economic stimulus, all-out efforts were made to restore confidence and fully overhaul the financial system. Managing change needed is a concerted and coordinated approach to the crisis that crippled an inextricably linked system.

Stimulus saved 3 Million US Jobs

Obama mentioned the dire state of the economy he inherited when he took office in January 2009, and claimed credit for stopping an economic freefall in which employers were shedding workers at a rate of 700,000 a month.

The American economy had been creating private-sector jobs in the years following the crisis, but at a slow pace. But, for quite some time, US unemployment rate remained at a stubbornly high 9.5 per cent, fueling Americans' frustrations with the lackluster recovery.

The $18 bn Jobs Stimulus Package

The US Congress approved $18-billion package of incentives to revive the struggling US labour market. According to Barack Obama "It is the first of what I hope will be a series of jobs packages that help to continue to put people back to work all across America."

The US unemployment rate stood at 9.7 per cent in February 2010, near a quarter-century high, even as the world's largest economy had begun growing again after a deep recession. The high jobless rate put pressure on Obama and his fellow Democrats to take further steps to encourage hiring. The package included tax credits for small businesses that hire workers and extends infrastructure spending.

"Obama did exactly the opposite of what should have been done," Taleb said in Montreal in a speech as part of Canada's Salon Speakers series. "He surrounded himself with people who exacerbated the problem. You have a person who has cancer and instead of removing the cancer, you give him tranquilizers. When you give tranquilizers to a cancer patient, they feel better but the cancer gets worse," he continued.

Obama proposed a package of $180 billion in business tax breaks and infrastructure outlays to boost spending and job growth. That would come on top of the $814 billion stimulus measure enacted last year. The US government's total outstanding debt is about $13.5 trillion, according to US Treasury Department figures.

Obama inherited what the National Bureau of Economic Research said was the deepest US recession since the Great Depression. Even after the stimulus measure and other government actions, the US unemployment rate is 9.6 per cent.

The Challenge and the Response—Calibrated Policy Moves for Close Performance Monitoring

The central bank of USA and Japan, i.e. the Federal Reserve and the Bank of Japan slashed their policy rates to zero and the British and European central banks also followed similar paths. Central banks also bought back large quantities of bonds from banks. This triad of infusion of cash, low rates and the fact that banks began to trust each other again restored a modicum of order, a thaw in inter-bank markets and halted the southward movement of lending rates. In line with such global policy initiatives, India responded to the challenge through fiscal stimulus injected by the Government and the RBI's policy of monetary accommodation and adoption of counter-cyclical regulatory measures to provide ample rupee liquidity, comfortable foreign exchange liquidity and credit flow to productive sectors.

The Government's strategic options and choices were constrained because of heavy fiscal stress emanating from oil, fertiliser, food subsidies; pay commission, debt waiver and the stimulus packages implemented in the face of a GFD/GDP ratio: 5.5-6.0 per cent. There were also large increases in market borrowings.

The RBI adopted both conventional measures such as reduction in the Repo rate from 9 per cent to 5 per cent, reduction in Cash Reserve Ratio from 9 per cent to 5 per cent, relaxed norms for external borrowings, raised interest rate ceilings on NRI deposits and unconventional measures, such as, Rupee-dollar swap facility for Indian banks, the effective reduction in the SLR from 25 per cent to 21.5 per cent with 1.5 per cent points of the reduction earmarked for liquidity support by banks to mutual funds and NBFCs. But these measures were not good enough. In an extremely insightful paper, Jahangir Aziz, Ajaya Shah and Ila Patnaik made wide-ranging suggestions such as cutting CRR to 5 per cent and SLR to 20 per cent, making oil and fertiliser bonds SLR-eligible, increasing the range of repo-eligible assets and even providing insurance against counterparty risk in interbank transactions, setting up a weekly dollar-swap facility against rupee-denominated assets and investing part of the foreign exchange reserves in one-year deposits in foreign branches of Indian banks. While these suggestions did not find universal acceptance, there is no doubt that given the enormity of the crisis, innovative and 'out-of-box' solutions were seriously considered to shore up the financial system. The success of the monetary stimuli was reflected in growth in advances and deposits by 24 per cent (year on year) and 22 per cent (year on year), respectively in FY09 because of a sharp expansion in term deposits and growth in agricultural and large corporate credit.

It is widely agreed that by the end of 2009, the worst was over but considerable damage had been done leading to debt restructuring, a rise in delinquency levels in retail credit and higher NPAs. Consequently, the banks in India perforce became more risk-averse, which had implications for credit disbursement and a focus on analyzing borrowers' financial health rather than capability. The banking sector also lost its pricing power. The risk of higher inflation because of excess liquidity led to higher bond yields and losses on bond portfolios.

Gross NPAs to gross advances ratio of SCBs declined from the high of 14 per cent in 2000-01 to 2.3 per cent in 2008-09. Foreign banks and the private sector banks grew faster than the industry from 2002-03 to 2008-09 primarily due to lower base effect and the rapid growth of these banks. In 2008-09, the total growth in lending and deposits was led by the PSBs. However, the growth of private and foreign banks was significantly lower in 2008-09 because of their high exposure to sensitive sectors.

Unsecured bank credit increased over the years, reaching 23.3 per cent of bank lending in 2008-09, compared with only 10.9 per cent in 2000-01. Lending to sensitive sector also grew by 46.1 per cent CAGR over 2004-05 to 2008-09. Against this backdrop, it was expected that future credit growth will be led by spending on infrastructure, while the retail credit will grow moderately.

The significance of retail lending, particularly housing loans, which constituted a significant portion of the portfolio for most banks, reduced because of higher risk weightage and provisioning requirements. The banks, however, mobilised a higher proportion of low cost deposits with a greater outreach in the semi urban and rural areas. This helped them to reduce the cost of funds. Apart from streamlining their processes through technology initiatives such as ATMs, telephone banking, online banking and web-based products, banks also resorted to greater cross selling of financial products such as credit cards, mutual funds and insurance policies to augment their fee based income.

Indian banks benefitted from higher levels of money supply, credit and deposits as a proportion of GDP in FY09 as compared to that in the preceding year.

China's Stimulus Package

According to Chen Demius, China's Minister of Commerce, China's stimulus package not only spurred up domestic demand, but also benefited world economic recovery and global policy coordinating.

He said at a press conference held on the sidelines of the annual session of the National People's Congress (NPC), the country's top legislature, "China's stimulus incentives on domestic consumption and exports abide by the rules of the World Trade Organization and bear no protectionism". "Although China's exports have regained momentum since the beginning of this year, it would take two or three years for exports to return to the level of 2008, as uncertainties would remain in global recovery," he said. Chen noted the pro-consumption measures implemented in 2009 including subsidies to the auto and home appliance buyers also invited the participation of foreign businesses. "...more than 20 business leaders of the Fortune 500 companies told me their business in China outshined their performance in other countries last year," he said. It is pertinent to mention here that China's exports slipped 16 per cent in 2009 as global recession sapped demand for Chinese goods.

Japan's $81 billion Economic Stimulus

Japan's government agreed on a $81 billion stimulus package in December 2009, aimed at preventing the economy from tipping back into recession as deflation persists and a strong yen threatens exports. Economists said the 7.2 trillion yen plan, equal to about 1.5 per cent of gross domestic product, would not provide a significant lift to an economy dependent on overseas demand for machinery, electronics and cars.

While several other economies were already debating phasing out economic stimulus deployed to fight the financial crisis, Japan continued to struggle amid chronically weak consumer demand and falling prices.

The budget highlighted the balancing act faced by Prime Minister Yukio Hatoyama and his Democratic Party. The Democrats were keen to avoid a recession but were also under pressure to make good on their pledge of fiscal discipline as the country's public debt nears 200 per cent of GDP, by far the worst among G7 nations.

"This may help the economy somewhat," said Yasunari Ueno, chief market economist at Mizuho Securities. "But it doesn't even begin to address the more fundamental issues facing Japan, such as weaknesses in the global economy and deflation." Japan pulled out of recession in April-June 2009 thanks to a recovery in exports.

However, Japan's growth slowed further in the first half of 2010 as the effect of nearly 27 trillion yen stimulus agreed by the previous Liberal Democratic Party government, weared off.

The new package, earmarked for low-interest mortgages for new home buyers, incentives for users of "green" technologies and extended subsidies for energy-efficient cars and household appliances, aimed to encourage reluctant Japanese consumers to spend more.

Analysts, however, were skeptical about the plan's impact and while most expected Japan to avoid a double-dip recession, those who predicted another slump were not swayed by the latest spending plan.

Financial markets showed a muted reaction to the package that was to be mostly funded with contingency funds and money redirected from what the Democrats described as wasteful spending in an earlier plan drawn up by the LDP. The Democrats pledged to fund their policies without any extra borrowing, but Finance Minister Hirohisa Fujii said that the new package would require issuing more than 100 billion yen in new bonds. While that would add only marginally to overall debt supply, Fujii also said an expected shortfall in tax revenues of more than 9 trillion yen would drive this fiscal year's new debt supply to around 53 trillion yen, up 20 per cent from the initial estimate.

Global Initiatives Imperative for Structural Reforms of the World's Financial System

The global financial system proved to be woefully inadequate, particularly in view of the manifest structural deficiencies in meeting the regulatory requirements of the present-day international financial system of the Bretton Woods architecture, which led to the establishment of the International Monetary Fund in 1945. The crisis drove home the significance of broad multilateral collaboration and cooperation in economic and financial policymaking and thus brought to the fore the imperative necessity of coordinated and concerted efforts by all countries to make the financial systems healthier and more resilient to global financial sector risks. Cross-country analysis clearly brings out the need for the international financial institutions' need to be made more robust in order to enable them to meet the financial needs of poor developing countries badly affected by the crisis. The world's financial architecture must change drastically because world unemployment could remain high at least for a couple of years, with the vulnerable being particularly hit. Hence, while highlighting the key challenges and variables that need to be addressed, developing countries need to understand social outcomes and devise appropriate social protection schemes.

The extraordinarily synchronized nature of the sub-prime crisis is necessary to launch the creation of a "global monitoring authority to promote global supervision" of cross-border investment, trade and banking with the fast-growing economies such as China, India and Brazil playing a far more important role in the new global financial architecture and ensuring that the results trickle down to the grassroots level. The world's financial architecture must change drastically in conformity with the transformed realities, particularly because, as cogently argued by Juan Somavia, world unemployment could increase by 20 million in the process surpassing the 200-million-mark for the first time. What lends urgency to the need to devise effective remedies is the near certainty that the poor, the deprived and the vulnerable are affected much more severely than the better-off and the crisis could throw 200 million additional people into poverty. Hence, the developing countries need to understand the social outcomes and provide appropriate social protection schemes to reduce the devastating impact of the crisis.

While devising a new global financial system we need a broad spectrum strategy to surmount this crisis and move ahead on the road back to solvency by initiating a series of developmental measures such as sustaining liquidity, reducing volatility in foreign exchange rate, allowing capital inflows and keeping domestic and external financing available. Towards this end of providing a long-term solution, the contours of the new regulatory paradigm necessitate designing more effective early warning systems; strengthening transparency and accountability; enhancing regulation including underwriting standards; coordinated actions and reinforcing international cooperation between countries and multilateral institutions, e.g. G7, IMF, IBRD, WTO; reinforced international institutions; assessment of the role of sovereign wealth funds as providers of capital in the context of inadequacy of financial institutions' capital cushions; examination of the role of the big three rating agencies, particularly Standard & Poor's, Moody's and Fitch, in structuring and rating securities; good central bank governance and effective public communication; and continuous evaluation and effectiveness of policy tools.

The financial stability process needs to grapple with the challenges of regulatory failure in the US, draw lessons from this regulatory failure and implement a transparent and effective framework in conformity with the growth and diversification of our economy and financial sector. But financial stability, particularly in the wake of technological innovation, structural changes in banking, and the evolution of central bank policies is a process, not a one-off miracle to be attained by sudden policy shifts and operational measures. It was felt that domestic reforms must be accompanied by prudential norms, efficient regulatory systems and healthy capital adequacy norms with a focus on prudent investments and quality lending. Since institutional resilience can effectively reduce the severity and duration of economic shocks and dislocations, it was well recognized that there has to be an accent on institutional strengthening to ensure that exercise regulation does not stifle innovation.

Juan Somavia, Director-General of the International Labour Organisation correctly stressed "the current search for better financial regulation and a global surveillance mechanism of checks and balances was a welcome step. But we must reach beyond the financial system. This is not simply a crisis on Wall Street; it is a crisis on all streets". Given that it was an overarching crisis, building a post-crisis global economy needed creation of an effective multilateral agency, including a new global regulatory agency. In view of the inherent limitations of unilateralism in a world of economic interdependence, support from a truly global polity with a focus on internationally coherent and decisive policy measures was sorely needed to restore confidence in the global financial system. As the G-7 Summit stressed, what was needed was "a coherent framework that will direct our individual and collective policy steps to provide liquidity to markets, strengthen financial institutions, protect savers, and enforce investor protection".

Apart from taking concrete steps to revive growth, bringing a boost in funding for the IMF, longer-lasting changes in the character of banking and investment banking and initiating an exploration of the ways to reshape the world's financial and economic order to restore trust in the financial system, developed countries must not resort to protectionism and global capital flows must remain unimpeded. A paradigm shift of the system must be based on the realization that the unprecedented budgets for structural policies are neither economically efficient nor politically acceptable. Hence, all markets, all territories, and all actors putting the global financial system at risk should be regularly monitored with zero tolerance for non-compliance with the rules of finance. Streamlined and transparent auditing standards must come into force and the rating agencies must be effectively regulated with stricter rules, a specific rating scale for complex products and regular publication of their returns.

The World Bank and the IMF identified measures to strengthen economic and financial stability, improve market functioning and, in turn, boost market confidence in the pursuit of sustained global recovery. The IMF in its "Global Financial Stability Report: Responding to the Financial Crisis and Measuring Systemic Risks" stressed the need to redefine global financial regulation and revamp the financial architecture.

The basic challenge in financial stability, from a diagnostic viewpoint, relates to breaking what the IMF described as the "downward spiral between the financial system and the global economy". Central to this will be the effectiveness of the multilateral bodies in redesigning the financial system, specifically the monitoring and regulatory functions, with the IMF estimating the worldwide losses for financial institutions at $4.1 trillion. As lax regulation contributed significantly to the crisis, the IMF report's call for bolder steps by governments, including nationalization, where necessary, needs serious consideration.

A well-informed understanding of the various aspects that go into the making of financial stability, the role of global cooperation in rejigging the international financial rules and systems, the identification of the most appropriate development rules and the role of developing countries in minimising financial contagion must constitute important building blocks in the road back from the crisis. There should be implementation of mechanisms to protect developing countries from the impact of the economic meltdown to ensure that the projected slower growth rates do not mean reduced allocation for the social sector in national budgets. The World Bank's decision to triple its investment in social protection programmes for 2009-10 from about $4 billion two years before the economic crisis was a welcome step. The Bank estimated in the "Global Monitoring Report, 2009" that close to 90 per cent of the developing countries were highly or moderately exposed to the impact of the crisis, as they faced slowing economic growth, high levels of poverty, or both.

Experience from the Latin American countries brought out the effectiveness of well-designed social protection programmes in stimulating public spending, apart from boosting human development through better education and healthcare. The vulnerable sections in the developing world, e.g. those without any form of social safety nets, has to be the focus of such programmes. Ban Ki-moon, the UN Secretary General, argued "Now more than ever we must be bold. In these times of crisis, when we are tempted to look inward, it is precisely the time when we must move pursuit of the common good to the top of the agenda. While recently we have heard much in the US about how problems on Wall Street are affecting innocent people on Main Street, we need to think more about those people around the world with no streets".

Role of Monetary and Fiscal Measures

Even in this era of sweeping globalization, the free play of the unfettered market mechanism (*laissez faire* economic theory) is fraught with great danger and there are inherent limitations to the theory that "state intervention is always flawed". Conventional microeconomics and the theory of "market fundamentalism", which have their origins in the work of Adam Smith, would have us believe that the objective relations between supply and demand bring about the desired equilibrium point with regulation being not only unnecessary but also detrimental. But, as the events showed, the markets did not oscillate around an equilibrium point but injected an upward bias into the system through speculation.

While monetary policy has to respond effectively to asset prices, manage capital flow volatility, discourage over-leveraging and promote active dynamic financial regulation with capital buffers and dynamic provisioning together with reduced regulatory arbitrage incentives/possibilities, attempts have to be made to avoid high volatility in monetary policy. In the words of Joseph Stiglitz "the reason that the invisible hand often seems invisible is that it is not there". In the present world, where all elements are critically in ferment, the market on its own is not enough and the market mystique needs to be examined with caution, the governments must play an important role in shaping the economic policies and the broader frame of reference. The Keynesian thesis of "pump-priming" continues to be relevant today and fiscal stimulus has an important part in the route back from the precipice. Given the overarching fiscal stress and the kinds of predicaments faced, what is needed is not just larger but also smarter and highly selective investment prioritized on national goals and on performance outcomes. Investments in infrastructure and technology in general and speedy implementation of various components of the National Highways Development Projects power projects and airport privatisation in non-metro cities will stimulate the economy in the short run and enhance growth in the long run.

Both economic theory and cross-country experiences strongly suggested that in such turbulent times, a proactive and responsive monetary policy and fiscal policy with timely, targeted, and temporary measures could provide the much needed stimulus to the economy and mitigate the severity of recession. Indeed this is what both the Government and the RBI attempted to do in India.

While the RBI reversed its earlier stance of a tight monetary policy, the government announced a series of fiscal stimulus packages to step up overall economic activity. Banks must put in place a constellation of measures both on interest rates and liquidity because of the implications for development policy. Towards this end, banks must ensure both the timeliness and reasonable pricing of credit, particularly to the SMEs and the housing sectors in India. SMEs must be allowed credit at close to BPLR rates depending on the creditworthiness of the unit and the project.

Sound Enterprise Risk Management (ERM)

In today's business environment, managing risk constitutes an integral part of an organization's long-term strategy impacting long-term profitability and sustainability. The ERM process involves establishing context, identifying risks, analyzing/quantifying risks, integrating risks, assessing/ prioritizing risks, treating/exploiting risks, monitoring and reviewing. The success of a firm depends on the right balance between enhancing profits and adroitly managing risk. Since successful firms manage risk effectively, risk management process must provide reasonable assurance of achieving corporate objectives such as alignment of existing programmes to the corporate objective, alignment to strategic goals through project prioritisation, "glocalisation" (think global, act local), effective marshalling of resources, reliable reporting, tracking of progress, costs and benefits and compliance with applicable laws and regulations.

Following are the key themes for moving towards sustainable growth:

- Putting in place changed risk framework encompassing risk governance, organisations and processes.
- Reexamination of instruments of Central Banks for emergency liquidity support and convergence by Central Banks to best practices. Central banks must continue to work in unison during this period of market stress and take steps in conformity with emerging need and requirements.
- Avoiding high volatility in monetary policy; appropriate response of monetary policy to asset prices.
- Having a sharper focus of financial firms on liquidity risk management and risk transmissions and check on credit derivatives.
- Restricting the spread of dislocations to other markets and to repair banks' balance sheets through greater capital infusions into banks and

recapitalization of institutions to boost confidence and avoid further undermining of credit channels.

- Monitoring over-leveraging; effecting changes in the design of regulation of mortgage to prevent the recurrence of a supply overhang.
- The traditional virtues of savings and thrift need to be encouraged. There is a clear need to strictly adhere to well-defined policies and procedures of decision-making and not to undertake imprudent risk in the future. Banks and financial institutions should extend loans to households on the basis of the traditional canons of disposable income, security norms and repayment capacity.
- Fostering a risk culture throughout the business-risk is too important to be left to risk managers alone.
- There should be a changed design of regulation of mortgage to prevent recurrence of a supply overhang leading to painfully corrected housing prices.
- Active dynamic financial regulation is needed with thrust on capital buffers, dynamic provisioning and reduced regulatory arbitrage incentives/possibilities.
- Desisting from imprudent risk, following sanction of household loans on the basis of the traditional canons of disposable income, security norms and repayment capacity.
- There should be a focus on business sense for risk monitoring changed risk measures and capital adequacy ratios, redesigned incentive schemes and preparation for the worst.

Three stimulus packages made obsolete the notion that we have fiscal changes through a budget once a year. Instead, radical budgetary changes for eight months have eclipsed anything proposed in regular budgets. The stimulus packages have cut standard excise duty from 14 per cent to 10 per cent and then further to 8 per cent. Service tax has been cut from 12 per cent to 10 per cent. Import and countervailing duties have been raised on steel and cement. Duty drawback rates have been increased for exporters. Besides, a host of monetary measures have reduced interest rates, increased liquidity, and directed credit to sectors in need.

CII Recommendations

The Confederation of Indian Industry (CII) made recommendations to the new Government on the 100 days action plan. Titled "Economic Agenda for Action: CII Suggestions", the paper aimed at addressing resilience and competitiveness of the Indian economy. Key recommendations included monetisation of fiscal deficit and reducing interest rates to counter large government borrowings which are negating efforts of RBI. The report stated that the Government would have to undertake policy measures for the short term as well as for medium and long term.

Releasing the paper, Mr. Venu Srinivasan, President, CII said, "During the last year, the economy has had to face significant challenges due to the onset of the global financial and economic crisis. It is imperative that the Government takes concrete steps in strengthening policies that will promote employment and growth across the key sectors of agriculture, industry and services along with driving investment in infrastructure and manufacturing. We would volunteer for an opportunity to work with the Government in a spirit of collaboration."

Mr. Chandrajit Banerjee Director General, CII said, "We would urge the government to take the lead in creating an enabling environment on the roadmap for economic recovery. Our recommendations in the 'Economic Agenda for Action' is targeted at supporting government initiative in that direction."

Some key recommendations in the report included the following:

(i) Quick disinvestment of profit-making PSUs as it will immediately help soften interest rates and assist fiscal management.

(ii) Repo and reverse repo rates must be reduced by at least 50 basis points to 4.25 per cent and 2.75 per cent respectively.

(iii) Monetise fiscal deficit.

(iv) Reduce interest rates by at least 50 basis points Labour reforms: Raise IDA limits for workers from 100 to 500.

(v) Allow Government to acquire land for industrial purposes and establish land banks for non-cultivable land.

(vi) Raise FDI limit in insurance to 49 per cent and allow 26 per cent FDI in pension fund management.

(vii) Implement GST at 12 per cent by April 2010.

(viii) Allow disinvestment in PSUs to raise Rs 30,000 crores.

(ix) Liberalise higher education.

The paper urged the government to promote public-private partnership in infrastructure by easing norms and financing mechanisms. It also mooted the establishment of Land Bank Corporations to acquire non-cultivable land to ease land acquisition. In the power sector the CII suggested concerted initiatives to alleviate the constraints, with immediate changes to pricing and tax policies and longer term measures such as coal sector reforms, for adding capacity.

The paper also called for Electronic Data Interchange to be enabled at all customs stations and concessional marketing assistance loans to reputed exporters, especially in the SME sector and incentives for investments in Africa and Latin America aimed at boosting exports.

In agriculture sector the paper called for effective redesigning of The Model APMC Act for particular sectors like horticultures for uniform implementation. It also recommended moving towards a common market for farm produce. CII called for the incentivisation of private investment in agriculture, agri-infrastructure and extension services and creation of policies for building linkages between farms and markets. Food safety and quality regulations should also be implemented, added CII.

CII strongly recommended the introduction of GST at 12 per cent in order to increase the share of manufacturing in the economy and also generating employment. The paper called for a National Manufacturing Policy focusing on domestic value addition and promotional measures that would help meet targets for employment and technology. Private sector participation in defence production was also recommended to be encouraged by creating a 'level playing field' between private and public manufacturers and increasing projects in the 'Make' category.

In a special section on MSME competitiveness, the paper asked for funds to be designated for technology adaptation and full depreciation on IT equipment to mitigate the effects of economic crisis on this group. Other procedural and administrative matters were also to be rationalised by Central and State Governments and local bodies. According to CII, to reach advanced country levels there was a need to stimulate industrial technology, R&D and innovation through facilitative fiscal policies and incentives through adoption of a comprehensive approach.

GDP Growth and Stimulus Package

According to the Associated Chambers of Commerce and Industry of India (ASSOCHAM), government's top priority should be to initially earmark 1.5 per cent of national GDP in stimulating demand as part of its 3rd stimulus package to the nation and revive its sagging economy.

Demand stimulation, according to ASSOCHAM was possible by slightly making adjustments in India's existing direct and indirect tax structure and lend purchasing power to consumer, which is the need of hour.

Earmarking 1.5 per cent of GDP would initially mean ₹ 50,000 crore's burden on government kitty as it would be required to further slash excise, customs, personal income and corporate tax and other levies and provide relief to consumers to enable them purchase goods and services.

ASSOCHAM President, Sajjan Jindal said, "the proposed move would also amount in reducing input costs and accelerate manufacturing to provide for cheaper goods and services, which is what consumers want."

The industrial reality during 2009-10 was that industry had production but few buyers as there was no purchasing power with them. Buyers can acquire purchasing power provided through tax cuts, it can save some liquidity and buy goods and services at competitive rates for, plenty of them were available in the market. In addition to relaxing taxes and inadvertent duty structure, it was suggested that government should also lay out clear cut guidelines for revising its tax slabs to boom time economy period after it has succeeded in bringing back economy on proper tax.

The ASSOCHAM Chief also pointed out that demand creation should follow growth in jobs which was possible with manufacturing getting a priority treatment. Success of manufacturing would depend on government's policies on infrastructure investment both overseas and domestic. Therefore, new investment guidelines needed to be rolled out with clarity and transparency as investors have resources but waiting for clarity in investment's guidelines through which existing urban and rural divide can be bridged.

According to ASSOCHAM, ongoing National Rural Employment Guarantee Programme (now Mahatma Gandhi National Rural Employment Guarantee Programme) needed further consolidation. According to the statistics, 50 per cent of rural folks were beneficiaries to this programme which goes to show that this popular scheme needed further improvement to make rural poor self-reliant to some extent.

ASSOCHAM also stated that the process of reforms should be hastened and especially these were needed for labour, insurance, civil aviation, banking and administration. Government expenses were still on higher side which needed to be re-looked at to divert wastages towards productivity.

Is it Time to Withdraw Stimulus Package?

After the end of financial year 2010-11, the Reserve Bank of India felt that time had come for fiscal consolidation after a period of generous stimulus packages which pumped in huge money supply into the economy last year. This indeed helped in pushing the GDP growth to a modest 6.7 per cent GDP growth in 2008-09 when the crisis was at its peak. This happened at a time when other countries were facing recession and shrinking economies.

There were clear positive indications. According to the figures released by the Central Statistical Organisation (CSO) the Industrial growth in December 2009 was about 18 per cent, after registering 11.7 per cent growth in November which could mean a growth rate in this sector in the whole year, of about 9 per cent. The Exports which suffered the most and kept on falling consistently in the last 13 months had begun picking up since November 2009. Exports recorded an increase of 9.3 per cent in December 2009 for the second consecutive month. The Agricultural sector also started looking up with prospect of a good Rabi crop. Farm output in 2010-11 was expected to be better than initial estimates as post monsoon rains were good.

According to ASSOCHAM, the stimulus packages offered, had significantly turned around the job creation activity of India Inc. by fuelling a growth of 19 per cent in employment generation during in the latter half of 2009-10.

The Study entitled "Impact of Fiscal Stimulus in Job Creation" revealed that when the global financial crisis hit the Indian shore in October 2008 and manufacturing sector was majorly impacted due to the decline in export orders, the domestic employment situation deteriorated sharply. However, a year later, there was a significant turnaround in new job creation accruing to the fruits of stimulus. The three installment stimulus packages offered an immediate opportunity to the beneficiary industrial sectors. Many industries took advantage not only in growth in profitability but also in terms of job creation. The strong pickup in domestic industrial production and improving export orders led to acceleration in the job creation process. This was evident from the fact that the index of industrial production rose 12.9 per cent during October 2009 to January 2010 period on an annualised basis while exports grew 8.1 per cent and employment 18.8 per cent.

ASSOCHAM President said that out of 32 sectors analyzed by the Study, some sectors registered robust recovery like academics, advertising and IT hardware while others like logistics, printing and packaging and energy sector lagged behind with very slow pace in job creation. Job creation growth was highest in academics with 137 per cent followed by advertising and event management (111 per cent), IT/Hardware (106 per cent), Research and Consultancy (65 per cent) and engineering (63 per cent). Among the sectors that saw major decline in job creation include—logistics (33 per cent), printing and packaging (28 per cent), Biotech/Pharma (22 per cent), Construction (12 per cent) and energy (10 per cent).

A number of incentives were announced in the economic stimulus package of India. These were drawn up by government to infuse a sense of optimism in the minds of investors and industrialists. Incentive schemes in Indian economic stimulus amounting to $70 million were allocated to boost exports. Measures were taken to boost exports of labor intensive commodities like textiles and handicrafts to provide stimulus to Indian economic retrieval. Lending rates on housing loans for low and middle income segments were reduced. Medium and small businesses were provided tax exemptions and tax holidays. Value added tax was cut at different levels and across products to increase spending. Reserve Bank of India has reduced its lending rate to 6.5 per cent and its borrowing rate to 5 per cent.

Central Value Added Tax (CENVAT) reduced by 4 per cent brought down prices of cement, textiles, and cars. CENVAT on non-petroleum products was slashed by up to 10 per cent, thereby significantly affecting Indian economic recovery.

Customs duty on naphtha, an intermediary product for power industry, was completely revoked. To provide an impetus to export, duty on export of iron ore was removed and levy on iron lump exports was reduced from 15 per cent to 5 per cent.

A 10-point India economic stimulus package program, charted by Prime Minister Manmohan Singh, targeted at reviving most badly affected sectors of Indian economy like housing, automobiles, infrastructure, power and medium and small industries. A funding of ₹ 300 billion was earmarked for this. An additional funding of ₹ 100 billion in the form of tax free bonds was earmarked for India Infrastructure Finance Company Limited. Montek Singh Ahluwalia, Deputy Chairman of Planning Commission, commented that the 10-point package was set to force manufacturers to operate in a competitive environment and pass on taz benefits to end users.

According to Finance Minister, India will keep unwinding economic stimulus deployed during the financial crisis and continue raising interest rates despite uncertainty linked to the euro zone's debt woes. Pranab Mukherjee pointed towards a deepening debt crisis in Europe which could hit India's and other emerging economies' exports and growth, but such a risk was not stopping India from gradually reversing loose fiscal and monetary policies.

Reserve Bank of India raised rates in March 2010 and again April by 25 basis points and signalled more hikes would follow, when it last met for a regular quarterly policy review in April 2010. However, the market volatility and worries that Europe's efforts to rein in debt may sap global growth, cast aspersion on the scope of monetary tightening by major central banks.

Such worries also gave rise to suggestions that major emerging markets economies such as China, India, Brazil and Russia, should help sustain global recovery by delaying the exit from loose policies put in place during the global downturn.

Mukherjee, however, was of the opinion that Asia's third-largest economy would continue to consolidate its finances and underscored the contrast between the relative fiscal health of emerging economies and debt-laden euro-zone members. "You need fiscal prudence and in the developing countries, we are doing so."

The Finance Minister said that India, which has pumped an equivalent of 3 per cent of gross domestic product into its economy to shield it from the global crisis, planned to withdraw that stimulus from 2011 onwards. "I hope to have next year a total exit policy," he said.

India Inc United against Stimulus Package Rollback

Whether to rollback the stimulus package or wait for some more time is a big policy dilemma facing India today India Inc, which feels that the stimulus should continue till economic recovery takes firm roots. Businesses and markets are worried that a premature withdrawal of the stimulus could put the nascent economic recovery at risk.

Essentially, industry and trade want Finance Minister Pranab Mukherjee to retain the tax cuts and interest rate subsidies that came as part of the ₹ 1,86,000 crore fiscal stimulus, amounting to 3.5 per cent of India's GDP.

In 2009-10, the economy expanded at 7.4 per cent, recovering from a slowdown in growth to 6.7 per cent in 2008-09. The growth rate, however, was still much below the average of 8.6 per cent clocked in the four years before the downturn. The industry's main argument, therefore, was that the stimulus must not be abandoned prematurely.

President of Confederation of Indian Industry (CII) voiced the opinion of the industry when he said, "The stimulus needs to be sustained until growth is robust and all sectors perform well. It needs to be there for at least another six months and be linked to the introduction of GST," Venu Srinivasan, TVS Motor Company CMD and President of the Confederation of Indian Industry, said.

There is no denying the fact that ₹ 8,700 crore stimulus in the form of tax cuts has worked wonders with a whole lot of troubled industries—from automobiles to consumer durables and from FMCG to aviation. Besides, real estate and export sectors like textiles, gems & jewellery, handicrafts, chemicals and engineering goods have also benefited from the interest rate subsidies.

The centre effected a 6 percentage point cut in CENVAT in two phases—by 4 percentage points in December 2008 and another 2 percentage points in February 2009—and brought down the service tax rate to 10 per cent from 12 per cent. It introduced interest rate subsidies on export credit for a number of labour-intensive products and also on home loans for dwellings costing below Rs. 20 lakh, inducing banks to go in for a general reduction in lending rates. Industries, which benefited directly, and even those which got an indirect fillip, want to hold on to these concessions.

The automobile industry wanted the stimulus package to continue for at least another year. While Maruti said it did not want to give up the concession in excise duty that has resulted in higher sales, Hyundai said the stimulus should be withdrawn only in phases. Mahindra felt that unless the industry replicated performance for at least two to three more quarters, the stimulus should not be withdrawn. Ashok Leyland feared that a withdrawal of life support could kill recovery.

Maruti Suzuki Chairman R.C. Bhargava said, "The exact benefit of the stimulus package is obviously higher sales. Who wants to give up a concession? Sales in the coming years will be higher if prices remain low as a result of the lowering of excise duties by 4 percentage points. If the stimulus is withdrawn, it will be a negative for the car industry."

Pawan Goenka, President of Mahindra & Mahindra and the Society of Indian Automobile Manufacturers stated, "Unless the automobile industry replicates the December 2009 quarter performance for at least the next two three quarters, the government should not withdraw the stimulus."

Demand arrival in consumer goods industry due to stimulus package and other policy changes has worked as a tonic for the double-digit growth of the entire manufacturing sector since August 2009 from a sharp slowdown a year ago. Sales of FMCG companies got a fillip from excise duty cuts as well as from the huge amount of money pumped into consumer pockets through enhanced spending sparked by the government pay hike, farm loan waivers and social schemes like the rural employment guarantee scheme. The industry has come a long way from a situation when people were postponing their purchases of white goods to that of robust consumer confidence in recent months. The fiscal measures boosted consumer sentiments after the companies passed on the duty benefits to the consumers and lowered the prices.

But no sector was in greater need of the stimulus than exports, the worst hit in the global meltdown. After declining for straight 11 months, India's mercantile exports saw a turn-around in the third quarter of 2009-10. But overall, the exports in 2009-10 were $165 billion, down 10 per cent from $185 billion in 2008-09. Exporters feel that it is too early to withdraw the support as they are yet to recover fully. "Only gems & jewellery and pharmaceuticals have shown positive results from the stimulus. The other sectors are still struggling," the Federation of Indian Export Organisations President, A Sakthivel said.

Exporters say that the interest rate subsidy has helped in cutting costs and thus facing competition from countries like China. "Withdrawing the benefits now will be detrimental to the textile industry. The main problem with Indian exporters is the challenge to keep costs low and meet competition," the CMD of the garment exporting firm, Orient Craft, Sudhir Dhingra said.

Demand from overseas markets continues to be subdued as economic recovery in the US and Europe is still weak. Gitanjali group Chairman Mehul Choksi said, "If the government pulls back the interest subvention, it will be disastrous for the industry. If it still withdraws the concession, it must make sure that all exporters get dollar credit at 4 per cent."

The fundamental growth constraint in the economy continues to be its poor infrastructure. The massive infrastructure investment plans announced as part of the stimulus package are yielding result. Infrastructure companies could derive only limited benefits from the enhanced cash availability in the system through a softening of interest rates and easing of the overseas borrowing window.

"Infrastructure did not receive any major direct benefits," said the GMR group Chief Financial Officer, A Subbarao. "If the package is withdrawn and the situation worsens again, the stimulus has to be brought back again," he said.

Tax-free bonds of ₹ 10,000 crore raised as a part of the plan to leverage investments worth ₹ 1,00,000 crore in infrastructure, mainly roads and ports, are also being utilized. It will bring further infrastructure development in the country.

Early Stimulus exit may Hit Global Recovery: PM

Prime Minister Manmohan Singh said the manner of Europe's handling of its debt problems would be "a major determinant of which way the world economy evolves".

He said the Group of 20 major and emerging economies should not rein in budget deficits too fast but coordinate policy to ensure a sustained economic recovery. "My own feeling is that early fiscal retrenchment carries very considerable global risks," Singh told the *Toronto Star* in an interview 26 and 27 June 2010, shortly before his arrival for the G-20 summit in Toronto.

The G-20 meeting took place amid a debate over how to improve public finances without compromising the uneven recovery from the global financial crisis. India has begun its own process of rolling back stimulus measures announced in the wake of the financial crisis. It has outlined a roadmap to cut its deficit to 4.1 per cent of GDP by end-March 2013, from a budgeted 5.5 per cent in the current fiscal year to end-March 2011, helped by buoyant revenues from accelerating growth.

Government Economic Power in the Post-Crisis World

The economic abilities of nations and governments have always been a force to reckon with. This was proved by the fact that the governments all over the world were able to rescue their respective economies through stimulus packages. According to Ministry of Finance, while the process of globalization saw government's economic power supplementing the forces of the market, the global economic crisis witnessed governments playing a crucial role in stabilizing financial markets and managing to coordinate responses in order to prop up the world economy.

Governments also play a critical role in ensuring redistributive equity and development. Motivated by the need to develop a set of metrics to encompass this important phenomenon, an index of government economic power was developed. The index can also be of value in deciding on the voting rights and other powers the governments of various countries ought to have in international organizations like the IMF and the World Bank. The index was created for 10 years (2000-09) covering 112 economies.

The index of government economic power (IGEP) endeavours to capture the ability of a government to project itself in the international sphere. There is also a normative content to this. Since the index shows the extent of charge a government has, it also can be used to determine how much say the government should have in multilateral fora. The index is composed of four variables: government revenues, foreign currency reserves, export of goods and services, and human capital. These variables broadly capture a government's ability to raise resources, its creditworthiness and credibility in international financial markets, its influence on global economic activity, and its representational strength, i.e. how much of the global economy, including global manpower, it can claim to represent. In order to ensure use of standard data, the index has been constructed using three widely accepted datasets; the IFS and WEO of the IMF, and the United Nations Development Programme's (UNDP's) Human Development Index (HDI).

The 2009 results show that the top ten ranks are occupied by (1) the United States, (2) China, (3) Japan, (4) Germany, (5) India, (6) Russia, (7) Brazil, (8) France, (9) Italy, and (10) the United Kingdom. In 2000 the top ten places were held by (1) the United States, (2) Japan, (3) China, (4) Germany, (5) France, (6) the United Kingdom, (7) Italy, (8) (Republic of) Korea, (9) Canada, and (10) India. Among the top ranking economies, some of the most dramatic rises in rank have been Brazil's ascent from 13th place in 2000 to 7th in 2009 and India's rise from 10th position in 2000 to 5th in 2009.[2]

"There is", the Ministry added, "a strong positive correlation between the growth in economic power (percentage change in index value between 2000 and 2009) and the change in GDP across the post-crisis period (between 2009 and 2010) indicating a link between growth in economic power as measured by the index and the ability to recover from the crisis. This does not establish a direct causal relationship between the two variables but is of descriptive interest.[3]

(Economic Division, Department of Economic Affairs, Ministry of Finance, working paper: 'The Evolving Dynamics of Global Economic Power in the Post-crisis World: Revelations from an Index of Government Economic Power'.)

Notes

1. "Report on Trend and Progress of Banking in India 2008-09." RBI.
2. The Evolving Dynamics of Global Economic Power in the Post-Crisis World: Revelation from an Index of Government Economic Power." Economic Division, Department of Affairs.
3. *Ibid.*

5

Role of Central Banks in Financial Stability

The global financial crisis 2008 forced the countries and institutions worldwide to review the financial stability frameworks and within that, the role of central banks in maintaining financial stability. Such a process involved the following:

(i) A review of the tools at the disposal of central banks, including monetary policy.

(ii) An assessment of the benefits and costs of an enhanced role of central banks in financial regulation.

(iii) An exploration of the objectives and scope of financial regulation.

(iv) An evaluation of general principles that can inform the design of the existing financial structure and relative strengths and weaknesses thereof.

Since the solutions suggested by such reviews and assessments were path-dependent and specific to the development of the financial sector in any given country, the degree of success of their applications may also vary. Moreover, the reviews may lead to different conclusions in different countries, and as such, different measures were expected to be taken by different countries.

The magnitude of global economic meltdown made experts think that there has been a collective failure to address the key objective of mitigating systemic risk. International Monetary

Fund in its Working Paper outlined the following weaknesses in the functioning of central banks and treasury departments:

- Central banks and supervisory agencies have not put enough energy into the development of macro-prudential tools that can, alongside monetary policy, be used to address the build-up of exposures to aggregate risks.
- Treasury departments have been slow to introduce and adjust the scope of special resolution regimes that mitigate the systemic impact of failure and that can address moral hazard incentives arising from implicit safety nets.
- Prudential supervisors have not developed and applied heightened prudential standards for large and complex institutions whose failure can have a major disruptive effect on financial markets.
- Central banks have not always been successful in promoting systemically robust procedures for the clearing and settlement of trades in rapidly-envolving financial markets. The example highlighted by the crisis is a lack of a robust infrastructures for credit derivatives.
- The overall framework does not appear to have been fully conductive to achieving its objectives, often leaving ill-defined the responsibilities and tools of central banks in their pursuit of financial stability.[1]

This observation though made in hindsight contains a fair degree of truth. The main issues involved in the process of reviewing the financial stability have been taken up below.

Monetary Policy

It has been observed, and was proved true by the crisis that, by aiming a price stability objective, central banks neglect developments in credit growth and asset prices. Thus, they miss a build-up of credit and leverage system, which proves unsustainable over a long-term period.

According to Bank for Settlement (BIS), the existing financial system is procyclical and prone to bubble-like behavior. As has frequently happened, very rapid credit growth has brought increase in asset prices more than their fundamental values, fuelling a boom in consumption and investment. All crises, be it the Great Depression in the US and Japan in the 1990s, or the East Asia in 1997, were preceded by rapid credit creation that manifested itself in higher asset prices and higher collateral values, leading to further increases in credit. One of the possible solutions suggested is "shading of the interest policy, termed as 'leaning against the wind'". But some experts like Ben Bernanke and Gartler have argued that using interest rate policy in this way may not be powerful enough to arrest the upswing of asset prices and leverage. Moreover, asset bubbles are not easy to detect, nor is their impact on the economy easy to assess. Further, interest rate policy that "leans against the wind is costly as compared with the cost of dealing with the fall-out."[2]

As a result of experiences gained during the financial crisis 2008-09, central banks are now reviewing the contribution that monetary policy can make to counter financial imbalances, by finding ways and means to bring greater developments in credit, leverage and asset prices. The Federal Reserve and Bank of England have called for a closer investigation of macro-prudential tools that may focus on financial sector and that could be used in addition to interest rate to respond to the challenges of financial cycles.

Efforts to design a countercyclical regulatory tool are already underway. Some proposals in this regard are enumerated below:

(i) To celebrate capital buffers above Basel minima to the loan growth at each individual firm. (Goodhart and Persand)

(ii) To introduce a dynamic provisioning framework like the one that Bank of Spain has adopted since 2000.

(iii) Building up a maximum leverage rates is another tool that may restrict the building of financial imbalances.

The Financial Stability Forum (FSF), and the Basel Committee are actively engaged in finding out which of these tools will prove most promising. It should also be kept in mind that such countercyclical prudent measures pose several practical difficulties. They need to strike a fine balance between pursuing the objective to counter financial excesses and develop a dynamic financial sector capable of supporting the growth of the economy. There are several advantages of designing such policy rules as may reduce supervisory discretion and introduce pre-commitment, but such rules must be updated periodically so that they are not arbitraged, and more importantly, they are able to keep pace with the new developments in financial sector.

Systemic Liquidity

After the onset of financial crisis, the central banks provided liquidity in interbank markets. They brought some changes in their monetary operations to remove liquidity stress. Most of the central banks, for example, reduced the penalties on banks not achieving their reserves targets. The discount rates at which banks could access standing facilities were reduced. Besides, central banks changed the terms of open market operations to more illiquid and credit risky securities. While earlier when such actions were taken, the aggregate amount of reserves provided to the system were kept constant, now the distinction between liquidity position and unconventional monetary policy was increasingly blurred. The central banks, as providers of market liquidity during different times of crunch, became the "market makers of last resort".

Taking actions to mitigate the impact of systemic risk on the financial system and the economy is, however, not without adverse effects on the central banks themselves. Providing liquidity in the interbank markets against credit-risky securities weakens the balance sheets of central banks. It also makes it difficult for them to implement properly the conventional monetary policy. For example, they have to choose between following the envisaged monetary policy and objectives of liquidity provision. "In small open economies...systemic liquidity provision can lead to a sharp depreciation of the exchange rate and in the longer run, increase inflation" (Jacome 2008).

It has been argued that since the containment of systemic risk proves costly for central banks, it is also in their interest if the frequency of systemic liquidity stresses is reduced. This calls for greater regulation of key private liquidity providers like commercial banks as well as proper regulation of markets.

Central Banks as Lenders of Last Resort

It has also been seen that in their extended function of being the lenders of last resort, central banks tend to become involved in the resolution of individual systemically-important institutions that are under severe liquidity stress. Examples include Bank of England in case of Bear Stearns. Federal Reserve even extended a line of credit to JPMorgan Chase in the latter's bid to take over Bear Stearns. Federal Reserve also acted as a bridge bank, taking temporary control of American Insurance Group (AIG). Central banks becoming involved in the resolution of institutions was prompted by the following four considerations:

(i) Since the central banks may have to lend when the long run viability of the institution is in doubt, it is necessary for them to obtain "knowledge that goes beyond what is known by the market", which is possible only if they get involved with the institution at deeper level.

(ii) Access to supervisory information enables the central bank to assess the impact on other institutions and as such, "broader economy of the failure of a stricken institution".

(iii) Central banks have an interest in the "prudential liquidity regulation and the effectiveness of supervision", in the absence of which some institutions may seek help on fake or flimsy grounds.

(iv) Not only central funds, but also their reputation is at stake, which "translates into an interest in the capital regulation of systemically important financial institutions".

Central banks may even prompt such review of prudential policies as conducted by the Financial Services Authority (FSA) in the wake of failure of Northern Rock, and by Securities and Exchange Commission (SEC) in the wake of failure of Bear Stearns and some other investment banks in the US. According to IMF, since central banks have to act in crisis situations, they should be given an influence on the prudential control of systemically important institutions within the design of overall financial stability framework.

Central banks have played an important role in the oversight of systemically-important payment and settlement systems and have endeavored to reduce counter party credit risk inherent in these systems. A fair degree of success has been achieved in removing the systemic risk in national and international payment and settlement systems. According to IMF:

> Due in no small part to these initiatives, the main payment and settlement systems in developed economies have proved remarkably resilient to the stress put on them during the crisis.

It would, however, be a gross misrepresentation of facts if the credit for developing economies faring strongly during global recession 2008 is given to the national and international payment and settlement systems. Economies like China's and India's were perhaps among the least affected by global recession 2008 because of their inherent strengths and resourcefulness. India, for example, has a strong financial system regulated by ever-vigilant Reserve Bank of India, and based on strong lending principles backed by tangible securities, which left no room for bubbles to develop and then bust.

Coming to the main point, there is need for central banks not only to have formal powers of oversight over systemically-important clearing and settlement systems, but also a stronger power over users of such systems. Mere moral suation that they usually have to rely on is not going to help any longer.

Costs and Benefits, Central Bank's Role in Financial Regulation

An expanded role of central banks in financial regulation will increase the effectiveness of financial regulation. Some envisaged benefits of such expanded role are enumerated below:

(i) Evolving a system to cover economic risk is costly for central banks. This creates incentives on their part to reduce the frequency of systemic crises, and to develop tools to reduce macro-systemic risk, and micro-prudential tools to reduce the frequency and impact of crises on individual systemic institutions.

(ii) A central bank's expertise in financial infrastructure proves useful in crises management and can be harnessed in the development of micro-prudential tools that reduce the systemic impact of failure, by encouraging the use of systems that pose far less systemic risk.

(iii) A role in financial regulation can harness central banks' expertise in macro-financial analysis that can in turn inform the design of macro-prudential tools. This role in macro-prudential policy adds to the central bank's tool set when both monetary policies and macro-prudential policies are used in complementary ways.

However, the experts feel that a regulatory role of the central bank brings potential costs. A comparison of benefits and costs of an expanded role of central banks in financial regulation needs to be considered Goodhart has suggested that the central bank may have the resources and discretion to sustain an insolvent institution under its supervision even when it is not necessary or desirable. Turner (2009) also holds the same opinion. The practical validity of such a supervision however remains doubtful.

Economists like Buiter believe that lender of last resort (LOLR) support may cause more uncertainty in the market. This can be supported by an example:

(i) When the crisis broke the UK in 2007, Bank of England believed Northern Rock to be solvent but immediately made public its LOLR-support of Northern Rock. While, because of the stigma attached to receiving support, emergency lending could benefit from being kept secret, Bank of England believed that a covert operation was likely to be leaked, creating further dislocations in the market.[3]

(ii) It has been seen that once the central bank takes a decision to put an institution in the public domain, the government officials, key persons in public and private sector as well as the public at large tend to indulge in an enormous amount of scrutiny on all its moves, operations, future prospects, making it risky for the central bank to become an LOLR.

(iii) Extending an LOLR operation in favour of an insolvent institution may prove undesirable for the central bank as it may affect its own balance sheet.

Notwithstanding above, many economists feel that the conflict between supervision and becoming LOLR ignores a number of aspects that give rise to the synergies between supervision and resolution. Supervisory information helps guage the systemic impact of failure of an institution as well as the effect of being LOLR, on central bank's balance sheet. A role in resolution also urges the central bank to adopt a tough supervisory stance from the beginning, as it is concerned with its own balance sheet, and would try to avoid reputational costs arising out of any mistake in handling the crisis. Such a stance by the central bank is also said to "sharpen their eyes in the supervision of individual systemic institutions".

Goodhart and Shoenmaker (1995) suggested that micro-prudential objectives may conflict with the macroeconomic objectives of a central bank and force them to compromise the conduct of monetary policy, particularly when the banking system is under stress. The monetary authority may then be hesitant to impose the appropriate degree of tightening through concern for the solvency of the banks it supervises. But, there are also counter arguments to the view, some of which are discussed below.

The monetary policy must not be concerned about bank solvency per se. It needs to be concerned about the impact of strains in the banking sector on the supply of credit to the economy, and the impact it can make on the outlook for output and inflation.

A policy of monetary easing will, for all intents and purposes, be appropriate in response to strains in the banking system, and this will hold whether the central bank is the supervisor of individual institutions or not. In response to the 2008-09 financial crises, central banks around the world reduced interest rates which may be said to have been motivated in part by a desire to counter the effect on the economy of dried-up credit markets.

A supervisory role also creates benefits in informing the central bank's response to banking sector stresses. According to Bernanke, "during the...financial turmoil the ability of the Fed to obtain information directly from key institutions and from supervisory reviews has been invaluable for understanding financial developments and their impact on the economy." Peek, Rosengren and Tootell (2003) are also of the opinion that the desirability of access to supervisory information has been emphasized by other central banks such as the European Central Bank, particularly to inform the monetary response to crisis situations. Empirical research confirms that access to supervisory information proves advantageous in assessing the outlook for output and inflation.

The concern that a supervisory role may compromise the conduct of monetary policy does not appear totally convincing. There are several considerations which imply that the central bank's role in monetary policy can create important benefits for macro-prudential policies, that are related to both central banks incentives and their expertise.

According to IMF Working Paper 2009, some economists have noted the difference in the speed of policy easing across advanced economies in response to the financial crises. But there could be several determinants of these differences, which may have been due to differences in the macroeconomic data faced by different central banks. They might also have been due at least in part to differences as regards whether or not the central bank has a supervisory role. But even if this could be established, it is not clear whether differences in the decisiveness of monetary easing may have been because of biases arising from a potential conflict of interest between supervision and monetary policy or owing to better access to supervisory information and a better understanding of the interaction between financial stresses and the macroeconomic outlook.

Goodhart states that if a central bank is responsible for prudential supervision of individual institutions as well as monetary policy, it is possible that highly visible failure in the former may undermine people's confidence in the latter. But, again, this may have been an exaggeration because in the case of the supervision and resolution of an individual institution, the type of judgement that needs to be made, the people including staff involved, and the processes followed in formulating policy are not the same as in the course of monetary policy. The cases of Bear Stearns, Northern Rock, Lehman Brothers, and American Insurance Group have amply illustrated this and it is plausible that the public is able to appreciate the differences, especially when monetary policy is delegated to an institutionally separate monetary policy committee. But even if it is accepted that failures in supervision could create reputational risks for monetary policy when central banks have a supervision role, it is not necessary that the supervision and monetary control would be better conducted by separate agencies. A central bank's concern for its reputation in monetary policy can create strong incentives to seek uninhibited implementation of supervisory standards which may lessen the frequency of crisis events such as the recent recession.

Some experts are of the opinion that a central bank's role in the supervision and resolution of individual institutions may politicize the central bank, affecting its independence from the government, making its position less secure. The following points may be noted in this regard:

(i) It neglects central bank's de facto involvement, including through being the lenders of last resort to institutions, providing liquidity for the market at large.

(ii) The crises such as recession may itself undermine central bank's institutional independence. As such, a formal role can strengthen the central bank and enable it to reduce systemic risk, thus decreasing the likelihood of political interference in crisis situation.

(iii) It is also advisable that where central bank's policy independence is less secure, instead of shielding it from a formal responsibility for financial stability, steps should be taken to increase its policy independence by giving the central bank a clear mandate for both monetary and financial stability, even by reaffirming its policy independence in law.

(iv) The most influential argument against what is termed as prudential role of the central bank has been that "it can lead to an undue concentration of powers, especially when the central bank also undertakes an independent monetary policy."[4]

This is a genuine concern, but there are also arguments against it. Some of such arguments are enumerated below:

(i) The crisis affects the development of an overall policy framework that necessitates the complementary use of monetary and micro-prudential tools. Synergies between supervision and monetary policies have many benefits such as getting valuable information, using central bank's expertise in informing the formulation of micro-prudential policies, etc.

(ii) According to Goodhart, politicians tend to oppose disinflationary monetary policies and countercyclical macro-prudential policies, especially in good times. This problem can be addressed by assigning responsibility for macro-prudential policies to an independent agency.

(iii) It is believed that large institutions have the means to influence politicians and are thus able to ensure that they are subjected to soft regulatory constraints. Political pressures on regulatory agencies become stronger in periods of recession to prevent any harsh measures in financial control. Thus, assigning responsibility for prudential regulation of large financial firms to an independent agency is always beneficial, because such firms are free from outside pressures.

(iv) A concentration of power has one distinct advantage that a combined agency can benefit from increasing doubt and credibility in formulating macro- and micro-prudential policies, enhancing its ability to resist the pressure created by politicians and financial industry.

It is necessary to study the major implications of benefits and costs of central bank's role in financial regulation. It is necessary to make it clear at the outset that the perceived costs apply only when the central bank's actions in monetary policy are heavily constrained, e.g. when a country is part of a currency unions, or operates a currency board. There are strong complementarities between monetary and prudential policies, and many economic benefits may arise from a combination of powers. Thus, the central bank may play an important role in financial regulation when it also conducts monetary policy. Some conflicts of interest also arise from central bank's supervisory role, which also increases costs. However, better supervision of systemically important institutions also beings huge benefits for the economy. It is also important to note that some of the benefits of a central bank's role in financial regulation may not require a supervisory role, but may come only through its role in regulatory design. It is also alleged that perceived costs are larger when the central bank is involved only ex post or de facto rather than in response to a formal mandate that may reduce these costs." Different countries may come to different conclusions in weighing all costs and benefits. Thus, country-specific situations need to be taken into account before reaching a conclusion in this regard. It is important to ensure that powers given to the central bank are supported with strong mechanisms that bring transparency and independent accountability of central bank's actions in safeguarding financial stability.

Financial Stability Frameworks

There is a worldwide debate after the global economic crisis of 2008-09, on how the existing financial stability frameworks can be improved. There are several commonalities in the problems faced during the recession and in the proposed policy responses, but there are also many differences that need to be looked into while analyzing the financial stability frameworks.

It is interesting to note that attempts to introduce a new financial regulatory structure had started in some countries before the conditions prevailing in 2008 erupted into a recession in September 2008, which engulfed all parts of the globe. In the US, the Treasury issued a blueprint for a modernized financial regulatory structure as early as March 2008, which pointed out that much of the existing regulatory structure was created more than 70 years ago, and that this structure now struggles to keep pace with market evolution, and faces increasing difficulties in preventing and anticipating financial crisis. It was revealed that the US regulation of deposit taking institutions had a complex web of ineffectual agencies, with five federal agencies needing to coordinate between each other in the regulation and resolution of national banks and state authorities, particularly with regard to the oversight of mortgage markets.

After the recession, there is an attempt worldwide to simplify and consolidate the existing regulatory structure. The organizing principle as stated by IMF is "regulation by objective", and the major objectives are: overall market stability, business conduct regulation, market discipline and consumer protection. Under the blueprint proposals brought in the US, Federal Reserve is to "become the overall market stability regulator". It will be given a formal "responsibility for overall financial stability" as well as "broad powers", including the authority to collect information from individual institutions, interact and collaborate with other institutions to make rules and take such corrective actions as deemed necessary, oversee payment systems, and designate specific systems to formal oversight. There will be a separate Federal prudential regulator to oversee all deposit-taking institutions and insurance companies. As a business regulator, it will oversee market practices across the financial industry, securities, insurance and banking included.

It is necessary to recall that a prompt corrective action framework was introduced in the US as early as in 1991, providing a resolution regime for commercial banks. But, it did not take in its fold, investment houses and other financial institutions.

Which type of financial institutions need to be regulated depends largely upon the functions performed or financial services offered by them such as 'banking', 'insurance', and 'securities services'. But the fact that the financial services are changing, and that institutions are doing a mixture of various types of services makes it difficult to classify them on this basis. The experts have therefore suggested an alternative method, i.e. that of asking the critical question as to which kind of financial institution might pose a threat to the two objectives of financial regulation—mitigating systemic risk and protecting customers and investors, and taking a decision on the basis of reply thereto.[5]

Ensuring effective regulation of systemic risk is not easy. First we need to make a distinction between macro-systemic risk and micro-systemic risk. Macro-systemic risks revolve around macroeconomics or aggregate risks. It is believed that the realization of risk manifests itself in changes in asset prices attached to aggregate developments. Usually, the holder of a leveraged position is tempted to increase his/her leverage when the development in prices is favourable. In such a situation, according to Brunnermeier et al. (2009), the provision of further leverage may cause a bubble, viz. an unjustified upward spurt in asset prices. When there is a sudden reversal in asset prices, the leveraged position will default, associated with the offloading of the asset, which, in turn, creats a downward spiral in asset price—termed as busting of the bubble. It puts solvency of leverage providers under pressure, especially when such providers themselves are leveraged financial institutions like commercial or investment banks.[6] Housing prices, share prices, exchange rates and interest rates have been identified to be vulnerable to aggregate risks. Leveraged exposure to stock market led to an unprecedented boom and then bust in the Great Depression (1929-33). The Japanese crisis of 1990s too was associated with leveraged position exposure to both real estate and stock market. In Iceland, the leveraged exposure to exchange rate, which fell sharply, led to a crisis. It is thus necessary to bring "leveraged providers of liverage" under regulation.

Quite different type of financial institutions come into the picture while discussing mitigation of risks that arise from the point of view of microeconomic level, though some overlap cannot be ruled out.

The impact of failure of an individual institution on the financial system at large depends on various factors that we have to consider while assessing the systemic threat posed by such individual institution. These factors can be studied under the following heads:

Magnitude

The magnitude of the impact of failure of an institution on the system as a whole ;s taken to be proportional to the size of its balance sheet. The size, in turn, determines the value of claims in currency terms, viz. dollars in the case of the US, pounds for UK and rupees for India.

Roll-over Short-term Finding

Some institutions rely on their ability to roll over short-term funding, which may trigger an unwinding of positions held, exposing the market to risks. This has happened in case of many hedge funds, which are also vulnerable to margin calls on the additional credit provided by their prime brokers.

Leverage

An institution having more debts, i.e. which is highly leveraged, has higher probability of failure.

Critical Placement

Institutions that are critically placed in the financial market pose a greater threat to financial stability. It was believed that insurance companies which receive regular premia from retail customers are not vulnerable, but the example of USA's American International Group (AIG) which came on the verge of failure during the global economic meltdown shows that insurance companies too may have a critical interconnectedness due to their activities in financial market, and thus impact the broader system.

Thus, it is not the characteristics that determine the impact of failure of a particular institution but also the strength of the financial infrastructure, its ability to "facilitate the orderly unwinding of positions". The decision to bring the institutions under financial regulation to mitigate micro-systemic risk must consider these two factors.

Another important means of achieving financial regulations is to have an effective agency structure.

Agency Structure

Any agency structure for financial regulation has to achieve two major objectives: (i) consumer protection, and (ii) mitigation of systemic risk. Such structure may not be uniform and may differ in different countries. But the experts are of the opinion that the structure should not be arbitrary. According to the IMF Paper 2009, an ideal agency structure should have the following features:

(i) It should be able to achieve both the objectives stated above.

(ii) It should be capable of avoiding internal conflicts, if any.

(iii) It should give the agencies proper tools to perform their tasks and should be accountable for their work.

(iv) Agencies should be able to create synergy across tools so that there are no conflicting objectives.

(v) If and where possible, the number of agencies should be reduced to mitigate the potential for inter-agency friction.

(vi) The new objectives assigned to the agencies must be consistent with the pre-existing objectives.

(vii) When more than one agencies are involved in the same activity, there are chances of duplicacy. It should be avoided.

(viii) The structure must ensure that the compliance costs on the industry are not heavy.

(ix) The structure should be sensitive to the state of development of financial system in a given country.

The agency structure having these features is likely to be successful in achieving the objectives of mitigation of systemic risk and consumer protection. Much will however depend on what type of risks are encountered in future and how they are tackled with the help of such structure. It is pertinent to mention here that the structure should not be so rigid in its regulations and approach that it creates roadblocks in the way of smooth functioning of the financial system. In other words, it should not overkill in its anxiety to bring financial regulation.

Conclusion

Central banks play a significant role in maintaining financial stability. After the global financial crisis (2008-09) the central banks are being equipped to play a greater role in financial stability. The world has perhaps taken a cue from India which is one of the few countries which were not affected to as great an extent as most countries of America and Europe, including the advanced countries like the US,

UK, France, Germany and Asian giants like Japan, among others. One of the reasons of India's relatively better performance during the financial crisis is said to be its central bank, the Reserve Bank of India which not only framed the financial policies for the country, but also kept a strong vigil on the entire financial market, so that the situation, though not very good in the times of turmoil, still remained within control. Not a single bank or financial institution in India failed or became insolvent or was ever in the danger of being so.

The US Federal Reserve and the European Central Bank (ECB) are "the agencies responsible for monetary policies underpinning the world's most important economies and markets."[7] They are being held responsible for the financial turmoil that struck the world during 2008 and lingered into 2009 and 2010. Their "lax supervision of the financial markets" is said to be one of the major causes of the crisis. Some experts have alleged that these two central banks were slow to take timely measures like lowering interest rates before the crisis snowballed. Once the rates had been cut to the lowest-possible levels, critics say, the Federal Reserve and ECB erred in the opposite direction and exceeded their statutory authority by using "quantitative monetary easing" facilities to inject massive amounts of liquidity into virtually all financial markets.[8] All this suggests that the role of central banks in maintaining financial stability cannot be over-emphasized. We need to give them adequate tools, power and means to ensure that the situation of severe economic crisis faced by the world during 2008-09 is not repeated.

Notes

1. Erlend Walter Nier. "Financial Stability Frameworks and the Role of Central Banks: Lessons from the Crisis" (IMF Working Paper), 2009.
2. *Ibid.*
3. Treasury Select Committee (2008).

4. Ereland Walter Nier. “Financial Stability Frameworks and the Role of Central Banks: Lessons from the Crisis” (IMF Working Paper 2009).
5. *Ibid.*
6. *Ibid.*
7. J. Paul Horne. “Independence and Regulatory Roles of US and European Central Banks Get a Fiery Political Trial”.
8. *Ibid.*

6

The Communist Perspective

In the social production of their existence, men inevitably enter into definite relations, which are independent of their will, namely relations of production appropriate to a given stage in the development of their material forces of production. The totality of these relations of production constitutes the economic structure of society, the real foundation, on which arises a legal and political superstructure and to which correspond definite forms of social consciousness.

The mode of production of material life conditions the general process of social, political and intellectual life. It is not the consciousness of men that determines their existence, but their social existence that determines their consciousness. At a certain stage of development, the material productive forces of society come into conflict with the existing relations of production or—this merely expresses the same thing in legal terms—with the property relations within the framework of which they have operated hitherto. From forms of development of the productive forces these relations turn into their fetters. Then begins an era of social revolution. The changes in the economic foundation lead sooner or later to the transformation of the whole immense superstructure.

In studying such transformations, it is always necessary to distinguish between the material transformation of the economic conditions of production, which can be

> determined with the precision of natural science, and the legal, political, religious, artistic or philosophic—in short, ideological forms in which men become conscious of this conflict and fight it out. Just as one does not judge an individual by what he thinks about himself, so one cannot judge such a period of transformation by its consciousness, but, on the contrary, this consciousness must be explained from the contradictions of material life, from the conflict existing between the social forces of production and the relations of production. No social order is ever destroyed before all the productive forces for which it is sufficient have been developed, and new superior relations of production never replace older ones before the material conditions for their existence have matured within the framework of the old society.
>
> –*Karl Marx*

The global financial imbroglio, which was characterized by weak economic environment, low liquidity and volatile debt, commodities and forex markets, was triggered by the subprime mortgage crisis in the US. Financial crisis implies sudden erosion in large part of the value of some financial institutions or assets. The violent disruption in the global financial markets, which had been in the making for over a year, erupted in September 2008, when major US and European financial institutions were about to go under and had to be bailed out by their governments and central banks. The crisis, which "was not caused by some external shock…the crisis was generated by the system itself" (George Soros), highlighted the vulnerabilities of many financial systems and corporate sectors that had experienced credit booms and had borrowed short and in foreign currencies. These and other disquieting features led to questions such as whether the economy was in a dangerous downward spiral, or was this a painful but ultimately healthy adjustment, leading to a sustainable growth path.

According to the IMF's *Global Financial Stability Report* (GFSR), the widening and deepening fallout from the US subprime mortgage crisis had profound financial system and macroeconomic implications. Financial markets remained considerably stressed because of a combination of weakening balance sheets of financial institutions, process of deleveraging, free fall in asset prices and difficult macroeconomic environment caused by debilitating global growth. Jaime Caruana, Head of the IMF's Monetary and Capital Markets Department maintained as under:

> The recent Fed actions in solving the Bear Stearns case and also in providing liquidity to a broader range of counterparties have reduced the probability of a tail event, although there are still funding pressures that continue.

IMF's Report warned that many of the lax lending practices of the past few years will have to change and economic growth will be crimped by the correction. This observation acquired a sharp poignancy in the wake of the collapse of the world capitalist system—widely acknowledged to be portending a catastrophe of dimensions not seen since the Great Depression of the 1930s and leading to another Great Depression.

Similarities with the 1930s

Almost all the errors of the 1930s were rooted in contextual economic orthodoxies. Nobel Laureate Milton Friedman demonstrated that the cause of the Great Depression was not stock market crash but a great contraction of credit due to bank failures. Similarly, Liaquat Ahamed highlighted in his book *Lords of Finance*,

> During a three-year period, real GDP (gross domestic product) in the major economies fell by over 25 per cent, a quarter of the adult male population was thrown out of work.... The economic turmoil created hardships in every corner of the globe, from the prairies of Canada to the teeming cities of Asia.

But the war irretrievably damaged the system. The debt-riddden and inter-linked global financial system "cracked at the first pressure" after 1928, when a rise in American interest rates forced other countries to follow, and ultimately led to the

1929 stock-market crash. With weakening of economies, a vicious cycle was set into motion: debts went into default, bank panic ensued, credit and industrial production declined and unemployment rose. In other words, weakness became self-perpetuating.

Clearly, there were common concerns of the 1930s and the recent global crisis. Such concerns included a worldwide credit collapse, the interconnectedness of global stock, bond and bank markets and the likelihood of losses in one market inducing withdrawal of money from other markets. According to an estimate of the Institute of International Finance, money flows to 28 emerging-market countries in 2009 dropped 80 per cent from 2007 levels. Currency misalignments reminiscent of the 1920s distorted trade.

There were, however, important features, which distinguished this crisis from that of the 1930s. Such features included easing of credit and pumping liquidity, support to financial institutions, deposit insurance by most countries to reduce the possibility of run on the banks, synchronized action by governments and central banks, huge deficits across countries to arrest an economic free fall and resort to unconventional measures.

Increasing complexity, loss of control and lack of regulation (Kregel 2008, Crotty 2008) were clearly reflected in a broad range of indicators. Such indicators included the meltdown of the rich world's financial system, plummeting stock markets, stoppage by banks of lending to one another, closure of money markets and credit markets with skyrocketing interest rates, fear of a generalised run on the banking system and the shadow banking system—broker-dealers, non-bank mortgage lenders, structured investment vehicles and conduits, hedge funds, money market funds, and private equity firms—being particularly vulnerable on their short-term liabilities. The collapse devastated ever wider layers of the population with the debris left behind devastating the working class through rapid growth of unemployment, poverty, homelessness and social misery. All the advanced economies were characterized not just by recession and a severe financial and banking crisis but also a severe political crisis, a crisis of leadership for capitalism. While crises have been endemic in capitalism, the ramifications of this crisis led to the eruption of severe financial problems simultaneously in many different countries, and the economic impact reverberated globally because of the increased interconnectedness of the global economy.

Since there is still absence of clarity and the myriad dimensions of the global financial crisis continue to be riddled with controversies, let us attempt to "connect the dots". Despite a clear consensus on the severity of the global financial meltdown, both the causes of the crisis and the possible solutions evoked acrimonious debates. True, there could be differing perceptions and important variations in looking at practices, which caused such widespread ruin and destruction. But the basic approach must factor in both the micro-prudential approaches to regulate individual institutions and macro-prudential strategies to manage the overall financial system risks. There was significant variation in country-specific experiences because of varying socio-economic, techno-financial developments, demographic transition, economic and legal prescriptions, etc. Most proponents of "saving the system", however, insisted that despite the turmoil in the markets escalating to a level, which completely derailed the global economy, there was "no alternative" to global capitalism. Hence, such proponents sought to convince—not fully successfully—persons such as working people and the poor, most hit by the crisis, to make major sacrifices to help restore the system's health. This is quite dangerous because as Karl Marx stressed in his book *The Communist Manifesto*, "the proletarians have nothing to lose but their chains".

The theoretical underpinnings of this school of thought ranged from the greed and myopic vision of the Wall Street financial elite and the failure of various government agencies to adequately regulate the markets to the excesses of "neoliberal ideology", urging a retreat from "free market fundamentalism" and to make a case for social-democratic "mixed economy" with a significantly expanded public sector. While "greed" and "reckless irresponsibility" are customarily associated with the capitalist class, particularly its financial aristocracy, right wing elements of the "mainstream" spectrum blamed the working class and the socially marginalized in causing the deflation in housing prices, which precipitated the financial crisis. It was contended that these "irresponsible" persons took advantage of the absurdly low subprime mortgage rates and subsequently defaulted on their mortgages, when rates shot through the roof.

The apparent dichotomy between the two approaches has often led to conflicting theoretical formulations and policy prescriptions. There could not have been any "one-size-fits all" approach to the omnipresent signs of strain starkly reflected in the liquidity crisis that afflicted the financial system in the autumn of 2008. Hence, there is a manifest need not to lose a sense of balance and proportion and examine aspects of development in a proper historical and comparative perspective and a broader framework. The remarkable success of investment banks and their subsequent collapse clearly demonstrates the success of the multi-pronged strategy put in place in an era of complete devastation of investment banks, which were dependent on volatile, market-linked businesses. It is, therefore, necessary not to be swayed by temporary gains but to adopt a balanced and long-term approach.

While markets across the development spectrum were adversely impacted by the escalation of delinquencies and defaults leading to systemic risks, the US mortgage market was particularly susceptible to growing macroeconomic debilities and the depth of the abyss that opened up for world capitalism. The markedly different institutional settings in the US and elsewhere influenced different responses to global financial developments and the interaction between these institutional details largely accounted for different outcomes. The uniqueness of the US mortgage market gathering storm stemmed from the triad of the US housing construction in excess of the underlying needs; much greater easing in US's lending standards, e.g. documentation, loan-to-valuation (LTV) ratios, including second mortgages and loans, (where principal was not paid down in the early stages of their lives) than elsewhere, and quick rise in mortgage arrears rates leading to higher foreclosures and defaults. Soros (2008) demonstrated that the super-bubble combined three major trends of (a) the long-term trend towards ever increasing credit expansion as indicated by rising loan-to-value ratios in housing and consumer loans, and rising volume of credit to gross national product ratios, (b) the globalization of financial markets, and (c) the progressive removal of financial regulations and the accelerating pace of financial innovations.

Casino Capitalism—Making Money from Money with Other People's Money

In the book *Irrational Exuberance*, Professor Robert J. Shiller of Yale University linked the subprime crisis to the irrational exuberance that caused the stock bubble in the 1990s and housing bubble between 2000 and 2007. He demonstrated how these bubbles led to the runaway growth in credit, trigerring large-scale foreclosures, bankruptcies, and write-offs, and a global credit crunch. Since illiquid, opaque toxic assets congested the credit and broader capital markets, Professor Shiller made a strong case for "truly aggressive measures". The structural and contextual changes driving the restoration of an orderly system include a restructuring of the institutional foundations of the financial system to induce people once again to transact homes and provide the enabling conditions for greater prosperity not just in America but across the world because of the inextricably inter-linked nature of the global economy.

Double Whammy—The Making of a Bubble

While the genesis of the US property bubble has a long history, the basic contributory factor of this credit implosion was the "easy money" policies of government. Whenever cyclical economic downturns seemed inevitable, governments slashed interest rates and injected liquidity into the banking system. Lending institutions with access to cheap money (often at sub-inflation interest rates) lent it out. The need for new investments overrode common sense leading to laxity in lending standards, inflation of real estate markets and proliferation of leveraged buyouts. None of these activities were productive investments, no new wealth was created, but more money entered circulation and more debt incurred in the razzle-dazzle of "sophistication" and "computer modelling". Remarkably, this entire process was visualized by Karl Marx when he stressed in his classic *The Communist Manifesto* that "the need of a constantly expanding market for its products chases the bourgeoisie over the whole surface of the globe. It must nestle everywhere, settle everywhere, establish connexions everywhere".

The "marketisation" of loans, i.e. the conversion of loans into tradable securities together with ineffective regulation, dubious credit ratings, large exposures on the part of highly leveraged institutions dependent on wholesale funding, information asymmetries and negative externalities—all hastened the journey to a perilous crossroads. In absolute terms, the credit boom on top of the housing bubble was unparalleled. In America, private-sector debt soared from $22 trillion in 2000 (or the equivalent of 222 per cent of GDP) to $41 trillion (294 per cent of GDP) in 2007.

Historical Perspective—Countdown to Armageddon?

Considered in a proper historical and comparative perspective, the seamless progression to the dangerous manipulation of American financial markets did not erupt overnight, it was clearly in the making for some time. The recent global financial crisis did not occur in a vacuum, but rather was superimposed and intimately related to a broader set of economic processes fast reaching a flashpoint. These processes, which caused a huge disequilibrium, included the imbalance between finance and the real economy; an overarching presence of debt, particularly private debt in the form of personal loans and corporate borrowing; and the "global imbalance" reflected in high savings and large current account surpluses in China and some other countries co-existing with debt financed over-consumption, leading to large US deficits. Clearly, the situation, which was unsustainable in the long term, was exacerbated by soaring oil prices, lower spending by the corporate sector and rising unemployment. The situation is reminiscent of Marx's views, as powerfully articulated in *German Ideology* (1845):

> We know only a single science, the science of history. One can look at history from two sides and divide it into the history of nature and the history of men. The two sides are, however, inseparable; the history of nature and the history of men are dependent on each other so long as men exist. The history of nature, called natural science, does not concern us here; but we will have to examine the history of men, since almost the whole ideology amounts either to a distorted conception of this history or to a complete abstraction from it. Ideology is itself only one of the aspects of this history.

Some of the signposts in the historic failure of American and world capitalism could be identified as the downgrading of General Motors' bonds by rating agencies from investment grade to non-investment grade or "junk"; HSBC sacking head of its US mortgage lending business with losses reaching $10.5 billion (February 22, 2007); suspension of shares in New Century Financial on fears of bankruptcy (March 12, 2007); heavily discounted sale by cash-strapped firm Accredited Home Lenders Holding of $2.7 billion of its subprime loan book (March 16, 2007); and filing of bankruptcy by New Century Financial (April 2, 2007).

Other chronological indicators of the implosion of major corporations, the devastating consequences of a greed-driven culture and dubious or illegal corporate accounts and standards of behaviour included heavy losses of GM finance unit on subprime mortgages and closure of UBS's US subprime lending arm, Dillon Read Capital Management (May 3, 2007); bailout package of $3.2 billion by investment bank Bear Stearns of two of its funds exposed to the subprime market (June 22, 2007); announcement by Bear Stearns to its investors to write-off the money invested in two of its hedge funds (July 18, 2007); and Bear Stearns' ban on cash withdrawal from a third fund because of heavy redemption requests and filing of bankruptcy protection for the two funds bailed out earlier (July

31, 2007). Filing of bankruptcy by American Home Mortgage (August 6, 2007), and BNP Paribas' announcement regarding its inability to fairly value the underlying assets in Parvest Dynamic ABS, BNP Paribas ABS Euribor and BNP Paribas ABS Eonia, because of exposure to US subprime mortgage lending markets (August 9, 2007), were climatic moments in a protracted process and clearly reflected the terrifying rise of financial skullduggery and the systemic damage wreaked.

Convulsive Crisis of Capitalism—A Sense of Déjà Vu!

The thesis of the inherent nature of the crisis in the capitalist system, systemic banking crises, financial volatility and the inevitability of the boom-and-bust cycles can be substantiated both by the incisive analysis of Karl Marx and the fact that not just the capitalist system but also even relatively mature financial systems have lurched from one crisis to the other with disruptive effects. As Karl Marx pithily wrote in *The 18th Brumaire of Louis Bonaparte*, "All great historical facts and personages occur, as it were, twice...the first time as tragedy, the second time as farce". This crisis also brought to the fore the inherent dysfunctionalities in the very nature of capitalism (Patnaik 2008).

Market economies faced 124 "systemic" banking crises, i.e. episodes in which bad debts soared across the economy and much of the banking sector was insolvent since 1970. Of the various banking crises, stock market collapses and credit crunches, the collapse of Overend and Gurney in May 1866, the Barings Crisis in 1890, the Wall Street crash of 1929 contributing to the Great Depression of the 1930s, US Savings and Loan Scandal, 1985, the US stock markets crash of 1987, the collapse of hedge fund Long-Term Capital Market (LTCM), which originated in Asia in 1997 and spread to Russia and Brazil in 1998, and the Dot Com Crash, 2000 are noteworthy. With global capital markets, investment banks and derivatives such as credit swaps, currency swaps, credit linked notes, interest rate swaps, etc. becoming more complex than ever before, it is important to fit all pieces of the jigsaw puzzle together for a holistic assessment. For, as Marx insightfully pointed out in *The 18th Brumaire of Louis*

Bonaparte "the past lies like a nightmare upon the present". Thus the discussion clearly brings out the need for an incisive analysis of disruptions to periods of financial stress that rocked the world. This is important because *The Communist Manifesto* (1848) of Marx and Engels highlighted as below:

> In bourgeois society, therefore, the past dominates the present; in Communist society, the present dominates the past. In bourgeois society capital is independent and has individuality, while the living person is dependent and has no individuality.

Privatizing Profits, Socializing Losses!

It can justifiably be maintained that despite the frequency of the crisis in the capitalist system, the financial crisis of 2008 had more severe and longer-lasting consequences than similar crises in the past, except the crisis of 1929. This stark reality check, which needs to be looked at against the broader macro-economic canvas, prompted the US treasury secretary Henry Paulson and the Federal Reserve to announce a slew of measures to move troubled assets from the balance sheets of American financial companies into a new institution in an attempt to avoid a downward spiral in the markets and to make the wheels of finance turn again. In line with Greenspan's scathing comments of "privatizing profits, socializing losses", the Fed lent to banks to meet redemption demands from money market mutual funds and bought debt from bond houses to aid financial market liquidity. The evolving tale of state activism was also a parable of hypocrisy: these foes of light regulation were, till the onset of the crisis, its champions. Some "financial socialism" this! No wonder, then, Martin Luther King justifiably maintained that "capitalism is socialism for the rich and free enterprise for the poor".

"Pump-priming" and "Animal Spirits"

Historically, the pursuit of financial stability goes way back to the 1920s. The genesis of the spiral versus stability dispute lies in the economic conditions of the Great Depression and the seminal work of John Maynard Keynes, who observed in 1931 during the Great Depression:

> A sound banker, alas, is not one who foresees danger and avoids it, but one who, when he is ruined, is ruined in a conventional way along with his fellows, so that no one can really blame him.

In the pre-Keynesian era, there was a widely held belief that economies naturally veered towards full employment. Keynes demonstrated that an industrialized economy can move downward when job reductions depress consumer spending, causing businesses to slash jobs and decrease investment, etc. The Keynesian thesis of "pump-priming", which stressed that the vicious cycle could be smashed only by the government spending to enhance demand, dominated economic thought till the late 1960s. But it emerged in the 1970s that consumers and businesses are rational and far-seeing, and not likely to be rushed into recession. Further, the government could not spend its way out of a recession because consumers realize that extra government spending now would necessitate higher taxes in the future, thereby inducing consumers to save more to prepare for that eventuality and thus offsetting the stimulus.

Some of the main strands of this seven-decade long debate were brought to the fore by this global economic crisis. There is a strong body of thought, as for example, reflected in the works of George A. Akerlof of the University of California at Berkeley (Nobel Prize Winner 2001) and Professor Shiller of Yale University that showed that the Keynesian thesis continued to be contextually relevant and fiscal stimulus had an important part in the route back from the precipice. Akerlof and Shiller argued that conventional macroeconomics is based on people and businesses being rational actors. But this model crumbles during booms and busts. Hence, the only way to understand the crisis was to focus on non-economic motivations and irrational behavior, or what they called "animal spirits" (i.e., the optimism and confidence that allow business owners to invest for the future) in the Keynesian terminology. Akerlof and Shiller's much broader definition of animal spirits included "confidence, fairness, corruption and antisocial behavior" as well as "stories", or the natural inclination of people to put together tales about the way the world works.

In conformity with a confluence of events and developments, a significant modification of the conventional strategy for growth and structural transformation is urgently needed. Akerlof and Shiller advanced the notion of a "confidence multiplier" (government action to boost confidence can have an impact far in excess of the original effort) analogous to the concept of a "fiscal multiplier" (government spending can have a wide-ranging impact on growth). The moral of the story that emerges from Akerlof and Shiller's fascinating analysis was that government needed to act forcefully to tame animal spirits, almost like enforcing rules on a child. This necessitates a fundamental change in relationship between government, banks, industry and consumers.

The worsening subprime crisis of illiquid loans and accounting for on an accrual basis in the "banking book" rather than on a mark-to-market basis in the "trading book", the frenzied speculation that caused cataclysmic disruptions in the international stocks and money markets could conceivably cause a liquidity crunch aggravating the slowdown and precipitating a recession. A key theme and driver was the "suboptimal, duplicative and out-of-date" regulatory forbearance (a case of the watchdog becoming the lap dog!) that characterised the ostensibly "transparent" but actually opaque markets, which are typical of modern finance. To quote Engels in *Anti-Dühring* (1877):

> The principles are not the starting-point of the investigation, but its final result; they are not applied to nature and human history, but abstracted from them, it is not nature and the realm of man which conform to these principles, but the principles are only valid in so far as they are in conformity with nature and history. That is the only materialist conception of the matter.

There is a fair measure of consensus that the genesis of the financial sector imbroglio lay in the "global imbalance", which was characterized by high savings and large current account surpluses in China and some other countries co-existing with debt financed over-consumption leading to large US deficits. Plainly, this situation of imbalance in the real economy, marked by a huge disequilibrium in the American economy because of excessive consumerism, which rose from two-thirds of the GNP to almost three-fourths of the GNP and the benign macroeconomic environment of high global output growth, low inflation and absurdly low interest rates, was unsustainable over the long haul. In the interregnum, the explosion of world macro-imbalances led to a general carelessness or a tendency to underprice risks, and the elusive search for better and progressively rising yield fostered financial innovation. In other words, wealth and income imbalance, current account imbalance, and financial sector imbalance together with financial innovations made up for the heady mix that caused the crisis. Engels justifiably maintained in his book *Socialism: Utopian and Scientific* (1880) as below:

> The materialist conception of history starts from the proposition that the production of the means to support human life and, next to production, the exchange of things produced, is the basis of all social structure; that in every society that has appeared in history, the manner in which wealth is distributed and society divided into classes or orders is dependent upon what is produced, how it is produced, and how the products are exchanged. From this point of view, the final causes of all social changes and political revolutions are to be sought, not in men's brains, not in men's better insights into eternal truth and justice, but in changes in the modes of production and exchange.

Explosive growth in both scale and complexity of innovations in the financial market were clearly reflected in the American runaway growth in the value of the total stock of credit securities, enhanced complexity of the securities sold, with the growth of the alphabet soup of structured credit products; and sharp rise in the volume of credit derivatives, enabling investors and traders to hedge underlying credit exposures, or to create synthetic credit exposures. The ludicrous situation was foreseen by Marx in his book *Capital*, when he stressed as under:

> A spider conducts operations that resemble those of a weaver, and a bee puts to shame many an architect in the construction of her cells. But what distinguishes the worst architect from the best of bees is this, that the architect raises his structure in imagination before he erects it in reality.

Michael Lewis cogently argues "the striking thing" about the current financial meltdown "is how egalitarian it has been". This crunch involved millions of oblivious persons "who have never heard of the Black-Scholes options-pricing models"—the financial theory that Lewis believes induced investors to take more risks than they should have, precisely by leading them to think they understood complicated financial risks and could price them accurately, when in fact they could not.

Sergio Focardi, Professor of Finance at EDHEC Business School has, however, demonstrated that the crisis had deep financial and economic roots, e.g. tremendous asset inflation, including the level of leverage in the market, which had clearly become unsustainable. Hence, it would be wrong to attribute the crisis to the use of defective mathematical models.

Changing the Rules of the Game

The financial debts rattled the world markets and gravely caused concern globally. In fact there are still no definitive answers on tackling this crisis. But undoubtedly the severity of the global financial crisis and the long, hard task of fixing the financial system require streamlining of financial regulations and supervision. As Marx cogently argued in Preface to the *Critique of Political Economy* (1859),

> There is in every social formation a particular branch of production which determines the position and importance of all the others, and the relations obtaining in this branch accordingly determine the relations of all other branches as well. It is as though light of a

particular hue were cast upon everything, tingeing all other colours and modifying their specific features.

The Future of Capitalism

The bastions of communist block have blamed capitalists for dragging the world into the biggest financial turmoil after the Great Depression of 1930s. Addressing the world Economic Forum at Davos, Switzerland, the Russian Prime Minister, Vladimir Putin spoke of a "perfect storm that... decimated the old system, rendering it obsolete," whereby "the investment banks, once considered the pride of Wall Street, have virtually ceased to exist". The Chinese premier, Wen Jiabao also blamed the United States for global economic meltdown: "Inappropriate macroeconomic policies... unsustainable model of development characterized by prolonged low savings...and high consumption...the blind pursuit of profit and the failure of financial supervision—all have contributed to the crisis." These and many other leaders of the communist block felt, at least in the latter half of 2008-09 that the future of capitalism was uncertain.

Talking of stimulus packages that were announced by one country after the other to save their respective economies, Jiabao remarked: "Suddenly, the invisible hand that is supposed to guide the goods and people in a free market economy has vanished, and the visible hand of the government is back in action." While some economists called the use of taxpayers' money to cover the private sector losses a strange thing to have happened, others described it as a significant policy shift at the international level. The boilouts also created a huge public outery dubbing it as "the socialization of private sector losses". According to CPI(M),

> Public pressures forced the governments of capitalist countries to partly nationalise the banks and financial companies, which were being bailed out using taxpayers' money. The deepening of the crisis eventually caused a significant policy shift at the international level. Governments across the world began abandoning fiscal conservation and expanding public expenditure on a big scale, abandoning neoliberal policies.[1]

Some economists went to the extent of saying that Adam Smith's 'hand money' had vanished into the air, and the world was returning to the good old days of big government as recommended by John Maynard Keynes who was an advocate of state intervention in economic activities. There were even beliefs, when the crisis was at its peak in the last quarter of calendar year 2008, that Karl Marx's prophecy that "capitalism will be replaced by communism just as feudalism was replaced by capitalism" may come true in the foreseeable future.

Marx saw the power of unbridled capitalism as a kind of myth which became more real than it actually is. However, in the present era of unchallenged capitalism, the only reality is money and its purchasing power. People want money in their pockets and their accounts, and the liberty to buy what they want to. That is how they understand the system. People believe in capitalism as it talks about profits, incentive and consumers' sovereignty.

Global Economic Crisis and Imperialist Globalization

The communist leaders allege that the global economic crisis was a direct outcome of imperialist globalization and the neoliberal policies pursued under its ambit by governments across the capitalist world. All the major capitalist centres—the US, the EU and Japan witnessed recession simultaneously and in huge magnitude, before it spread to the other parts of the world and clearly, in not as large proportion as in the capitalist world. The argument of these leaders is based on the following points:

1. There has been a wide gap in the distribution of income and wealth. In the US, for example, the wealthiest one per cent have earned over 20 per cent of all incomes in the last decade, whereas the bottom 50 per cent earned about 13 per cent of all incomes. This gap created a mismatch in the economy, making many of the low-income people to go for costlier and much riskier subprime loans, which exposed the financial institutions including banks to a great risk.

2. Capitalism has thrived on globalization, which, inter alia, has led to an increasing concentration of wealth and capital in the hands of business elite which indulged in a phenomenal increase of speculative businesses and activities. Unprecedented rise in the prices of select equities in the share market and the mushrooming of realtors in the wake of very high prices of properties before the economic meltdown are examples. It is pertinent to mention here that when the earnings and living standards of low-income groups worsened, the growth process became largely dependent on speculative bubbles in the financial markets, including equity markets, property markets as well as credit-driven consumption growth of affluent classes.
3. There have been unbridled privatization and liberalization in the capitalist countries. This, the imperalist world claims has led to fast economic growth, and it may be right in claiming so, but at the same time this has also meant the withdrawal of state intervention in most economic activities and "dismantling of market regulation."[2] In this regard it may be mentioned that it has now been universally accepted that poor financial regulation in the capitalist economies was at the root of global economic crisis. There were no financial stability frameworks to mitigate the systemic risks inherent in capital markets. IMF's Working Paper (2009) has this to say regarding the situation that developed into a worldwide crisis: "The depth and breadth of the financial crisis has given fresh impetus for authorities around the world to rethink existing financial stability frameworks. Such revision needs to start from reconnecting with the objectives of financial regulation. With hindsight, there has been a collective failure to address a key objective—mitigation of systemic risk."[3] The Paper has highlighted five important points that may well be

called a synopsis of the main reasons that led to the global economic meltdown:

(i) Central banks and supervisory agencies have not put enough energy into the development of macroprudential tools that can, alongside monetary policy, be used to address the build-up of exposures to aggregate risks.

(ii) Treasury departments have been slow to introduce and adjust the scope of special resolution regimes that mitigate the systemic impact of failure and that can address moral hazard incentives arising from implicit safety nets.

(iii) Prudential supervisors have not developed and applied heightened prudential standards for large and complex institutions whose failure can have a major disruptive effect on financial markets.

(iv) Central banks have not always been successful in promoting systemically robust procedures for the clearing and settlement of trades in rapidly-evolving financial markets. The example highlighted by the crisis is a lack of a robust infrastructure for credit derivatives.

(v) The overall framework does not appear to have been fully conducive to achieving its objectives, often leaving ill-defined the responsibilities and tools of central banks in their pursuit of financial stability.[4]

The questions that come to mind, and the arguments that capitalists make in reply the above arguments are: If capitalism is the root cause of the crisis because of its policies, then why should the communist economies like those of Russia and China be impacted in a major way? Why do we have failures and recessions in communist regimes also? Though China has done very well during the crisis, yet Russia—a communist economy has been greatly impacted by the crisis, why? If

China, which is a communist economy has stood very well during the crisis, so has India, which is by no means a communist economy, and which has embraced a policy of privatization and liberalization since the 1990s; what are the reasons? It is not easy to answer these questions in entirety. But this much can be stated with a fair degree of credibility that in the present world of globalization, the impacts of events like financial crisis do not remain confined to one country or region. The ripple effect is felt in all parts of the globe, whatever the nature of economy. Nevertheless, not much can be taken away from the point made by the communists that the financial crisis was perhaps the inevitable outcome of a distorted and unsustainable growth process, which was not based on broad-based economic expansion. Lack of financial regulation was a serious lapse in this whole episode.

Severe economic crises have occurred and recurred in many countries in the past few decades, notably in South-East Asia, Russia, Mexico, Brazil, Argentina and Turkey. But what was striking about the recession of 2008-09 crisis was that it hit the US—the leader of the capitalist world the most. It engulfed huge financial institutions like Lehman Brothers which had survived even the Great Depression of 1930s. The insurance companies like AIG, banks like Bear Stearns and a large number of companies, including financial companies, which had indulged in reckless speculation, became bankrupt. Once the US economy came on the verge of collapse, the entire capital world, which in the present age of globalization had become increasingly dependent on the US, sank into recession.

India and Global Economic Meltdown

It is widely believed that the Indian economy was not as severely impacted by the meltdown as those of America and Europe. In fact, India is said to have performed well even during the recession. However, the impact on India at least initially was quite large. There were large lay-offs, erosion of profits, credit crunch, share market crash and a drastic fall in demand and thus prices of various types of goods and services, decrease in exports, among other things.

Those with communist ideologies feel that the government's response to the global crisis was neither prompt nor adequate. At first it was in the denial mode. The officials claimed that the fundamentals of the economy were strong. Though it proved to be so, yet the impact was clearly visible as explained above. Though the government increased Plan expenditure for 2009 by ₹ 20,000 crore, it was only 0.5 per cent of the country's GDP, and which, according to IMF, was the fourth lowest fiscal stimulus package in proportion to GDP, among the G-20 countries. In comparison, China's fiscal stimulus for 2009 was 2 per cent of its GDP; that of the US was 1.9 per cent of its GDP; Russia's was 1.7 per cent; Germany, Canada and South Korea had stimulus packages equivalent to 1.5 per cent of their respective GDPs; Japan's was 1.4 per cent; Indonesia, South Africa and Argentina had 1.3 per cent and Mexico one per cent (IMF). A higher stimulus package by the Indian government would have served the economy better. But the government expressed its helplessness in doing so, citing constraints. Nonetheless, it doled out ₹ 30,000 crore in tax concessions to big corporate houses though even these concessions were not linked to protecting the workers from lay-offs and retrenchment.

The Indian financial system has remained relatively immune to the global meltdown which rocked the advanced capital countries, principally because of regulations and public sector domination of the financial sector, which the Left claims has struggled hard to defend. It did not allow the passage of the Banking Regulation (Amendment) Bill which would have allowed the takeover of Indian private banks by foreign banks. If this had happened, the Indian banks would have been severely affected by the crisis. Similarly, the Left defended the insurance sector by preventing the passage of legislation to increase foreign direct investment (FDI) in the insurance sector from 26 per cent to 49 per cent.

The Left also claims to have protected the pensions of government employees by opposing the Pension Fund Regulatory and Development Authority (PFRDA) Bill which would have led to pension funds being privatized and invested in the stock market. But for the Left's opposition, the unhindered financial liberalization that the government was recklessly pursuing, would have exposed the banking and insurance sectors to the same catastrophe witnessed in the western capitalist world. Indian people's savings remained safe and secure because of Left's intervention.[5]

When major financial institutions, including the financial giant Lehman Brothers failed, there was a stock market crash all over the world. BSE SENSEX and Nifty index in India also experienced a huge fall. Between September and December 2010, the Bombay Stock Exchange (BSE) index fell from over 20,000 to less than 10,000. The investors lost a sizeable amount of their investment. The major reason was that the foreign institutional investors (FIIs) took ₹ 67,000 crore out of India in 2008, and another ₹ 12,000 crore till mid-March 2009. This bears testimony to the speculative capital flows to India. The government was keen to push capital account convertability which the Left opposed. If the government were allowed to go for greater capital account liberalization, the FIIs and other investors would have taken larger sums of money out of the country causing a sharper fall in the stock market and a severe currency crisis.

There is no question that the global financial crisis crippled economic growth around the world. But there is a lesson in this crisis. The rumours about the demise of capitalism may be exaggerated but the warning signs are clear and scary. In the present age of globalization, an unregulated market—which is susceptible to manipulation by a few rogue characters—can plummet and send out strong ripples. Capitalism may have an in-built self-correcting mechanism, but how painful such mechanism is, can be realized from the global economic conditions which have jolted the entire world.

The financial crisis that rocked the world was the result of serious shortcomings in domestic financial governance that have exposed gaps in the global governance of institutional finance and capital. Its immediate roots lie in the excessive and not so transparent leverage of complex securities and derivatives that inflated the real economy to excessive proportions. The US regulatory regime governing its financial and banking worlds—which had far-reaching repercussions for the entire globe—can be euphemistically described as light, incomplete and fragmentary. Thus, the need for efficient, effective and transparent regulatory and surveillance instruments and institutions is quite obvious. The importance of the role of global governance institutions, is being increasingly felt now more than ever before. Only a new regulatory regime will reassure the world at large that the balance has been restored between the risks and the benefits of integrating with an open world economy.

There is a growing recognition that the system to manage the modern world of banking, capital and finance has to be redesigned. The corporations, markets and financial flows are global, but regulatory and financial systems are national—or in a few cases like Europe—regional. The world at this juncture needs "some sort of visionary internationalism" like Bretton Woods Conference in 1944 that founded the IMF and the World Bank and restructured the international monetary system.

Debt Crisis in Europe

Two years after the crisis hit the world there have been talks of economic recovery at least in some parts of the world. But this does not mean that the debate regarding the real causes of meltdown, i.e. capitalism or regulatory failure, privatization or gross speculative activities by financial institutions, has ended decisively. While recovery itself is partial, some European nations are facing a severe sovereign debt crisis. Since early 2010, a sovereign debt crisis has developed in some European states like Greece, Ireland, Italy, Portugal and Spain. Stefan Schultz, a staff writer for *Spiegel*, has discussed the issue in detail.[6] The situation has led to a crisis of confidence in the entire Eurozone. Since Greece has been under the most severe debt crisis, a brief account is necessary here to drive home the point being made.

From 2000 to 2007, the Greek economy grew at an annual rate of 4.2 per cent as foreign capital flooded the country. A strong economy and falling bond yields allowed its government to run large structural deficits. It is believed that large public deficits are one of the features that have marked the Greek social model since the restoration of democracy in 1974. After the removal of the right leaning military junta, the government wanted to bring disenfranchised left leaning portions of the population into the economic mainstream.[7] In order to do so, successive Greek governments have, among other things, run large deficits to finance public sector jobs, pensions, and other social benefits. Since 1993, its debt to GDP has remained above 100 per cent. Thus, it can be deduced that socialist policies can put huge pressure on a country's debt situation.

There was a strong fear that the debt crisis could spread beyond Greece as it reduced the confidence of other European economies. Ireland with a government deficit of 14.3 per cent, UK with 12.6 per cent, Spain with 11.2 per cent and Portugal at 9.4 per cent were considered most vulnerable.[8]

Shortly after the announcement of the EU's new "emergency fund" for Eurozone countries in early May 2010, Spain's socialist government announced new austerity measures designed to further reduce the country's budget deficit. It had hoped to avoid such deep cuts, and weak economic growth as well as domestic and international pressure forced the government to expand on cuts already announced in January 2010. As one of the largest Eurozone economies, the condition of Spain's economy remained of particular concern to international observers, and faced pressure from the United States, the IMF, other European countries and the European Commission to cut its deficit more aggressively. Thus, it is not just the system of government that causes a crisis but the overall conditions, locally and globally that are largely responsible for it.

It is also being felt that the existing political or economic institutions like IMF and G7 have not proved equal to the task of coordinating an adequate response to global crisis. The way things are, it is hard to imagine that any major global challenge can be effectively addressed without involving all three Asian giants—China, India and Japan. But two of them, viz. India and Japan are not permanent members of the UN Security

Council, and two, viz. China and India are not part of the G7. These anomalies need to be removed to give these countries more say in international economic activities so that a balance is created in the financial affairs of the world and crisis situations are effectively dealt with before they assume catastrophic proportions.

Notes

1. "The Global Economic Crisis and India: Need for Pro-People Policies." CPI(M): 2009.
2. *Ibid.*
3. Ereland Walfer Neir. "Financial Stability Frameworks and the Role of Central Banks: Lessons from the Crisis." IMF Working Papers (2009).
4. *Ibid.*
5. "The Global Economic Crisis and India: Need for Alternative Pro-People Policies." CPI(M): 2009.
6. Stephan Schultz. "Five Threats to the Common Currency."
7. Demetrius A. Flouda. "The Greak Financial Crisis 2010: Chimerae and Pandaemonium."
8. "2010 European sovereign debt crisis." Wikipedia.

7

Revival and Recovery 2009-10

The economic crisis leading up to recession in a number of developed economies pushed back their GDP growth during 2008-09 and 2009-10. However, Indian economy displayed a degree of resilience although the rate of economic growth witnessed a deceleration from the pre-recession level.

Industrial activity in India slowed down since the beginning of the second half of FY09. However, there were a few positive signs which indicated a recovery in some sections of the economy. Revival in auto sales, relatively high growth in infrastructure industries, easing interest rates inducing consumption demand were a few cheering factors. But it was still too early to get a sense of direction in which way the economy was heading during that period though the growth story was intact.

Economic Outlook 2009-10

The impact of the economic crisis initially was widespread. It not only affected businesses, but also consumers, both in urban and rural regions. A survey conducted by IMRB among 2,440 households across urban and rural areas revealed that consumers cut expenditure on high-end products and entertainment in order to survive in the crisis. The survey showed that consumers had a negative outlook on the future of the economy. But towards the end of 2009-10, the conditions greatly improved. The experts were optimistic about the future economic outlook. All regions except a few saw improvement in the economic situation in the near future.

Improvement in Expenditure Outlook

When economic slowdown gripped the economy, the consumers adopted a cautious outlook on their spending. Expenditure on big-ticket items such as buying new home or vehicle, and on entertainment, went drastically down. On the other hand, spending on essential items such as FMCG products, apparels and telecommunication actually improved significantly. But in 2009-10 consumers' expenditure on high-end products started looking up.

Industrial Output Clawed back to Positive Territory

Industrial output clawed back into positive territory to rise by a better-than-expected 1.4 per cent in April 2009, its best performance in five months and providing the clearest signal yet that the country may have seen the back of the slowdown.

The index for industrial production (IIP) bounced back from a revised negative 0.8 per cent in the preceding month on the back of a resilient domestic demand, after slipping into negative terrain in December 2008, February as well as March 2009.

Pronab Sen, the country's chief statistician, attributed the jump to industries building their inventory levels in anticipation of an increase in demand. According to him, the strength of the recovery would be evident in the ensuing months. "By July, we will have a clearer picture about the strength of the recovery," he said, adding that a lot will depend on whether private investments will remain robust.

In a research note after the IIP data was released, Goldman Sachs said: "Historical peak-to-trough declines in the investment cycle suggest a bottoming out in the first half of 2009, and the economy continues to have a significant pent-up demand for investment, especially in infrastructure and in affordable housing."

Economists had forecast IIP to rise on an average by 0.5 per cent in April 2009. Many economists had expected the negative trend to continue. They said the excess liquidity in the system, easing of financial tightness and the pickup in key indicators like the purchasing managers index, infrastructure index and rise in cement dispatches pointed to a recovery. A strong show by intermediate goods segment and an expansion in 11 out of 17 manufacturing sub-sectors showed that the recovery was broad-based and sustainable, they said. Intermediate goods are inputs for production of other goods and growth in this segment suggest that manufacturers were expecting demand for finished goods to rise. The IIP figures show encouraging signs of recovery and the stimulus packages may be having some impact. It is critical to sustain this pace of recovery," said Harsh Pati Singhania, president of industry lobby group FICCI.

Table 7.1: Trend in IIP Growth

		March		April-March	
	Weight	2009	2010	2009	2010
IIP	100.0%	0.3%	13.5%	2.8%	10.3%
Mining	10.5%	1.9%	11.0%	2.6%	9.7%
Manufacturing	79.4%	-0.3%	14.3%	2.9%	10.8%
Electricity	10.2%	6.3%	7.7%	2.7%	6.0%
Use-Based Classification					
Basic	35.6%	1.9%	10.1%	2.7%	7.1%
Capital	9.3%	-6.3%	27.4%	8.1%	18.0
Intermediate	26.5%	1.9%	12.7%	-1.9%	13.8%
Durables	5.4%	8.4%	32.0%	4.5%	26.3%
Non-Durables	23.3%	-1.0%	3.3%	5.1%	1.8

Source: Central Statistical Organisation (CSO).

Table 7.1 reveals that the Index of Industrial Production (IIP) showed a growth of 10.3 per cent during the year ended March 2010 as compared to 2.8 per cent in 2008-09. Mining, which had a growth of only 2.6 per cent in 2008-09, registered a growth of 9.7 per cent in 2009-10. Manufacturing and electricity showed a growth of 10.8 per cent and 6.00 per cent respectively during 2009-10 as compared to 2.9 per cent and 2.7 per cent respectively during 2008-09. As per use based classification, durables showed a robust growth of 26.3 per cent in 2009-10 as against just 4.5 per cent in 2008-09. When the economic crisis was at its peak, i.e. in 2008-09, intermediate goods had a negative growth of –1.9 per cent. It not only came in the positive territory during 2009-10 but showed a good growth at 13.8 per cent.

Table 7.2: Significant Contributors to Manufacturing Growth

Sector	Weight March 2009	Growth March 2010	Contribution to Manuf.	Growth
Machinery and Equipment other than				
Transport equipment	9.57	0.5%	22.1%	4.3%
Transport Equipment and Parts	3.98	11.3%	23.0%	1.7%
Food Products	9.08	-36.0%	26.2%	1.6%
Basic Metal and Alloy Industries	7.45	-4.5%	15.8%	1.5%
Other Manufacturing Industries	2.56	-20.3%	40.1%	1.4%
Others	—	—	3.6%	—
Manufacturing	79.36	—	—	14.3%

Source: CSO

Machinery and equipment, transport equipment and parts thereof, food products, basic metal and alloy industries are the main constituents of manufacturing sector in India. Table 8.2 shows growth trends in these industries in March 2009 and March 2010. Machinery and equipment other than transport equipment had a meager growth of 0.5 per cent in March 2009, but registered a growth of 22.1 per cent in March 2010. Transport equipment and parts did not have as much variation in growth as other industries, growing 11.3 per cent and 23.0 per cent in March 2009 and March 2010 respectively. Growth in food products showed the biggest variation. It remained in the negative territory and decelerated at –36.0 per cent during March 2009, but came out strongly by registering a growth of 26.2 per cent in March 2010. Basic metals also had a negative growth at –4.5 per cent in March 2009. However, it grew by 15.8 per cent in March 2010. Other manufacturing industries which had a negative growth of –20.3 per cent in March 2009, came up strongly with a growth of 40.1 per cent in March 2010. The comparison given in Table 7.2 above bears testimony to three important things. One that when the global economic meltdown was at its peak, i.e. in the second half of 2008-09, all the industries in the manufacturing sector in India experienced a fall in growth, some showing a negative growth, Secondly, that manufacturing in India was affected by the global economic crisis despite all the claims of decoupling. Thirdly, that the things had improved vastly by March 2010 when all the industries showed a much better growth.

Specific Components of Capital Inflow

With regard to specific components, net equity flows fell from $297 billion in 2007 to $241 billion in 2008 before edging up to $250 billion in 2010, the bulk of it foreign direct investment. Portfolio equity investment, which witnessed a capitulation of $8 billion in 2007 and $92 billion in 2008, came back to positive territory of around $25 billion in 2009 and 2010. Net new debt-creating private credits shifted from $591 billion in 2007 to net repayments of $100 billion in 2009 before resuming net inflows of $123 billion in 2010.

Asia led in FDI inflow among all the emerging markets of the world. Net private flow to Asian emerging markets fell from $296 billion in 2007 to $88 billion in 2009 before rising to $120 billion in 2010. As a percentage of the total for all emerging markets, Asia's share rose to 63 per cent in 2009 before reverting to 32 per cent in 2010. The jump in 2009 reflects the sharp retrenchment in flows to Eastern Europe, Russia and Turkey, which experienced output contraction of 7 per cent.

In addition to somewhat more favourable global backdrop, capital flows to India were bolstered during 2009-10. Net private flows had reached a record $90 billion in the fiscal year ending March 2008 before retrenching to $8 billion in 2008-09, but were likely to rebound to $27 billion in 2009-10. Net private flows to India was 10 per cent of the total of all emerging markets in 2007-08, which improved in 2009-10 after the major impact of economic slowdown was over.

Stabilization of Financial Markets

India needed to push reforms in the banking, insurance and pension sectors so that corporates can have access to more long-term funds, prime minister's economic advisory council chairman Suresh Tendulkar said at a conference organised by United Nations Conference on Trade & Development (UNCTAD) that banks were unnecessarily affected by the irrational import of the psychology of gloom and doom. Conditions in India were different from industrialised nations of the West which were over-leveraged and less-capitalised. During 2008-09 the interest rates were reduced by banks to maintain money supply and boost demand. However, after a ceratin limit, banks could not lower interest rates which would affected their profitability. Some of the banks had taken deposits at higher rates before the financial crisis hit. While the fact can be explained, the declining credit-deposit ratio by banks cannot be explained, he added. After the global financial crisis, external sources of funds had dried up for the corporate sector. But, there was no immediate danger. Before the financial crisis, companies had accumulated resources to meet their finance requirements and this would last for sometime.

India Maintained Steady GDP

In one of his speeches, Prime Minister Manmohan Singh said that India will return to 8-9 per cent growth in the medium term, since the country was on a strong wicket on many fronts. Once the global economy started to recover in 2009-10, the return on capital will also be higher in an economy like India, which was poised to grow faster than its Western counterparts. And the increase in FDI flow into the country was a clear sign of easing capital situation.

Although the Prime Minister stated that India will bounce back to 8-9 per cent growth in the medium term even if developed economies do not recover, yet we have to understand what are the conditions necessary to achieve this. It is important to remember the supply-side constraints. A lot of people are concerned about the global economy. The impact of the global economy on India, primarily on the demand side, is less than would otherwise be the case. But as long as on the supply side, we are in a situation where productivity and domestic savings and the growth of capital and the growth of investment leading to the growth of capacity take place the way we want it, we should be able to grow at 8-9 per cent. The focus is on savings and whether we are investing enough, if there will be enough inflow of foreign investment and whether domestic capital will be able to achieve the productivity gains is what we have to look at. All known cases of high growth are not those where you just expand capital stock but also where you have high levels of productivity. On all these counts, India is in a very strong position. What has happened, though, is that the global economy will grow slowly, but over a medium term, we can overcome that problem.

In the context of India needing more foreign savings, it has to be ascertained whether capital flows have already begun to ease?

After the collapse of Lehman Brothers, there was an atmosphere of uncertainty and a huge premium on liquidity. Global financial institutions were pulling back capital to reconstitute their own balance sheets. Then there was some restoration of confidence that the system was not going to collapse. The news that came from the West was that perhaps, by the second half of the calendar year 2010, the global economy will bottom out and start a gentle upswing. There won't be robust growth but there will be growth in the world economy 2010-11. This puts an end to fear and uncertainty. Once the confidence is restored, global investors will look for returns. But since the West will grow slower, the return on capital will be higher in economies which grow faster, like India and China. Referring to reforms the PM said that it is not enough to talk about reforms that will have an impact in the next six months. Psychologically, we also have to look at the reform signal for the medium term; the actual impact of those decisions will be seen only after two to three years. The signals given today change investor expectations, and that's not necessarily to do with foreign investor expectations. Foreign investment is important but domestic investment is much larger.

Signs of Economic Revival on the Anvil

The economic meltdown was at its peak during 2008-09. Financial year 2009-10 however began on a positive note. The gloom that prevailed on the economies, world over, finally seemed to be ebbing a bit.

While the markets and the economy started to show some signs of revival, the corporate world continued to adopt a cautious approach and appeared skeptical about a quick upturn in the overall economic conditions. The skepticism was clearly reflected in the declining Business Confidence Index (BCI), which went down for five consecutive quarters in a row before relenting. After that the firms began to see some ray of hope. This optimism stemmed from the recovery expected by these firms in their turnover and profitability in the near term.

Some sectors of the economy started hoping to see their top line graph move in the upward direction, albeit slowly. Consumer non-durables led this race with most respondents expecting a surge in the domestic sales by 5 per cent to 10 per cent. Interestingly, this was the only sector where not a single respondent was expecting a decline in sales in the near future. The same, however, could not be said about the consumer durables and the capital goods sector where the confidence level clearly reflected the ebbing demand conditions in the domestic market with both households and businesses having safely put their long-term and heavy expenditures on hold. But the situation started improving in this area too during 2009-10 and afterwards.

The services sector was believed to be somewhat neutral in its view and most respondents under this category did not expect things to change much in the following months. The export forecasts continued to be lackluster in most of 2009-10. The overall scenario was not much exciting with only a marginal increase in the number of respondents expecting to see a hike in export sales. And even those who were hopeful expected only a trivial increase in sales by up to 5 per cent. As sales were expected to move, though slowly, it seemed that the firms would leave no stone unturned to meet the demand with adequate supply. With firms using their capacities to the optimum levels, most respondents wanted to maintain their production levels for the next six months. There was a sharp decline in the number of respondents who thought of cutting down their production.

It was surprising to see marginal increase in the number of respondents expecting a surge in the import of raw materials given their neutral perception with respect to production. This pattern seemed to have been influenced by the fact that a large portion of imported goods are used as inputs in exports. While there had been an increase in those who anticipated rise in imports, it was only vis-à-vis the previous quarter. For majority, the current pattern of raw material imports remained the same for 2009-10 and the initial months of 2010-11.

Forecasts about US Economy

Experts from some of the top banks believed that the US economy would emerge from recession by the end of third quarter of 2009. The American Bankers Association's Economic Advisory Committee said it expected economic activity to increase by 0.5 per cent between July and September 2009. But committee head, Bruce Kasman said the economy would "return to growth [in the quarter] but not to health". The bankers also said US unemployment would hit 10 per cent early 2010. Separately, the Secretary-general of the Organisation for Economic Co-operation and Development (OECD) stated that economic recovery within the group's 30 countries will begin at the end of 2009. Speaking in Mexico, Angel Gurria added that the US would be one of the first countries to come out of recession. From hindsight we can say now that it did not happen.

US consumer spending, which accounts for about two-thirds of economic growth in the US, was expected to increase in the second half of 2009 and help to moderate lay-offs and cuts in investment spending, the Economic Advisory Committee said. "Coupled with support from policy stimulus and an improvement in financial market conditions, these developments have made it likely that the overall economy will expand in the second half of the year," it predicted. This prediction however did not come off.

Mr. Kasman, the chief economist for JP Morgan Chase, also said that a recovery in the housing market would be an "important contributor" to economic growth. But he cautioned against too much optimism. "Growth in the coming quarters is likely to gather momentum but will not prove sufficiently robust to undo much of the severe damage done to our labour markets and public finances," he said. This meant that growth would not return to "trend pace" until the middle of 2010, he added. For this reason, unemployment would remain at or above 9.5 per cent for the whole of next year. The current unemployment rate (October 2011) in the US is 9.1 per cent. Thus, this prediction, though not entirely true, was more realistic.

There were mixed calls on the US economy. The US economy contracted by an annual rate of 5.7 per cent in the first three months of 2009. The figures that came during 2009-10 sent out mixed messages about the timing of any recovery. Earlier, the figures showed that the number of new houses being built in the US in May bounced from record lows in April 2009. But separate figures showed that industrial production fell by more than analysts had expected.

India Inc Set to Ride the Growth Wave

India Inc expected the country to be back on the growth track during 2009-10 and Third World countries to become more powerful as a fall-out of the global economic slowdown, a survey by research firm IMRB International revealed.

The survey commissioned by All India Management Association (AIMA) showed that nearly two-thirds of the managers, who took part in the survey, had positive views about India's economic growth and believed that India Inc will bounce back with renewed profits. As per the survey conducted among 450 middle-level managers across sectors such as pharmaceuticals, automobile, energy and power, telecom and IT, the respondents feel that the sub-prime crisis in the US and weak corporate governance were the main causes of slowdown. Low sentiment brought down the consumer expenditure although there wasn't a steep decline in income levels. Consumer spending had come down, mainly in lifestyle.

While the spending on children and food products went up, there had been no significant change in the spending on automobile and household durables, the survey said. "With a stable government in power again, reforms will be unstoppable. A special focus should be laid on employment generating projects and increasing money flow in the economy, besides reducing taxes to bring back both consumers' and investors' confidence," said AIMA's research committee chairman B.S. Sahay.

The optimism was higher among managers in the pharmaceuticals, telecom, IT/ITeS and textile sectors, while it was low in automobile and financial services. Almost half of the respondents felt that liquidity crunch was the major problem facing corporate India. Despite higher optimism towards the Indian economy, around 35 per cent of those surveyed believed that economic recovery in India and elsewhere will not be too spaced out. This reflected, as stated earlier, the fact that Indian economy was not isolated from the global market.

According to the survey, besides the US, BRIC countries, particularly India and China, will be the primary growth drivers in the global recovery. Managers working with public sector companies were more optimistic about the economy than those in the private sector, the survey revealed. While most Indian private companies were trying to minimise risks by pulling back investments and cutting costs, public sector firms were taking steps to bring down operational expenses.

Promising Show by Core Sector

In the very first month of 2009-10, thought to be the Revival and Recovery fiscal, six core industries together clocked the fastest growth rate in 10 months, emboldening the prime minister Manmohan Singh's key economic advisor to hint at the possibility of an upward revision of the growth forecast for the year. Power, crude oil, refinery products, coal, cement and finished steel grew 4.3 per cent year-on-year, recovering from the low of 1.1 per cent in December 2008, according to a release by the ministry of commerce and industry. The April 2009 figures raised hopes of a brighter industrial output, as these six industries had a combined weightage of 26.7 per cent in the Index of Industrial Production (IIP).

Suresh Tendulkar said, "The growth in core sectors is on expected lines. Upside risk for economic growth projections made by EAC is emerging with a stable government coming to power, and the business confidence slowly returning," The Economic Advisory Council (EAC) had earlier projected a growth rate of 7 per cent, plus or minus 0.5 per cent, for 2009-10. The figures of April 2009 were the highest since July 2008, when the global financial meltdown pushed the Indian economy into rough waters. Consequently, the growth rate had dipped to 2.7 per cent for the last fiscal against 5.9 per cent for 2007-08. Coal, followed by cement, clocked the highest growth, and the annual growth rate in steel production moved into positive territory after a month-long gap.

The economists had forecast that the revival in cement and steel production would pick up further after April 2009 on the back of boosted public spending. Data on cement despatch for May from major manufacturers, including Ambuja Cement, Grasim Industries and its subsidiary UltraTech Cement, showed robust growth. However, the regular lull in construction activity during monsoon appeared to dampen this momentum thereafter.

The private investment activity was expected to pick up further, with business confidence making a comeback. However, it was felt that while signs of stability were becoming visible in terms of business confidence as well as modest improvement in investment growth, it may take some more time for the revival phase to set in, given the weakness in exports. In this regard, Yashika Singh, head, economic analysis, Dun & Bradstreet India stated thus:

> Easing liquidity conditions and interest rates in the domestic as well as global financial markets should help Indian corporates in raising funds, thereby providing support to investment and industrial activity in the revival phase.

With electricity generation also picking up, crude and petroleum refinery products were the only segments that showed an annual drop in production in April 2009. This was the fifth straight month for which crude production witnessed a year-on-year contraction while the output of petroleum refinery products showed the sharpest contraction in the past four months.

According to analysts, Indian oil wells were ageing, thus bringing down crude oil production. But with ONGC working on enhancing the productivity of these wells, we can expect production to move into positive territory, the experts said.

Global Consumer Confidence Stabilizing

Global consumer confidence was stabilizing after falling for 18 months, providing a glimmer of hope for a shattered world economy in which three quarters of households cut spending, a survey showed.

A Reuter's poll of 23 countries found that about 40 per cent of consumers blamed the banking and finance industry for the worst economic downturn since the Great Depression, while 19 per cent also held former U.S. President George W. Bush's administration and their own governments responsible for the crisis.

"It looks like we have hit bottom and so there are glimmers of hope," said Clifford Young of Ipsos Global Public Affairs, the international market research and polling company that carried out the online poll. "What we're seeing is that consumers for the most part have been scared, they have cut expenditures and increased savings," he said. "The uptick won't be as fast as the decline, but if the United States is stabilized that's really important in the global sense," he added. Ipsos polled people in the United States, Canada, Brazil, Mexico, Argentina, South Korea, China, Japan, Australia, India, Russia, Czech Republic, Poland, Hungary, Turkey, Sweden, Italy, the Netherlands, Belgium, Germany, France, Spain, and Britain. "The stabilization is basically happening in the United States, India and China and that has staunched a bit the bleed around the world," Young said. "That being said

Europe is still dicey as well as Brazil and Russia." This observation too wasn't entirely true for though China and India were recovering well from whatever effects they had on their industries, exports and economies in 2009-10, the US was still struggling and the Eurozone too looked uncertain.

In the United States, which sparked the global economic downturn, consumer confidence rose two percentage points to 13 per cent, while in China it jumped to 61 per cent from 46 per cent and in India it increased five points to 70 per cent. The effect of the financial crisis had lagged in Brazil, but consumer confidence in Latin America's largest economy dropped to 56 per cent from 61 per cent at the start of 2009-10, while Russian optimism fell to 35 per cent from 52 per cent and Europe dropped nine points to 23 per cent. "It's an issue of confidence in institutions," Young said of the continued fall in Europe. "For better or worse in the United States the people saw the government taking extreme actions. Though this happened in Europe it happened less so." The 23 countries, polled as mentioned earlier, make up 75 per cent of the world's gross domestic product. Cuts in household spending continued during the first half of 2009-10.

US Economic Recovery

Nearly half of 300 CEOs surveyed in the newly released fifth annual NYSE Euronext CEO Report, entitled "The Road to Recovery," conducted by Opinion Research Corporation, were of the opinion that a broad U.S. economic recovery in 2010 would be followed by a slower global rebound in 2011 or later.

While a large majority of CEOs were in favour of business tax cuts, low interest rates and lending to spur the economic recovery, U.S. and non-U.S. CEOs were divided in their opinion with respect to the intervention of government in business. However, they agreed on the need to restructure America's financial regulatory system, streamline corporate governance measures, and align U.S. and international accounting standards.

"The NYSE Euronext CEO Report 2010 reveals how CEOs have been forced to analyze their past habits and significantly change the way they operate today and plan for tomorrow," according to Jeff Resnick, President of Opinion Research Corporation. "Despite the troubled economy, CEOs have been able to find silver linings, from retaining and hiring skilled staff to strengthening corporate governance. US CEOs and their non-US counterparts have different views on government intervention and other matters, but they generally agree on the needs to be innovative yet disciplined to successfully emerge from the economic crisis," said Duncan L. Niederauer, CEO, NYSE Euronext. "Global CEOs are responsibly addressing the challenges brought on by the financial crisis, and are employing genuine operational discipline and planning for the future. They are focused on maintaining a strong balance sheet and on corporate competitiveness, and are identifying new growth opportunities and ways to build stakeholder value. I share their concerns on the recession's impact on entrepreneurship and venture capital investment. Moreover, the results show that CEOs throughout the world want to do their utmost to contribute to the recovery and to be part of the solution," he continued to say.

Unlike previous surveys, the fifth annual NYSE CEO Report had one dominating theme which emerged on almost every question—the economy. The global economic crisis, combined with the ensuing credit crunch, had forced companies to make changes in many areas of their business. While economic difficulties were the focus of studies during 2008-09 and were largely confined to the financial services sector, in 2009-10 they revolved around companies in all industries, globally.

It was noticed that CEOs of US-based companies were gloomier than CEOs based at companies outside the US. This phenomenon is sharply different from just two years ago, when 84 per cent of CEOs at U.S.-based companies thought the US economy was in excellent or good shape, significantly more positive than the evaluation of CEOs based outside the US during the same time period. Besides, earlier there was a strong dichotomy of opinion concerning the appropriateness of government intervention in business—U.S. CEOs normally disapproved while their non-U.S. counterparts generally approved. But it was seen that after the global economic crisis, the US government brought several stimulus packages—an action approved by majority of companies and people, though opposition was there by some who said that taxpayers money was being used to pay for poor financial management by big business houses.

Another significant point is that while companies were making across the board budget cuts, customer relations and shareholder relationship management remained much less affected. This meant that the CEOs are taking a long-term view of the importance of these areas, regardless of the current financial restraints.

Despite the downturn, most CEOs acknowledged that their companies had gained some benefits from the downturn. Getting a larger market share, contract renegotiations on easy terms and acquiring new employee talent at not so high packages in contrast with pre-crisis period were among the most commonly mentioned positives.

With a view to guiding their companies through the current turmoil, the CEOs focused on reducing expenses and debt through a variety of means including large lay-offs. This they said would strengthen the balance sheets of the companies. The HRD experts however were of the opinion that resorting to large lay-offs would not be in the long-term interests of the companies.

When the CEOs were asked what change they would make to help their companies through future market turmoil, the majority of them answered that they would put controlling costs and debt and remaining highly liquid at the top. Securing finance was the highest priority as the internal factor having a greater impact on revenue growth through 2010, while the strength of the management team a close second. As was the case in 2008, operational efficiency and management stood out as the internal factors expected to have more impact on profitability. CEOs downgraded the importance of new technology and products, partnerships and advertising and marketing. The expected impact of compliance costs also declined by 22 points since 2006.

The expected impact of health care costs dropped 23 points in 2009 and 2010, indicating that CEOs believe they may had done all they could to reduce these costs. CEOs viewed U.S. and global economic conditions as the most important external influences on their companies' overall growth through 2010, with the proportion of CEOs who rank these as 'much more important' having increased markedly since last year. This is quite significant in today's globalised world where the economies of individual countries are integrated to the world economies as well as those of other countries to a varying degree.

CEOs also thought that the metrics related to company's financial soundness such as outstanding debt, credit ratings, and cash flow, are much more important to shareholders than they were prior to the crisis, while various types of growth parameters such as sales, operating, earnings-per-share are less important.

Trends in interest rates continued to have the most influencing factor on business planning, although CEOs are including a greater number of new measures than several years ago. About eight in ten CEOs think that market opportunities in mergers and acquisitions (M&A) were 'exceptional' or 'good' through 2010, with CEOs of companies based outside the US being particularly upbeat about M&A potential. One-fourth of CEOs saw the M&A opportunities as 'exceptional.' It is pertinent to recall that during the peak period of the economic slowdown, M&A suffered quite a lot.

In contrast with previous years, when CEOs expected net budget increases for almost all areas, in 2010 they anticipated net increases only in areas like customer-relationship management, health care, technology, environmental compliance and investor relations. The results for customer-relationship management and investor relations indicated that CEOs are well aware of the importance of preserving goodwill towards their companies during lean times so they can capitalize on it in good times.

Throughout 2010, CEOs expected significant reductions in capital expenditures, raw materials, executive compensation and recruitment costs. Unlike three years ago, CEOs said they were experiencing much more difficulty attracting investors and retaining and customers. Conversely, it was a buyers' market for human talent.

As in the pre-crisis period, the United States was the region CEOs most frequently cited as crucial for their business through 2010. The U.S. was followed by Western Europe and China. This trend however is undergoing a change as the US and Europe are not recovering from the downturn as fast as many were expecting them to and the companies in other regions like Asia are performing better. But as in previous years, companies based outside the U.S. are more influenced by the trade environment, which is currently affecting them very unfavorably.

About half of CEOs viewed emerging markets like China and Korea and India as an opportunity for their companies, while only 3 per cent said they were a threat. About 50 per cent of those who viewed emerging markets as opportunities, were establishing or expanding local marketing and sales activities in these countries to draw maximum benefit of the opportunity, while most of the rest were investing in locally-owned facilities or partnering with local vendors.

Nearly one-third of CEOs believed that outsourcing offered less economic value during 2009 and 2010 than it did five years ago. CEOs of U.S. companies in particular thought outsourcing offered less value, while those at companies based outside the U.S. tended to differ.

It may be recalled that there was a hue and cry during financial turmoil about huge compensation being given to the executives of private companies. President Obama also criticized this and asked the American companies to reduce it.

Seeking to "restore trust" in the nation's financial industry, President Obama imposed a $500,000 pay cap for top executives at teetering firms needing federal payout money.

"This is America. We don't disparage wealth. We don't begrudge anybody for achieving success. And we certainly believe that success should be rewarded," Obama said. "But what gets people upset—and rightfully so—are executives being rewarded for failure, especially when those rewards are subsidized by U.S. taxpayers, many of whom are having a tough time themselves," he added. Obama lambasted top executives who grant themselves enormous compensation packages while turning to the American taxpayer when their firms are in trouble. He described the practice as a "shameful," "bad taste" and the "height of irresponsibility."[1]

During the survey, half of CEOs said their companies had made changes to executive compensation plans in 2009. Most of the companies have put in place cuts or freezes rather than increases in executive salaries, bonuses, raises and benefits and perks. The most common perks targeted for cuts or elimination were air travel expenses, club memberships, pensions, etc. But after the crisis, these perks were reduced considerably to control expenditure.

Business Confidence Rises in India despite Concerns

According to Confederation of Indian Industry-bi-annual Business Confidence Index (CII-BCI), India Inc's business confidence improved considerably for April-September 2009 period compared to the previous six months. CII-BCI was recorded at 58.7 for April-September 2009-10, which reflected an increase after two consecutive periods of decline. "The rise in the index reflects better expectations for the coming six months and confirms our belief that the worst is likely to be over for the economy", Director General, CII Chandrajit Banerjee, said. However, uncertain global economic outlook and slackening consumer demand still remained major concerns for the business community.

The CII-BCI is constructed as a weighted average of the Current Situation Index (CSI) and the Expectations Index (EI).

The CSI that reflects current business conditions lost 2.5 points for the period April-September 2009-10 when compared with the previous six months. In comparison with the corresponding period of previous year, the CSI was down 6.9 points, reflecting a decrease in current business sentiments due to global financial and economic meltdown.

The EI that reflects the expectation of Indian industry with regard to performance of their company, sector and the economy for the period April-September 2009-10 gained 4.9 points as compared to the second half of 2008-09. The CII survey, which was based on a sample size of 374 companies, showed that 83 per cent of the respondents expected GDP growth for the year 2009-10 to exceed 5 per cent, with the majority expecting it to remain between 5 and 6 per cent. On inflation, 86 per cent of the respondents expected it to be above 2 per cent in 2009-10, thus ruling out the possibility of sustained deflation in the economy. Given the global slowdown, 96 per cent of the respondents felt that it was only in the second half of 2009-10 and beyond, that the Indian economy may witness a turnaround and begin returning to normal growth.

In the survey there was also focus on the prospects for investment, capacity utilization, production, employment and exports as elements that build up the business confidence. It revealed that 30 per cent of the respondents planned to increase investments during April-September 2009-10. Capacity utilization had improved and 50 per cent of the respondents said that capacity utilization for April-September 2009-10 was expected to be in the range of 75-100 per cent compared to 39 per cent of respondents who said that capacity utilization was below 75. The CII survey also revealed that 23 per cent of the respondents expected the inventory levels to increase, lower than the 33 per cent that reported an increase for the past six months.

Nearly 50 per cent of the respondents felt that the value of production would increase in the next six months. Further, increase in production was likely because of expected increase in new orders. Over 50 per cent of the respondents were hopeful that new orders would increase in the next six months, compared to about 30 per cent of the respondents who were of the opinion that new orders had increased in the second half of 2008-09.

On exports, over 30 per cent of the respondents expressed confidence in expansion of exports for the period April-September 2009-10. Regarding procedural delays, over 90 per cent of the respondents felt that the delays have not reduced. This has been a long-standing hurdle for exporters, which raises transaction costs and needs to be addressed urgently.

The CII Business Outlook Survey also asked respondents what were their main concerns and the majority said that they were global economic instability, high interest rate, cost and availability of labour, infrastructure and institutional shortages, currency risks, slackening consumer demand, cost of compliance, surge in imports and risk of deflation.

Did Global Slowdown Bottom out in 2009-10?

It was felt, particularly in the latter half of financial year 2009-10, that the financial markets were coming out of a deep freeze, but it was too early to say that the global slowdown had bottomed out, said Standard & Poor's Ratings Services in a report. The report, titled "Fiscal Health of Asian Sovereigns If 'Green Shoots' Wither," was a "what-if" scenario analysis, looking at potential evolutions of selected Asian sovereign fiscal performance over the next few years in two scenarios.

One scenario was Standard & Poor's baseline projections of economic development, in which Asian economies would recover sometime in 2010 after steep declines in many of them. "In this scenario, the negative impact on sovereign credit ratings would be minimal, with the possible exceptions of those with a negative outlook—Thailand, Vietnam, and India," said Standard & Poor's credit analyst Kim Eng Tan.

The other scenario was an extended recession, in which eventuality, most of Asia would drag through four consecutive years of contraction. However, this scenario was considered to be a remote possibility by most of the economists. According to Tan, even in this scenario, "our simulation indicates that fiscal pressures are not likely to lead to default although sovereign credit quality in many cases would deteriorate markedly."

Organization of Petroleum Exporting Countries (OPEC) in its Monthly Oil Market Report (2009) pointed out that the world economy has seen some positive developments with the rally in the stock markets, improved confidence and a more positive sentiment. However, volatility remains high and large uncertainties persist as the world economy struggles to emerge from recession.

International Monetary Fund (IMF) was not very hopeful in the year 2009 and predicted a fall of 2.5 per cent in the GDP as compared to a fall of just 0.4 per cent a year earlier. The IMF figures suggested that, unless an investment-grade sovereign makes major policy mistakes, most would remain in that category after an extended-recession scenario, even though their credit ratings could slip by one to four notches. The resilience of these investment-grade sovereigns, with a few exceptions, stems from their relatively strong fiscal positions prior to the crisis. "These governments have years of fiscal consolidation and debt reduction, a sounder banking sector with higher capitalization and better risk management, and stronger external liquidity enhanced by more flexible exchange rate regimes," Tan said.

Standard and Poor's came up with a new level of innovation for investors looking to gain exposure to the US and Australian markets while limiting their risk. The rating agency launched risk controlled versions of its widely followed S&P 500 and S&P/ASX 200 indices. The S&P 500 Risk Control 10% Index and the S&P/ASX 200 Risk Control 15% Index tracked the return of a strategy which dynamically adjusted the exposure to each underlying index in order to control the level of risk. The S&P 500 Risk Control 10% Index targeted a volatility level of 10 per cent and the S&P/ASX 200 Risk Control 15% Index targeted a volatility level of 15 per cent. If the risk level reached a threshold considered too high, the exposure to the index would be decreased in order to maintain the target volatility.

If the risk level reached a level considered too low then the index will employ leverage to maintain the targeted level of volatility.

Indian Industry shows Marginal Recovery Signs

Indian manufacturing sector shows marginal signs of recovery with a few sectors moving from negative growth to moderate growth and a few other moving from moderate to positive growth compared to the previous quarters of 2008-09, said CII in a press release issued based on the CII's Ascon survey for the period April 2008-09 over April 2007-08.

The sectors that moved from negative growth group to moderate growth group between the third and fourth quarters of 2008-09 are fertilisers, LDPE, HDPE, pig iron, steel and mopeds.

High growth in production was reported by 18.75 per cent of the 80 sectors for April-Mar 2009. The percentage of sectors reporting high growth declined in the last two quarters from 40 per cent to 26.73 per cent to 15.63 per cent. However, the year-to-year comparison reveals that manufacturing sector has significantly slowed down during 2008-09 when compared to 2007-08. "While on a yearly basis the manufacturing sector has slowed down, there are some green shoots from a few sectors that have demonstrated a marginal pickup during the second half of 2008-09 when compared to the first half. These demonstrate a cautious optimism on signs of recovery", said Mr Chandrajit Banerjee, Director General CII.

Sectors reporting high growth are asbestos cement, switch gears, power cables, capacitors, industrial gases like argon, carbon dioxide and hydrogen. While the sectors reporting negative growth are edible oils, bus & truck tyres, M&HCVs, LCVs, MPVs, capital goods like textile machinery, distribution transformer, industrial valves, energy meters and motors starters. Other sectors such as cement, polymer like HDPE, LDPE, LLDPE, sponge iron, circuit breakers, auto components, electric motors, transmission line towers, vehicle industry including cars, scooters, motor cycles, other consumer durables like colour TV, refrigerators, electric fans and consumer non-durables like soya were in moderate growth category. Sectors reporting excellent growth are industrial gases like nitrogen and oxygen, power transformers, electric two wheelers, etc.

Out of the 32 sectors reporting sales, 17 sectors recorded moderate growth while 12 sectors were in negative growth category. Sales growth for electric two wheelers was nearly 50 per cent while for asbestos cement it was almost 22 per cent. Sectors reporting declining sales were ball and roller bearings, industrial valves, tractors, machine tools, textile machinery and utility vehicles. The sectors such as cement, sponge iron, automotive tyres, cars, electric fans, and vehicle industry indicate a moderate sales growth.

On the export side, 11 out of 22 sectors reported negative growth. Ball and roller bearing and vehicle industry including cars and motorcycles, etc. were the sectors in the excellent growth category. Industrial valves, textile machinery and commercial vehicles reported negative growth.

Weak Recovery in Europe

According to a UN report, "World Economic Situation and Prospects 2011" , the GDP of the European Union grew by 1.7 per cent in 2010 and is expected to slow to 1.5 per cent in 2011. The report said that Europe's economic discord had resulted in an uneven economic performance with some countries showing positive growth and others still remaining in recession. Fiscal and austerity measures dominated the region's economic landscape.[2]

The report also said that economic activity in Western Europe picked up well in the first half of 2010 due to an export-driven industrial rebound, fiscal support measures and inventory restocking. But in the second half of 2010, the output growth slowed as the rebound in global trade weakened, fiscal stimuli were phased out and the inventory cycle was complete. There were weaknesses in industrial production and high unemployment rates in many countries. There were fiscal crises in countries like Greece, Ireland, Portugal and Spain. All this indicated that recovery was far from complete.[3]

Notes

1. *Daily News*: 4 February 2009.
2. "World Economic Situation and Prospects 2011": UN Report.
3. *Ibid*.

8

India and the Global Financial Crisis What have We Learnt?

D. Subbarao, Governor, RBI

23 June 2011

...

President Narayanan

2. Late President Narayanan was a distinguished diplomat, a reputed parliamentarian, a capable minister and above all an erudite scholar. Born at the very bottom of India's social pyramid, he rose on to occupy the highest office in the country with no assets other than hard work, integrity and humility. 'A working President', as he described himself, he never allowed dogma to overwhelm his beliefs and convictions.

3. President Narayanan was in office from 1997 to 2002, a time when globalization, as we are experiencing it in the current times, was taking root. At the banquet he hosted for the visiting US President Bill Clinton in New Delhi in March 2000, President Narayanan remarked: "Mr. President, we do recognise and welcome the fact that the world has been moving inevitably towards a one-world.... But, for us, globalization does not mean the end of history and geography, and of the lively and exciting diversities of the world." This was a thoughtful remark. As much as globalization may be inevitable, history and geography need not be destiny. If we learn the lessons of experience, we will not repeat the same mistakes. This indeed is the topic for my oration, and my

tribute to late President Narayanan—to seek the lessons of the crisis that we have just gone through so that we can make this a better world of all of us.

Is this Time Different?

4. By all accounts the 2008-09 crisis has been the deepest financial crisis of our times. It has taken a devastating toll on global output and welfare. Arguably, the fundamental causes of all financial crises are the same—global imbalances, loose monetary policy and high levels of leverage driven by 'irrational exuberance'. In that respect this crisis has been no different.

5. Where this crisis has been different, however, is in its manifestation. Most recent crises had occurred in individual emerging economies or regions, and they were, at their core, traditional retail banking or currency crises. The countries in trouble could be rescued by multilateral interventions; besides, the advanced countries provided a buffer for trade and financial support. In contrast, this crisis originated in the most advanced economy, the United States, and hit at the very core of the global financial system. With virtually no buffers to fall back on, the crisis rapidly engulfed the whole world. Much to their dismay, emerging market economies too were soon pulled into the whirlpool.

How was India Hit by the Crisis?

6. India was no exception. We too were affected by the crisis. Output growth which averaged 9.5 per cent per annum during the three year period 2005-08 dropped to 6.8 per cent in the crisis year of 2008-09. Exports which grew at 25 per cent during 2005-08 decelerated to 12.2 per cent in the crisis year (2008-09) and declined by 2.2 per cent in 2009-10. In the pre-crisis years, we had capital flows far in excess of our current account deficit. In contrast, during the crisis year, net capital flows were significantly short of the current account deficit and this put downward pressure on the rupee. The exchange rate depreciated from ₹ 39.37 per dollar in January 2008 to ₹ 51.23 per dollar in March 2009.

7. Notwithstanding our sound banking system and relatively robust financial markets, India felt the tremors of the tectonic shocks in the global financial system. The first round effects came through the finance channel by way of sudden stop and then reversal of capital flows consequent upon the global deleveraging process. This jolted our foreign exchange markets as well as our equity markets. Almost simultaneously, our credit markets came under pressure as corporates, finding that their external sources of funding had dried up, turned to domestic bank and non-bank sources for credit.

8. By far the most contagious route for crisis transmission was the confidence channel. For weeks after the Lehman collapse in mid-September 2008, everyday there was news of yet another storied institution crashing. In this global scenario of uncertainty, the lack of confidence in advanced country markets transmitted as hiccups to our markets too. The net result was that all our financial markets—equity, debt, money and foreign exchange markets—came under varying degrees of pressure. Finally, the transmission of the crisis through the real channel was quite straightforward as the global recession that followed the financial crash resulted in a sharp decline in export demand for our goods and services.

Why was India Hit by the Crisis?

9. There was dismay in India that we too were affected by the crisis, and this dismay arose mainly on two counts. First, the exposure of our banks to toxic sub-prime assets was marginal and their off balance sheet activities were limited, and so, the argument went, we should not have been affected by a financial sector crisis that originated from these causes. Second, India's growth is driven by domestic demand and a drop in external demand, it was contended, should have caused no more than a small dent in output growth. Yet the crisis hit us, and did so more ferociously than we thought possible. The reason for this is globalization: India is more integrated into the global system than we tend to acknowledge. Let me illustrate that point with some broadbrush numbers.

10. India's two way trade (merchandize exports plus imports), as a proportion of GDP, more than doubled over the past decade: from 19.6 per cent in 1998-99, the year of the Asian crisis, to 40.7 per cent in 2008-09. Note that global trade declined by 11 per cent in 2009 as a result of the crisis in contrast to a robust average growth of 8.6 per cent during the previous few years 2004-07. Such a sharp collapse in world trade had an impact on our export demand demonstrating that our trade integration was quite deep.

11. If our trade integration was deep, our financial integration was even deeper. A measure of financial integration is the ratio of total external transactions (gross current account flows plus gross capital account flows) to GDP. This ratio had more than doubled from 44 per cent in 1998-99 to 112 per cent in 2008-09 evidencing the depth of India's financial integration. In sum, the reason India was affected by the crisis, despite mitigating factors, is its deepened trade and financial integration with the world.

Managing Globalization

12. What the experience of the crisis demonstrated clearly was the power of globalization. Globalization is a double edged sword; it opens up incredible opportunities but also poses immense challenges. India surely benefitted from opening up to the world but had also incurred costs on that count. The challenge for India, and indeed for all Emerging Market Economies (EMEs), is really to minimize the costs and maximize the benefits of globalization.

Lessons of Crisis

13. A lot is being written about how this crisis has been too important to waste, how we should learn the lessons of the crisis and apply them in a Schumpeterian creative destruction mode. Some people have, however, questioned the wisdom of drawing lessons even before the crisis is fully behind us. When Zhou Enlai, former Chinese Prime Minister, was asked what he thought of the French Revolution, he said it was too early to say. Historians who take a long view may agree with Zhou Enlai but practical policymakers do not enjoy that luxury. So,

let me use the opportunity of this platform to draw out eight big picture lessons of the crisis.

LESSON 1: IN A GLOBALIZING WORLD, DECOUPLING DOES NOT WORK

14. The crisis challenged many of our beliefs, and among the casualties is the decoupling hypothesis. The decoupling hypothesis, which was intellectually fashionable before the crisis, held that even if advanced economies went into a downturn, EMEs would not be affected because of their improved macroeconomic management, robust external reserves and healthy banking sectors. Yet the crisis affected all EMEs, admittedly to different extents, bringing into question the validity of the decoupling hypothesis.

15. Some analysts argue against such an outright dismissal of the decoupling hypothesis and suggest a more nuanced evaluation. Recent IMF research[1] in fact illustrates that the transmission of distress from advanced economies to EMEs took place in three distinct phases. The first phase runs from the time early signs of the crisis appeared in mid-2007 till the Lehman collapse in September 2008. During this period, the growth performance of EMEs outshone that of advanced economies indicating decoupling. The second phase, starting with the Lehman collapse till the first quarter of 2009 was one of 'recoupling' when advanced economies pulled EMEs too into the downturn. The third phase started in the second quarter of 2009 when EMEs started recovering from the crisis ahead of advanced economies suggesting a shift once again to decoupling.

16. So, have EMEs decoupled from the advanced economies? The answer has necessarily to be nuanced. A useful way to visualize decoupling in the wake of the crisis is to distinguish between 'trend' and 'cycle' decoupling. 'Trend' decoupling is reflected by the widening gap between the trend rates of growth of EMEs and of advanced economies. This is evidently owing to the growing weight of domestic factors, mainly consumption, in the EMEs' growth process. However, given that there is still significant integration between the two

groups of countries, cycles are still coupled. From a 'lessons' perspective, what this means is that EMEs should focus on strengthening domestic drivers of demand and instituting automatic stabilizers to buffer themselves against cyclical shocks from advanced economies.

LESSON 2: GLOBAL IMBALANCES NEED TO BE REDRESSED FOR THE SAKE OF GLOBAL STABILITY

17. No crisis as complex as this has a simple or a single cause. In popular perception, the collapse of Lehman Brothers in mid-September 2008 will remain marked as the trigger of the crisis. At one level that may well be true. Indeed, I can visualize future textbooks in finance dividing the world into 'before Lehman' and 'after Lehman'. But if we probe deeper, we will learn that at the heart of the crisis were two root causes—the build up of global imbalances and developments in the financial markets over the last two decades. And received wisdom today is that these two root causes are interconnected, and that financial market developments were in a sense driven by the global imbalances.

18. Global macro imbalances got built up because of the large savings and current account surpluses in China and much of Asia in wake of the East Asian Crisis a decade ago. These were mirrored by large increases in leveraged consumption and current account deficits in the US. In short, Asia produced and America consumed. Between the US consumption boom and the Asian savings glut, there is a raging debate on what was the cause and what was the effect. Regardless, the bottom line is that one was simply the mirror of the other and the two share a symbiotic relationship.

19. And how did these imbalances build up? The answer lies in globalization—globalization of trade, of labour and of finance. The world witnessed a phenomenal expansion in global trade over the last three decades; global trade as a proportion of global GDP increased from 34 per cent in 1980 to 51 per cent in 2007, just before the crisis hit us.[2] Globalization of finance was even more prolific, especially over the last decade. For the world taken together, the ratio of

foreign assets and foreign liabilities to GDP rose from 133 per cent in 1994 to over 300 per cent in 2008.[3] The impact of globalization of labour was by far more striking. Emerging Asia added nearly three billion to the world's pool of labour as it integrated with the rest of the world over the last two decades thus hugely improving its comparative advantage. Together, the three dimensions of globalization—trade, finance and labour—helped emerging Asia multiply by a factor its exports to the advanced economies. The result was large and persistent current account surpluses in the Asian economies and corresponding current account deficits in the importing advanced economies.

20. The chain of causation from these imbalances to the financial crisis is interesting although not obvious. As Asia accumulated savings and simultaneously maintained competitive exchange rates, the savings turned into central bank reserves. Central banks, in turn, invested these savings not in any large, diversified portfolio but in government bonds of the advanced economies. This in turn drove down risk free real interest rates to historically low levels triggering phenomenal credit expansion and dropping of the guard on credit standards, erosion of credit quality and search for yield, all of which combined to brew the crisis to its explosive dimensions.

21. It is argued that if the US Fed had refused to supply the incipient demand for liquidity in the late 1990s and early 2000s, higher interest rates could have prevented the borrowing boom and the follow on widespread deterioration of financial standards and the subsequent melt down. But this also would have meant lower growth in the US and the rest of the world. The short point is that even as macroeconomic imbalances should not be allowed to proliferate, it is necessary to balance the need for global economic growth against the disruptions which follow the unwinding of such imbalances.

22. So, where do we go from here? The G-20 is now actively engaged in the challenging task of redressing structural imbalances in the global economy. At their Pittsburgh Summit in September 2009, the G-20 leaders agreed on a 'Framework

for Strong, Sustainable and Balanced Growth' and committed to a 'Mutual Assessment Process' (MAP) which is a peer review of each country's progress towards meeting the shared objectives underlying the framework. Recognizing that global imbalances which had narrowed during the crisis started widening again in the exit phase, driven mainly by the uneven recovery around the world, the G-20 resolved that promoting external sustainability should be the focus of the next stage of the MAP and entrusted this task to a Framework Working Group (FWG).

23. India is privileged in co-chairing, together with Canada, the FWG for managing the task of developing the indicative guidelines for assessing and addressing persistent global imbalances. The FWG has adopted a two-stage approach: a limited number of indicators will guide the initial assessment process, while a broader set—including qualitative ones—will be used in the second stage to inform an in-depth external sustainability assessment. The success of this initiative is critical for redressing the problem of global imbalances.

LESSON 3: GLOBAL PROBLEMS REQUIRE GLOBAL COORDINATION

24. The crisis demonstrated the interconnectedness of the world through trade, finance and confidence channels. What originated as a bubble in the US housing sector soon snowballed into a crisis and radiated in two different ways—first, in a geographical sense, from the US to other advanced economies and then to the rest of the world; and second, in a sectoral sense, from housing to all productive sectors. Even as each country started dousing the fires on its own, it was soon realized that the effort was in vain and that global coordination is a necessary condition for managing a global crisis.

25. From that perspective, the London G-20 Summit in April 2009 will go down in history as a clear turning point when the leaders of the world showed extraordinary determination and unity. Sure, there were differences, but they were debated and discussed and compromises were made

without eroding the end goal—that is to end the crisis. This resulted in an agreed package of measures having both domestic and international components but all of them to be implemented in coordination, and indeed in synchronization where necessary. The entire range of crisis response measures—accommodative monetary stance, fiscal stimulus, debt and deposit guarantees, capital injection, asset purchases, currency swaps—all derived in varying degrees from the G-20 package.

26. Now, as we exit from the crisis, there are concerns and apprehensions that the vaunted unity that the G-20 had shown during the crisis is dissipating. But might it also be a tad unrealistic to expect the degree of unity shown in managing the crisis to also be shown in addressing 'peace time' issues? The focus of G-20 now is to flesh out the agenda for economic and financial restructuring at national and international levels so that the world can prevent, or at any rate minimize the probability of, another crisis of the type we have gone through. Differences of opinion, when the agenda is so broad, are not only to be expected, but may in fact have a positive influence in determining what is collectively optimal.

27. The common thread running through the entire G-20 agenda is the need for global cooperation in solving our most pressing problems of today. The crisis has taught us that no country can be an island and that economic and financial disruptions anywhere can cause ripples, if not waves, everywhere. The crisis also taught us that given the deepening integration of countries into the global economic and financial system, uncoordinated responses will lead to worse outcomes for everyone.

28. The global problems we are facing today are complex and not amenable to easy solutions. Many of them require significant and often painful adjustments at the national level. Because short-term national interests conflict with globally optimal solutions, it is quite understandable that there are differences of views within the G-20. We must remember though that in a world divided by nation-states, there is no natural constituency for the global economy. At the same time, the global crisis has shown that the global economy as

an entity is more important than ever and that global coordination to solve global problems is critical.

LESSON 4: PRICE STABILITY AND MACROECONOMIC STABILITY DO NOT GUARANTEE FINANCIAL STABILITY

29. The years before the crisis were characterized by steady growth and low and stable inflation in advanced economies and rapid growth and development in EMEs. The so-called 'Great Moderation' prompted a growing consensus around the view that the best practice in monetary policy framework is the pursuit of a single target (price stability) by means of a single instrument (short-term policy interest rate). The success of the Great Moderation fortified the argument that price stability is a necessary and (a nearly) sufficient condition for economic growth and for financial stability. Central bankers believed they had discovered the holy grail.

30. That sense of triumph was deflated by the unravelling of the crisis. As the global financial sector came to the brink of a collapse even in the midst of a period of extraordinary price stability, it became clear that price stability does not necessarily guarantee financial stability.

31. Indeed the experience of the crisis has prompted an even stronger assertion, that there is a trade off between price stability and financial stability, and that the more successful a central bank is with price stability, the more likely it is to imperil financial stability. The argument goes as follows. The extended period of steady growth and low and stable inflation during the Great Moderation lulled central banks into complacency. Only with the benefit of hindsight is it now clear that the prolonged period of price stability blindsided policy-makers to the cancer of financial instability growing in the underbelly.

32. A dominant issue in the wake of the crisis has been the role of central banks in preventing asset price bubbles. The monetary stance of studied indifference to asset price inflation stemmed from the famous Greenspan orthodoxy which can be summarized as follows. First, asset price bubbles are hard to identify on a real time basis, and the fundamental factors that

drive asset prices are not directly observable. A central bank should not therefore second guess the market. Second, monetary policy is too blunt an instrument to counteract asset price booms. And third, central banks can 'clean up the mess' after the bubble bursts. The surmise therefore was that the cost-benefit calculus of a more activist monetary stance of 'leaning against the wind' was clearly negative.

33. The crisis has dented the credibility of the Greenspan orthodoxy. The emerging view post-crisis is that preventing an asset price build up should be within the remit of a central bank. Opinion is divided, however, on whether central banks should prevent asset bubbles through monetary policy action or through regulatory action. On one side, there is a purist view questioning the efficacy of resorting to monetary tightening to check speculative bubbles. Opposed to this is the argument that a necessary condition for speculative excesses is abundant liquidity, and that controlling liquidity which is within the remit of monetary policy should be the first line of defence against 'irrational exuberance'.

34. No matter how this debate settles, a clear, if also disquieting lesson of the crisis is that price stability and macroeconomic stability do not guarantee financial stability.

LESSON 5: MICROPRUDENTIAL REGULATION AND SUPERVISION NEED TO BE SUPPLEMENTED BY MACROPRUDENTIAL OVERSIGHT

35. The crisis has clearly demonstrated that a collection of healthy financial institutions does not necessarily make a healthy financial sector. This is because there are complex interconnections in the financial sector across banks, other financial institutions, markets, and geographies and a problem in any part of the system can rapidly transmit through the system, cascade across layers and develop into a crisis. Systemic safety can also be jeopardized by procyclicality. As the crisis demonstrated, there is a strong collective tendency among financial entities to overexpose themselves to the same type of risk during an upturn and become overly risk averse during a downturn. Importantly, individual institutions, and indeed microprudential oversight too, fail to take into account

the spillover impact of the actions of the rest of the financial system on them. This raises the paradox of the fallacy of composition. What is good from an individual institution's point of view can become disruptive, and even destructive, if all institutions act in a similar way.

36. That a bubble that started in the US housing sector snowballed into a major crisis is a vivid illustration of the risks arising from the interconnectedness of the global financial system and the risks of procyclicality. The lesson clearly is that as much as microprudential supervision is necessary, it needs to be supplemented by macroprudential oversight to prevent systemic risk building up.

37. Macroprudential oversight requires both analytical sophistication and good judgement. Regulators need to be able to analyze the nature and extent of risk and be able to make informed judgement on when and what type of countercyclical buffers they must impose. Both type I and type II errors—imposing buffers too early out of excessive caution or delaying imposition of buffers till it is too late to avert an implosion—can be costly in macroeconomic terms.

LESSON 6: CAPITAL CONTROLS ARE NOT ONLY UNAVOIDABLE, BUT ADVISABLE IN CERTAIN CIRCUMSTANCES

38. As EMEs started recovering from the crisis earlier than advanced economies, they also began exiting from the crisis driven accommodative monetary stance ahead of the advanced economies. This multi-speed recovery and the consequent differential exit have triggered speculative capital flows into EMEs resulting in currency appreciation unrelated to economic fundamentals. This poses complex policy management challenges. Currency appreciation erodes export competitiveness. Intervention in the forex market to prevent appreciation entails costs. If the resultant liquidity is left unsterilized, it could potentially fuel inflationary pressures. If the resultant liquidity is sterilized, it puts upward pressure on interest rates which not only hurts competitiveness, but also, in a curious variation of the Dutch disease, encourages further flows.

39. Capital inflows far in excess of a country's absorptive capacity could pose problems other than currency appreciation. Speculative flows on the look out for quick returns can potentially lead to asset price build up. Also, in the current juncture, one of the driving forces behind hardening commodity prices in recent months is the excess liquidity in the global system which has possibly triggered financialization of commodities.

40. Quite unsurprisingly, the old debate about whether capital controls are a legitimate policy option has resurfaced again. This is a debate that has traditionally frowned on moderation. Critics maintain that capital controls are distortionary, largely ineffective, difficult to implement, easy to evade and that they entail negative externalities. On the other hand, supporters of capital controls argue that controls preserve monetary policy autonomy, save sterilization costs and tilt the composition of foreign liabilities toward long-term maturities and ensure macroeconomic and financial stability.

41. The debate on capital controls resurfaced after the Asian crisis of the mid-1990s, especially as one of the root causes of the crisis was the open capital accounts of the East Asian economies. However, as the Asian economies recovered in quick order, regained their export competitiveness and started building up external reserves for self-insurance, the debate was not pursued to its logical conclusion, and the orthodoxy that capital controls are undesirable persisted.

42. The recent crisis has, however, been a clear turning point in the worldview on capital controls. Notably, the IMF put out a policy note[4] in February 2010 that reversed its long held orthodoxy that capital controls are inadvisable always and everywhere. The note has referred to certain "circumstances in which capital controls can be a legitimate component of the policy response to surges in capital flows". The World Bank and the Asian Development Bank Outlook - 2010 too echoed these views.

43. A useful way of assessing the capital account management of an EME is to draw a distinction between 'strategic' and 'tactical' controls. Strategic controls would

involve defining. a long-term policy indicating the *inter se* preference, or the hierarchy of preferences as it were, across different types of capital flows and the controls that will be deployed to operationalize that policy. Strategic controls give stakeholders a clear and predictable framework of rules to make informed choices and to manage risks, and they give policymakers sufficient levers to calibrate the flows; in essence they define the boundaries of the playing field. Tactical controls, on the other hand, introduce barriers into the playing field itself. They are deployed opportunistically to stem a surge in inflows or outflows. By their very nature, tactical controls introduce a new element of uncertainty into the calculations of both domestic and foreign stakeholders.

44. India's approach to capital account management is typically strategic. For example, we have an explicitly expressed preference for long-term over short-term flows and equity over debt flows, and we have used both price based and quantity based controls to operationalize this policy. We have, of course, periodically recalibrated elements of the strategy in pursuit of capital account liberalization. An important lesson from India's experience is that even with relatively large swings in capital flows during the crisis, the pressure to use tactical controls did not build up because the strategic controls provided automatic buffers.

45. Even as we debate what EMEs should or should not do to manage excess capital flows, we should remember that to the extent that lumpy and volatile flows are a spillover from policy choices of advanced economies, managing capital flows should not be treated as an exclusive problem of emerging market economies. How this burden is to be shared raises both intellectual and practical challenges. The intellectual challenge is to build a better understanding of the forces driving capital flows, what type of policy instruments, including capital controls, work and in what situations. The practical challenge is the need to reach a shared understanding on a framework for cross border spillovers of domestic policies in capital-originating countries, and the gamut of policy responses by capital receiving countries.

LESSON 7: ECONOMICS IS NOT PHYSICS

46. A few months into the crisis, the Queen happened to be at the London School of Economics and asked a perfectly sensible question: How come none of the economists saw the crisis coming? The Queen's question resonated with people around the world who felt that they had been let down by economics and economists. As economists saw their profession discredited and their reputations dented, the economic crisis soon turned into a crisis in economics.

47. What went wrong with economics? It now seems that by far the most egregious fault of economics, one that led it astray, has been to project it like an exact science. The charge is that economists suffered from 'physics envy' which led them to formulate elegant theories and models—using sophisticated mathematics with impressive quantitative finesse—deluding themselves and the world at large that their models have more exactitude than they actually did.

48. Admittedly, in a limited sense there may be some parallels between economics and physics. But similarity in a few laws does not mean similarity in the basic nature of the academic discipline. The fundamental difference between physics and economics is that physics deals with the physical universe which is governed by immutable laws, beyond the pale of human behaviour. Economics, in contrast, is a social science whose laws are influenced by human behaviour. Simply put, I cannot change the mass of an electron no matter how I behave but I can change the price of a derivative by my behaviour.

49. The laws of physics are universal in space and time. The laws of economics are very much a function of the context. Going back to the earlier example, the mass of an electron does not change whether we are in the world of Newton or of Einstein. But in the world of economics, how firms, households and governments behave is altered by the reigning economic ideology of the time. To give another example, there is nothing absolute, for example, about savings being equal to investment or supply equalling demand as

maintained by classical economics but there is something absolute about energy lost being equal to energy gained as enunciated by classical physics.

50. In natural sciences, progress is a two-way street. It can run from empirical findings to theory or the other way round. The famous Michelson-Morley experiment that found that the velocity of light is constant led to the theory of relativity—an example of progression from practice to theory. In the reverse direction, the ferocious search now under way for the Higgs Boson—the God particle—which has been predicted by quantum theory is an example of traversing from theory to practice. In economics, on the other hand, where the human dimension is paramount, the progression has necessarily to be one way, from empirical finding to theory. There is a joke that if something works in practice, economists run to see if it works in theory. Actually, I don't see the joke; that is indeed the way it should be.

51. Karl Popper, by far the most influential philosopher of science of the twentieth century, propounded that a good theory is one that gives rise to falsifiable hypotheses. By this measure, Einstein's General Theory was a good theory as it led to the hypothesis about the curvature of space under the force of gravity which indeed was verified by scientists from observations made during a solar eclipse from the West African islands of Sao Tome and Principe. Economics, on the other hand, cannot stand the scrutiny of the falsifiable hypothesis test since empirical results in economics are a function of the context.

52. The short point is that economics cannot lay claim to the immutability, universality, precision and exactitude of physics. Take the recent financial crisis. It is not as if no one saw the pressures building up. There were a respectable number of economists who warned of the perilous consequences of the build-up of global imbalances, said that this was simply unsustainable and predicted a currency collapse. In the event, we did have the system imploding but not as a currency collapse but as a melt down of the financial system.

53. We will be better able to safeguard financial stability both at global and national levels if we remember that economics is a social science and real world outcomes are influenced at a fundamental level by human behaviour.

LESSON 8: HAVING A SENSE OF ECONOMIC HISTORY IS IMPORTANT TO PREVENT AND RESOLVE FINANCIAL CRISES

54. Let me finish with the last lesson which is on a larger canvas—that having a sense of economic history is important to prevent and to resolve financial crises. In their painstakingly researched book, *This Time is Different: Eight Centuries of Financial Folly*, Kenneth Rogoff and Carmen Reinhart argue that every time a crisis occurs and experts are confronted with the question of why they could not, based on past experience, see it coming, they would argue that past experience was no guide as circumstances had changed. Yet this 'this time is different' argument does not hold. Reinhart and Rogoff put forward impressive evidence showing that over eight hundred years, all financial crises can be traced to the same fundamental causes as if we learnt nothing from one crisis to another. If only teaching in economics had included a study of economic history, perhaps we can avoid repeating history, never mind as a farce or a tragedy.

Notes

1. Llaudes, Ricardo, Ferhan Salman, and Mali Chivakul, "The Impact of the Great Recession on Emerging Markets". IMF Working Paper 237, October 2010.
2. Calculations based on IMF Direction of Trade Statistics, June 2010.
3. Calculations based on IMF Balance of Payments Year Book, 2010.
4. Ostry, Jonathan D. and Others (2010), "Capital Inflows: The Role of Controls", IMF Staff Position Note, SPN/10/04, February 19, 2010.

K.R. Narayanan Oration by Dr. Duvvuri Subbarao, Governor, Reserve Bank of India at the South Asia Research Centre of the Australian National University, Canberra on June 23, 2011) • *Courtesy*: www.rbi.org.in

9

India and the Global Financial Crisis Transcending from Recovery to Growth

D. Subbarao, Governor, RBI

April 26, 2010

India clocked average growth of 9 per cent per annum in the five years to 2007/08. That growth momentum was interrupted by the financial crisis which impacted India too, more than we had originally thought but less than it did most other countries. Despite falling below 6 per cent for one quarter, the growth for the full year 2008/09 was a resilient 6.7 per cent. Current estimates are that the economy had grown between 7.2 and 7.5 per cent for the just ended fiscal year 2009/10 and that growth for 2010/11 will be 8+ per cent. The quick turn in sentiment following the uncertainty and anxiety of the crisis period has seen the return of the FAQ: When will India get on to double digit growth?

2. For policymakers, the FAQ translates to three nuanced questions:

(i) In the short term, how do we restore the economy to its trend rate of growth while maintaining price stability?

(ii) In the medium term, how do we raise the trend rate of growth itself without compromising financial stability?

(iii) How do we ensure that growth is inclusive?

3. India is such an over analyzed country that it is difficult to be original. The answers to all the three questions above are all out there in the open, and they involve moving on with a host of structural and governance reforms. I want to use this platform provided by the Peterson Institute to comment on a few issues on the reform agenda that are relevant to the Reserve Bank of India.

Capital flows

4. Volatile capital flows have been a central issue during the crisis, and continue to be so now as the crisis is ebbing. Emerging market economies (EMEs) saw a sudden stop and reversal of capital flows during the crisis as a consequence of global deleveraging. Now the trend has reversed once again, and many EMEs are seeing net inflows—a consequence of a global system awash with liquidity, the assurance of low interest rates in advanced economies over 'an extended period' and the prospects of robust growth in EMEs. The familiar question of how EMEs can maximize the benefits and minimize the costs of volatile capital flows has returned to haunt the policy agenda.

5. One little known aspect of capital flows, what could perhaps be called the law of capital flows, is that they never come in at the precise time or in the exact quantity you want them. Managing these flows, especially if they are volatile, is going to test the effectiveness of central bank policies of semi-open EMEs. If central banks do not intervene in the foreign exchange market, they incur the cost of currency appreciation unrelated to fundamentals. If they intervene in the forex market to prevent appreciation, they will have additional systemic liquidity and potential inflationary pressures to contend with. If they sterilize the resultant liquidity, they will run the risk of pushing up interest rates which will hurt the growth prospects. Capital flows can also potentially impair financial stability. How EMEs manage the impossible trinity—the impossibility of having an open capital account, a fixed exchange rate and independent monetary policy—is going to have an impact on their prospects for growth, price stability and financial stability.

6. India has followed a consistent policy on capital account convertibility in general and on capital account management in particular. Our position is that capital account convertibility is not a standalone objective but a means for higher and stable growth. We believe our economy should traverse towards capital convertibility along a gradual path—the path itself being recalibrated on a dynamic basis in response to domestic and global developments. Post-crisis, that continues to be our policy. We will continue to move towards liberalizing our capital account, but we will revisit the road map to reflect the lessons of the crisis.

7. India's approach to managing capital flows too has been pragmatic, transparent and contestable. We prefer long term flows to short-term flows and non-debt flows to debt flows. The logic for that is self-evident. Our policy on equity flows has been quite liberal, and in sharp contrast to other EMEs which liberalized and then reversed the liberalization when flows became volatile, our policy has been quite stable. Historically, we have used policy levers on the debt side of the flows to manage volatility. This has been our anchor when we had to deal with flows largely in excess of the economy's absorption capacity in the years before the crisis. This has been our policy when we saw large outflows during the crisis. And I believe this will continue to be our policy on the way forward.

8. The surge in capital flows into some EMEs even as the crisis is not yet fully behind us has seen the return of the familiar question—the advisability of imposing a Tobin type tax on capital flows. Both before and after the crisis, there are examples of countries, notably Chile, Colombia, Brazil and Malaysia, which have experimented with a Tobin tax or its variant. Even as there are some lessons to be drawn from the country experience, on the aggregate, it does not constitute a sufficient body of knowledge for drawing definitive conclusions.

9. Critics of Tobin tax contend that the tax is ineffective, is difficult to implement, easy to evade and that its costs far exceed the potential benefits, and all this because financial markets always outsmart policy makers. Supporters of the tax

argue that if designed and implemented well, the tax can be effective in smoothing flows and that evading controls is not such a straight forward option as efforts to evade require incurring additional costs to move funds in and out of a country which is precisely what the tax aims to achieve.

10. In India, given the overall thrust of policy, we are quite agnostic on the choice of different instruments. The stereotype view is that we have an express preference for quantity based controls over price based controls. A critical examination of our policy will show that this view is mistaken. For example, on bonds we impose both a limit on the amount foreigners can invest as well as a withholding tax. Similarly, our policy on external commercial borrowing employs both price and quantity variables. We have not so far imposed a Tobin type tax nor are we contemplating one. However, it needs reiterating that no policy instrument is clearly off the table and our choice of instruments will be determined by the context.

11. The recent crisis has clearly been a turning point in the world view on capital controls. The Asian crisis of the mid-90s demonstrated the risk of instability inherent in a fully open capital account. Even so, the intellectual orthodoxy continued to denounce controls on capital flows as being inefficient and ineffective. The recent crisis saw, across emerging economies, a rough correlation between the extent of openness of the capital account and the extent of adverse impact of the crisis. Surely, this should not be read as a denouncement of open capital account, but a powerful demonstration of the tenet that premature opening hurts more than it helps.

12. Notably, the IMF published a policy note in February 2010[1] that reversed its long held orthodoxy. The note has referred to certain "circumstances in which capital controls can be a legitimate component of the policy response to surges in capital flows". Now that there is agreement that controls can be "desirable and effective" in managing capital flows in select circumstances, the IMF and other international bodies must pursue research on studying what type of controls are appropriate and under what circumstances so that emerging economies have useful guidelines to inform policy formulation.

Exchange Rate Management

13. Just as on capital flows, on exchange rate too, our policy has been consistent which is that we do not target a specific rate or level for the exchange rate. The Reserve Bank intervenes in the market only to smooth volatility which is harmful to trade and investment. The 'volatility centric approach' to exchange rate also stems from the source of volatility which is capital flows. Despite not having a fully open capital account, we have experienced large volatility in capital flows as the following figures for the external sector for the four years to 2009-10 demonstrate.

Trends in India's External Sector

	2006/07	2007/08	2008/09	2009/10
CAD (% of GDP)	1.0	1.3	2.4	2.5
Net Capital flows (% of GDP)	4.8	8.7	0.6	3.8
Capital flows in excess of CAD ($ billion)	36	92	(–) 20	14
Rupee appreciation (+) depreciation (–) vis-à-vis US$ during the year	2.3	9.0	(–) 21.5	12.9

Note: Numbers for 2009/10 are rough estimates.

14. The above numbers show that capital flows were in excess of the current account deficit in the years before the crisis during India's growth boom and that they had abruptly reversed in the crisis year 2008/09. The full balance of payments for the just completed fiscal year 2009/10 is not yet available but latest data show that the net accretion to reserves was modest.

15. The above numbers and trends are a demonstration of our policy stance. First, the two way movement shows that we have a flexible exchange rate, and also evidences the increasing flexibility of the rate over time in relation to the magnitude of flows.

16. Second, India does not have a deliberate strategy of building up reserves for 'self-insurance'. The variations in our foreign exchange reserves are an offshoot of our exchange rate policy which is to intervene in the market only to smooth

exchange rate volatility and prevent disruptions to macroeconomic stability. Third, even as our reserves got built up over the years owing to capital flows, the same reserves have been used to contain volatility in the event of capital reversals. Importantly, given our persistent trade and current account deficits, our foreign exchange reserves comprise borrowed funds which are qualitatively different from accumulation of reserves through trade and current account surpluses. Even so, it is clear that the reserves have helped us better cope with external sector vulnerabilities.

17. Our fairly flexible exchange rate policy has not been without costs. Importantly, because inflation in India has typically been higher than that in our trading partners in the recent period, the real effective exchange rate has appreciated significantly more than the nominal rate. This has implications for our external competitiveness, that too at a time when the world trade is recovering amid concerns relating to protectionism. Also if we have a flexible exchange rate, and if other countries which are our trading partners or those which compete for the same export markets have a fixed exchange rate, we get disadvantaged.

Inflation targeting

18. The Reserve Bank is not a pure inflation targetter. Some people have suggested that the economy will be better served if the Reserve Bank becomes a pure inflation targetter. The argument is that inflation hurts much more in a country like India with hundreds of millions of poor people and that the Reserve Bank will be more effective at combating inflation if it is not burdened with other objectives. This argument is contestable.

19. Inflation targeting, characterized by a single target (price stability) and a single instrument (short-term policy interest rate), has respectable academic credentials. An exclusive commitment to inflation enhances operational effectiveness and enforces accountability. The success of several developed economy central banks in maintaining price stability in the years before the crisis has also given it intellectual credibility. The unravelling of the 'Great Moderation' during

the crisis has however diluted, if not dissolved, the consensus around the minimalist formula of inflation targeting. The crisis has shown that price stability does not necessarily ensure financial stability. Indeed there is an even stronger assertion—that there is a trade-off between price stability and financial stability, and that the more successful a central bank is with price stability, the more likely it is to jeopardize financial stability.

20. Inflation targeting is neither desirable nor practical in India for a variety of reasons:

- First, it is inconceivable that in an emerging economy like India, the central bank can drive a single goal oblivious of the larger development context. The Reserve Bank must be guided simultaneously by the objectives of price stability, financial stability and growth.
- Second, food items which have a large weight (46-70 per cent) in the various consumer prices indices are subject to large supply shocks, especially because of the vagaries of the monsoon, and are therefore beyond the pale of monetary policy. An inflation targeting RBI cannot do much to tame a supply driven inflation except as a line of defence in an extreme situation.
- Third, which inflation index do we target? In India, we have one wholesale price index and four consumer price indices. There are ongoing efforts at a technical level to reduce the number of consumer price indices, and I believe the technical issues are not insurmountable. But that still will not give us a single representative inflation rate for an emerging market economy with market imperfections, diverse geography and 1.2 billion people.
- Fourth, the monetary transmission mechanism in India is impeded because of a number of structural factors. Inflation targetting can be efficient and

effective only after monetary transmission becomes streamlined.

- Finally, we need to manage the monetary fall-out of volatile capital flows that queer the pitch for a single focus monetary policy. A boom-bust pattern of capital flows can lead to large disorderly movements in exchange rates rendering both inflation targeting and financial stability vulnerable. Like other emerging economies, India too will have to navigate the impossible trinity as best as it can.

21. Post crisis, the 'new environment hypothesis' which says that flexible inflation targetting, rather than pure inflation targetting, is more efficient is gaining ground. According to this hypothesis, if inflation is way off target, a central bank's first call is to bring it within the acceptable range, and if inflation is within the range, the central bank can focus on other objectives.

22. The Reserve Bank's 'multiple indicator framework' adopted in 1998 and refined since then, in fact, subsumes a flexible inflation objective framework over the medium-term. Under this framework, while we strive for a balance among multiple objectives with the relative weights assigned to each objective varying as dictated by the prevailing macroeconomic context, we aim to achieve a medium-term inflation target. Our commitment in this regard is clearly defined in our own policy documents where we say our objective is to "contain perception of inflation in the range of 4.0 to 4.5 per cent in line with the medium-term objective of 3.0 per cent inflation consistent with India's broader integration with the global economy". Admittedly, our communication strategy is not yet best practice. We need to work, and indeed we are working, on improving dissemination, both at technical and non-technical levels. In the dissemination, we need to explain the inflation outlook, the priority assigned to different objectives, what impact our policy actions are intended to have and how they will take us towards the stated objectives.

Harmonizing Monetary and Fiscal Policies

23. One of the mega trends in macroeconomic management world over in the last few decades has been the gradual abatement of the fiscal dominance of monetary policy. This has been the trend in India too. The ebbing away of fiscal dominance has been a continuous process but two discrete events marked significant milestones. The first was the agreement between the Reserve Bank and the Government to completely phase out ad-hoc treasury bills from April 1997, a move that saw the termination of the egregious practice of automatic monetization by the central bank of the government's fiscal deficit. The second was the enactment of the Fiscal Responsibility and Budget Management (FRBM) Act which, among other things, prohibited the Reserve Bank from financing government debt in the primary market with effect from April 2006. These trends got a further boost as a result of the fiscal consolidation during 2004-08 which yielded space for monetary policy. The healthy transition of monetary policy from fiscal dominance to functional autonomy was halted, if not reversed, by the response to the crisis, which necessitated fiscal expansion and monetary accommodation of that higher fiscal deficit.

24. In India, both the Government and the Reserve Bank have begun the process of exit from the expansionary stances of the crisis period. The Government has programmed a reduction in the gross fiscal deficit from 6.8 per cent of GDP in fiscal year 2009/10 to 5.5 per cent of GDP in 2010/11. The Reserve Bank began the reversal of its crisis response accommodative stance by terminating sector-specific liquidity facilities, incrementally raising the cash and liquidity reserve ratios and the policy interest rates. Going forward, the challenge for India, as it indeed is for every country, is to unwind the expansionary policies harmoniously since inconsistencies between fiscal and monetary policies can be costly in economic terms.

25. As indicated earlier, the two crisis years—2008/09 and 2009/10—saw government borrowing rising sharply and abruptly. Even so, the Reserve Bank, as the Government's

debt manager, could manage the borrowing programme by maintaining easy liquidity conditions. Surely, yields on government securities had firmed up, but only modestly. Even as fiscal deficit this year (2010/11), as a percentage of GDP, is lower, the absolute amount of government borrowing in gross terms is roughly of the same order as in last year. Indeed, measured by the metric of fresh supply of government paper, the borrowing this year will be higher than in last year, and this perhaps will be a more influential determinant of the yield trajectory. Meanwhile, the economic conditions have changed since last year in important ways. First, inflationary pressures are stronger, thereby restraining the flexibility for infusing liquidity through open market operations (OMO). Second, last year banks held significant quantities of Market Stabilization Scheme (MSS) bonds issued earlier for sterilizing the liquidity arising from capital flows. The Reserve Bank bought back those bonds to infuse systemic liquidity. That option is not available this year as the quantum of MSS bonds remaining is very marginal. Finally and importantly, as recovery is taking hold, private credit demand is reviving. But the upward pressure on yields on government securities and the consequent pressure on interest rates makes 'crowding out' a potential possibility.

26. Even setting aside crisis related developments, 'fiscal dominance' of monetary policy continues to be a concern. The long term interest rates are influenced significantly by the yields on government securities and hence on the size of the government borrowing programme, thereby eroding to some extent the efficacy of monetary transmission. The credibility of the Reserve Bank's inflation management, therefore, is critically dependent on the credibility of Government's fiscal consolidation.

27. Fiscal consolidation is important for a number of other weighty reasons apart from the inflation dimension. The Government has initiated action on the recommendations of the Thirteenth Finance Commission (TFC) on the revised road map for fiscal responsibility. In drilling down the road map, the Government should also keep in view two

relevant objectives. First, fiscal consolidation should shift from exclusive reliance on increasing revenues to focus on restructuring expenditures. The consolidation effort should target slashing recurring expenditures rather than one-off items. Second, it is important, even as targeting quantitative indicators, to pay equal attention to the quality of fiscal adjustment.

Improving Monetary Policy Transmission

28. The standard tool of central banks is the short term interest rate which they use to influence interest rates across financial markets, and thereby steer the financial conditions in the economy. During the crisis, central banks around the world reduced policy rates ferociously, and in many advanced economies the rates are at or near zero. However, financial markets refused to respond and remained in seizure reflecting the near total collapse of monetary transmission.

29. The effectiveness of monetary transmission, the process by which the central bank's policy signals influence the financial markets, is a function of both tangible and intangible factors. It depends on the depth and efficiency of the financial markets. It also depends on the overall confidence and sentiment in the financial system. Typically, monetary transmission in emerging economies tends to be slower, reflecting shallow financial markets and inefficient information systems.

30. The monetary transmission mechanism in India has been improving but is yet to fully mature. There are several factors inhibiting the transmission process. First, India has a government sponsored small savings programme characterized by administered interest rates and tax concessions. Operating through a huge network of post offices and field agents, the small savings scheme has an enormous and impressive reach deep into the hinterland. Banks are typically circumspect about reducing deposit rates in response to the central bank's policy rate signals for fear of losing their deposit base to small savings. The government too has not adjusted the rates on small savings on a regular basis to offset their competitive edge.

31. Second, depositors enjoy an asymmetric contractual relationship with banks. When interest rates are rising, depositors have the option of withdrawing their deposits prematurely and redepositing at the going higher rate. On the contrary, when deposit rates are falling, banks do not have the option of repricing deposits at the lower rate because of the asymmetry of the contract. This structural rigidity clogs monetary transmission. Banks are typically unable to adjust their lending rates swiftly in response to policy signals until they are able to adjust on the cost side by repricing the deposits in the next cycle. Third, and importantly, monetary transmission is also impeded because of large government borrowings and illiquid bond markets.

32. There is a stereotype view that monetary transmission broke down during the crisis in India too like in advanced economies. This is incorrect. Monetary policy signals transmitted to the money and bond markets reasonably efficiently. Monetary transmission in the credit market was admittedly slower but this had more to do with the structural rigidities explained above rather than any crisis related impediments in the financial markets.

33. In evaluating monetary transmission during the crisis, it should be remembered that the contagion of the crisis transmitted to India though largely the confidence channel; the financial markets were affected more by a perception of scarcity than actual scarcity. As such, market conditions improved markedly in fairly quick order since the Reserve Bank's assurance that it will maintain 'abundant' liquidity inspired widespread confidence in the markets. It is important to recognize that in India, the crisis transmitted from the real to the financial sector unlike in the advanced economies where the transmission was from the financial sector to the real sector. The implication of this is that the decline in credit flow, as banks have asserted, was due more to a decline in credit demand from the private sector rather than any increased risk aversion on the part of the banks.

34. It should be recognised that the clogs in monetary transmission in India are possibly exaggerated because of the

current system of loan pricing. Banks are required to declare a benchmark prime lending rate (BPLR) but they enjoy the freedom to lend at rates below their BPLR. Over time, sub-BPLR lending has become a rule rather than an exception. Currently about two thirds of bank lending takes place at rates below the BPLR. As many interest rates are indexed to the BPLR, banks have been reluctant to adjust their BPLRs in response to policy rate changes as changes erode their discretionary flexibility in pricing loans. The BPLR system has therefore become an inadequate tool to evaluate monetary transmission.

35. Improving monetary transmission is important if the Reserve Bank's efforts at promoting growth with price stability are to be effective. The problems indicated above suggest obvious solutions. An important reform initiative post crisis has been the replacement of the BPLR system by a new base rate [BR] system which will come into effect on July 1, 2010. Each bank will determine its own BR reflecting all those cost elements which are common across borrowers. A bank will then charge its borrowers the base rate plus a premium on top of that reflecting customer specific risk. The BR will thereby set the floor for all lending rates. Concurrently, the ceiling interest rate on export credit and small loans up to Rs. 200,000 has been withdrawn making deregulation of lending rates complete. The new system is expected to be transparent, fair and contestable and will help in improving monetary transmission to credit markets.

Conclusion

36. In the course of my comments, I have spoken about five specific issues:

(i) Capital flows

(ii) Exchange rate management

(iii) Inflation targeting

(iv) Harmonizing monetary and fiscal policies

(v) Improving monetary policy transmission

37. My effort has been to indicate our priorities and clarify our policy stance on some issues thrown up by the crisis. This is by no means an exhaustive list of our challenges or tasks. That I am sure will be a much longer listing.

38. The final thought that I want to leave with you as I finish is that the growth drivers that powered India's high growth in the years before the crisis are all intact. The challenge for the Government and the Reserve Bank is to move on with reforms to steer the economy to a higher growth path that is sustainable and equitable.

Note

1. Ostry, Jonathan D. and Others (2010), "Capital Inflows: The Role of Controls", IMF Staff Position Note, SPN/10/04, February 19, 2010.

Comments of Dr. D. Subbarao, Governor, Reserve Bank of India at the Peterson Institute for International Economics, Washington DC, April 26, 2010 • *Courtesy*: www.rbi.org.in

10

Impact of Global Financial Crisis on Financial Consumers—Global and Indian Perspective on Need for Consumer Protection—Role of Ombudsmen

K.C. Chakrabarty, Deputy Governor, RBI

21 September 2011

Introduction

...

2. The focus of current international discourse is on financial sector stability. It may not be out of place to recall what the great American President Abraham Lincoln had to say "If we could first know where we are, and whither we are tending, we could better judge what to do and how to do it". Financial sector stability, as we all know, in simple terms, is the absence of instability in the financial system. As a policy objective, it refers to the avoidance of financial crisis as also to the ability of the financial system to limit, contain and deal with the emergence of imbalances before they constitute a threat to the economic processes. Financial sector stability also has deep linkages to the principle of financial consumer protection.

Securing the Customer

3. ...I would like to convey the message of Mahatma Gandhi who said "A customer is the most important visitor on

our premises. He is not dependent on us. We are dependent on him. He is not an interruption in our work—he is the purpose of it. We are not doing him a favour by serving him. He is doing us a favour by giving us the opportunity to serve him". Thus, irrespective of whether the business has good or bad times, the consumer and his protection are central to the existence of business. Consumer protection is achievable by having appropriate commercial laws and open competition. But our experience in dealing with provision of financial products and services indicates that the law is heavily loaded in favour of the financial services industry. As far as competition is concerned, it has no implications for the most vulnerable sections of the society. Further, the legal processes tend to be expensive and unaffordable in terms of both time and money. The good times for the financial services industry have meant expensive services and products for the common person while bad times have meant inadequate or no supply of even basic financial services.

4. Can the above contradictions be balanced without having consumer protection at its core? What did the consumer gain when the times were good for the financial services industry and why is he made to suffer today, for no fault of his, just because the industry has fallen into bad times? The disconnect between business strategy and consumer protection can only be a recipe for disaster. When Mr. Bill Gates made the famous statement "world needs banking but it does not need banks" everyone perhaps was euphoric that we would soon breach the final frontier of banking. But it is going to be quite some time before we say good bye to banks. The recent past has seen product innovation and product penetration through use of technology. The challenge posed by the rapid changes in products and service delivery models is our ability to scale up our efforts regarding financial education and customer awareness. A financially literate and enlightened customer would be able to better judge the suitability of a product to meet his requirements.

5. The question I am often asked is: "Why as a regulator, are you concerned about customer care and protection? Why is

it not left to the market forces and competition to take care of? The answer to this lies in the fact that in a service industry where market forces and competition play out freely, this may well be the case. However, banking/financial services industry being a highly regulated service industry with very stiff entry norms, consumer protection cannot entirely be left to the market forces. Hence, the regulator has a role. Availability of financial services/products at affordable prices on an uninterrupted basis is the purpose and result of financial sector stability. Responsible marketing, responsible lending, responsible grievance redress mechanism and responsible consumer protection are not mutually exclusive but are inter-dependent. The public deposits and the funds available to the financial services industry represent a nation's wealth. As such, the least we can think of is protecting the owners of this wealth, not merely in terms of deposit insurance but also in terms of day-to-day transactions and contractual relationships a consumer has with the banking and financial services industry.

6. Consumer trust and protection has always been an issue of interest and concern for policymakers and the entire financial industry. The debate has become particularly acute over the last few years in view of the recent market developments. In times of globalization, new opportunities in terms of new financial products, new instruments and technologies became available posing new challenges for the consumers such as understanding the risks associated with complex products. The current levels of transparency and the consequent difficulty of consumers in identifying and understanding the fine print from a large volume of information leads to an information asymmetry between the financial intermediary and the consumer. From the perspective of policymakers, including the Reserve Bank of India and other financial sector regulators, financial literacy is a must to gauge the needs of the population and financial institutions, so that financial resources can be translated into higher economic growth while minimizing the financial stability risks.

7. It is widely believed that the complex financial instruments that contributed to the financial crisis essentially had their basis in the boom period home loans, the credit quality of which was poorly assessed. Apart from the credit quality issues which went against the interest of the lenders, the interest of the borrowers were also severely compromised as they were lured into the complex yet alluring deals without being assessed for their repaying capacity based on their prospective income and net worth. Costs of such irresponsible lending and borrowing were borne by tens of millions of tax payers in the form of bailout of beleaguered institutions.

8. The financial services industry players need to evolve efficient consumer policies that must be based on two main pillars: financial education and transparent information on one side and competition on the other. These aspects are central to foster the confidence of consumers and help them make informed financial decisions and select the products best suited for their needs. Competition is an important dimension of consumer policy which has a positive impact on prices, quality of service and choice of products. Was this evident when we were going through turmoil in the global financial services industry? Perhaps not. We, therefore, have to harmonize the role of regulation, competition and financial education to achieve the twin objectives of consumer protection and financial sector stability.

9. Financial consumers need protection because they are at a structural disadvantage inasmuch as they have difficulty in exercising their market power since their heterogeneity and mass make it difficult for them to organize themselves into pressure groups. Additionally, the fixed costs of procuring information can be high. A greater degree of protection may therefore make sense. Information asymmetry between financial service providers and customers, especially in emerging economies, works to the advantage of the former. Therefore, transparency rules or disclosure regulations should, at the minimum, seek to create standardized and comparable information about pricing, suitability of the product to different population groups, terms and conditions and risks

to customers and supervisory authorities. Full disclosure of quality information should be combined with mechanisms to ensure that clients properly understand the information provided and their impact on their personal financial decisions.

10. For countries where banking with formal institutions is still emerging, consumer protection measures must be a top priority. In all such cases the targeted client groups come from the most vulnerable and low income segments. This is a major challenge for the credibility and sustainability of the whole financial sector. If not properly addressed, some of the problems faced by these consumers could lead to a long-term mistrust in formal financial institutions and loss of confidence in the banking system. It is, therefore, imperative that all consumers should benefit from the same level of security and protection, whatever be the institution they operate with. Unchecked market forces and lax policies, combined with relaxed regulatory oversight, can result in customers being exploited while efforts to open financial markets to serve the bottom of the pyramid are made through financial inclusion measures. While financial inclusion is a necessary pre-condition for financial stability and inclusive economic development, the negativities that may affect a poor ill-informed new customer can be enormous—from high level of indebtedness due to excessively high prices and predatory lending, to complete loss of savings and assets created out of loans and those collaterally charged to the banks. Hence, the financial services industry cannot blindly follow a strategy of customer acquisition without providing new accesses to new customers by using the ICT led financial inclusion models or brick and mortar structures or the business correspondent model. These initiatives must not be seen as costs but need to be reckoned as investment necessary for business stability.

11. It is important to highlight that customers have rights but responsibilities also. While financial service providers have to ask the relevant questions to their prospective customers and ensure that the proposed products and services are the most appropriate according to their needs and means, it is the customers' responsibility also to provide relevant, complete

and accurate information on their financial situation and taking their personal as well as financial circumstances into account when making their decisions. The responsibility of the financial service provider may, therefore, be read and assessed in the light of the customer's responsibilities. Financial service providers need to understand that for their businesses to survive, their customers must survive and for that, they need to understand the appropriateness of the products themselves to be able to explain it to their customers.

12. The financial entities must not use the vulnerable sections to cross-subsidize the clientele with power to bargain and command a price of their choice. The reasonableness of service charges/interest rates must be ensured by way of commitment to the cause of financial inclusion. Further, the service charges/penalties must not be disproportionate to the level of default. The bundling of products by banks with a view to generate more non-interest income would fall in the category of exploitative pricing. Every bank/financial service provider, in order to expand its customer base, needs to understand the requirements of their customers, the risks involved and return to be achieved.

13. The USA, which was affected the most by the crisis, had, in the aftermath of the crisis, initiated exemplary policy and other structural reforms to guard against financial instability (Dodd—Frank Wall Street Reform and Customer Protection Act). Among the measures initiated, the customer protection aspect had received prime attention resulting in enactment of Customer Protection Act and creation of Customer Financial Protection Bureau (CFPB) to assure that markets for financial products and services worked in a fair, transparent, and competitive manner and were subject to meaningful and consistent oversight. In India, setting up of Financial Stability and Development Council has also been with a similar view to strengthen and institutionalize the mechanism for maintaining financial stability by way of macro-prudential supervision together with focus on developmental aspects of customer protection, viz. financial literacy and financial inclusion.

Where the Banking Ombudsman Comes In

14. The role of the Ombudsmen adjudicating financial consumer disputes is onerous and the recent upheavals in the marketplace have only heightened the consumers' expectations. The existence of a legal framework is a must for consumer protection. The Ombudsmen, by definition, deal with individual grievances about which the common person is agitated. They cannot substitute effective legal and regulatory systems. Expecting them to bring about systemic improvements of a sustainable nature by resorting to class action may be to expect too much from the schemes. The Ombudsman Schemes achieve two important objectives, viz. timely disposal of grievances and continuing the relationship between the financial service provider and the consumer. While the courts of law decide cases in finality, many a times bringing contractual relations to an end, the decisions or awards passed by Ombudsmen generally do not have such implications.

15. What needs to be done is to have a constant interaction between law makers, regulators, standards and codes setting bodies and the Ombudsmen to sort out systemic issues that may be leading to individual grievances. The regulators also need to be aware of their responsibility of protecting the vulnerable sections of the poor in matters of pricing, fair treatment, non-discriminatory approach to consumer care and transparency in dealings with customers. Very often, the Ombudsmen are bogged down with issues of jurisdiction, either pecuniary or physical. This should not hinder them from encouraging a conciliatory approach to redress the grievances. We just cannot leave it to the care of the market forces and competition and expect them to serve the cause of the consumers. The standards and codes setting bodies must evaluate the quality and effectiveness of consumer care measures including the financial education initiatives taken by the service providers. The Ombudsmen need to move out of their offices to spread awareness about existing redress systems available within the framework of the financial services industry. All the initiatives must be aimed at empowering the customer to be able to make a studied and reasonable choice of

a financial product or service. The effectiveness of the Ombudsmen is not to be judged by the number of complaints handled every year but by the cases that resulted in bringing about sustainable continuous systemic improvement.

16. In this age of networking, fora like the INFO play an important role in broadening our outlook and understanding of issues from a local as well as global perspective. While globalization has had its share of success in improving markets and competition, it has also exposed the limitations of national regulators in protecting their consumers from actions arising out of trans-border transactions. Hence, the Ombudsmen who are part of INFO and the regulators must adopt the high level principles on financial consumer protection that have been put in public domain by G-20 OCED.

What are We Doing in India

17. In India, for the banking industry, we have the following broad structure for consumer protection that is underpinned by deposit insurance. India has the statutory framework for consumer protection by way of a Consumer Protection Act. We also have the Banking Codes and Standards Board of India and a Banking Ombudsman Scheme. The Banking Ombudsman Scheme has been in existence for over fifteen years and is cost free for access by the common person. The Banking Ombudsman Scheme (BOS) is fully funded and managed by India's central bank, i.e. the Reserve Bank of India. As of now, bank customers can lodge a complaint with any of the fifteen offices of the Banking Ombudsman situated across the country, on twenty-seven different grounds of deficiency in banking services. These grounds of complaint cover all the delivery channels as also customer touch points. The number of complaints handled under the BO Scheme during the year 2010-11 was 71274 as against 79266 during 2009-10. Though these numbers may not reflect the true picture about the quality of consumer care or the hardships faced by the common persons, given the vastness of our country and the large customer base numbering over 800 million, we are seized of the need for bringing about greater awareness about the Ombudsman Scheme, especially in small

towns and villages. The bigger challenge facing us is that of financial inclusion and financial education. To address these issues, we have embarked on an ambitious plan of financial inclusion and are committed to providing access to financial services to every village with a population of 2000 or above by March 2012. The challenge of financial education, in a multi-lingual and multi-ethnic country like India, poses many operational difficulties, given the low levels of financial literacy and a population of 30 per cent which is uneducated. We are trying to tide over this situation by adopting multi-disciplinary and multi-channel strategies.

18. Despite having undertaken a number of initiatives for ensuring fair treatment to customers, it was realized that the efficacy of the tiered mechanism for customer grievance redress in banks was far from satisfactory. It was necessary to further develop a credible and effective functional system of attending to customer complaints by strengthening banks' internal structures to attend not only to the basic customer needs but the special needs of disadvantaged groups such as pensioners and small borrowers, including farmers. Taking into account these considerations, a committee was constituted by the Reserve Bank. The committee was to look into the banking services rendered to retail and small customers and pensioners, structure and efficacy of the existing grievance redress mechanism, the functioning of BOS, possibility of leveraging technology for better customer service in the light of increasing use of Internet and IT for bank products and services, etc. and to recommend steps for improvements.

Conclusion

19. The lessons that the global financial crisis had to teach us have been expensive and painful. Let us not blindly believe in the ability of the markets and competition to take care of all segments of the population. There are sections of financial consumers who always have the highest sense of protection and there are the vulnerable sections of the society who feel left out. We, therefore, have to move to an order where the market forces, competition, effective regulation and a vibrant Ombudsman scheme all co-exist and handle matters

concerning financial consumers' protection in a harmonized way.

....

Address by Dr. K.C. Chakrabarty, Deputy Governor, RBI at the Annual Conference of the International Network of Financial Services Ombudsman Schemes—INFO 2011 at Vancouver, Canada on September 21, 2011 • *Courtesy*: www.rbi.org.in

11

G-20 After the Crisis: An Indian Perspective

Subir Gokarn, Deputy Governor, RBI

1 November 2010

Introduction

.... While the title of the session is "What India expects from the G-20", I think it would be extremely presumptuous of me to speak on behalf of the country as a whole. I have, of course, been involved with the G-20 process as the Central Bank deputy and, in that capacity have had the opportunity to contribute to the shaping of the Indian position on various issues. So, rather than assert a national position, I would prefer to share some of the thinking that underlies the stance that is taken at various G-20 forums. With this in mind, my presentation is divided into three broad segments. First, I look at what the G-20 did to avert a potentially severe crisis a couple of years ago, which essentially provides the context to whatever role it may play in more 'normal' circumstances. Second, I explore the inherent differences within the group, which will naturally impose limits on what it can realistically hope to achieve by way of global co-ordination on structural issues. Third, I build on these two foundations to try and articulate a general "emerging market economy" position, which, I think, would be reflective of the Indian stance on a range of issues.

The Context of Crisis

The G-20 had its origins in a previous crisis that also began in the financial sector and which threatened to spill over from one country to the next. This was the East Asian crisis of 1997-98, the roots of which lay in the increasing presence of foreign capital in economies that perhaps did not quite have the capabilities to handle it. The fact that one of the factors underlying the crisis—foreign capital—linked the advanced and emerging economies provided the basis for countries from both groups coming together to look for ways to minimize the vulnerability of emerging economies on the one hand and global financial institutions domiciled in advanced economies on the other.

Of course, the East Asian crisis wound down, with the affected countries showing strong resilience in the years following. The need for collective solutions such as those which might have been provided by the G-20 was felt less and less as emerging economies, both those most impacted by the crisis and those which escaped it, found their own, individual buffers against the next crisis. Since the crisis had had no significant macroeconomic impact on the advanced economies, they also had no particular interest in pursuing any collective strategy for structural change, which might have helped to stabilize the global economy and make it less vulnerable to a crisis. Of course, one important outcome of keeping the group going despite the absence of a particularly significant agenda was that the institutional representatives from the member countries got to know each other, making communication during the most recent crisis when the group really came into its own perhaps a little easier and more effective than otherwise.

In effect, then, a group that was born in the wake of one crisis really got the opportunity to demonstrate its effectiveness when another one precipitated. This crisis also had its genesis in the financial sector, which helped retain the relevance of the group's structure, with its core constituencies being finance ministries and central banks. This time round, however, the origins of the crisis lay squarely in the financial sectors of the advanced economies, a factor that has created some special challenges for the group's attempts to deal with post-crisis structural issues, a point that I shall return to later.

My essential point is that the origins and structure of the group made it an appropriate and, eventually, effective mechanism to deal with a crisis that threatened to spiral into a deep global recession. There have been many questions raised about what exactly the group did that contributed to mitigating the impact of the crisis. Some have argued that the measures that each country took to deal with the crisis would have essentially been the same even without the coming together of the G-20. That may well be the case, but I would argue that it was precisely the show of strength and collective resolve of the group that helped reinforce the confidence of global stakeholders that the crisis would indeed be averted. Individual, uncoordinated responses, to my mind, would not have had the same impact on global perceptions that the G-20 solidarity did, even if the policy measures in each country had been exactly the same.

Beginning with the Washington Summit in November 2008 and through 2009, the visible focus of the group on both the proximate aspects of the crisis and the more fundamental causes was, I believe, a major reason for the restoration of global confidence. The economic recovery has been slow and somewhat choppy, but potential disruptions have also been met with collective responses, which have, in turn, reinforced the belief that the recovery can be sustained. Further, the prominence that the group gave to structural reforms of various kinds sent the signal that it was committed not just to dealing with the immediate crisis but to putting in place measures that would significantly reduce the probability of recurrence. As we know from our own experience with structural reform, crisis always presents a window of opportunity to obtain a consensus on reform measures that would just not be possible under normal circumstances. It is for the leadership to grasp this and to push through reforms that meet the needs of changing global circumstances. The group's focus on structural issues was itself an important reason for the credibility it gained for its efforts to manage the crisis.

In short, I think that it is a reasonable assessment that the global economy would have been in somewhat different shape today if the G-20, or any collective process involving the world's largest economies, had not taken place. The group can certainly draw strength from this as it now shifts focus from dealing with the crisis to dealing with the structural issues that are perceived to have caused it. But it is precisely at this stage in the process that the challenges to change management arise. As the crisis abates, the common threat perception and collective responsibility inevitably begins to dissipate and the consensus that was visible in the crisis management phase gives way to more individualistic priorities and agendas. How are these manifesting in the G-20?

Dividing Lines

A number of factors have contributed to the emergence of differences within the group. This should not be surprising in and of itself, given the fact that this is an enormously disparate set of countries. The 20 countries in the group can be classified into categories based on a large number of parameters, each of which implies different policy priorities and, consequently, different approaches to deal with domestic and global conditions. Large or small, more or less affluent, net importers or exporters, commodities producers or manufacturers, aging or young populations—whichever way one looks at it, the composition of the group should not inspire much confidence that it can agree on common approaches to the structural issues that confront the global economy. Let me explore a few of these dividing lines and their implications for the group.

At this juncture, the variability of the recovery across the members of the group is a critical difference. In fact, with some economies having consolidated their domestic recoveries while others struggle to do so, there are legitimate concerns about whether the crisis has actually abated; in other words, whether the primary objective of the group has actually been achieved.

Perceptions about the robustness of the global recovery have oscillated quite widely during the past several months and the outlook today is somewhat more negative than it was at the beginning of 2010. But within this overall shift, while the outlook for several economies has deteriorated, it has remained constant or improved for others. This has immediate implications for the domestic policy priorities of each country. In a group that is ostensibly committed to doing no harm to each other, these differences may pose a challenge.

The most visible dilemma is on the issue of continued quantitative easing by advanced economies whose recoveries are showing some signs of stalling. As the capacity for further fiscal stimulus abates, more so as countries attempt to pull back from huge fiscal overhangs, more liquidity being pumped in appears to be the only avenue remaining for stimulating the economy. From the viewpoint of individual countries, there is not much choice; not using the instrument significantly increases the risks of the recovery reversing course. Apart from the domestic impact of this, given the relative size of the economies involved, this could clearly have global implications as well. So, it may well be that individual and collective interests are aligned on this issue.

But, while there may be alignment over a somewhat longer time horizon, in the immediate future, there are signs of misalignment. More liquidity, even the prospect of it, in some advanced economies, is spilling over into fast-recovering emerging economies, introducing several complications into their domestic policy environment. Some are worried about currency appreciation and the impact that this might have on their recovery as domestic producers lose competitiveness. Others are worried about the short-term nature of the inflows and the disruption that might be caused if there is a sudden exit in response to a global shock or new developments in the source countries. There are widespread concerns among energy and commodity importers that global liquidity is flowing into commodities and driving up prices, with consequent inflationary implications. In short, the immediate impact of quantitative easing may represent a dividing line within the group, even if, over time, it may be in the collective interest.

Financial safety nets represent another potential dividing line, not necessarily on principle, but on the different approaches that groups of countries have used to develop them. Self-insurance by way of reserve accumulation may be the safest way to protect oneself from global shocks from the viewpoint of individual countries. But, beyond some threshold levels of magnitude, it begins to generate externalities. To return to a point that was made earlier in the context of the East Asian crisis of the late 1990s, the effective choice made by countries affected or threatened by that crisis to build up self-insurance capacity was both a response to perceived inadequacies in the collective safety nets available at the time and a contributory factor to some of the imbalances that have been associated with the global transmission of the recent crisis.

The analytical debate on this issue will go on, but the practical implication for many countries is to decide on their acceptable mix of insurance options within the overall consideration of doing no harm to other countries. Even while collective options such as those that have recently been introduced by the International Monetary Fund become more accommodating of individual country requirements, the benefits of self-insurance that many countries experienced first-hand during the recent crisis are difficult to deny. Meanwhile, the perceived link between the building up of individual safety nets and global imbalances makes this issue a dividing line within the group.

Another example of a dividing line is financial regulation. It is now generally accepted that a significant contributory factor to the recent crisis was the opportunity that the existing regulatory and supervision framework in some advanced economies provided for highly risky investments to be made. However, even as this was happening, there are several countries in the group whose regulatory frameworks did not provide such opportunities and whose financial systems emerged from the crisis relatively unscathed. Notably, there seems to be a significant correlation across countries between the degree of damage that domestic financial systems suffered and the speed and robustness of their recoveries.

However, there is little question that there is a strong and inexorable process of global financial integration, which, with all the risks it entails, does have large potential benefits for all countries concerned. One important requirement for realizing these benefits is a set of common regulatory principles, standards and practices across countries. These are necessary to ensure that capital flows across the world based on genuine consideration of fundamental returns and risks and not on arbitrage between different regulatory environments. Certainly in theory, this should not be the cause of any division; there is a clear common and shared interest in the outcome. In practice, however, divisions could arise on what exactly these standards and practices should be; whether they are driven by the specific conditions prevailing in the worst hit financial systems and, therefore, inappropriate and burdensome for the relatively healthy ones; and, the knowledge and human capital requirements to implement them effectively across a diverse set of countries.

I have tried to provide some examples of potential dividing lines, drawing on my experience and observations of the process in the finance track. Let me conclude this segment of the presentation by reiterating the point on which it began. This is an extremely differentiated and heterogeneous set of countries, whose conditions and priorities differ both in the short-term and over the long run. It would be extremely naive to expect that such a group would be able to reach agreement on anything beyond the immediate crisis at hand, despite their ambition to tackle structural issues. From this perspective, any consensus on any issue is an achievement. It reflects the recognition that, notwithstanding differences between countries, global integration is a process that can be chaotic and disruptive if not handled in a collective and coordinated way. What is true for crisis management is also valid for the range of structural issues that the G-20, as well as those which other multilateral processes are dealing with.

An Emerging Market Economy/Indian Perspective

Against this backdrop, let me now attempt to articulate what I would call an "Emerging Market Economy" perspective, but which also reflects my characterization of the Indian perspective. An important premise in this perspective is the point I concluded the last segment with. The process of globalization has enormous potential benefits for EMEs in all its forms. But it also brings with it significant risks such as the vulnerability to shocks which emanate outside their sphere of control. The best way to optimize on the "risk-return" tradeoff from globalization is to adhere to a common set of standards and rules, which, as I said earlier, forces the process to be driven by fundamental factors rather than by regulatory arbitrage, broadly speaking. On the basis of this argument, EMEs will see a clear benefit from engaging in any process that can develop and enforce such common standards and practices. The G-20 is one such process, with the distinct advantage that, being a relatively small group, reaching consensus where it can be found is not too difficult a task.

However, EMEs have significant domestic objectives and challenges and these must take priority in their policy decisions. Many are dealing with the critical challenge of providing a large proportion of their population access to the most basic necessities, let alone education, health and financial services. An integrated and balanced development strategy makes several demands of the financial system. This, in turn, requires a careful balancing between rapid expansion in capacity and the kinds of products and services offered on the one hand and safety and prudence on the other. This balancing act, at one level common to EMEs, but at another, differentiated by the vastly different conditions within the EMEs themselves may not be amenable to a reasonable set of common standards, except at a lowest common denominator level, which is then unlikely to serve the purpose of achieving a safe and secure global financial system.

The financial safety nets issue is also one on which a distinct EME perspective may emerge. The difference in concerns between advanced and emerging economies is heightened in the current environment in which increasing liquidity in some advanced economies is driving possibly short-term capital flows into emerging economies. In such a situation, self-insurance needs to be given due consideration. When economic fundamentals are sound, would reserves not constitute the most effective way of dealing with reversals in short-term capital flows? If self-insurance were done away with, reliance on external insurance mechanisms might conceivably have two negative implications. One, procedure and due diligence might take time, thereby diluting the effectiveness of the safety net. Two, global investors may suspect that something is fundamentally wrong, aggravating the pressure of exit.

I have used the issues of financial regulation and safety nets to illustrate my point about the balancing act that EMEs need to perform between addressing domestic priorities and aligning with a meaningful set of global standards or mechanisms. However, this can be taken as a more general issue for EMEs as they engage in global forums on a whole range of issues on which the benefits of integration have to be viewed in conjunction with the pursuit of domestic policy objectives.

Essentially, from the emerging market perspective, the value of the G-20 process lies in how effectively it is able to accommodate this need for balance. As I have tried to argue through this presentation, both on short-term and long-term issues, the differences and divergences between countries in the group are wide and, perhaps, inevitable. This puts the group at an immediate disadvantage when it comes to addressing issues, because, given the differences, even agreeing on a common objective, let alone a common approach may be a difficult, if not impossible task.

However, it is reassuring that, in the face of these inherent handicaps, the group seems to have made significant achievements, which go beyond the immediate compulsions of crisis management and address some of the key structural issues. The underpinning for this progress, as I have alluded to earlier in the presentation, is the recognition by all parties involved that the process of globalization has potential benefits for everybody as long as it is controlled in some way. The basis of control is, as the G-20 demonstrates, common principles, on which are based common, or at least compatible standards for both conduct and enforcement. But control does not mean homogenization. As long as common standards can be reconciled with differences in practices and institutions, which allow individual countries to effectively address their domestic priorities, the arrangement is eminently workable.

Just as each country needs to maintain a balance between acceptance and adherence to global standards, the group needs to accommodate a possibly thin and blurred line between conformity and autonomy. Its effectiveness on all the issues that it seeks to address, but particularly on the structural ones, will depend heavily on this accommodation. Every member of the group must feel that there are some tangible benefits from continuing to associate and in turn, that perception depends on the space that the is available to pursue legitimate domestic priorities, which do not impinge on the interests of the other members of the group.

By this benchmark, the group has done quite well. In the midst of significant differences, some of which I have pointed out, meaningful consensus on, for example, safety nets, financial regulation and reform of the International Monetary Fund suggest that it has found a way to accommodate the balance on a number of significant issues. The nature of this consensus has been widely reported on and debated in the wake of the recent Finance Ministers and Central Bank Governors' meeting in Gyeongju, Korea, so I do not want to go into the details here. The point I want to emphasize, though, is that the common feature of both the process of arriving at consensus and the agreements themselves was precisely the acceptance of common principles and standards, which do not come in the way of allowing each country to organize its internal systems in ways that it thinks is best.

This is not to say that there are no disagreements or unresolved issues within the group. It would be naive to expect that there would not be. However, as in the case of all collective activity, the presence of disagreements, even intractable ones, does not in any way undermine the legitimacy of the process. It should be judged by what it is able to achieve, not by what it is not.

Concluding Remarks

At the very least, the G-20 provides a compact forum for knowledge and experience sharing between the largest economies in a structured way. The network that it creates certainly facilitates co-ordination on policy actions, should an occasion for this arise. In this respect, it is certainly a useful and effective crisis management mechanism.

But from an emerging market perspective, its utility can and has gone beyond crisis management. These countries do recognize that the benefits of globalization will not be fully realized and the risks will be heightened in the absence of some meaningful collective activity. The effectiveness of this collective activity is, in turn, enhanced by its emphasis on common principles and standards, its recognition of national autonomy in deciding on policy priorities and strategies and, very importantly, its insistence on the principle of "do no harm". A realistic assessment of the performance of the group over the past two years would suggest that, while it may not have had equal success on all fronts, its achievements are significant and, in many ways, a vindication of its approach.

....

Keynote Address by Dr. Subir Gokarn, Deputy Governor, Reserve Bank of India at ICRIER/InWEnt/DIE Conference "Policies for Growth and Financial Stability Beyond the Crisis—The Scope for Global Cooperation" at Mumbai on October 27, 2010. • *Courtesy*: www.rbi.org.in